Lecture Notes in Computer Science 14587

Founding Editors

Gerhard Goos
Juris Hartmanis

Editorial Board Members

The series Lecture Notes in Computer Science (LNCS), including its subseries Lecture Notes in Artificial Intelligence (LNAI) and Lecture Notes in Bioinformatics (LNBI), has established itself as a medium for the publication of new developments in computer science and information technology research, teaching, and education.

LNCS enjoys close cooperation with the computer science R & D community, the series counts many renowned academics among its volume editors and paper authors, and collaborates with prestigious societies. Its mission is to serve this international community by providing an invaluable service, mainly focused on the publication of conference and workshop proceedings and postproceedings. LNCS commenced publication in 1973.

Martin Andreoni
Editor

Applied Cryptography and Network Security Workshops

ACNS 2024 Satellite Workshops
AIBlock, AIHWS, AIoTS, SCI, AAC, SiMLA, LLE, and CIMSS
Abu Dhabi, United Arab Emirates, March 5–8, 2024
Proceedings, Part II

Springer

Editor
Martin Andreoni
Technology Innovation Institute
Abu Dhabi, United Arab Emirates

ISSN 0302-9743   ISSN 1611-3349 (electronic)
Lecture Notes in Computer Science
ISBN 978-3-031-61488-0   ISBN 978-3-031-61489-7 (eBook)
https://doi.org/10.1007/978-3-031-61489-7

This Springer imprint is published by the registered company Springer Nature Switzerland AG
The registered company address is: Gewerbestrasse 11, 6330 Cham, Switzerland

Preface

These proceedings contain the papers selected for presentation at the ACNS 2024 satellite workshops and the poster session, which were held in parallel with the main conference (the 22nd International Conference on Applied Cryptography and Network Security) from 5 to 8 March 2024.

Eight satellite workshops, two of which were new, were held in response to this year's call for workshop proposals. Each workshop provided a forum to address a specific topic at the forefront of cybersecurity research.

- 6th ACNS Workshop on Application Intelligence and Blockchain Security (AIBlock 2024), chaired by Weizhi Meng and Chunhua Su
- 5th ACNS Workshop on Artificial Intelligence in Hardware Security (AIHWS 2024), chaired by Stjepan Picek and Shivam Bhasin
- 6th ACNS Workshop on Artificial Intelligence and Industrial IoT Security (AIoTS 2024), chaired by Neetesh Saxena and Bong Jun Choi
- 5th ACNS Workshop on Secure Cryptographic Implementation (SCI 2024), chaired by Jinggiang Lin and Bo Luo
- 1st Workshop on Advances in Asymmetric Cryptanalysis (AAC 2024), chaired by Elena Kirshanova and Andre Esser
- 6th ACNS Workshop on Security in Machine Learning and its Applications (SiMLA 2024), chaired by Ezekiel Soremekun
- 1st Workshop on Low-Latency Encryption (LLE 2024), chaired by Shahram Rasoolzadeh and Santosh Ghosh
- 4th International Workshop on Critical Infrastructure and Manufacturing System Security (CIMSS 2024), chaired by Chuadhry Muieeb Ahmed and; Rajib Ranian Maiti

This year, we received a total of 61 submissions. Each workshop had its own Program Committee (PC) in charge of the review process. These papers were evaluated based on their significance, novelty, and technical quality. The review process was double-blind. Ultimately, 33 papers were selected for presentation at the eight workshops, with an acceptance rate of 54%.

ACNS also awarded the best workshop paper to Marina Krček and Thomas Ordas, *"Diversity Algorithms for Laser Fault Injection"* from the AIHWS workshop. The winning paper was selected from among the nominated candidate papers from each workshop. The authors also received the monetary prize sponsored by Springer.

Besides the regular papers presented at the workshops, there were 12 invited talks.

- "Hard-Hat Cryptanalysis - Drilling Down into Real-world TLS Protocol Failures" by Robert Merget (TII, UAE) and "Attacks Against the CPA-D Security of Exact FHE Schemes, and Threshold-FHE schemes" by Damien Stehlé (Cryptolab, South Korea) at the AAC workshop

- "Building a Low-Latency Pseudorandom Function" by Joan Daemen (Radboud University, The Netherlands), "Designing Low-Latency Primitives and Modes" by Gregor Leander (Ruhr University Bochum, Germany), and "Automated Security Analysis of Symmetric-Key Primitives Using Tools" by Yu Sasaki (Nagoya University, Japan) at the LLE workshop
- "Attacking Machine Learning Models" by Yang Zhang (CISPA, Germany) at the SiMLA workshop
- "Searchable Symmetric Encryption and its attacks" by Kaitai Liang (TU Delft, The Netherlands) at the SCI workshop
- "Hardware Security through the Lens of Dr AI" by Debdeep Mukhopadhyay (IIT Kharagpur, India), and "Touching Points of AI and Cryptography" by Moti Yung (Columbia University & Google, USA) at AIHWS workshop
- "Cybersecurity in the 3D and IoT Era of Power Systems: Load Altering Attacks Unleashed!" by Charalambos (Harrys) Konstantinou (King Abdullah University of Science and Technology, Saudi Arabia) and "The Future of IoT Security: AI/ML and Lightweight Cryptography countering emerging threats" by Hoda Alkhzaimi (NYU Abu Dhabi, UAE) at the AIoTS workshop
- "Securing the Future: Advanced Safety and Resilience in Autonomous and Autonomic Systems" by Shreekant (Ticky) Thakkar (TII, UAE) and "Security of Advanced Machine Learning Features in Autonomous Systems" by Muhammad Shafique (NYU Abu Dhabi, UAE) at the CIMSS workshop

Charalambos Konstantinou also chaired a poster session, and 11 posters are included in the proceedings as extended abstracts. The following poster was recognised with the ACNS 2024 Best Poster Award.

- Francesco Antognazza, Alessandro Barenghi, Gerardo Pelosi, Ruggero Susella, "A Versatile and Unified HQC Hardware Accelerator"

The ACNS 2024 workshops were made possible by the joint efforts of many individuals and organizations. We sincerely thank the authors of all submissions. We thank each workshop's program chairs and PC members for their great effort in providing professional reviews and interesting feedback to authors on a tight schedule. We thank all the external reviewers for assisting the PC in their particular areas of expertise. We are grateful to Springer for sponsoring the best workshop paper award and the local organizing team for sponsoring the best poster award. We also thank the General Chairs, Michail Maniatakos and Ozgur Sinanoglu, and the organizing team members of the main conference and each workshop for their help in various aspects. A special acknowledgment goes to Jianying Zhou for his guidance and suggestions on the workshop organization.

Last but not least, we thank everyone else, speakers, session chairs, and attendees, for their contribution to the success of the ACNS 2024 workshops.

Martin Andreoni

AAC 2024

First Workshop on Advances in Asymmetric Cryptanalysis

07 March 2024

General Chair

Javier Verbel   Technology Innovation Institute, UAE

Program Chairs

Elena Kirshanova   Technology Innovation Institute, UAE
Andre Esser   Technology Innovation Institute, UAE

Program Committee

Leo Ducas	CWI, The Netherlands
Eamonn Postlethwaite	King's College London, UK
Luca de Feo	IBM Research, Switzerland
Markku-Juhani O. Saarinen	Tampere University, Finland and PQShield, UK
Philippe Gaborit	University of Limoges, France
Paolo Santini	Università Politecnica delle Marche, Italy
Ján Jančár	Masaryk University, Czech Republic
Damien Stehlé	CryptoLab, South Korea
Alexander Karenin	Technology Innovation Institute, UAE
Jean-Pierre Tillich	Inria de Paris, France
Péter Kutas	Eötvös Loránd University, Hungary
Alexander May	Ruhr University Bochum, Germany
Monika Trimoska	Radboud University, The Netherlands
Semyon Novoselov	I. Kant Baltic Federal University, Russia
Alexander Wallet	Inria Rennes, France
Lorenz Panny	Technical University of Munich, Germany
Violetta Weger	Technical University of Munich, Germany
Juliane Krämer	University of Regensburg, Germany

SiMLA 2024

Sixth Workshop on Security in Machine Learning and its Applications

06 March 2024

Program Chair

Ezekiel Soremekun   Royal Holloway, University of London, UK

Web Chair

Badr Souani   University of Luxembourg, Luxembourg

Publicity Chair

Salijona Dyrmishi   University of Luxembourg, Luxembourg

Program Committee

Ahmed Rezine	Linköping University, Sweden
Alexander Bartel	Umeå University, Sweden
Amin Aminifar	Heidelberg University, Germany
Christopher M. Poskitt	Singapore Management University, Singapore
Jingyi Wang	Zhejiang University, China
Salah Ghamizi	University of Luxembourg, Luxembourg
Salijona Dyrmishi	University of Luxembourg, Luxembourg
Sudipta Chattopadhyay	Singapore University of Technology and Design, Singapore
Thibault Simonetto	University of Luxembourg

LLE 2024

First Workshop on Low-Latency Encryption

07 March 2024

Program Chairs

Shahram Rasoolzadeh   Radboud University, The Netherlands
Santosh Ghosh   Intel Labs, USA

Program Committee

Christof Beierle   Ruhr University Bochum, Germany
Elif Bilge Kavun   University of Passau, Germany
Christoph Dobraunig   Intel Labs, USA
Maria Eichlseder   Graz University of Technology, Austria
Fukang Liu   Tokyo Institute of Technology, Japan
Bart Mennink   Radboud University, The Netherlands
Thorben Moos   Université Catholique de Louvain, Belgium
Siwei Sun   University of Chinese Academy of Sciences, China

CIMSS 2024

Fourth Workshop on Critical Infrastructure and Manufacturing System Security

07 March 2024

Program Chairs

Chuadhry Mujeeb Ahmed   Newcastle University, UK
Rajib Ranjan Maiti   BITS-Pilani, India

Web Chair

Chenglu Jin   CWI Amsterdam, The Netherlands

Program Committee

John Henry Castellanos   CISPA Helmholtz Center for Information Security, Germany

Yuqi Chen   ShanghaiTech University, China
Qin Lin   Cleveland State University, USA
Nagendra Kumar   IIT Indore, India
Kanchan Manna   BITS Pilani Goa Campus, India
Weizhi Meng   Technical University of Denmark, Denmark
Venkata Reddy Palleti   Indian Institute of Petroleum and Energy, India

Contents – Part II

Contents – Part I

AIoTS – Artificial Intelligence and Industrial IoT Security

SCI – Secure Cryptographic Implementation

AAC – Workshop on Advances in Asymmetric Cryptanalysis

Forging Tropical Signatures

Lorenz Panny[✉]

Technische Universität München, Munich, Germany
lorenz@yx7.cc

Abstract. A recent preprint [3] suggests the use of polynomials over a tropical algebra to construct a digital signature scheme "based on" the problem of factoring such polynomials, which is known to be NP-hard. This short note presents two very efficient forgery attacks on the scheme, bypassing the need to factorize tropical polynomials and thus demonstrating that security in fact rests on a different, empirically easier problem.

Keywords: Cryptanalysis · tropical algebra · digital signatures · factorization

1 Introduction

Tropical algebra is concerned with the *min-plus semiring*, or *tropical semiring*: an algebraic structure over the extended reals defined by the two binary operations "min" and "+". Multiple candidate cryptographic constructions using the tropical semiring in various ways have been suggested in a series of papers starting about ten years ago, and, to a large extent, broken. Readers may wish to consult the introduction of [2] for an overview of past proposals and corresponding attacks.

The most recent proposal [3] in the tropical-cryptography family is a signature scheme building on multiplication of polynomials over the tropical semiring. In this note, we give two fairly simple, yet very effective forgery attacks against the scheme and show that the attacker is in fact not required to solve the claimed hard problem underneath the construction. We provide implementations of both attacks, confirming that they work in practice.

These results also highlight the need for clear problem statements and unambiguous claims concerning the relationships between them: The signature scheme of [3] may be "based on" the factorization problem for tropical polynomials in the sense that it is *inspired by* that problem. However, there is no known result indicating that breaking the signature scheme is as hard as factoring tropical polynomials (e.g., a reduction from that factoring problem to breaking the EUF-CMA security of the scheme), and indeed, our attacks strongly suggest the opposite.

As a side remark, we also note that the emphasis of [3] on the NP-hardness of factoring tropical polynomials misses the point: Cryptography requires computational problems that are hard *for almost all instances*, while the notion of

Date of this document: 2024-01-13.

NP-hardness only says something about the hardest, possibly very few instances. See the classic paper [5] for an informal overview of average-case complexity.

Parallel and Subsequent Work. Soon after this note first appeared online, a larger set of attacks against [3] and some countermeasures (insufficient to prevent all known attacks) were presented in [1]. Yet another attack which was not covered by [1] was presented in [6]; it bypasses the countermeasures of [1] too.

1.1   Tropical Polynomials

The *tropical semiring* is defined as the set $\mathbb{R} \cup \{+\infty\}$ with two binary operations $a \oplus b = \min\{a, b\}$ and $a \otimes b = a + b$. With this, *tropical polynomials* are simply symbolic expressions of the form

$$f(x) = c_0 \oplus (c_1 \otimes x) \oplus (c_2 \otimes x^{\otimes 2}) \oplus \cdots \oplus (c_n \otimes x^{\otimes n})$$

where x is a variable and the coefficients $c_0, ..., c_n$ lie in the tropical semiring; they too form a semiring under the operations $\oplus$ and $\otimes$ extended to polynomials in the usual way. Note that "missing" coefficients are interpreted as $+\infty$.

Example 1. In more usual notation, $f(x) = \min\{c_0, c_1 + x, c_2 + 2x, ..., c_n + nx\}$.

Example 2. The tropical polynomial product $f(x) \otimes g(x)$ has coefficients $c_0 + c_0'$, $\min\{c_0 + c_1', c_1 + c_0'\}$, $\min\{c_0 + c_2', c_1 + c_1', c_2 + c_0'\}$, etc., where c_i and c_j' are the coefficients of $f(x)$ and $g(x)$ respectively. Generally, the kth coefficient equals

$$\min\left\{c_i + c_{k-i}' : i \in \{0, ..., k\}\right\}.$$

Remark 3. Beware that there are at least two notions of "tropical polynomial" in the literature: One is the algebraic viewpoint employed in [3] and here. The other identifies polynomials with the *functions* they define on $\mathbb{R}$. In the latter formalism, all tropical polynomials split uniquely into linear tropical polynomials and the factors can be found in polynomial time; see for instance [4].

1.2   Signatures from Tropical Polynomials

The signature scheme proposed by [3] features two integer parameters d and r; the values suggested in [3, § 4] are $d = 150$ and $r = 127$. Let $T_{d,r}$ denote the set of tropical polynomials of degree d and with all coefficients in $\{0, ..., r\} \subseteq \mathbb{Z}$, and let H be a collision-resistant hash function from bit strings to $T_{d,r}$.

The <u>public key</u> is a tropical product $M = X \otimes Y$, where (X, Y) are tropical polynomials sampled uniformly from $T_{d,r}$. A valid <u>signature</u> for a message m is a triple (S_1, S_2, N) of tropical polynomials with $S_1, S_2 \in T_{3d,3r}$ and $N \in T_{2d,2r}$, such that $S_1 \otimes S_2 = P \otimes P \otimes M \otimes N$ where $P = H(m)$; in addition, neither S_1 nor S_2 may be a constant (tropical) multiple of $P \otimes M$ or $P \otimes N$.

For the sake of completeness, here is how [3] computes such a signature using the private key $(X, Y) \in T_{d,r} \times T_{d,r}$: Sample $U, V \leftarrow T_{d,r}$ and let $N := U \otimes V$. The signature is $(P \otimes X \otimes U, P \otimes Y \otimes V, N)$.

Remark 4. By definition (cf. Example 2), multiplying a tropical polynomial by a constant amounts to shifting each coefficient by that constant. Hence, constant multiples can easily be detected using ordinary subtraction on the coefficients.

2   The Attacks

The problem of recovering a secret key for a given public key really is factoring (with some extra constraints on the degree and coefficient sizes). However, the problem of forging a signature gives significantly more power to the attacker: Their task is to factor *when another factorization is already known!*

In more detail, recall that a signature consists of a triple (S_1, S_2, N) of tropical polynomials such that $S_1 \otimes S_2 = P \otimes P \otimes M \otimes N$, where M is the public key and P is a hash value of the message encoded as a tropical polynomial in a suitable way. Setting $S_1 = P \otimes M$ and $S_2 = P \otimes N$ solves the verification equation but clearly does not require knowledge of the secret; hence, this pair and its constant (tropical) multiples are excluded as "trivial forgeries" in [3]. However, in tropical algebra, polynomial multiplication is highly non-cancellable, and a tropical polynomial typically has a very large number of distinct product decompositions. All attacks explained in the sequel are based on different methods of discovering new product decompositions starting from a given one.

Note that we focus on the most basic version of each attack for simplicity, and that the forged signatures produced by those methods look rather different from honestly generated signatures. We can (and will) however speculate that any particular method of detecting forgeries can be fooled by carefully combining and adjusting the basic forgery techniques. Indeed, since chaining these basic strategies may prove useful, it is helpful to view them not just as one-shot forgery attacks, but as *transformations* on pairs (S_1, S_2) of tropical polynomials which produce another pair (S_1', S_2') such that $S_1' \otimes S_2' = S_1 \otimes S_2$, while preserving superficial properties like the degrees and bounds on the coefficients.

2.1   Warmup: "Trivial Forgeries"

The most trivial forgery would be $(P \otimes M, P \otimes N, N)$ for any N with the correct degree and coefficient bounds. A mild generalization is to (tropically) multiply the three components by constants in such a way that the verification equation and coefficient bounds remain satisfied; this yields signatures of the form $(c_1 \otimes P \otimes M, c_2 \otimes P \otimes N, c_1 \otimes c_2 \otimes N)$. Forgeries of this type are detected and rejected by the verification algorithm specified in [3]. However, they form a big part of the following stronger attacks in the sense that they provide the initial product decomposition $(S_1, S_2) = (P \otimes M, P \otimes N)$ of $P \otimes P \otimes M \otimes N$.

2.2   Attack #1: Morphing Products

The starting point for the first attack is to recall Example 2 and notice that there will almost certainly be coefficients c_i and c_j' in the inputs (S_1, S_2) which effectively do not contribute to the result at all: Only the smallest sum $c_i + c'_{k-i}$ in each coefficient of the product matters; the remaining information disappears under the minimum. This phenomenon is particularly pronounced for the middle coefficients, where each minimum runs over a large number of individual sums $c_i + c'_j$.

Hence, the idea is to search for small modifications to the coefficients of both $S_1 = P \otimes M$ and $S_2 = P \otimes N$ which do not spoil the final product. The simplest conceivable approach is to first find a single coefficient c_i in S_1 such that setting $c_i \leftarrow c_i \pm 1$ preserves the product with S_2, and then find a single coefficient c'_j in S_2 such that setting $c'_j \leftarrow c'_j \pm 1$ preserves the product with that modified S_1. Experimentally, for the parameter choices suggested in [3], there appears to be plenty of freedom in S_1 and S_2 to produce a forgery that passes verification.

We stress again that there is no reason to stop at modifying a single coefficient in each value by ± 1 only; hence, the obvious countermeasure of banning values of S_1 and S_2 which are "close to" $P \otimes M$ or $P \otimes N$ is insufficient.

2.3   Attack #2: Swapping Divisors

The second attack is based on the simple observation that divisors of S_1 can be moved over to S_2, and vice versa, without changing the value of the product $S_1 \otimes S_2$. Notably, a full factorization of the respective polynomials is not needed, and finding small-degree divisors appears to be significantly easier — if they exist. Empirically, generic constraint solvers are capable of computing (or ruling out) divisors of reasonably small degree very quickly; see Sect. 2.4.

Forging signatures thus works as follows: Search for a message such that $P \otimes M$ can be decomposed as $D_1 \otimes R_1$ with $\deg(D_1) \ll \deg(R_1)$. Once found, search for a nonce N as in the legitimate signing algorithm that can be decomposed as $D_2 \otimes R_2$ with $\deg(D_2) = \deg(D_1)$. The signature is $(D_1 \otimes R_2, D_2 \otimes R_1, N)$. In practice, executing this forgery becomes a little easier by directly assembling N with a suitable pre-existing known factor, rather than searching randomly.

2.4   Attack Implementation

We provide Python code for both attack varieties, using the proof-of-concept implementation of [3] to check that forgeries were successful. While the script for attack #1 is entirely elementary, the script for attack #2 makes use of the Python interface to the *z3* solver [7] to find divisors of tropical polynomials up to degree 5. (This cutoff was chosen pretty arbitrarily.)

Both attacks require no more than a few seconds of computation on average.

Code: https://yx7.cc/files/tropical-attack.tar.gz

References

1. Brown, D.R.L., Monico, C.: More forging (and patching) of tropical signatures. IACR Cryptology ePrint Archive 2023/1837 (2023). https://ia.cr/2023/1837
2. Buchinskiy, I., Kotov, M., Treier, A.: Analysis of four protocols based on tropical circulant matrices. IACR Cryptology ePrint Archive 2023/1707 (2023). https://ia.cr/2023/1707
3. Chen, J., Grigoriev, D., Shpilrain, V.: Tropical cryptography III: digital signatures. IACR Cryptology ePrint Archive 2023/1475 (2023). https://ia.cr/2023/1475
4. Grigg, N., Manwaring, N.: An elementary proof of the fundamental theorem of tropical algebra (2007). arXiv: 0707.2591
5. Impagliazzo, R.: A personal view of average-case complexity. In: Proceedings of Structure in Complexity Theory, pp. 134–147 (1995)
6. Kim, M.: Tropical Santa (2023). https://soon.haari.me/2023-christmas-ctf/#tropical-santa
7. de Moura, L., Bjørner, N.: Z3: an efficient SMT solver. In: Ramakrishnan, C.R., Rehof, J. (eds.) TACAS 2008. LNCS, vol. 4963, pp. 337–340. Springer, Heidelberg (2008). https://doi.org/10.1007/978-3-540-78800-3_24, https://github.com/Z3Prover/z3

Quantum Circuit Design
for the Lee-Brickell Based Information Set
Decoding

Simone Perriello$^{(\boxtimes)}$ ⓘ, Alessandro Barenghi ⓘ, and Gerardo Pelosi ⓘ

Department of Electronics, Information and Bioengineering - DEIB,
Politecnico di Milano, 20133 Milan, Italy
{simone.perriello,alessandro.barenghi,gerardo.pelosi}@polimi.it

Abstract. In the race for quantum-safe cryptography, fostered by the ongoing National Institute of Standards and Technology (NIST) post-quantum standardization process, it is crucial to assess the security of the emerging schemes. In this work, we propose a fully quantum algorithm to accelerate the Lee-Brickell's Information Set Decoding (ISD)—one of the main cryptanalytic techniques used for assessing the security of code-based schemes—on binary error correcting codes. Our solution relies on a careful scheduling of the quantum gates included in the circuit design, coupled with a strategy that applies multiple times the oracle-reflection, from a Grover-like search, within a single Grover iteration. Compared with the state-of-the-art alternatives, our solution shows a reduction of the circuit depth ranging between 2^3 and 2^{26}, when considering the parameters sets for code-based cryptosystems advanced to the fourth round of the NIST process. Denoting as t and $t-p$ the two sets of bit flips tackled by the Lee-Brickell's strategy, as an additional noteworthy fact we show that our solution exhibits 1 as the best value for p instead of 2 as it is the case for the classic ISD, for all concrete parameter sets considered.

Keywords: code-based cryptography · post-quantum cryptography · quantum computing · Information Set Decoding · ISD

1 Introduction

Shor's quantum algorithm [1], capable of factoring integers and computing discrete logarithms in polynomial time, threatens widely used public-key cryptosystems like RSA and ECC. Acknowledging this threat, prominent organizations like the **National Institute of Standards and Technology (NIST)** are engaging in standardizing cryptographic primitives for **Post-Quantum Cryptography (PQC)**, aiming to safeguard classical data against quantum-accelerated attacks. Among the PQC options, **Code-Based Cryptography (CBC)** has emerged as a promising alternative. Its security hinges on hard problems coming from coding theory, among which the **Syndrome Decoding Problem (SDP)** is

M. Andreoni (Ed.): ACNS 2024 Workshops, LNCS 14587, pp. 8–28, 2024.
https://doi.org/10.1007/978-3-031-61489-7_2

arguably one of the most studied ones. Notably, NIST advanced to the fourth round of its standardization call [2] all the remaining CBC systems, further underlining their potential as alternatives to lattice-based schemes. The relevance of CBC is particularly evident in the proposals submitted to the first (latest at the time of writing) round of NIST's additional call for digital signature schemes [3]. Therefore, it is essential to precisely assess the computational complexity needed to break CBC schemes for concrete parameter values. Classically, the most effective cryptanalytic tool to solve the SDP is the **Information Set Decoding (ISD)** technique, dating back to Prange's proposal [4] that was later slightly improved in several ways [5–13]. On the quantum front, attacks relying on Grover's framework or quantum-walk frameworks exhibit only an asymptotic quadratic speed-up compared to classical ISD approaches.

Related Works. The first work showing a reduced computational complexity of a quantum-accelerated adaptation of the Prange's ISD with respect to its classical counterpart was proposed in [14]. This proposal, relying on Grover's framework, inspired quantum circuit designs for Prange's [15–17], and Lee-Brickell's ISD [16–18]. Notably, the design in [19] offers, to the best of our knowledge, the best figures in terms of all the relevant cost metrics related to quantum circuits (namely, number of qubits, number of gates, depth and depth×width). In [19], the authors additionally argue that the quantum Lee-Brickell's ISD is unlikely to produce significant improvements on the plain Prange's ISD. This assertion is supported by the analyses of quantum circuit in [18], showcasing a design of a hybrid classical-quantum approach based on Lee-Brickell's ISD, and [16], proposing instead a full-quantum approach for both Prange's and Lee-Brickell's ISD. On a parallel research path, the quantum-walk based approaches [20, 21], aiming to accelerate more advanced ISD variants, were shown to provide a theoretical speed-up with respect to the Grover's based approaches. However, to the best of our knowledge, the literature still lacks concrete gate-based circuits design for these approaches, making therefore challenging a precise assessment of their complexity in the finite regime.

Contribution. We describe a quantum circuit adapting the Lee-Brickell's ISD [5] using Grover's quantum framework [22]. By relying on a computational model akin to [23], in which the quantum unit acts as a memory peripheral controlled by the classical unit, we show how a careful design of the classical algorithm generating the quantum circuits reduces the complexity metrics. Our design shows a significantly reduced computational complexities compared to the state-of-the-art designs, with gains ranging from 2^4 to 2^{22} in the depth and depth×width metrics with respect to all the CBC schemes advanced to the fourth round of NIST's standardization call [24]. We additionally present an implementation of Grover's oracle operator diverging from the traditional compute-uncompute pattern employed in its implementation. Finally, as an interesting side result, we report that the optimal value of the parameter p used in our quantum adaptation of the Lee-Brickell's ISD variant is equal to 1, for all concrete cryptosystem parameters considered; this result differs from the expectation on classical ISD solvers, where the asymptotically optimal value is equal to 2.

2   Background

Notation. We denote sets using calligraphic capitalized letters, as in $\mathcal{S}$, and their cardinality as $|\mathcal{S}|$. The notation $[x]$ represents the set of all integers within the range $[0, x-1]$. For sets composed of all the size-y subsets containing integers within $[x]$, we use the notation $\binom{[x]}{y}$. Vectors are denoted with lowercase bold letters, as in v, and intended as column vectors. Matrices are denoted with uppercase bold letters, as in M. Elements within vectors and matrices belong to F_2. The notation $v_{|i}$ denotes the element at index i of the vector v, while $v_{|\mathcal{S}}$ denotes the projection of the elements of v on the indexes of $\mathcal{S}$. The number of elements of v is denoted as $|v|$. Similarly, the subscript $M_{|i,j}$ denotes the element of M at row i and column j, while $M_{|\mathcal{S}_1,\mathcal{S}_2}$ denotes a selection of the rows indexed by the elements in $\mathcal{S}_1$ and of the columns indexed by the element in $\mathcal{S}_2$. In this context, we use the symbol $*$ to represent the set of all rows or columns, as in $M_{|i,*}$, representing the selection of all the elements at row i. Given v_1 and v_2, the notation $[v_1 \, v_2]$ denotes their row-wise concatenation. On the other hand, given A_1 and A_2 of appropriate sizes, the notation $[A_1 \, A_2]$ denotes their column-wise concatenation. Finally, we denote as $\mathsf{Hw}(v)$ the Hamming weight of v, i.e., the number of non-null entries in v, and we denote as $\mathcal{B}_y^x$ the set of all the length-x binary vectors having Hamming weight y. To conclude, we extend the vector notation to array objects by employing Greek letters as labels, as in α, and a 0-based indexing, as in $\alpha_{|i}$, with $0 \le i < |\alpha|$.

2.1   Code-Based Cryptography

Code-Based Cryptography relies on computationally hard problems involving objects from the theory of error-correcting codes. A binary linear code, denoted as $\mathcal{C}$, is a linear mapping from the vector space F_2^k into the vector space F_2^n, with $n > k$, used to encode a k-bit *message*, represented as the vector $m \in F_2^k$, into an n-bit *codeword*, represented as the vector $c \in \mathcal{C} \subset F_2^n$. The encoding adds $r = n-k$ redundant bits to the message m through a linear transformation described by a generator matrix $G \in F_2^{k \times n}$, that is such that $\mathcal{C} = \{c \in F_2^n : c = G^T m\}$. Alternatively, the linear code $\mathcal{C}$ can be characterized by a parity-check matrix $H \in F_2^{r \times n}$, that is such that $\mathcal{C} = \{c \in F_2^n : Hc = 0\}$, being $HG^T = 0_{r \times k}$.

The definition of H provides a straightforward test for the integrity of a potentially corrupted codeword $y = c \oplus e$, where $e \in F_2^n$ represents the error vector. Indeed, since $Hy = Hc \oplus He = He$, if the product Hy is not a null vector, the fact indicates the presence of an error. The vector $s = He$ is known as the *syndrome* of the error e. If no restriction is placed on the values of e, many different values may satisfy $He = s$ for a given H, s pair. In the following we will consider only error vectors with a Hamming weight equal to t, where t is chosen to be small enough that a single error vector satisfies the equation above. While, for appropriately chosen parity-check matrices, it is possible to obtain e given $He = s$ and H, a computation known as *syndrome decoding*, there is no known polynomial time algorithm solving the Syndrome Decoding Problem (SDP) for a random H. The decision version of the SDP (i.e., determining if a

---

Algorithm 1: Lee-Brickell Algorithm

Input   : H: a $r \times n$ binary parity-check matrix
$\quad\quad\quad$ s: a r-bit long syndrome (column vector)
$\quad\quad\quad$ t: the weight of the error vector to be recovered
$\quad\quad\quad$ p: the weight of the first k bits of $\widehat{e}$, $0 \le p \le t$
Output : e: $n \times 1$ column vector s.t. $He = s$, $\mathsf{Hw}(e) = t$

1 **repeat**
2 $\quad$ **repeat**
3 $\quad\quad$ $\mathcal{I} \xleftarrow{\$} \binom{[n]}{r}$
4 $\quad\quad$ $P \leftarrow \mathsf{GetPermutation}(\mathcal{I})$
5 $\quad\quad$ $\widehat{H} \leftarrow HP$ // implies $\widehat{e} = P^T e$
6 $\quad\quad$ $\left[\widehat{H} \mid \widehat{s}\right] \leftarrow \mathsf{GJE}\left(\left[\widehat{H} \mid s\right]\right)$
7 $\quad\quad$ $[W_{r \times r} \mid V_{r \times k}] \leftarrow \widehat{H}$
8 $\quad$ **until** $W = I_r$
9
10 $\quad$ **foreach** $\mathcal{J} \in \binom{[k]}{p}$ **do**
11 $\quad\quad$ $e_1 \leftarrow \widehat{s} \oplus \left(\bigoplus_{j \in \mathcal{J}} V_{|*,j}\right)$
12 $\quad\quad$ **if** $\mathsf{Hw}(e_1) = t - p$ **then**
13 $\quad\quad\quad$ $e_2 \leftarrow \mathbf{0}_{k \times 1}$
14 $\quad\quad\quad$ **foreach** $j \in \mathcal{J}$ **do**
15 $\quad\quad\quad\quad$ $e_{2|j} \leftarrow 1$
16 $\quad\quad\quad$ **return** $P \left[e_1 \, e_2\right]$

---

value for e exists) was shown to be NP-complete in [25], while its search version is NP-hard with a straightforward search to decision reduction algorithm [26]. From now on, we consider the computational variant of the SDP, which is the one solved by ISD based cryptanalytic approaches, defined as follows:

Definition 1 (Computational Syndrome Decoding Problem (CSDP)). *Given a parity-check matrix $H \in F_2^{r \times n}$, a syndrome $s \in F_2^r$, and an integer $t > 0$, find an error vector $e \in F_2^n$ such that $\mathsf{Hw}(e) = t$ and $s = He$.*

Our analysis focuses on the case in which the solution to the CSDP is unique.

The complexity of the SDP paved the way to the design, in the mid-20th century, of two asymmetric cryptosystems: McEliece [27] and Niederreiter [28]. In these systems, the trapdoor function relies on an obfuscated version of a non-random, efficiently decodable parity-check matrix H'. The obfuscation is achieved through the selection of a random secret, non-singular matrix A, along with a random permutation matrix P, obtaining an apparently random parity-check matrix $H = AH'P$ to be used as a public key. The matrix H enables any party wishing to transmit a message, encoded as an error vector e of Hamming weight t, to compute its syndrome $s = He$ and transmit it over a public channel. An adversary aiming to recover e must then find a solution to the SDP.

2.2   Information Set Decoding

Information Set Decoding is a technique to solve the CSDP, with a significant speed-up with respect to a straightforward exhaustive search for the value of e. Lee-Brickell's ISD [5], shown in Algorithm 1, builds upon Prange's initial proposal [4]. The algorithm starts by guessing uniformly at random a set from $\binom{[n]}{k}$, known as *information set* and denoted as $\mathcal{I}$, representing a random guess on the k indexes of the elements of the error vector e of Hamming weight p. In the remaining r positions, which are indexed by the complement of the information set, $\overline{\mathcal{I}}$, e has the remaining Hamming weight $t-p$. The set $\overline{\mathcal{I}}$ (line 3) is employed to obtain a permutation matrix P (line 4), that is used to bring the matrix obtained packing the columns of H indexed by $\overline{\mathcal{I}}$, $H_{|*,\overline{\mathcal{I}}}$, to the leftmost part of H (line 5), resulting in the permuted matrix $\widehat{H}$. Using the original equation of the syndrome $s = He$, the permutation produces the equivalent formulation $s = (HP)\left(P^T e\right)$ that, by renaming the two components enclosed in parentheses, describes a system of linear equations $s = \widehat{H}\widehat{e}$, with $\widehat{e} = P^T e$. We denote the topmost $r{\times}1$ portion of $\widehat{e}$ as e_1, and the bottommost $k{\times}1$ portion as e_2; that is, $\widehat{e} = [e_1 \, e_2]$. Lee-Brickell's assumption can be restated as $\mathsf{Hw}(e_1) = t-p$, and $\mathsf{Hw}(e_2) = p$. The next step of Algorithm 1 executes a **Gauss-Jordan Elimination (GJE)** (line 6) on the augmented matrix $\left[\widehat{H} \; s\right]$, verifying if the resulting matrix $\left[\widehat{H} \; \tilde{s}\right]$ contains an identity submatrix in its leftmost $r{\times}r$ portion. If the condition is not met, the algorithm iterates the random guess of $\overline{\mathcal{I}}$. Conversely, if the condition is met, we can rewrite the equation of the syndrome as:

$$\tilde{s} = [I V] \, [e_1 \, e_2] = e_1 \oplus V e_2 \leftrightarrow e_1 = \tilde{s} \oplus V e_2 \, .$$

The last product represents the sum of the columns of V indexed by the p asserted bits of e_2. For this reason, the algorithm performs an exhaustive search through all the sets belonging to $\binom{[k]}{p}$ (line 10). If, for one such set $\mathcal{J}$, the sum of $\tilde{s}$ to the p columns of V indexed by the elements of $\mathcal{J}$ results in a vector of Hamming weight $t-p$, the algorithm reports a success.

Computational complexity of Algorithm 1. The time complexity of Algorithm 1 is

$$\frac{\mathrm{T_{Iter}}}{\mathrm{Pr_{Succ}}} \approx \frac{\binom{n}{t}}{0.288\binom{r}{t-p}\binom{k}{p}} \left(\mathrm{T_{GJE}}(n,r) + \mathrm{T_{ES}}(k,p,r) \right) \tag{1}$$

Lee-Brickell's algorithm is indeed a Las Vegas algorithm, that is, a randomized algorithm that ensures the correct result (the value of e) with a probabilistic runtime. To compute the expected runtime, we focus on determining the probability of success $\mathrm{Pr_{Succ}}$ for a single iteration of the outer loop (line 1). Notably, each iteration operates independently, randomly selecting a set $\overline{\mathcal{I}}$, making the success probability for one iteration unaffected by others. The probability of success, $\mathrm{Pr_{Succ}}$, is split into two components. The first component is the probability that the submatrix $H_{|*,\overline{\mathcal{I}}}$ is invertible, which is given by $\prod_{i=1}^{n}(1 - 2^{-i})$, which converges to ≈ 0.288 as the value of r increases. The second component is the probability of guessing a set $\overline{\mathcal{I}}$ generating, among all the total number of length-n error vectors having Hamming weight t (i.e., $\binom{n}{t}$), the ones for which $e_{|\overline{\mathcal{I}}}$ has Hamming weight $t-p$ (i.e., $\binom{r}{t}$). The main factor influencing the cost $\mathrm{T_{Iter}}$ of a single iteration of Algorithm 1 is $\mathrm{T_{GJE}}$, representing the cost of executing the GJE algorithm, for which [26] reports a bit complexity of $\mathrm{T_{GJE}}(n,r) = \mathcal{O}\left(\frac{nr^2}{2} + \frac{nr}{2} - \frac{r^3}{6} + r^2 + \frac{r}{6} - 1\right)$. The next component of the cost, $T_{ES}(k, p, r)$, pertains to the exhaustive enumeration of all the $\binom{k}{p}$ possible sets that belong to $\binom{[k]}{p}$. In [26], the authors report a bit complexity of $\mathcal{O}\left(\binom{k}{p}\left((2k - p)\log_2^2\binom{k}{p} + pr\right)\right)$, obtained by generating, at each iteration, the combinatorial representation of the iteration number—that is, the unique $\binom{k}{p}$ combination corresponding to that number—(cost $(2k - p)\log_2^2$), followed by p sums of length-r columns (cost pr).

2.3   Quantum Computing

In quantum computing, the state of a computation is a column vector belonging to a finite-dimensional Hilbert space—that is, a complex vector space equipped with an inner product—spanned by 2^n orthonormal basis states. A state of such a system is denoted as $|\alpha\rangle = \sum_{i \in \{0,1\}^n} a_i |i\rangle$, where each $|i\rangle$ is a basis column vector labelled with an n bit string; $a_i \in \mathbb{C}$ represents its *amplitude*. The state $|\alpha\rangle$ is thus described as a linear combination, called *superposition*, of the basis states. Each digit of a basis state $|i\rangle$ is called *qubit*. When the state is observed, the superposition collapses to one of the basis states $|i\rangle$ with probability $\|a_i\|^2$.

The state of a quantum system is manipulated using quantum *operators*, described through unitary matrices in $\mathbb{C}^{2^n \times 2^n}$. A matrix U is called unitary if $UU^\dagger = U^\dagger U = I$, in which $U^\dagger$ denotes the adjoint of U. The state obtained applying U to a state $|\alpha\rangle$ is described through the matrix vector multiplication $U|\alpha\rangle$. If we partition the qubits into k disjoint subsets, and have k operators $U_1, \ldots, U_k$ each acting on a subset, the global operator acting on the quantum state is $(U_1 \otimes \ldots \otimes U_k)|\alpha\rangle$, in which $\otimes$ denotes the Kronecker products between matrices. On the other hand, the sequential application of the operators $U_{t_1}, \ldots, U_{t_k}$ to a quantum state $|\alpha\rangle$ is expressed as $(U_{t_k} \ldots U_{t_1})|\alpha\rangle$. Fig. 1 (top left) shows an example of operators applied to a state $|\alpha\rangle$.

As an alternative to the algebraic formulation, a sequence of operators can be visualized using a *quantum circuit*, in which each wire corresponds to a qubit, and operators are seen as *quantum gates* sequentially applied, from left to right, to qubits. When considering a circuit implementing U, deriving the circuit for $U^\dagger$ involves reversing the order of the gates used for U, additionally replacing each gate with its adjoint. Such a circuit is commonly called *uncomputation* of U. Figure 1 (top centre) shows the circuit corresponding to the same sequence of operations described in the previous example.

Assuming the computational model of [23], in which the quantum unit is a memory peripheral whose operations are governed by a classical controller, we employ a pseudocode notation to accommodate both quantum and classical operations. To tighten the connection between classical and quantum computation, we refer to a set of qubits as *quantum register*, and we employ the same notation as the one for classical arrays, using an underline to remark the difference between their quantum behaviour, as in $\underline{\alpha}$ and $\underline{\alpha}_{|i}$. Moreover, we use the function notation $G(\underline{\alpha})$ to express that the gate G operates on the quantum register $\underline{\alpha}$. In contrast, classical routine names follow PascalCase notation, capitalizing each word in the compound name of the routine. For instance,

$$\underbrace{(U_Z \otimes U_{SWAP})}_{U_{t_1}} \underbrace{(U_{C^2X})}_{U_{t_2}} \underbrace{(I_2 \otimes U_X \otimes U_{R_Y(\theta)})\,|\alpha\rangle}_{U_{t_3}}$$

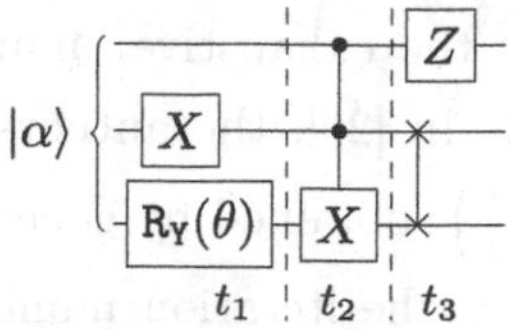

Algorithm: Circuit($\underline{\alpha}$)
X($\underline{\alpha}_{|0}$)
R$_Y$(θ)($\underline{\alpha}_{|2}$)
C^{2}X($\underline{\alpha}_{|2}$ | $\underline{\alpha}_{|0}$, $\underline{\alpha}_{|1}$)
Z($\underline{\alpha}_{|1}$)
SWAP($\underline{\alpha}_{|1}$, $\underline{\alpha}_{|2}$)

$$\texttt{X, NOT} = \begin{bmatrix} 0\,1 \\ 1\,0 \end{bmatrix} \quad \texttt{Z} = \begin{bmatrix} 1 & 0 \\ 0 & -1 \end{bmatrix} \quad \texttt{SWAP} = \begin{bmatrix} 1\,0\,0\,0 \\ 0\,0\,1\,0 \\ 0\,1\,0\,0 \\ 0\,0\,0\,1 \end{bmatrix} \quad \texttt{R}_\texttt{Y}(\theta) = \begin{bmatrix} \cos(\theta/2) & -\sin(\theta/2) \\ \sin(\theta/2) & \cos(\theta/2) \end{bmatrix} \quad \texttt{C}^2\texttt{X, CCNOT} = \begin{bmatrix} I_6 & 0 \\ 0 & U_X \end{bmatrix}$$

Fig. 1. (Top) Three different conventions to represent a sequence of operations applied to a quantum state: mathematical representation (left), gate-based circuit model (center), pseudocode (right). (Bottom) Unitary matrices associated to the gates in the top circuit. Note that I_k denotes the identity matrix of size $k \times k$.

GenerateCircuit($\underline{\alpha}$, a, $\boldsymbol{\alpha}$) denotes a classical routine taking as inputs a quantum register $\underline{\alpha}$, a classical variable a and a classical vector $\boldsymbol{\alpha}$, using them to generate a sequence of quantum gates. Figure 1 (top right) shows the pseudocode corresponding to the same running example.

Finally, we say that a quantum gate—and, by extension, the classical routine generating it—has one or more control qubits to indicate that the gate acts on the target qubits only if all the control ones are 1. In the circuit model, the control qubits are denoted by a black circle, while in the pseudocode, they are separated from the target qubits by the symbol |. For a generic multi-controlled gate, we use the notation C^{n}G to denote an arbitrary gate G having n control qubits and a single target qubit. When $n = 1$ the exponent is omitted. Additionally, since the X gate is commonly interpreted as the quantum analogous of the NOT gate, it is common to refer to the CX and C^{2}X as CNOT and CCNOT respectively.

Reflection Operators. We use the notation $U_{\mathrm{ref}(\alpha)}$ to represent the operator performing a reflection of a quantum state around the subspace defined by $|\alpha\rangle$. Its action is such that $U_{\mathrm{ref}(\alpha)}|\alpha\rangle = |\alpha\rangle$, while $U_{\mathrm{ref}(\alpha)}|\alpha^{\perp}\rangle = -|\alpha\rangle$, in which $|\alpha^{\perp}\rangle$ is any state orthogonal to $|\alpha\rangle$. Analogously, $U_{\mathrm{ref}^{\perp}(\alpha)}$ is the operator performing a reflection around the subspace spanned by $|\alpha^{\perp}\rangle$. We define as $U_{\mathrm{ref}^{\perp}(1)}$ the operator inverting the sign of the amplitude associated to the basis state labelled with the all-one's bitstring, while leaving all the other amplitudes unchanged. The operator corresponds to a C^{n}Z gate involving all the n qubits describing the state $|1^n\rangle$. Similarly, $U_{\mathrm{ref}^{\perp}(0)}$ inverts the sign of the amplitude associated to the basis state labelled as the all-zero's bitstring. The operator can be implemented using a layer of X gates on each of the n qubits describing the basis state $|0^n\rangle$, followed by a C^{n}Z gate, followed by another layer of X gates. Figure 2a shows both.

2.4 Grover's Framework

Grover's algorithm [22] can be phrased in terms of a quantum framework searching for the unique value x^* for which the Boolean function $f : D \mapsto \{0,1\}$

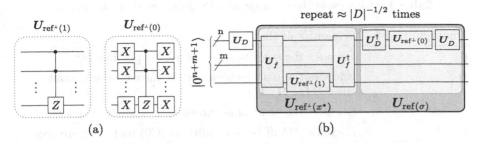

Fig. 2. (a) Circuit for the $U_{\mathrm{ref}^\perp(1)}$ and $U_{\mathrm{ref}^\perp(0)}$ reflection operators. (b) Circuit for Grover's framework in terms of the input preparation U_D, and the reflections $U_{\mathrm{ref}^\perp(x^*)}$ and $U_{\mathrm{ref}(\sigma)}$. The reflections can be decomposed in terms of the simpler reflections $U_{\mathrm{ref}^\perp(1)}$ and $U_{\mathrm{ref}^\perp(0)}$, and the unitary U_f, corresponding to the quantum circuit implementation of the function f, that stores in the last qubit the result of the function evaluation.

evaluates to 1, with $D \subseteq \{0,1\}^n$ representing a subset of all length-n bitstrings. The framework, whose circuit description is given in Fig. 2b, relies on three operators.

1) *Input preparation* (U_D). It corresponds to a quantum circuit preparing a uniform superposition of all the basis states labelled as the bitstrings belonging to the function domain D; that is, $|\sigma\rangle = \sum_{i \in D} \frac{1}{\sqrt{|D|}} |i\rangle$.

2) *Oracle* ($U_{\mathrm{ref}^\perp(x^*)}$). It is a reflection operator that changes the sign of the basis state labeled as x^*. This operator is typically stated in terms of an auxiliary quantum operator U_f, corresponding to a quantum implementation of the Boolean function f. For all the non-trivial functions, the circuit requires a number m of auxiliary qubits, plus an additional single qubit that will store the result of the evaluation of $f(x)$. The U_f operator is then followed by the application of the reflection $U_{\mathrm{ref}^\perp(1)}$ operator on the previous qubit—that is, a Z gate—that, by inverting the sign of the basis state containing a 1 in the output qubit, achieves the reflection $U_{\mathrm{ref}^\perp(x^*)}$. Finally, following a compute-uncompute pattern, the operator $U_f^\dagger$ restores all the qubit labels to their previous states, with the only difference being in their amplitudes.

3) *Diffusion* ($U_{\mathrm{ref}(\sigma)}$). It is a reflection around the superposition state prepared by the U_D circuit, that can be decomposed as $U_{\mathrm{ref}(\sigma)} = U_D U_{\mathrm{ref}^\perp(0)} U_D^\dagger$.

Grover demonstrated how repeating steps 2) and 3) approximately $\frac{1}{\sqrt{|D|}}$ times results in a probability of observing the basis state $|x^*\rangle$ close to 1. In [29], the authors showed that the optimal number of iterations is $\approx \frac{0.58}{\sqrt{|D|}}$, leading to a probability of observing $|x^*\rangle$ close to 0.84. Additionally, they generalized the framework to the case of M multiple solutions, for which the number of iterations is reduced by a factor of $\sqrt{M}$.

Table 1. Overview of the main quantum registers used in our circuit.

Quantum register	Semantics of the content
$\underline{\delta}$	Encodes the superposition of all the possible $\mathcal{B}_r^n$
$\underline{\eta}$	Encodes the parity-check matrix through the various stages $(\boldsymbol{H}, \widehat{\boldsymbol{H}}, \widetilde{\boldsymbol{H}})$
$\underline{\sigma}$	Encodes the syndrome through the various stages $(\boldsymbol{s}, \tilde{\boldsymbol{s}})$
$\underline{\alpha}$	Encodes $|11\rangle$ iff both conditions (C0) and (C1) are true

3   Lee-Brickell Circuit to Speed-Up ISD Iterations

To accelerate the Lee-Brickell's ISD, we frame it as a search procedure to find the unique solution x^* to a Boolean function $f : \mathcal{B}_r^n \mapsto \{0, 1\}$, where the domain $\mathcal{B}_r^n$ is the set of all binary vectors of length n and Hamming weight r, representing all the possible choices for the Information Set complement $\overline{\mathcal{I}}$. Indeed, given a binary vector $\boldsymbol{x} \in \mathcal{B}_r^n$, the set $\{\, i \mid \boldsymbol{x}_{|i} = 1 \,\}$ is an admissible value for the set $\overline{\mathcal{I}}$. In line with the assumptions of Lee-Brickell's algorithm (see Sect. 2.2), the function f evaluates to 1 if and only if both the following conditions are met:

(C0) the corresponding set $\overline{\mathcal{I}} \in \binom{[n]}{r} = \{\, i \mid \boldsymbol{x}_{|i} \,\}$ selects a non-singular subma-trix $\boldsymbol{H}_{|*,\overline{\mathcal{I}}}$ (line 8 of Algorithm 1);
(C1) the sum of a selection of p columns of $\boldsymbol{V}$ and the vector $\tilde{\boldsymbol{s}}$, obtained after the GJE procedure, results in a vector having Hamming weight equal to $t-p$ (line 12 of Algorithm 1).

Employing Grover's framework to speed up the Lee-Brickell's ISD requires a circuit generating a uniform superposition of all the basis states labelled as the bit strings of $\mathcal{B}_r^n$, and another one implementing $\boldsymbol{U}_f$. In the following, we detail the design of the required subcircuits, mapping them to the operators introduced in Sect. 2.4. Table 1 summarizes the quantum registers we employ.

3.1   Input circuit: superposition of all $\overline{\mathcal{I}}$ on $\underline{\delta}$

The $\boldsymbol{U}_D$ operator in Grover's algorithm creates a uniform superposition of all the basis states labelled by bitstrings within the domain $\mathcal{B}_r^n$. This superposition corresponds to the Dicke state $|D_r^n\rangle$, defined as the equal superposition of all n-qubit basis states labelled as bitstrings of Hamming weight r; that is, $|D_r^n\rangle = \binom{n}{r}^{-\frac{1}{2}} \sum_i |i\rangle$, with $i \in \mathcal{B}_r^n$. The first deterministic quantum circuit to generate such a state was presented in [30]. The Dicke state preparation procedure follows an inductive approach, building a Dicke state starting from another one with one less qubit, with a procedure depending on whether the qubit being added is equal to 1 or 0. The authors of [31] reduced the gate count metric from [30], obtaining a circuit consisting of k X gates, $5nk-5k^2-2n$ CX gates, and $4nk-4k^2-2n+1$ R_Y gates. The whole circuit only requires n qubits to store the Dicke state. The complexity of the circuit by [30], was further analysed in [18] obtaining a tighter upper bound on its depth being $\leq \frac{27nk-12n-27k^2+3}{k-2} \in \mathcal{O}(n)$.

3.2 A Grover Oracle Circuit for Lee-Brickell's ISD

We now describe the oracle circuit realizing Lee-Brickell's approach from Algorithm 1, rewritten in terms a Boolean function f. Our design for the oracle operator $U_{\mathrm{ref}^\perp(x^*)}$ diverges from the standard formulation of Grover's framework given in Sect. 2.4 in two ways. Firstly, our reflection operator $U_{\mathrm{ref}^\perp(1)}$ does not act on a single qubit, but on a pair of qubits belonging to a register denoted as $\underline{\alpha}$. The first qubit, $\underline{\alpha}_{|0}$, will be put in state 1 by the subcircuits composing the oracle if and only if condition (C0) is true; the second one, $\underline{\alpha}_{|1}$, will instead be put in state 1 if and only if condition (C1) is true. As a consequence, as explained in Sect. 2.3, the circuit implementation in terms of gates for $U_{\mathrm{ref}^\perp(1)}$ corresponds to a CZ gate involving the two qubits of $\underline{\alpha}$. Secondly, our oracle operator $U_{\mathrm{ref}^\perp(x^*)}$ diverges from the standard compute-rotate-uncompute pattern shown in Sect. 2.4, and instead is implemented by splitting the single $U_{\mathrm{ref}^\perp(1)}$ subcircuit into a sequence of repeated $U_{\mathrm{ref}^\perp(1)}$ operator applications. In the following, we describe all the subcircuits composing our proposal for the oracle implementation. The complexity metrics related to all the oracle subcircuits are reported in Table 2.

Basis Encoding: H into $\underline{\eta}$, s into $\underline{\sigma}$. The first step of the oracle circuit involves the encoding of the parity-check matrix $H \in F_2^{r \times n}$ and the syndrome vector $s \in F_2^r$ within the circuit. This subcircuit maps them onto the qubits of two quantum registers, denoted as $\underline{\eta}$ and $\underline{\sigma}$, respectively. It does so by applying an X gate on the corresponding qubit whenever the value in the matrix or vector is equal to 1. This encoding technique, known as *basis encoding*, requires a number of qubits equal to the original data size, resulting in a total of $rn + r$ qubits. Given that both H and s are random looking, it is reasonable to anticipate that, on average, approximately half of them will be equal to 1. Consequently, this subcircuit needs a number of X gates approximately equal to $(r + rn)/2$. As all these gates can be applied simultaneously, the depth of this stage is 1.

Column Permutation: from H to $\widehat{H}$. The second subcircuit composing the oracle uses the qubits of $\underline{\delta}$, encoding a superposition of all the binary strings representing the possible sets $\overline{\mathcal{I}}$. By binding each of the n qubits of $\underline{\delta}$ to a group of r qubits in $\underline{\eta}$ encoding a single column of H, the value encoded in the qubits of $\underline{\delta}$ represents a binary choice on where to put the qubits tied to them. Specifically, whenever $\underline{\delta}_{|i}$ is equal to 1, the r qubits $\underline{\eta}_{|*,i}$ encoding the column $H_{|*,i}$ are brought in the positions of $\underline{\eta}$ encoding the leftmost $r \times r$ submatrix of H.

For this operation, we use the quantum sorting network, initially proposed in [15] and later expanded in [19]. Its design relies on a quantum adaptation of the classical bitonic sorting network [32], and operates sorting the n qubits labelling a quantum state. As per its classical counterpart, the quantum sorting network employs a fixed number of compare-and-swap units. The comparator required inside the compare-and-swap unit checks if the values of two qubits are not sorted in e.g., increasing order. The authors of [19] show a quantum implementation for this component using 1 CX gate, 2 X gates, and one auxiliary qubit, that is set to 1 if the label of the first qubit is smaller than the one of the

---

Algorithm 2: QGJE — classical generation procedure

Data : η: Encodes $\widehat{H}$ at the start and $\widetilde{H}$ at the end of the algorithm
$\underline{\sigma}$: Encode s at the start and $\tilde{s}$ at the end of the algorithm
$\underline{\beta}$: Auxiliary quantum register initialized to $|\bar{0}\rangle$
$\underline{\gamma}$: Auxiliary quantum register initialized to $|\bar{0}\rangle$

```
 1  b ← 0      c ← 0
 2  for x to r−1 do                       10
       // Phase 1                              // Phase 2
 3     if x ≠ r − 1 then                  11   for i ← 0 to r−1 do
 4        for i ← x + 1 to r−1 do         12      if i ≠ x then
 5           IsEqual(η|x,x, 0, β|b)        13         IsEqual(γ|c, 1, η|i,x)
 6           for j ← 0 to r−1 do          14         for j ← 0 to r−1 do
 7            | Add(η|i,j, η|x,j, |β|b)    15          | Add(η|x,j, η|i,j | γ|c)
 8           Add(σ|i, σ|x | β|b)          16         Add(η|x, η|i | γ|c)
 9           b ← b + 1                     17      c ← c + 1
```

---

second. The result qubit is then used as the control qubit of a CSWAP gate having as target the pair of qubits previously being compared, that will be therefore swapped if and only if they are in the wrong order. The overall network requires $(n-1)\log_2(n)\,(\log_2(n)-1)$ comparators and the same amount of ancillary qubits, and it has a fixed depth of $\log_2(n)\,(\log_2(n)+1)$. Such a circuit can be used to reorder the qubits of $\underline{\eta}$ in such a way that this register will encode, after its computation, the basis encoding of $\widehat{H}$. To do so, while performing pairwise comparisons and swaps between the qubits of $\underline{\delta}$, we additionally perform a set of r CSWAP gates, each one having as control the qubit storing the result of the comparison, and as targets the r pair of qubits of $\underline{\eta}$ encoding the two matrix columns of V. Since the CSWAP can be interleaved between layers, the overall depth for this circuit is $\log_2(n)\,(\log_2(n)+1) + r$. At the end of this stage, we obtain in $\underline{\eta}$ the basis states encoding all the possible values of $\widehat{H}$.

Qgje: from $\left[\widehat{H}, s\right]$ to $\left[\widetilde{H}, \tilde{s}\right]$; Check (C0). This stage performs a **Quantum Gauss Jordan Elimination (QGJE)** on the qubits of $\underline{\eta}$ encoding, in superposition, all the possible values of $\widehat{H}$. To the best of our knowledge, [19] presents the most efficient circuit in terms of depth, number of gates and qubits for a QGJE. The plain version of the proposal is based on a quantum circuit presented in [15], which relies on the classical generation procedure described in Algorithm 2.

The QGJE generation algorithm, that relies on two auxiliary quantum registers denoted $\underline{\beta}$ and $\underline{\gamma}$, performs r distinct iterations. Each iteration, which we denote as x-iteration, focuses on the qubit $\underline{\eta}_{|x,x}$, corresponding to the candidate pivot element $\widehat{H}_{|x,x}$, and is split into two distinct phases. Phase 1 checks if the

value of the qubit encoding the pivot is 0 and, in that case, sets it to 1. Therefore, the loop starting at line 4 iterates on all the qubits encoding the rows of
$\widehat{H}$ below the pivot row. At each iteration, the IsEqual function corresponds to
a quantum circuit to check if the pivot encoded in $\eta_{|x,x}$ is equal to 0 and, in
that case, set an auxiliary qubit belonging to register β to 1 (line 5). Then, the
same qubit of β is used to control the addition of the qubits encoding the row
under analysis to the ones encoding the pivot row through the Add procedure
(line 7), which stores the result in the qubits encoding the pivot row. The same
operation is performed on the qubits of σ encoding the value of $\tilde{s}$ (line 8).

The goal of phase 2 is to put all the qubits encoding the elements of $\widehat{H}$
below and under the pivot to 0. For this reason, at line 11 we iterate over all
such elements. At each iteration, the IsEqual function (line 13) corresponds to
a circuit to check if the element under analysis is 1 and, if this is the case, set
the auxiliary qubit belonging to the quantum register γ to 1. This qubit is then
used to control the additions of the qubits encoding the pivot row to the ones
encoding the row under analysis through the Add function (line 15). The same
operation is performed on the qubits of σ encoding the value of $\tilde{s}$ (line 16).

In terms of standard quantum gates, the quantum circuit generated by the
two functions Add and IsEqual is simplified by the fact that we are working in
F_2. The IsEqual$(\gamma_{|c}, 1, \eta_{|i,x})$ function can be implemented through a simple
CX$\left(\gamma_{|c} \mid \eta_{|i,x}\right)$ gate. Similarly, the IsEqual$(\eta_{|x,x}, 0, \beta_{|b})$ circuit can be imple-
mented through the sequence of gates X$\left(\eta_{|x,x}\right)$, CX$\left(\beta_{|b} \mid \eta_{|x,x}\right)$, and X$\left(\eta_{|x,x}\right)$.
On the other hand, the circuit generated by the uncontrolled version of the Add
procedure can be implemented as a CX gate having as control qubit the first
argument of the function, and as target the second argument of the function.
The controlled version of the Add requires therefore an additional control qubit,
corresponding to the qubit of β in phase 1 and γ in phase 2. This plain version
of the QGJE algorithm was later improved in [19], in which the authors reduced
both the overall depth of the circuit and the number of additional qubits by carefully avoiding the generation of operations on qubits not significant for the final
result, and by rearranging gates across each iteration. Additionally, the authors
also remove all the QGJE operations on the rightmost portion of the register
η, since they only need the leftmost portion of the register. This optimization
cannot be applied to our algorithm, which needs instead the full matrix $\widehat{H}$.
Adapting their proposal to our case, even if the number of C^2X gates increases
by a factor of $\mathcal{O}(r^2k)$, the overall depth only increases by a factor of k, as shown
in Table 2.

At the end of the QGJE stage, we obtain the basis encoding of I_r on the $r \times r$
qubits within η if and only if the quantum register δ contains the encoding of a
set $\overline{\mathcal{I}}$ for which the matrix $H_{|*,\overline{\mathcal{I}}}$ is invertible. This condition, which corresponds
to condition (C0), can be verified by utilizing a multi-controlled gate C^rX, having
as control qubits all the ones within η that encode the leftmost diagonal of $\widehat{H}$,
while employing the ancillary qubit $\alpha_{|0}$ as the target.

Algorithm 3: Exhaustive Search — classical generation procedure

---

Data : r: Number of rows of $\widetilde{H}$ η: Encodes $\widetilde{H}$
$\underline{\sigma}$: Encodes $\tilde{s}$
$\underline{\alpha}$: Auxiliary, having $\underline{\alpha}_{|0}=1$ if (C0) is satisfied, and $\underline{\alpha}_{|0}=0$ before this
procedure starts

1	$\mathcal{J}_p \leftarrow \emptyset$	8	
2	**foreach** $i \in \binom{k}{p}$ **do**	9	**foreach** $j \in \mathcal{D}_r$ **do**
3	$\quad \mathcal{J}_c \leftarrow$ NextComb(i)	10	$\quad$ Add$(\eta_{|*,:j+r}, \underline{\sigma})$
4	$\quad \mathcal{D}_l \leftarrow \mathcal{J}_p \setminus \mathcal{J}_c$	11	IsHwEqual$(\underline{\sigma}, t-p, \underline{\alpha}_{|1})$
5	$\quad \mathcal{D}_r \leftarrow \mathcal{J}_c \setminus \mathcal{J}_p$	12	Reflection$(\underline{\alpha}_{|0}, \underline{\alpha}_{|1})$
6	$\quad$ **foreach** $j \in \mathcal{D}_l$ **do**	13	IsHwEqual$^\dagger(\underline{\sigma}, t-p, \underline{\alpha}_{|1})$
7	$\quad\quad$ Sub$(\eta_{|*,j+r}, \underline{\sigma})$	14	$\mathcal{J}_p \leftarrow \mathcal{J}_c$

Exhaustive sum of $\binom{k}{p}$ **columns of** V; **Check** (C1); **apply** $U_{\mathbf{ref}^\perp(1)}$ The goal of this stage is to find the group of p columns placed in the rightmost $r \times k$ portion of $\widetilde{H}$—corresponding to the submatrix V—and encoded in η satisfying condition (C1). Since p is a fixed value known at circuit generation time, the classical controller, fixing in advance a strategy to generate all the $\binom{k}{p}$ sets belonging to $\mathcal{B}_p^k$, can generate, for each of them, the quantum gates performing the sum of the columns of V indexed by the set and encoded in η to the vector $\tilde{s}$ encoded in $\underline{\sigma}$.

The pseudocode for the circuit generation strategy is given in Algorithm 3. Starting from the empty set $\mathcal{J}_p$, each iteration of the enumeration strategy first generates the next combination of integers through the NextComb function, storing the result in $\mathcal{J}_c$ (line 3), and then computes two additional sets, $\mathcal{D}_l = \mathcal{J}_p \setminus \mathcal{J}_c$ and $\mathcal{D}_r = \mathcal{J}_c \setminus \mathcal{J}_p$. Using them, the algorithm can reuse, in the current iteration, the sum of the columns computed in the previous iteration, and only performs the correct operations on the columns that changed across the two iterations. Hence, the algorithm first generates the quantum circuits to delete, from the sum computed in the previous iteration, the columns indexed by the integers that were present in the previous iteration but not in the current one (Sub procedure at line 7), and then generates the circuit to add the columns indexed by the integers that were not present in the previous iteration but are instead present in the current one (Add procedure at line 10). Note that, since we are working on F_2, both the Add and the Sub procedure are equivalent to XOR operations. The next step of the algorithm, corresponding to the procedure IsHwEqual (line 11), generates a quantum circuit to compute the Hamming weight of the qubits of $\underline{\sigma}$, setting the ancillary qubit $\underline{\alpha}_{|1}$ to 1 if such a weight is equal to $t-p$. Later, the Reflection procedure (line 12) generates a circuit applying the reflection operator $U_{\mathbf{ref}^\perp(1)}$ to $\underline{\alpha}$, whose qubit $\underline{\alpha}_{|0}$ was set to 1 during the stage C) if and only if condition (C0) was satisfied. Finally, the IsHwEqual† procedure generates the quantum circuit corresponding to the adjoint of the circuit generated by the IsHwEqual procedure, restoring the qubit $\underline{\alpha}_{|1}$ to 0 before the next

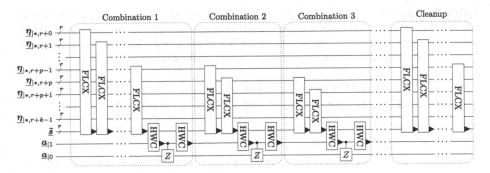

Fig. 3. Quantum circuit implementation of the exhaustive columns sum strategy of Lee-Brickell's ISD (compare to Algorithm 3).

iteration. This enumeration strategy, unlike what typically occurs in a standard adaptation of a Boolean function f to the Grover's framework, necessitates $\binom{k}{p}$ applications of the reflection operator $U_{\text{ref}^\perp(1)}$ at each iteration of Grover's, as opposed to just one. Given the unicity of the solution, the strategy still ensures that only one among the $\binom{k}{p}$ combinations actually sets the qubit $\boldsymbol{\alpha}_{|1}$ to 1, and therefore the sign of the amplitude is changed only once during a single Grover's iterations.

A naive enumeration strategy does not guarantee any pattern in two consecutive combinations of integers generated, resulting, in the worst case, in $|\mathcal{D}_l| = p$ and $|\mathcal{D}_r| = p$. That is, all the indices of the columns changed between two consecutive iterations of the enumeration strategy, and therefore we have to execute p times the procedure Sub and p times the procedure Add. Aiming to reduce both the gate count and the depth of this stage, we rely instead on a different enumeration strategy known as *revolving door algorithm* and detailed in [33, chap. 7.2.1.3]. This algorithm generates all the combinations of the subsets belonging to $\binom{[k]}{p}$ in such a way that, apart from the very first iteration, two consecutive subsets differ by only a single element. During the first iteration, on the other hand, $\mathcal{D}_r$ has size p, while $\mathcal{D}_l$ is empty. The procedures Add and Sub, therefore, are called only once each for all the $\binom{k}{p} - 1$ iterations following the first one.

Figure 3 shows the quantum circuit generated by using such a strategy. In the circuit, the quantum circuits generated by the Sub and Add procedures of Algorithm 3 are both denoted as First to Last CX (FLCX). Both of them apply r CX between the qubits of $\boldsymbol{\eta}$ and $\boldsymbol{\sigma}$, using the former as controls and the latter as targets. The two FLCX applied at each iteration following the first one results in a constant depth of 2, since all the r CX gates composing a FLCX acts on distinct pair of qubits. The Hamming Weight Check (HWC) abstract gate, on the other hand, computes the Hamming weight of the qubits of $\boldsymbol{\alpha}$, setting $\boldsymbol{\alpha}_{|1}$ to 1 if it is equal to $t - p$. The quantum circuit to perform the Hamming weight count can be realized through a quantum implementation of a fast population count circuit, similar to the one used in [19], in which the authors report a logarithmic depth circuit requiring $r - 1$ quantum adder, each one requiring an additional ancillary

Table 2. Complexity metrics for the subcircuits composing $U_{\text{ref}^\perp(x^*)}$, as a function of the linear code parameters (n, r), the wanted Hamming weight (t) and the Lee-Brickell parameter (p). Apart from D), all the other stages require an uncomputation at each Grover's iteration, and hence their values should be multiplied by 2.

Cost metric	A) Basis encoding	B) Columns Permutation	C) QGJE & Check (C0)	D) FLCX, HWCC & Check (C1)
X	$(r+rn)/2$	$2(n-1)\cdot\log_2(n)\cdot$ $(\log_2(n)-1)$	$2(r-1)$	$\binom{k}{p}\cdot(4r-\log_2(r/t)-3)$
CX	0	$(n-1)\cdot\log_2(n)\cdot$ $(\log_2(n)-1)$	$\frac{1}{2}r(r-1)$	$\binom{k}{p}\cdot(\frac{9}{2}r-5\log_2(r)-9)+2r-2p$
C²X	0	0	$\frac{r}{6}\cdot(r-1)\cdot(9n+9-1)$	$\binom{k}{p}\cdot(3r-2\log_2(r)-3)$
C^{a}X$^\Diamond$	0	1	$\binom{k}{p}$	
CZ	0	0	0	$\binom{k}{p}$
CSWAP	0	$(n-1)\cdot\log_2(n)\cdot$ $(\log_2(n)-1)(r+1)$	0	0
Depth	1	$\log^2(n)+$ $\log_2(n)+r-1$	$\frac{3}{2}r^2-\frac{1}{2}r+2$	$\binom{k}{p}\cdot(\log_2^2(r)+7\log_2(r)-2)$
Qubits	$r+rn$	$(n-1)\cdot\log_2(n)\cdot$ $(\log_2(n)-1)$	$\frac{1}{2}r(r-1)$	$r-1$

$\Diamond a$ is equal to r in stage C) and $\log_2(r)$ in stage D).

qubit for the carry. By using the adder of [34], the authors report a gate count of $5r - \log_2(r/t) -3$ X, $9r/2 - 5\log_2(r) -11$ CX and $3r - 2\log_2(r) -3$ C²X, with an overall depth of $\log_2^2(r) + 7\log_2(r) -4$. Moreover, the additional component setting the qubit $\alpha_{|1}$ to 1 if the weight is equal to $t - p$ can be realized by first performing a basis encoding of the value of the binary complement of $t - p$ on the $\log_2(r)$ qubits storing the result of the Hamming weight computation, and then applying the C$^{\log_2(r)}$X gate having all of them as controls, and the qubit $\alpha_{|1}$ as target. Finally, the CZ gate performs the reflection $U_{\text{ref}^\perp(1)}$ using both the qubits of $\underline{\alpha}$, whose qubit $\alpha_{|0}$ was set to 1 during stage C) if condition (C0) was true.

We note that this stage, differently from all the others, does not require an uncomputation circuit to clean up the state of the registers before the next Grover's iteration. Indeed, after the last possible iteration of the enumeration strategy, the classical controller holds all the values of $\mathcal{J}_c$ that, XORed together, gives the result stored in σ. To restore this register to the state in which it was before the enumeration strategy, the controller can just delete, one by one, the p columns of V encoded in $\underline{\eta}$ indexed by the elements of $\mathcal{J}_c$.

4 Experimental Evaluation

To evaluate the computational complexity of our solution with cryptographically relevant parameters, we focus on the CBC schemes that progressed to the fourth

Table 3. Parameter sets for the code-based candidates advanced to round 4 of NIST standardization process [24].

Scheme	Security Level	Code parameters			Scheme	Security Level	Code parameters		
		n	k	t			n	k	t
BIKE (key)	L1	24,646	12,323	142	HQC	L1	35,338	17,669	132
	L3	49,318	24,659	206		L3	71,702	35,851	200
	L5	81,946	40,973	274		L5	115,274	57,637	262
BIKE (message)	L1	24,646	12,323	134	Classic McEliece	L1	3,488	2,720	64
	L3	49,318	2,4659	199		L3	4,608	3,360	96
	L5	81,946	40,973	264		L5	6,688	5,024	128
						L5	6,960	5,413	119
						L5	8,192	6,528	128

round (the ongoing one at the time of writing) of the NIST standardization process [24]: Classic McEliece [35], BIKE [36] and HQC [37]. As per [38], for the BIKE scheme we consider both the message and the key variants to distinguish between the SDP instantiated for the syndrome s being equal to the all-zeros vector and to a random vector respectively. According to NIST's original submission requirements [39], cryptographic schemes were classified into three security levels: L1, L3, and L5. These categories correspond to a computational effort comparable to or greater than that required for a quantum key search on the block cipher AES 128, 192, and 256 respectively. Table 3 displays the parameter sets proposed for all the three CBC proposals under analysis.

NIST's initial submission requirement [39] makes a conservative assumption of an equal weight for all quantum gates involved in a quantum circuit. However, recent literature advocates for converting gates operating on more than 3 qubits into ones operating on at most 3 qubits in order to allow a more concrete assessment of the complexity of implemented quantum circuits. Therefore, we converted the multi-controlled X gates used at each Grover's iteration in both stages C) and D) to check for conditions (C0) and (C1), having a number of controls equal to r and $\log_2(r)$ respectively. While the $C^r X$ gate of stage C) is repeated once at each iteration of Grover's algorithm, the $C^{\log_2(r)} X$ gate of stage D) is instead repeated $\binom{k}{p}$ times at each Grover's iteration. The logarithmic-depth translation of the multi-controlled X gate proposed in [19] proved to offer better results for our proposal. Such a translation requires a number of auxiliary qubits linear in the number of controls. Nevertheless, all of them are restored to their original value, and thus the overall number of qubits of the whole circuit is not affected, since it is still dominated by the rn qubits required to store $\boldsymbol{H}$.

Table 4. Comparison of our quantum Lee-Brickell's ISD approach with: 1) the Prange's ISD quantum (**Q**) circuit design of [16, 19]; 2) the Lee-Brickell's ISD hybrid classical-quantum (**C+Q**) design of [18]; 3) the Prange's and Lee-Brickell's ISD classical (**C**) design employing a DOOM strategy and using the GJE complexity measures of [26]. For the quantum circuits, G denotes the number of quantum gates, D the depth, W the number of qubits, DW multiplies the depth by the width. For the classical circuits, T denotes the number of Boolean gates. All the values are expressed in base-2 logarithm.

Scheme and Sect. level		Prange								Lee-Brickell											
		Q [16]			Q [19]				C	C+Q [18]					This work					C	
		D	W	DW	G	D	W	DW	T	p	G	D	W	DW	p	G	D	W	DW	p	T
BIKE (key)	L1	113	28	141	108	93	29	123	177	3	161	159	15	174	1	105	90	29	119	1	173
	L3	148	30	178	142	127	31	158	244	3	228	225	16	241	1	140	123	31	154	1	239
	L5	184	32	215	178	162	33	195	313	3	295	291	17	308	1	175	158	33	191	1	308
BIKE (message)	L1	109	28	137	104	89	29	119	169	–	–	–	–	–	1	102	86	29	115	1	165
	L3	144	30	175	139	123	31	155	236	–	–	–	–	–	1	136	120	31	151	1	232
	L5	179	32	210	173	157	33	190	303	–	–	–	–	–	1	170	153	33	186	1	298
HQC	L1	110	29	139	104	89	30	119	169	–	–	–	–	–	1	102	86	30	116	1	164
	L3	146	31	177	140	125	32	157	239	–	–	–	–	–	1	138	121	32	153	1	234
	L5	179	33	212	173	157	34	190	303	–	–	–	–	–	1	171	153	34	186	1	297
Classic McEliece	L1	111	21	133	102	92	22	114	173	13	152	145	12	157	1	97	89	22	110	2	163
	L3	134	22	156	125	115	23	138	216	15	194	186	12	198	1	120	111	23	134	2	206
	L5	174	23	198	165	154	24	178	295	–	–	–	–	–	1	160	150	24	174	2	283
	L5	175	23	198	165	155	24	178	296	–	–	–	–	–	1	160	150	24	174	2	284
	L5	194	24	218	184	173	24	197	333	27	300	291	13	304	1	179	169	24	193	2	321

Table 4 shows the assessment of the effort needed to attack the three code-based cryptosystems being evaluated in NIST's PQC standardization call[1]. Note BIKE and HQC employ a quasi-cyclic structure that, as mentioned in [19], allows to reduce the number of Grover's iterations by a factor of $\sqrt{r}$.

In the table, considering an equal impact of all the gates involved, we report the aggregate number of gates (**G**), the depth (**D**), the number of qubits (also known as width (**W**)) and the depth×width (**DW**) metric proposed in [23]. In the same table, we conduct a direct comparison between our proposal and the state-of-the-art works approaching the SDP using a quantum-accelerated attack based on Grover's framework. To the best of our knowledge, the first comprehensive design and implementation of a quantum circuit to accelerate the SDP problem through a quantum ISD approach was presented in [18]. This proposal, based on a quantum adaptation of Prange's ISD [4], was later refined in [19]. The work presented in [16] offers a similar adaptation of Prange's ISD, and further sketches an algorithm for the Lee-Brickell's ISD relying on an exhaustive search strategy

---

[1] The source code used to generate the table measures is available at https://www.github.com/paper-codes/2024-ACNS-scripts.

similar to the one used in our proposal. The first difference between our strategy and the one employed in [16] is that the latter uses an additional accumulator register, which is increased by one, at each iteration of the enumeration, if the current sum of columns of V and $\tilde{s}$ is equal to $t - p$. The second and main difference is instead related to an unoptimized enumeration strategy in [16], leading to p applications at each Grover's iteration of the Sub and Add generation procedure of Algorithm 3. Since $p \ll r$, the $2pr$ CX gates required for each set generated by the enumeration strategy to sum the p columns of V to σ and then, after computing the resulting Hamming weight, delete them from σ, cannot be easily parallelized. Hence, the authors of [19] report, for such a strategy, a depth of the order of $\mathcal{O}(\binom{k}{p}2r)$. Since the proposal of [16] has already a depth for each Grover's iteration in the order of $\mathcal{O}(n^3 \log_2(n))$, the circuit performing the exhaustive strategy does not have a profound impact on the overall measures for $p \in \{1, 2\}$ with respect to the quantum Grover's proposal presented in the same work, while having an exponentially increasing worse complexity for $p > 2$. Lastly, we report in the same table the gate count obtained for the classical Prange's and Lee-Brickell's ISD in terms of standard Boolean gates. To obtain such measures, we employed the GJE complexity metrics reported in [26].

Table 4 shows that our design improves the state-of-the-art in all the metrics, with a gain in the DW metric going from 2^4 to 2^{22} with respect to all the quantum Prange's based proposals. With respect to the quantum Lee-Brickell's proposal made in [18], the gain in the depth and depth×width is still more pronounced. The substantially lower value in the number of qubits required by [18] is justified by the hybrid approach used in that work, that, in offloading only a portion of the Lee-Brickell's approach to the quantum unit, requires the basis encoding for only the matrix V. Finally, we remark that our experimental results show that the value of p giving the best results for all the cryptographic schemes under consideration is $p = 1$. Indeed, for all the values of $p \geq 2$, the computational cost of the oracle circuit in terms of both the depth and the number of gates of the exhaustive search portion of the oracle is greater than the ones of the QGJE, as Table 2 confirms. This result is in contrast to the classical case, for which the McEliece scheme has the best complexity measures for $p = 2$.

5   Concluding Remarks

In this work, we presented a Grover-based quantum circuit solving the SDP, focusing on Lee-Brickell's ISD and we assessed its computational complexities. By targeting CBC schemes that advanced to the final stage of NIST's PQC standardization call, we compared the complexity metrics of our proposal with existing state-of-the-art circuits designed for the same problem. Our results indicate substantial reductions in the computational effort required to attack these cryptosystems across key metrics. We highlight that our implementation of the quantum oracle, a crucial element in Grover's framework, diverges from traditional patterns, opting for a series of repeated rotations, closely mirroring the inner search procedure of Lee-Brickell's algorithm. This novel approach may be of independent interest.

A promising research path explored the adaptation of the quantum walk framework to the advanced ISD variants [20,21], with theoretical enhancements with respect to Grover's framework. However, a concrete quantum circuit design for this approach is yet to be proposed.

Acknowledgements. The activity was partially funded by the Italian *Centro Nazionale di Ricerca in HPC, Big Data e Quantum computing - SPOKE 10* and with partial financial support of the Italian MUR (PRIN 2022 project POst quantum Identification and eNcryption primiTives: dEsign and Realization (POINTER) ID-2022M2JLF2).

References

1. Shor, P.W.: Algorithms for quantum computation: discrete logarithms and factoring. In: 35th Annual Symposium on Foundations of Computer Science, Santa Fe, New Mexico, USA, 20-22 November 1994, pp. 124–134. IEEE Computer Society (1994). https://doi.org/10.1109/SFCS.1994.365700
2. National Institute of Standards and Technology (NIST). Announcing Request for Nominations for Public-Key Post-Quantum Cryptographic Algorithms. Federal Register **81**(244), 92787–92788 (2016). https://federalregister.gov/a/2016-30615
3. National Institute of Standards and Technology (NIST). Call for Additional Digital Signature Schemes for the Post-Quantum Cryptography Standardization Process (2022). https://csrc.nist.gov/csrc/media/Projects/pqc-dig-sig/documents/call-for-proposals-dig-sig-sept-2022.pdf
4. Prange, E.: The use of information sets in decoding cyclic codes. IEEE Trans. Inf. Theory **8**(5), 5–9 (1962). https://doi.org/10.1109/TIT.1962.1057777, http://ieeexplore.ieee.org/document/1057777/. ISSN: 0018-9448. Accessed 08 Sept 2020
5. Lee, P.J., Brickell, E.F.: An observation on the security of McEliece's public-key cryptosystem. In: Barstow, D., et al. (eds.) EUROCRYPT 1988. LNCS, vol. 330, pp. 275–280. Springer, Heidelberg (1988). https://doi.org/10.1007/3-540-45961-8_25. Accessed 08 Sept 2020
6. Leon, J.S.: A probabilistic algorithm for computing minimum weights of large error-correcting codes. IEEE Trans. Inf. Theory **34**(5), 1354–1359 (1988). https://doi.org/10.1109/18.21270
7. Stern, J.: A method for finding codewords of small weight. In: Cohen, G., Wolfmann, J. (eds.) Coding Theory 1988. LNCS, vol. 388, pp. 106–113. Springer, Heidelberg (1989). https://doi.org/10.1007/BFb0019850
8. Dumer, I.: On minimum distance decoding of linear codes. In: Proceedings of the 5th Joint Soviet-Swedish International Workshop Information Theory, Moscow, pp. 50–52 (1991)
9. Finiasz, M., Sendrier, N.: Security bounds for the design of code-based cryptosystems. In: Matsui, M. (ed.) ASIACRYPT 2009. LNCS, vol. 5912, pp. 88–105. Springer, Heidelberg (2009). https://doi.org/10.1007/978-3-642-10366-7_6
10. May, A., Meurer, A., Thomae, E.: Decoding random linear codes in $\tilde{\mathcal{O}}(2^{0.054n})$. In: Lee, D.H., Wang, X. (eds.) ASIACRYPT 2011. LNCS, vol. 7073, pp. 107–124. Springer, Heidelberg (2011). https://doi.org/10.1007/978-3-642-25385-0_6

11. May, A., Ozerov, I.: On computing nearest neighbors with applications to decoding of binary linear codes. In: Oswald, E., Fischlin, M. (eds.) EUROCRYPT 2015, Part I. LNCS, vol. 9056, pp. 203–228. Springer, Heidelberg (2015). https://doi.org/10.1007/978-3-662-46800-5_9

12. Both, L., May, A.: Decoding linear codes with high error rate and its impact for LPN security. In: Lange, T., Steinwandt, R. (eds.) PQCrypto 2018. LNCS, vol. 10786, pp. 25–46. Springer, Cham (2018). https://doi.org/10.1007/978-3-319-79063-3_2

13. Becker, A., Joux, A., May, A., Meurer, A.: Decoding random binary linear codes in $2^{n/20}$: how $1 + 1 = 0$ improves information set decoding. In: Pointcheval, D., Johansson, T. (eds.) EUROCRYPT 2012. LNCS, vol. 7237, pp. 520–536. Springer, Heidelberg (2012). https://doi.org/10.1007/978-3-642-29011-4_31

14. Bernstein, D.J.: Grover vs. McEliece. In: Sendrier, N. (ed.) PQCrypto 2010. LNCS, vol. 6061, pp. 73–80. Springer, Heidelberg (2010). https://doi.org/10.1007/978-3-642-12929-2_6. Accessed 08 Sept 2020

15. Perriello, S., Barenghi, A., Pelosi, G.: A complete quantum circuit to solve the information set decoding problem. In: Müller, H.A., et al. (eds.) IEEE International Conference on Quantum Computing and Engineering, QCE 2021, Broomfield, CO, USA, 17–22 October 2021, pp. 366–377. IEEE (2021). https://doi.org/10.1109/QCE52317.2021.00056

16. Esser, A., et al.: An optimized quantum implementation of ISD on scalable quantum resources (2021). https://eprint.iacr.org/2021/1608

17. Esser, A., et al.: Hybrid decoding - classical-quantum trade-offs for information set decoding. In: Cheon, J.H., Johansson, T. (eds.) PQCrypto 2022. LNCS, vol. 13512, pp. 3–23. Springer, Cham (2022). https://doi.org/10.1007/978-3-031-17234-2_1

18. Perriello, S., Barenghi, A., Pelosi, G.: A quantum circuit to speed-up the cryptanalysis of code-based cryptosystems. In: Garcia-Alfaro, J., Li, S., Poovendran, R., Debar, H., Yung, M. (eds.) SecureComm 2021, Part II. LNICST, vol. 399, pp. 458–474. Springer, Cham (2021). https://doi.org/10.1007/978-3-030-90022-9_25

19. Perriello, S., Barenghi, A., Pelosi, G.: Improving the efficiency of quantum circuits for information set decoding. ACM Trans. Quantum Comput. (2023). https://doi.org/10.1145/3607256. ISSN 2643-6809

20. Kachigar, G., Tillich, J.-P.: Quantum information set decoding algorithms. In: Lange, T., Takagi, T. (eds.) PQCrypto 2017. LNCS, vol. 10346, pp. 69–89. Springer, Cham (2017). https://doi.org/10.1007/978-3-319-59879-6_5

21. Kirshanova, E.: Improved quantum information set decoding. In: Lange, T., Steinwandt, R. (eds.) PQCrypto 2018. LNCS, vol. 10786, pp. 507–527. Springer, Cham (2018). https://doi.org/10.1007/978-3-319-79063-3_24

22. Grover, L.K.: A fast quantum mechanical algorithm for database search. In: Miller, G.L. (ed.) Proceedings of the Twenty-Eighth Annual ACM Symposium on the Theory of Computing, Philadelphia, Pennsylvania, USA, 22–24 May 1996, pp. 212–219. ACM (1996). https://doi.org/10.1145/237814.237866

23. Jaques, S., Schanck, J.M.: Quantum cryptanalysis in the RAM model: claw-finding attacks on SIKE. In: Boldyreva, A., Micciancio, D. (eds.) CRYPTO 2019, Part I. LNCS, vol. 11692, pp. 32–61. Springer, Cham (2019). https://doi.org/10.1007/978-3-030-26948-7_2

24. Moody, D.: Status report on the third round of the NIST post-quantum cryptography standardization process. NIST IR 8413. National Institute of Standards and Technology, Gaithersburg (2022). https://doi.org/10.6028/NIST.IR.8413, https://nvlpubs.nist.gov/nistpubs/ir/2022/NIST.IR.8413.pdf. Accessed 06 July 2022

25. Berlekamp, E.R., McEliece, R.J., van Tilborg, H.C.A.: On the inherent intractability of certain coding problems (corresp.). IEEE Trans. Comput.-Aided Design Integr. Circuits Syst. **24**(3), 384–386 (1978). https://doi.org/10.1109/TIT.1978.1055873

26. Baldi, M., et al.: A finite regime analysis of information set decoding algorithms. Algorithms **12**(10) (2019). https://doi.org/10.3390/a12100209, https://www.mdpi.com/1999-4893/12/10/209. ISSN 1999-4893

27. McEliece, R.J.: A public-key cryptosystem based on algebraic coding theory. In: The Deep Space Network progress report, pp. 114–116 (1978). https://ntrs.nasa.gov/api/citations/19780016269/downloads/19780016269.pdf

28. Niederreiter, H.: Knapsack-type cryptosystems and algebraic coding theory. Probl. Control Inf. Theory **15**(2), 157–166 (1986)

29. Boyer, M., et al.: Tight bounds on quantum searching. Fortschritte der Phys.: Progr. Phys. **46**(4-5), pp. 493–505 (1998). https://doi.org/10.1002/(SICI)1521-3978(199806)46:4/5<493::AID-PROP493>3.0.CO;2-P, arXiv: quant-ph/9605034

30. Bärtschi, A., Eidenbenz, S.: Deterministic preparation of Dicke states. In: Gąsieniec, L.A., Jansson, J., Levcopoulos, C. (eds.) FCT 2019. LNCS, vol. 11651, pp. 126–139. Springer, Cham (2019). https://doi.org/10.1007/978-3-030-25027-0_9

31. Mukherjee, C.S., et al.: Preparing Dicke states on a quantum computer. IEEE Trans. Quantum Eng. **1**, 1–17 (2020). https://doi.org/10.1109/TQE.2020.3041479

32. Batcher, K.E.: Sorting networks and their applications. In: American Federation of Information Processing Societies: AFIPS Conference Proceedings: 1968 Spring Joint Computer Conference, Atlantic City, NJ, USA, 30 April–2 May 1968, vol. 32. AFIPS Conference Proceedings, pp. 307–314. Thomson Book Company, Washington D.C. (1968). https://doi.org/10.1145/1468075.1468121

33. Knuth, D.E.: The Art of Computer Programming, Volume IVa: Combinatorial Algorithms. Addison-Wesley Professional (2011)

34. Takahashi, Y., Tani, S., Kunihiro, N.: Quantum addition circuits and unbounded fan-out. Quant. Inf. Comput. **10**, 872–890 (2010). https://doi.org/10.26421/QIC10.9-10-12

35. Bernstein, D.J., et al.: Classic McEliece: conservative code-based cryptography (2020). https://classic.mceliece.org/. Accessed 20 Aug 2023

36. Aragon, N., et al.: BIKE: bit flipping key encapsulation (2017). https://bikesuite.org. Accessed 20 Aug 2023

37. Melchor, C.A., et al.: Hamming quasi-cyclic (HQC) (2017). https://pqc-hqc.org/. Accessed 20 Aug 2023

38. Esser, A., Bellini, E.: Syndrome decoding estimator. In: Hanaoka, G., Shikata, J., Watanabe, Y. (eds.) PKC 2022, Part I. LNCS, vol. 13177, pp. 112–141. Springer, Cham (2022). https://doi.org/10.1007/978-3-030-97121-2_5

39. National Institute of Standards and Technology (NIST). Submission Requirements and Evaluation Criteria for the Post-Quantum Cryptography Standardization Process (2016). https://csrc.nist.gov/CSRC/media/Projects/Post-Quantum-Cryptography/documents/call-for-proposals-final-dec-2016.pdf

Projective Space Stern Decoding and Application to SDitH

Kevin Carrier[1]([✉]), Valerian Hatey[1], and Jean-Pierre Tillich[2]

[1] ETIS UMR 8051 - Cergy-Paris Université, ENSEA, CNRS, Cergy, France
kevin.carrier@cyu.fr, valerian.hatey@ensea.fr
[2] Project COSMIQ, Inria de Paris, Paris, France
jean-pierre.tillich@inria.fr

Abstract. We show that here standard decoding algorithms for generic linear codes over a finite field can speeded up by a factor which is essentially the size of the finite field by reducing it to a low weight codeword problem and working in the relevant projective space. We apply this technique to SDitH and show that the parameters of both the original submission and the updated version fall short of meeting the security requirements asked by the NIST.

1 Introduction

Code-based cryptography is based on the hardness of the decoding problem. In its syndrome (and fixed weight) version it is given for the Hamming metric (where we denote the Hamming weight of a vector $\mathbf{x}$ by $|\mathbf{x}|$) by

Problem 1.1 (Syndrome Decoding SD($\mathbf{H}, \mathbf{s}, t$)). *Given a matrix* $\mathbf{H} \in \mathbb{F}_q^{(n-k) \times n}$, *a syndrome* $\mathbf{s} \in \mathbb{F}_q^{n-k}$ *and a weight* $t \in [\![0, n]\!]$, *find a vector* $\mathbf{e} \in \mathbb{F}_q^n$ *such that* $\mathbf{He} = \mathbf{s}$ *and* $|\mathbf{e}| = t$.

In other words, it consists in solving a linear system with a constraint on the weight of the solution. This non-linear constraint is commonly believed to make the problem difficult on average over $\mathbf{H}$ for suitable values of t. Despite that many efforts have been spent over the last 60 years [Pra62, Ste88, Dum91, MMT11, BJMM12, MO15, BM17, BM18, CDMT22], the problem remains hard in the range of parameters given above, even with the help of a quantum computer [Ber10, KT17]. Thus, the decoding problem has raised interest among cryptosystem designers. It is today the heart of the security of PKE and signature schemes submitted to the NIST competitions[1] such as Classic McEliece

---

[1] https://csrc.nist.gov/projects/post-quantum-cryptography.

The work of KC, VH and JPT was funded by the French Agence Nationale de la Recherche through ANR JCJC DECODE (ANR-22-CE39-0004-01) for KC and VH and ANR-22-PETQ-0008 PQ-TLS for JPT.

© The Author(s), under exclusive license to Springer Nature Switzerland AG 2024
M. Andreoni (Ed.): ACNS 2024 Workshops, LNCS 14587, pp. 29–52, 2024.
https://doi.org/10.1007/978-3-031-61489-7_3

[AAB+22], BIKE [ABC+22], Wave [BCC+23] and SDitH [AMFG+23]. It is quite common to study the binary version of the decoding problem but the non-binary case also aroused interest [BLP10, BLP11] or more recently with the signature schemes Wave [DST19] or SDitH [FJR22] for instance. The security of Wave is based on ternary codes and SDitH addresses the syndrome decoding over the fields $\mathbb{F}_{256}$ and $\mathbb{F}_{251}$. In this article, we focus on the case where q is large, as is the case in SDitH.

The best known decoding algorithms are Information Set Decoders (ISD) initiated by Prange in [Pra62]. The idea of Prange basically consists in guessing that $\mathbf{e}$ is zero on an *information set*, that is a set of k positions that determines the whole vector $\mathbf{e}$ considering the linear relation $\mathbf{He} = \mathbf{s}$. If the guess does not allow to find a vector of weight t, then we repeat the process changing the information set until we make the right guess on it.

There have been numerous improvements to the Prange algorithm. One of the first breakthrough in this domain uses the *birthday paradox* [Ste88, Dum91]. Basically, the ISD template is used here to reduce the decoding problem to a collision search. Later, other techniques were introduced to improve ISD. For instance, [MMT11] and [BJMM12] exploit the fact that a low weight vector can be represented in multiple ways as the sum of two lower weight vectors, it is the so-called *representation technique* introduced by Howgrave-Graham and Joux in [HJ10]. In the SDitH specifications, it is noticed that the representation technique was originally designed for the binary case and that it loses its interest when q is large. This claim is supported by Meurer in his PhD thesis [Meu12] and also by Canto-Torres in [Can17] where he shows that the MMT [MMT11] and BJMM [BJMM12] complexity exponent tend to the Prange complexity exponent when q tends to infinity. This is the reason why the algorithm on which SDitH focuses on is Stern [Ste88] which is considered optimal by the authors of SDitH in their particular context.

1.1　Our Contribution

Our main observation here is that decoding over a big field can basically be speeded up by a factor which is the size of the field by a simple homogenizing trick (or what is the same by a reduction to the low weight codeword search problem). The idea is that instead of looking for a vector $\mathbf{e}$ of weight t satisfying $\mathbf{He} = \mathbf{s}$ we look for a vector $\mathbf{x}$ of weight t such that $\mathbf{Hx}$ is *proportional* to $\mathbf{s}$, *i.e.* is such that $\mathbf{Hx} = \lambda \mathbf{s}$ for some $\lambda \in \mathbb{F}_q$. If we find such a vector (and if $\lambda \neq 0$ which will happen with large probability as we will see in what follows) then we get from such an $\mathbf{x}$ our $\mathbf{e}$ by taking $\mathbf{e} = \lambda^{-1}\mathbf{x}$. The point is that basically all the collision search techniques used for solving the decoding problem get speeded by essentially a factor $q - 1$ by identifying all vectors which are proportional. This is particularly helpful in the case where we work with big field sizes as is the case for the NIST submission SDitH [AMFG+23]. We will adapt this idea to one of the simplest collision decoding technique, namely Stern's decoding algorithm over $\mathbb{F}_q$ [Pet10]. We call this variant, *projective Stern's algorithm* since we work here essentially in the projective space. We provide here a clean counting of the complexity of this variant of Stern's algorithm in the spirit of [Pet11, Ch. 6]. This precise complexity counting includes the use of the Canteaut-Chabaud technique [CC98] to gain in the complexity of Gaussian elimination. This part can not be neglected at all for giving tight security estimates in the case of SDitH because the list sizes in an optimal Stern algorithm are in this case really small. In SDitH there is also a variant of the decoding which is considered, which is the d-split variant: the support of the error is split into d equal parts and it asked to find an error $\mathbf{e}$ of weight t/d on each of the part. We give an adaptation of our projective Stern's algorithm to this case too.

We will study in detail the impact of this technique to SDitH both for the initial submission [AMFG+23] and for the recent update that can be found on https://sdith.org/. The initial submission was unfortunately affected by a mistake in the choice of parameters that corresponded to a region where there were several hundred of solutions to the decoding problem whereas the analysis implicitly assumed that there was just one. The security claims made in [AMFG+23] were incorrect because of this. The new algorithm presented here also reduces the security of this proposal. All in all, this shows that the security of the initial submission [AMFG+23] is below the NIST requirements by 9 to 14 bits depending on the SDitH variant. Three days after preliminary results of this work were made public [CTH23], new parameters of SDitH were released and announced on the NIST forum (see https://groups.google.com/a/list.nist.gov/g/pqc-forum/c/OOnB655mCN8/m/rL4bPD20AAAJ). This new parameter set corrected the initial error in the parameter choice (now the parameters are chosen such that there is typically just one solution to the decoding problem). The authors took a 4 bit security margin between the NIST security requirements and the estimate for the best attack provided in https://sdith.org/. We show here that this is still a little bit short of meeting the NIST requirements by roughly one bit. It should be noted that contrarily to [AMFG+23] which uses (i) a non tight reduction from standard decoding to d-split decoding which gives an overestimate on the attacks, (ii) neglects the cost of Gaussian elimination in the attack, our security estimate is based on a precise count of the complexity of the attack which does not neglect the cost of Gaussian elimination. It turns out that the optimal parameters for the projective Stern algorithm are in the regime where the cost of Gaussian elimination is non negligible.

2 Preliminaries

Vectors and Matrices. Vectors and matrices are respectively denoted in bold letters and bold capital letters such as $\mathbf{v}$ and $\mathbf{M}$. The entry at index i of the vector $\mathbf{v}$ is denoted by v_i. $\mathbf{M}^\mathsf{T}$ stands for the transpose of the matrix $\mathbf{M}$. To limit the use of transposition notation as much as possible, we consider in this paper that the vectors are column vectors; so $\mathbf{v}^\mathsf{T}$ represents a row vector. Let I be a list of indexes. We denote by $\mathbf{v}_I$ the vector $(v_i)_{i \in I}$. In the same way, we denote by $\mathbf{M}_I$ the submatrix made up of the columns of $\mathbf{M}$ which are indexed by I. The notation $\mathrm{supp}(\mathbf{v})$ stands for the support of $\mathbf{v}$, that is the set of the non-zero positions of $\mathbf{v}$.

The double square brackets stand for a set of consecutive integers. For instance, $[\![a, b]\!]$ are the integers between a and b.

Coding Background. A linear code $\mathcal{C}$ of length n and dimension k over the field $\mathbb{F}_q$ is a subspace of $\mathbb{F}_q^n$ of dimension k. We say that it is an $[n, k]_q$-code. It can be defined by a *generator matrix* $\mathbf{G} \in \mathbb{F}_q^{k \times n}$ whose rows form a basis of the code:

$$\mathcal{C} \stackrel{\text{def}}{=} \left\{ \mathbf{G}^\top \mathbf{u} \; : \; \mathbf{u} \in \mathbb{F}_q^k \right\}. \tag{2.1}$$

A *parity-check matrix* for $\mathcal{C}$ is a matrix $\mathbf{H} \in \mathbb{F}_q^{(n-k) \times n}$ whose right kernel is $\mathcal{C}$:

$$\mathcal{C} \stackrel{\text{def}}{=} \left\{ \mathbf{c} \in \mathbb{F}_q^n \; : \; \mathbf{Hc} = \mathbf{0} \right\}. \tag{2.2}$$

A set of k positions that fully defines a code $\mathcal{C}$ is called an *information set*. In other words, for $I \subseteq [\![1, n]\!]$ such that $|I| = k$ and $J \stackrel{\text{def}}{=} [\![1, n]\!] \smallsetminus I$, the subset I is an information set if and only if $\mathbf{G}_I$ is invertible or equivalently $\mathbf{H}_J$ is invertible. In that case, J is called *redundancy set*.

In this paper, we address the decoding Problem 1.1. We focus on the case where the decoding distance t is lower than $n - \frac{n}{q}$. We distinguish two particular regimes: when the decoding problem has typically less than one solution and when it has more. For $\mathbf{H} \in \mathbb{F}_q^{(n-k) \times n}$ and $\mathbf{s} \in \mathbb{F}_q^{n-k}$ that are drawn uniformly at random, the greatest distance t for which the decoding problem has less than one solution on expectation is called the *Gilbert-Varshamov distance* and it is denoted by:

$$d_{\mathsf{GV}}(n, k) \stackrel{\text{def}}{=} \sup \left(\left\{ t \in \left[\!\!\left[0, n - \tfrac{n}{q} \right]\!\!\right] \; : \; \binom{n}{t} (q-1)^t \leqslant q^{n-k} \right\} \right) \tag{2.3}$$

How We Measure Complexities. Because one of our goals is to compare our results to those of the SDitH specifications, we measure the complexities in the same way as they do. In particular, we assume that the additions and multiplications in $\mathbb{F}_q$ are implemented using lookup tables and that these two operations therefore have the same cost. In the SDitH specifications, this cost is considered as $\log_2(q)$ which is the estimated cost of a memory access. In the following, we count the complexities in number of additions/multiplications and therefore we ignore the factor $\log_2(q)$. However, the results of Sect. 7 are given with this factor.

3 The Stern Decoder and Peters' Improvements

In this section, we recall the main results of [Ste88] and [Pet10] that are used in SDitH specifications to solve the decoding problem $\mathrm{SD}(\mathbf{H}, \mathbf{s}, t)$. Stern's decoding algorithm is an iterative algorithm that is parametrized by two integers p and ℓ to optimize. Each iteration starts by selecting an information set $I \subseteq [\![1, n]\!]$ of size k. We denote $J \stackrel{\text{def}}{=} [\![1, n]\!] \smallsetminus I$. Then, we search for $\mathbf{x} \in \mathbb{F}_q^k$ of weight $2p$ such that:

$$|\mathbf{Px} - \mathbf{y}| = t - 2p \tag{3.1}$$

where

$$\mathbf{P} \overset{\text{def}}{=} \mathbf{H}_J^{-1}\mathbf{H}_I \quad \text{and} \quad \mathbf{y} \overset{\text{def}}{=} \mathbf{H}_J^{-1}\mathbf{s} \qquad (3.2)$$

We can easily verify that if we find such an $\mathbf{x}$, then the vector $\mathbf{e} \in \mathbb{F}_q^n$ defined by $\mathbf{e}_I \overset{\text{def}}{=} \mathbf{x}$ and $\mathbf{e}_J \overset{\text{def}}{=} \mathbf{y} - \mathbf{Px}$ is a solution to the decoding problem. By making the additional bet that the sought error $\mathbf{e}$ is such that $\mathbf{e}_I$ is of weight p on each half and $\mathbf{e}_J$ is $\mathbf{0}$ on its ℓ first positions, we can use collision search to find $\mathbf{e}$ more efficiently. Indeed, using lookup tables, one can find all pairs $(\mathbf{x}_1, \mathbf{x}_2) \in \mathbb{F}_q^k \times \mathbb{F}_q^k$ such that $\mathbf{x}_1$ is zero on its second half (resp. $\mathbf{x}_2$ is zero on its first half), $|\mathbf{x}_1| = p$ (resp. $|\mathbf{x}_2| = p$) and $\mathbf{Px}_1 - \mathbf{y}$ and $\mathbf{Px}_2$ collide on their ℓ first positions. Thus, for each of these collisions, the vector $\mathbf{e}$ such that $\mathbf{e}_I \overset{\text{def}}{=} \mathbf{x}_1 + \mathbf{x}_2$ and $\mathbf{e}_J \overset{\text{def}}{=} \mathbf{y} - \mathbf{P}(\mathbf{x}_1 + \mathbf{x}_2)$ is a potential solution to the SD problem because it has syndrome $\mathbf{s}$ and it is of particular low weight on at least $k + \ell$ positions. Finally, Algorithm 1 summarizes the Stern decoder.

Algorithm 1: Stern's algorithm to solve $\mathrm{SD}(\mathbf{H}, \mathbf{s}, t)$

Input: $\mathbf{H} \in \mathbb{F}_q^{(n-k) \times n}$, $\mathbf{s} \in \mathbb{F}_q^{n-k}$ and $t \in [\![0, n]\!]$.
Parameters: $p \in \left[\!\!\left[0, \frac{\min(t,k)}{2}\right]\!\!\right]$ and $\ell \in [\![0, n-k-t+2p]\!]$.
Output: $\mathbf{e} \in \mathbb{F}_q^n$ such that $\mathbf{He} = \mathbf{s}$ and $|\mathbf{e}| = t$.

1 **repeat as many times as necessary**
2   draw $I \subseteq [\![1, n]\!]$ of size k uniformly at random
3     $J \leftarrow [\![1, n]\!] \smallsetminus I$
4     $\mathbf{P} \leftarrow \mathbf{H}_J^{-1}\mathbf{H}_I$ /* if $\mathbf{H}_J$ is not invertible, go back to step 2 */
5     $\mathbf{y} \leftarrow \mathbf{H}_J^{-1}\mathbf{s}$
6     $\mathbf{R} \leftarrow$ the ℓ first rows of $\mathbf{P}$
7     $\mathbf{z} \leftarrow$ the ℓ first positions of $\mathbf{s}$
8     $\mathscr{L}_1 \leftarrow \left\{ \mathbf{Rx}_1 - \mathbf{z} : \mathbf{x}_1 \in \mathbb{F}_q^{\lfloor k/2 \rfloor} \times 0^{k-\lfloor k/2 \rfloor} \text{ and } |\mathbf{x}_1| = p \right\}$
9     $\mathscr{L}_2 \leftarrow \left\{ \mathbf{Rx}_2 : \mathbf{x}_2 \in 0^{\lfloor k/2 \rfloor} \times \mathbb{F}_q^{k-\lfloor k/2 \rfloor} \text{ and } |\mathbf{x}_2| = p \right\}$
10   **forall** $(\mathbf{Rx}_1 - \mathbf{z}, \mathbf{Rx}_2) \in \mathscr{L}_1 \times \mathscr{L}_2$ *such that* $\mathbf{Rx}_1 - \mathbf{z} = \mathbf{Rx}_2$ **do**
11   **if** $|\mathbf{P}(\mathbf{x}_1 - \mathbf{x}_2) - \mathbf{y}| = t - 2p$ **then**
12   **return** $\mathbf{e}$ such that $\mathbf{e}_I \overset{\text{def}}{=} \mathbf{x}_1 - \mathbf{x}_2$ and $\mathbf{e}_J \overset{\text{def}}{=} \mathbf{y} - \mathbf{P}(\mathbf{x}_1 - \mathbf{x}_2)$

Note that if a particular error vector $\mathbf{e}$ has the good weight distribution – that is $\mathbf{e}_I$ is of weight p on each half, $\mathbf{e}_J$ is $\mathbf{0}$ on its ℓ first positions and of weight $t - 2p$ on its $n - k - \ell$ other positions – then Stern's algorithm will find $\mathbf{e}$. So the probability to find a particular solution is

$$p_{\text{part}} = \frac{\binom{\lfloor k/2 \rfloor}{p}\binom{k-\lfloor k/2 \rfloor}{p}\binom{n-k-\ell}{t-2p}}{\binom{n}{t}} \qquad (3.3)$$

Moreover, in the case where **s** has been produced as the syndrome of an error $\widetilde{\mathbf{e}}$ of weight t – that means **s** has been drawn uniformly at random in $\{\mathbf{H}\widetilde{\mathbf{e}} : |\widetilde{\mathbf{e}}| = t\}$ – then, the expected number of solutions to the decoding problem we address[2] is

$$N_{\text{sol}} \overset{\text{def}}{=} \mathbb{E}_{\mathbf{H}}\left(|\{\mathbf{e} \in \mathbb{F}_q^n : |\mathbf{e}| = t \text{ and } \mathbf{H}\mathbf{e} = \mathbf{H}\widetilde{\mathbf{e}}\}|\right) \tag{3.4}$$

$$= 1 + \sum_{\substack{\mathbf{e} \in \mathbb{F}_q^n \setminus \{\widetilde{\mathbf{e}}\} \\ |\mathbf{e}| = t}} \mathbb{P}_{\mathbf{H}}\left(\mathbf{H}\mathbf{e} = \mathbf{H}\widetilde{\mathbf{e}}\right) \tag{3.5}$$

$$= 1 + \frac{\binom{n}{t}(q-1)^t - 1}{q^{n-k}} \tag{3.6}$$

Thus, the success probability of one iteration of Stern's algorithm is

$$p_{\text{succ}} = 1 - (1 - p_{\text{part}})^{N_{\text{sol}}} \tag{3.7}$$

So on average over the choice of **H**, we need to repeat Stern's procedure $\frac{1}{p_{\text{succ}}}$ times before finding a solution to the decoding problem. To determine the complexity of Stern's algorithm, we still have to measure the time complexity of one iteration. Using some of the tricks proposed in [Pet10], the designers of SDitH claim to be able to perform each iteration of Stern with a running time

$$\begin{aligned}
T_{\text{iter}} = \; & \tfrac{1}{2}(n-k)^2(n+k) \\
& + \ell\left(\tfrac{k}{2} - p + 1 + \left(\binom{\lfloor k/2 \rfloor}{p} + \binom{k-\lfloor k/2 \rfloor}{p}\right)(q-1)^p\right) \\
& + \tfrac{q}{q-1}(t - 2p + 1)2p\left(1 + \tfrac{q-2}{q-1}\right)\frac{\binom{\lfloor k/2 \rfloor}{p}\binom{k-\lfloor k/2 \rfloor}{p}(q-1)^{2p}}{q^\ell}
\end{aligned} \tag{3.8}$$

4   Reducing the Decoding Problem to the Low Weight Codeword Search

Working in projective spaces is only interesting if the syndrome is zero. In that case, we are actually looking for a low weight codeword instead of an error vector. This can be readily achieved by a well known reduction from decoding in an $[n, k]_q$ linear code to a low weight codeword search in an $[n, k+1]_q$ linear code (see for instance [NCBB10, Section 1, page 4]) that we now recall. Let **H** be a parity check matrix of a code $\mathcal{C}$. Without loss of generality, we can consider that **H** is in systematic form[3]:

$$\mathbf{H} \overset{\text{def}}{=} [\mathbf{A} | \mathbf{I}_{n-k}] \qquad \text{where } \mathbf{A} \in \mathbb{F}_q^{(n-k) \times k} \tag{4.1}$$

---

[2] Simulations can be found on https://github.com/kevin-carrier/SDitH_security to verify the Eq. (3.6).

[3] The first operation of Stern's algorithm precisely consists in putting the parity-check matrix in systematic form (up to a permutation). And therefore making this assumption does not induce any additional cost.

To solve the decoding problem $SD(\mathbf{H}, \mathbf{s}, t)$, one can find a low weight codeword in the new code

$$\mathcal{C}' \overset{\text{def}}{=} \langle \mathcal{C}, \mathbf{z} \rangle \overset{\text{def}}{=} \{\mathbf{c} + \alpha \mathbf{z} \; : \; \mathbf{c} \in \mathcal{C} \text{ and } \alpha \in \mathbb{F}_q\} \tag{4.2}$$

where $\mathbf{z} \in \mathbb{F}_q^n$ is any solution of the equation $\mathbf{Hz} = \mathbf{s}$ (without any weight constraint on $\mathbf{z}$). Because $\mathbf{H}$ is in systematic form, we can take $\mathbf{z}^\top \overset{\text{def}}{=} (\mathbf{0}^\top, \mathbf{s}^\top) \in \mathbb{F}_q^n$. Then a generator matrix of $\mathcal{C}'$ is

$$\mathbf{G}' \overset{\text{def}}{=} \begin{bmatrix} \mathbf{I}_k & -\mathbf{A}^\top \\ \mathbf{0}^\top & \mathbf{s}^\top \end{bmatrix} \tag{4.3}$$

By only one step of a Gaussian elimination (one column to eliminate), we can find a parity-check matrix $\mathbf{H}'$ of the augmented code $\mathcal{C}'$.

By looking for a low weight codeword in $\mathcal{C}'$ – *i.e.* a vector $\mathbf{e}$ such that $\mathbf{H}'\mathbf{e} = \mathbf{0}$ –, we actually find a low weight error $\mathbf{e}$ of $\mathcal{C}$ that has syndrome $\mathbf{He} = \alpha \mathbf{s}$ where α can be any scalar in $\mathbb{F}_q$. There are two possible situations: either $\alpha = 0$ or $\alpha \neq 0$. If $\alpha = 0$ then we have actually found a codeword in $\mathcal{C}$ instead of an error vector (we want to avoid this situation). On the contrary, if $\alpha \neq 0$ then a solution to our original decoding problem is simply $\alpha^{-1}\mathbf{e}$. We now claim that the probability to get $\alpha = 0$ is lower than $\frac{1}{q}$:

Theorem 4.1. *Let a code $\mathcal{C}$ be the right kernel of a parity-check matrix $\mathbf{H} \in \mathbb{F}_q^{(n-k) \times n}$ and let $\mathbf{s} \in \{\mathbf{H}\widetilde{\mathbf{e}} \; : \; |\widetilde{\mathbf{e}}| = t\}$ for $t \in [\![0, n]\!]$. Let $\mathcal{C}' \overset{\text{def}}{=} \langle \mathcal{C}, \mathbf{z} \rangle$ be the code generated by the codewords in $\mathcal{C}$ and any word $\mathbf{z} \in \mathbb{F}_q^n$ such that $\mathbf{Hz} = \mathbf{s}$. We denote by $\mathbf{H}'$ a parity-check matrix of this augmented code. Then we can solve the decoding problem $SD(\mathbf{H}, \mathbf{s}, t)$ by solving, on average over $\mathbf{H}$, at most $\frac{q}{q-1}$ low weight codeword searches $SD(\mathbf{H}', \mathbf{0}, t)$.*

The proof of Theorem 4.1 can be found in Appendix A.

5 Stern's Algorithm in Projective Space

In Sect. 4, we gave a reduction of decoding to low weight codeword searching. In this section, we address the second problem, that is given a parity-check matrix $\mathbf{H}' \in \mathbb{F}_q^{(n-k-1) \times n}$ of $\mathcal{C}'$, we want to find $\mathbf{e} \in \mathbb{F}_q^n$ such that $|\mathbf{e}| = t$ and $\mathbf{H}'\mathbf{e} = \mathbf{0}$.

We have to be careful about the distribution of $\mathbf{H}'$ which has not been drawn uniformly at random in $\mathbb{F}_q^{(n-k-1) \times n}$. Indeed, for an error $\widetilde{\mathbf{e}} \in \mathbb{F}_q^n$ of weight t, $\mathbf{H}'$ has been drawn such that $\widetilde{\mathbf{e}}$ is a codeword in $\mathcal{C}'$, so $\mathbf{H}'$ verifies $\mathbf{H}'\widetilde{\mathbf{e}} = \mathbf{0}$. Essentially, our method consists in running a Stern procedure in the projective space $\mathbb{F}_q^n/\sim$. In particular, we show that Peters' improvements of Stern [Pet11, Ch. 6] are still applicable in the projective space.

5.1 The Algorithm

When the syndrome is zero, Stern's algorithm essentially consists in finding pairs $(\mathbf{x}_1, \mathbf{x}_2) \in \mathbb{F}_q^{k+1} \times \mathbb{F}_q^{k+1}$ such that $\mathbf{x}_1$ (resp. $\mathbf{x}_2$) is of weight p on its first $\lfloor \frac{k+1}{2} \rfloor$ (resp. last $k + 1 - \lfloor \frac{k+1}{2} \rfloor$) positions, zero elsewhere and

$$\mathbf{R}'\mathbf{x}_1 = \mathbf{R}'\mathbf{x}_2 \tag{5.1}$$

where $\mathbf{R}'$ are the ℓ first rows of $\mathbf{P}' \overset{\text{def}}{=} \mathbf{H}_J'^{-1} \mathbf{H}_I'$. Each pair $(\mathbf{x}_1, \mathbf{x}_2)$ that collides gives a candidate codeword $\mathbf{e}$ defined by

$$\mathbf{e}_I = \mathbf{x}_1 - \mathbf{x}_2 \quad \text{and} \quad \mathbf{e}_J = \mathbf{P}'(\mathbf{x}_1 - \mathbf{x}_2). \tag{5.2}$$

One can remark that if the pair $(\mathbf{x}_1, \mathbf{x}_2)$ is a solution to the collision search, then for all $\alpha \in \mathbb{F}_q^*$, $\alpha\mathbf{x}_1$ and $\alpha\mathbf{x}_2$ also collide.

Remark 5.1. Note that this trick, inspired by Minder and Sinclair [MS09], is specific to the fact that the syndrome is zero. If the syndrome is non-zero, then given a pair $(\mathbf{x}_1, \mathbf{x}_2)$ that is such that $\mathbf{R}'\mathbf{x}_1 - \mathbf{y}' = \mathbf{R}'\mathbf{x}_2$, we can no longer guarantee that for any non-zero α, we still have $\alpha\mathbf{R}'\mathbf{x}_1 - \mathbf{y}' = \alpha\mathbf{R}'\mathbf{x}_2$. That is the reason why the reduction in Sect. 4 is essential. Note that a related trick is used in [NCBB10, Section 2] and [NPC+17, Section 3.1.1]. However, they do not use the reduction from Sect. 4 and so they need to deal with the non-zero syndrome; this leads to a different method which only allows to gain a factor of order $\sqrt{q-1}$ at best on the overall complexity. This gain is questioned by Peters in her PhD thesis [Pet11, Section 6.2.3, Remark 6.11] where it is argued that this trick is not likely to gain a lot in practice and that is not backed up by a proper operation count.

Moreover, $\alpha\mathbf{x}_1$ and $\alpha\mathbf{x}_2$ respectively share the same support as $\mathbf{x}_1$ and $\mathbf{x}_2$ so the Stern procedure enumerates all the collinear equivalents of $\mathbf{x}_1$ and $\mathbf{x}_2$ and consequently, it explores all the candidate codewords that are collinear to $\mathbf{e}$. However, we only need one of them. Indeed, if $\mathbf{e}$ is in $\mathcal{C}'$ but not in $\mathcal{C}$ – that is $\mathbf{H}'\mathbf{e} = \mathbf{0}$ but $\mathbf{H}\mathbf{e} \neq \mathbf{0}$ – then there is a unique $\alpha \in \mathbb{F}_q^*$ such that the syndrome $\alpha\mathbf{H}\mathbf{e}$ is exactly $\mathbf{s}$ and not a multiple of it. The solution $\alpha\mathbf{e}$ can be found from any vector that is collinear to $\mathbf{e}$ and so, we only need to find one of them.

From the discussion above, we remark that when the syndrome is zero, Stern's algorithm can be run in the projective space. For a space $\mathcal{E}$ over $\mathbb{F}_q$, the projective space $\mathcal{E}/_\sim$ is the quotient set of $\mathcal{E}$ by the *equivalence relation* $\sim$:

$$\forall \mathbf{x}, \mathbf{y} \in \mathcal{E}, \quad \mathbf{x} \sim \mathbf{y} \iff \exists \alpha \in \mathbb{F}_q^*, \ \mathbf{x} = \alpha\mathbf{y}. \tag{5.3}$$

The *equivalence class* of a vector $\mathbf{x} \in \mathcal{E}$ is denoted by:

$$[\mathbf{x}] \overset{\text{def}}{=} \{\mathbf{y} \in \mathcal{E} : \mathbf{y} \sim \mathbf{x}\}. \tag{5.4}$$

And so

$$\mathcal{E}/_\sim \overset{\text{def}}{=} \{[\mathbf{x}] : \mathbf{x} \in \mathcal{E}\}. \tag{5.5}$$

Now, if $\mathbf{x}_1, \mathbf{x}_2 \in \mathbb{F}_q^{k+1}$ are such that $\mathbf{R}'\mathbf{x}_1 = \mathbf{R}'\mathbf{x}_2$ then we also have $\mathbf{R}'[\mathbf{x}_1] = \mathbf{R}'[\mathbf{x}_2]$ where $[\mathbf{x}_1]$ and $[\mathbf{x}_2]$ live in $\mathbb{F}_q^{k+1}/\sim$. But we have to note that if $\mathbf{R}'[\mathbf{x}_1] = \mathbf{R}'[\mathbf{x}_2]$ then we do not necessarily have $\mathbf{R}'\mathbf{x}_1 = \mathbf{R}'\mathbf{x}_2$. So we need to choose representatives $\overline{\mathbf{x}_1} \in [\mathbf{x}_1]$ and $\overline{\mathbf{x}_2} \in [\mathbf{x}_2]$ which guarantee

$$\mathbf{R}'\overline{\mathbf{x}_1} = \mathbf{R}'\overline{\mathbf{x}_2} \tag{5.6}$$

To do that, we distinguish a particular class representative:

Definition 5.2 (Particular class representative). *Let* $\mathbf{R}' \in \mathbb{F}_q^{\ell \times (k+1)}$. *For all* $[\mathbf{x}] \in \mathbb{F}_q^{k+1}/\sim$, *if* $\mathbf{R}'\mathbf{x} = \mathbf{0}$ *then the vector* $\overline{\mathbf{x}}$ *is any representative of* $[\mathbf{x}]$, *otherwise it is the unique representative of* $[\mathbf{x}]$ *such that the first non-zero symbol of* $\mathbf{R}'\overline{\mathbf{x}}$ *is 1.*

Lemma 5.3. *For any* $\mathbf{x}_1, \mathbf{x}_2 \in \mathbb{F}_q^{k+1}$,

$$\mathbf{R}'[\mathbf{x}_1] = \mathbf{R}'[\mathbf{x}_2] \iff \mathbf{R}'\overline{\mathbf{x}_1} = \mathbf{R}'\overline{\mathbf{x}_2}. \tag{5.7}$$

Proof. If $\mathbf{R}'\mathbf{x}_1 = \mathbf{R}'\mathbf{x}_2 = \mathbf{0}$ then the proof is trivial. Otherwise, for either $i = 1$ or 2, $\mathbf{R}'[\mathbf{x}_i]$ is made of all the vectors that are collinear to $\mathbf{R}'\mathbf{x}_i$. Thus, all the elements in $\mathbf{R}'[\mathbf{x}_i]$ share the same support, in particular they have the same first non-zero position, and there is a unique vector in $\mathbf{R}'[\mathbf{x}_i]$ for which this first non-zero position contains a 1. So, we first notice that $\overline{\mathbf{x}_1}$ and $\overline{\mathbf{x}_2}$ exist and they are unique.

Assume $\mathbf{R}'[\mathbf{x}_1] = \mathbf{R}'[\mathbf{x}_2]$. That means $\mathbf{R}'\overline{\mathbf{x}_1} \in \mathbf{R}'[\mathbf{x}_2]$. On another hand, the first non-zero symbol in $\mathbf{R}'\overline{\mathbf{x}_1}$ is a one and the only element of this kind in $\mathbf{R}'[\mathbf{x}_2]$ is $\mathbf{R}'\overline{\mathbf{x}_2}$, so we necessarily have $\mathbf{R}'\overline{\mathbf{x}_1} = \mathbf{R}'\overline{\mathbf{x}_2}$.

Conversely, $\mathbf{R}'\overline{\mathbf{x}_1} = \mathbf{R}'\overline{\mathbf{x}_2} \Rightarrow [\mathbf{R}'\overline{\mathbf{x}_1}] = [\mathbf{R}'\overline{\mathbf{x}_2}] \Rightarrow \mathbf{R}'[\mathbf{x}_1] = \mathbf{R}'[\mathbf{x}_2]$. $\qquad \square$

Now we are ready to describe our adaptation of Stern's algorithm to the projective space. Algorithm 2 gives the pseudo code of the method. Note that unlike Algorithm 1, here the syndrome is zero and $\overline{\mathbf{x}_1}, \overline{\mathbf{x}_2} \in \mathbb{F}_q^{k+1}$ are some particular representatives of $[\mathbf{x}_1], [\mathbf{x}_2] \in \mathbb{F}_q^{k+1}/\sim$. Moreover, we must treat differently the case where $\mathbf{R}'\overline{\mathbf{x}_1} = \mathbf{R}'\overline{\mathbf{x}_2} = \mathbf{0}$ because this case generates $q - 1$ collisions that are not collinear with each other. Lemma 5.3 guarantees that a collision in projective space is still a collision when using the good representative so that guarantees the correctness of the algorithm.

5.2   Reducing the Cost of Gaussian Elimination

For large q and p, the Gaussian elimination step is negligible and so, we can afford to perform it on $n - k - 1$ columns drawn independently at each iteration. Thus, Gaussian elimination needs $(n - k - 1)^2(n + k + 2)$ operations. However, in the context of SDitH, we are far away from this regime and the Gaussian elimination is actually one of the most expensive operation we have to perform. In this sub-section, we present two modifications of our original projective Stern

---

Algorithm 2: Projective Stern's algorithm to solve $\mathrm{SD}(\mathbf{H}', \mathbf{0}, t)$

Input: $\mathbf{H}' \in \mathbb{F}_q^{(n-k-1)\times n}$ and $t \in [\![0, n]\!]$.

Parameters: $p \in \left[\!\!\left[0, \frac{\min(t, k+1)}{2}\right]\!\!\right]$ and $\ell \in [\![0, n-k-1-t+2p]\!]$.

Output: $\mathbf{e} \in \mathbb{F}_q^n$ such that $\mathbf{H}'\mathbf{e} = \mathbf{0}$ and $|\mathbf{e}| = t$.

1   **repeat as many times as necessary**
2   draw $I \subseteq [\![1, n]\!]$ of size $k+1$ uniformly at random
3      $J \leftarrow [\![1, n]\!] \setminus I$
4      $\mathbf{P}' \leftarrow \mathbf{H}_J'^{-1}\mathbf{H}_I'$ /* if $\mathbf{H}_J'$ is not invertible, go back to step 2 */
5      $\mathbf{R}' \leftarrow$ the ℓ first rows of $\mathbf{P}'$
6      $\mathscr{L}_1' \leftarrow \left\{ \mathbf{R}'\overline{\mathbf{x}_1} \ : \ [\mathbf{x}_1] \in \left(\mathbb{F}_q^{\lfloor \frac{k+1}{2}\rfloor} \times 0^{k+1-\lfloor \frac{k+1}{2}\rfloor} \right)/_\sim \text{ and } |\mathbf{x}_1| = p \right\}$
7      $\mathscr{L}_2' \leftarrow \left\{ \mathbf{R}'\overline{\mathbf{x}_2} \ : \ [\mathbf{x}_2] \in \left(0^{\lfloor \frac{k+1}{2}\rfloor} \times \mathbb{F}_q^{k+1-\lfloor \frac{k+1}{2}\rfloor} \right)/_\sim \text{ and } |\mathbf{x}_2| = p \right\}$
8   **forall** $(\mathbf{R}'\overline{\mathbf{x}_1}, \mathbf{R}'\overline{\mathbf{x}_2}) \in \mathscr{L}_1' \times \mathscr{L}_2'$ such that $\mathbf{R}'\overline{\mathbf{x}_1} = \mathbf{R}'\overline{\mathbf{x}_2}$ **do**
9   **if** $\mathbf{R}'\overline{\mathbf{x}_1} = \mathbf{0}$ and $\exists \alpha \in \mathbb{F}_q^*, |\mathbf{P}'(\alpha\overline{\mathbf{x}_1} - \overline{\mathbf{x}_2})| = t - 2p$ **then**
10   **return** $\mathbf{e}$ such that $\mathbf{e}_I = \alpha\overline{\mathbf{x}_1} - \overline{\mathbf{x}_2}$ and $\mathbf{e}_J^\top = \mathbf{P}'(\alpha\overline{\mathbf{x}_1} - \overline{\mathbf{x}_2})$
11   **else if** $|\mathbf{P}'(\overline{\mathbf{x}_1} - \overline{\mathbf{x}_2})| = t - 2p$ **then**
12   **return** $\mathbf{e}$ such that $\mathbf{e}_I = \overline{\mathbf{x}_1} - \overline{\mathbf{x}_2}$ and $\mathbf{e}_J^\top = \mathbf{P}'(\overline{\mathbf{x}_1} - \overline{\mathbf{x}_2})$

---

algorithm that allow to reduce the impact of the Gaussian elimination step. Those tricks are inspired by [Pet10] and [BLP08] and have been adapted to our situation.

Factorizing the Gaussian Elimination Step. An iteration of Algorithm 2 begins with selecting an information set I and a window of size ℓ. Let denote by I_1 (resp. I_2) the first half of I (resp. the second half of I) and J_ℓ the ℓ first positions of $J \stackrel{\text{def}}{=} [\![1, n]\!] \setminus I$. The iteration succeeds in finding the particular error vector $\mathbf{e}$ of weight t if it verifies

$$|\mathbf{e}_{I_1}| = |\mathbf{e}_{I_2}| = p \quad \text{and} \quad |\mathbf{e}_{J_\ell}| = 0. \tag{5.8}$$

To save some Gaussian elimination steps, we can test several partitions (I_1, I_2, J_ℓ) for one given information set. In other words, the main loop in Algorithm 2 can be divided into an *outer loop* and an *inner loop*. The *outer loop* consists in selecting an information set I and performing a Gaussian elimination on it (steps 2–4). The *inner loop* starts by partitioning I into (I_1, I_2) and selecting a window $J_\ell \subset J$ of size ℓ, then it performs the steps 5–12 with

$$\mathbf{R}' \stackrel{\text{def}}{=} \text{The rows of } \mathbf{P}' \text{ indexed by } J_\ell \tag{5.9}$$

$$\mathscr{L}_1' \stackrel{\text{def}}{=} \left\{ \mathbf{R}'\overline{\mathbf{x}_1} \ : \ [\mathbf{x}_1] \in \mathbb{F}_q^{k+1}/_\sim \text{ and } \operatorname{supp}(\mathbf{x}_1) \subseteq I_1 \text{ and } |\mathbf{x}_1| = p \right\} \tag{5.10}$$

$$\mathscr{L}_2' \stackrel{\text{def}}{=} \left\{ \mathbf{R}'\overline{\mathbf{x}_2} \ : \ [\mathbf{x}_2] \in \mathbb{F}_q^{k+1}/_\sim \text{ and } \operatorname{supp}(\mathbf{x}_2) \subseteq I_2 \text{ and } |\mathbf{x}_2| = p \right\} \tag{5.11}$$

For a given information set I, we choose the partition (I_1, I_2, J_ℓ) uniformly at random and independently from one iteration to another. Assuming we are looking for a t-weight codeword $\mathbf{e} \in \mathcal{C}'$ that verifies $|\mathbf{e}_I| = 2p$, then the success probability of finding this particular codeword during an iteration of the inner loop is

$$q_{\text{in}} = \frac{\binom{\lfloor \frac{k+1}{2} \rfloor}{p} \binom{k+1-\lfloor \frac{k+1}{2} \rfloor}{p} \binom{n-k-1-\ell}{t-2p}}{\binom{k+1}{2p} \binom{n-k-1}{t-2p}}. \tag{5.12}$$

So the number of trials needed to get $\mathbf{e}$ follows a geometric distribution of parameter q_{in} and so, by iterating $N_{\text{in}}^{\text{tmp}}$ times the inner loop, we will find $\mathbf{e}$ with probability

$$p_{\text{in}} \overset{\text{def}}{=} 1 - (1 - q_{\text{in}})^{N_{\text{in}}^{\text{tmp}}} \tag{5.13}$$

Note that taking

$$N_{\text{in}}^{\text{tmp}} \overset{\text{def}}{=} \frac{1}{q_{\text{in}}} \tag{5.14}$$

allows to achieve a success probability p_{in} for the inner loop that is exponentially close to 1.

Reusing Pivots in the Gaussian Elimination. In [CC98], Canteaut and Chabaud propose to simplify the Gaussian elimination step by changing only one index in the information set I. Thus, only one pivot is necessary from one iteration of the outer loop to another. This idea is generalized in [BLP08] where this time, the number of columns to eliminate from one iteration to another can be greater than 1. By doing this, we reduce the cost of Gaussian elimination but we also induce some dependencies between the selected information sets that impact the number of iterations of the outer loop that is needed.

To estimate the impact of the technique described above, we lean on the analysis in [BLP08, Pet10]. We first introduce the parameter c which represents the number of columns to eliminate in each iteration[4]. Thus, the cost of Gaussian elimination per iteration of the outer loop is

$$T_{\text{Gauss}} = 2 \sum_{i=1}^{c} (n - k - 1)(k + 1 + i) \tag{5.15}$$

$$= c(n - k - 1)(2k + c + 3) \tag{5.16}$$

Note that if a t-weight codeword $\mathbf{e} \in \mathcal{C}'$ is such that $|\mathbf{e}_I| = 2p$, then the corresponding iteration of the outer loop will find a representative of $[\mathbf{e}]$ with probability p_{in}. So we need to count the average number of iterations of the outer loop that we need for having this particular weight distribution. However, there are some dependencies between the iterations that must be taken into account. Indeed, we do not draw the $k + 1$ positions of the information set independently from one iteration to another ($k + 1 - c$ positions are kept).

The situation can be modeled by a $(t+2)$-state absorbing Markov chain. Given a t-weight codeword $\mathbf{e} \in \mathcal{C}'$, let X_i be the random variable that represents the

---

[4] In [BLP08], another parameter r is introduced but its interest is only for small field.

weight of e_I at iteration $i \in \mathbb{N}$ of the outer loop or "Done" if the previous iteration succeeds. For the first iteration, the information set I is chosen uniformly at random as a subset of $[\![1, n]\!]$ of size k. So the distribution of X_0 is given by

$$\forall v \in [\![0, t]\!], \quad \mathbb{P}\left(X_0 = v\right) = \frac{\binom{k+1}{v}\binom{n-k-1}{t-v}}{\binom{n}{t}} \quad \text{and} \quad \mathbb{P}\left(X_0 = \text{Done}\right) = 0. \quad (5.17)$$

Let $\mathbf{\Pi}$ be the transition matrix of the Markov chain. It is defined as the following stochastic matrix:

$$\forall (u, v) \in \{\text{Done}, 0, \cdots, t\}^2, \quad \mathbf{\Pi}[u, v] \stackrel{\text{def}}{=} \mathbb{P}\left(X_{i+1} = v \mid X_i = u\right) \quad (5.18)$$

The state Done is the absorbing state, that means when we are in this state, we cannot get out anymore. So we have

$$\forall v \in [\![0, t]\!], \quad \mathbf{\Pi}[\text{Done}, v] = 0 \quad \text{and} \quad \mathbf{\Pi}[\text{Done}, \text{Done}] = 1. \quad (5.19)$$

From an iteration to another, the information set I is updated by swapping c indexes drawn uniformly at random in I with c indexes drawn uniformly at random in J. So an iteration moves from state u to state v with probability

$$\mathbf{\Pi}[u, v] = \sum_j \frac{\binom{u}{j}\binom{k+1-u}{c-j}\binom{t-u}{v-u+j}\binom{n-k-1-t+u}{c-v+u-j}}{\binom{k+1}{c}\binom{n-k-1}{c}} \quad (5.20)$$

except for $u = 2p$ because then the algorithm succeeds with probability:

$$\mathbf{\Pi}[2p, \text{Done}] = p_{\text{in}}. \quad (5.21)$$

So for all $v \in [\![0, t]\!]$:

$$\mathbf{\Pi}[2p, v] = (1 - p_{\text{in}}) \cdot \sum_j \frac{\binom{2p}{j}\binom{k+1-2p}{c-j}\binom{t-2p}{v-2p+j}\binom{n-k-1-t+2p}{c-v+2p-j}}{\binom{k+1}{c}\binom{n-k-1}{c}}. \quad (5.22)$$

Finally, to determine the number of iterations needed to get the first success, one only has to compute the fundamental matrix associated to $\mathbf{\Pi}$:

$$\mathbf{F} \stackrel{\text{def}}{=} (\mathbf{I}_{t+1} - \mathbf{\Pi}')^{-1} \quad (5.23)$$

where $\mathbf{I}_{t+1}$ is the identity matrix of size $t + 1$ and $\mathbf{\Pi}'$ is the $(t + 1) \times (t + 1)$ sub-matrix of $\mathbf{\Pi}$ such that

$$\forall (u, v) \in \{0, \cdots, t\}^2, \quad \mathbf{\Pi}'[u, v] \stackrel{\text{def}}{=} \mathbf{\Pi}[u, v]. \quad (5.24)$$

Then, the average number of iterations of the outer loop needed to find a representative of $[\mathbf{e}]$ is

$$N_{\text{out}}^{\text{tmp}} = \sum_{u=0}^{t} \sum_{v=0}^{t} \mathbb{P}\left(X_0 = v\right) \mathbf{F}[u, v]. \quad (5.25)$$

Finding One Solution from Many. With $N_{\text{out}}^{\text{tmp}} \cdot N_{\text{in}}^{\text{tmp}}$ repetitions of the inner loop, we are able to find one particular t-weight projective codeword $[\mathbf{e}] \in \mathcal{C}'/_\sim$. But there is potentially more than one such projective codeword since this number is

$$N_{\text{sol}} = \mathbb{E}_{\mathbf{H}'}\left(\left|\left\{[\mathbf{e}] \in \mathbb{F}_q^n/_\sim \ : \ |\mathbf{e}| = t \text{ and } \mathbf{H}'[\mathbf{e}] = [\mathbf{0}]\right\}\right|\right) \tag{5.26}$$

$$= 1 + \frac{\binom{n}{t}(q-1)^{t-1} - 1}{q^{n-k-1}} \tag{5.27}$$

Because we want to find only one solution from the N_{sol} ones, we actually need to approximately iterate the outer loop N_{out} times and for each iteration of the outer loop, we iterate the inner loop N_{in} times where

$$N_{\text{out}} \stackrel{\text{def}}{=} \max\left(1, \frac{N_{\text{out}}^{\text{tmp}}}{N_{\text{sol}}}\right) \tag{5.28}$$

$$N_{\text{in}} \stackrel{\text{def}}{=} \max\left(1, N_{\text{in}}^{\text{tmp}} \cdot \min\left(1, \frac{N_{\text{out}}^{\text{tmp}}}{N_{\text{sol}}}\right)\right). \tag{5.29}$$

5.3 Complexity of Our Projective Stern Decoding

Finally, considering the modifications of the previous sub-section and using the implementation tricks of Peters [Pet10], we are able to state the following Theorem 5.4 that gives the complexity of Stern's algorithm in projective space.

Theorem 5.4. *Let $\tilde{\mathbf{e}} \in \mathbb{F}_q^n$ be such that $|\mathbf{e}| = t$. On average over the choice of $\mathbf{H}' \in \mathbb{F}_q^{(n-k-1)\times n}$ that is such that $\mathbf{H}'\tilde{\mathbf{e}} = \mathbf{0}$, we can solve the low weight codeword search problem $SD(\mathbf{H}', \mathbf{0}, t)$ with a running time of order*

$$T_{\text{Stern-proj}} = N_{\text{out}}\left(T_{\text{Gauss}} + N_{\text{in}}\left(T_{\text{lists}} + T_{\text{check}}\right)\right) \tag{5.30}$$

where N_{out}, N_{in} and T_{Gauss} are given by Eqs. (5.28), (5.29) and (5.16), and

$$L_1 = \binom{\lfloor \frac{k+1}{2} \rfloor}{p}(q-1)^{p-1} \tag{5.31}$$

$$L_2 = \binom{k+1-\lfloor \frac{k+1}{2} \rfloor}{p}(q-1)^{p-1} \tag{5.32}$$

$$T_{\text{lists}} = \ell\left(k + 2p - 1 + 2(L_1 + L_2)\right) \tag{5.33}$$

$$N_{\text{collisions}} = \frac{(q-1)L_1 L_2}{q^\ell} \tag{5.34}$$

$$T_{\text{check}} = \left(2p + \frac{q}{q-1}(t - 2p + 1)2p\left(1 + \frac{q-2}{q-1}\right)\right) \cdot N_{\text{collision}} \tag{5.35}$$

The proof of Theorem 5.4 follows the same approach as Peters in [Pet10]. More details are given in Appendix B.

6   The d-Split Decoding Problem

The security of SDitH is actually based on the d-split decoding problem. Before stating this problem, let us bring in the following notation:

Notation 6.1. *Let* $\mathbf{v} \in \mathbb{F}_q^n$. *For d that divides n and for all $i \in [\![1, d]\!]$, we denote by $\mathbf{v}_{[i]}$ the ith piece of $\mathbf{v}$ of length $\frac{n}{d}$. More formally,*

$$\mathbf{v}_{[i]} \overset{def}{=} \mathbf{v}_{[\![(i-1)\frac{n}{d}+1,\,i\frac{n}{d}]\!]} \overset{def}{=} (v_j)_{j \in [\![(i-1)\frac{n}{d}+1,\,i\frac{n}{d}]\!]} \tag{6.1}$$

Then the d-split syndrome decoding problem can be stated as follows:

Problem 6.2 (d-split Syndrome Decoding $\mathsf{SD}(d, \mathbf{H}, \mathbf{s}, t)$). *Given a matrix* $\mathbf{H} \in \mathbb{F}_q^{(n-k) \times n}$, *a syndrome* $\mathbf{s} \in \mathbb{F}_q^{n-k}$ *and a distance* $t \in [\![0, n]\!]$, *find a vector* $\mathbf{e} \in \mathbb{F}_q^n$ *such that* $\mathbf{He} = \mathbf{s}$ *and* $\forall i \in [\![1, d]\!]$, $|\mathbf{e}_{[i]}| = t/d$.

The d-split decoding problem is quite similar to the standard decoding problem but with the additional constraint that the error weight must be regularly distributed over d blocks. Note that the syndrome $\mathbf{s}$ was actually produced using an injected solution $\widetilde{\mathbf{e}}$ whose weight is precisely regularly distributed. In other word, there exists at least one $\widetilde{\mathbf{e}} \in \mathbb{F}_q^n$ such that $\mathbf{s} = \mathbf{H}\widetilde{\mathbf{e}}$ and $\forall i \in [\![1, d]\!]$, $|\widetilde{\mathbf{e}}_{[i]}| = t/d$.

In the SDitH specifications, the hardness of the d-split syndrome decoding problem is lower bounded by a quantity that depends on the complexity to solve the standard decoding problem. This lower bound is based on the following theorem:

Theorem 6.3 ([FJR22]). *Let* $\mathbf{H}$ *be drawn uniformly at random in* $\mathbb{F}_q^{(n-k) \times n}$ *and let* $\mathbf{s} \in \mathbb{F}_q^n$. *If an algorithm can find any particular solution of the d-split syndrome decoding problem $\mathsf{SD}(d, \mathbf{H}, \mathbf{s}, t)$ in time T with probability ε_d, then there is an algorithm that can find any particular solution of the syndrome decoding problem $\mathsf{SD}(1, \mathbf{H}, \mathbf{s}, t)$ in time T with probability ε_1 with*

$$\varepsilon_1 \geqslant \frac{\binom{n/d}{t/d}^d}{\binom{n}{t}} \varepsilon_d \tag{6.2}$$

Using Theorem 6.3, it can be argued that the best average complexity to solve $\mathsf{SD}(d, \mathbf{H}, \mathbf{s}, t)$ cannot be lower than $\binom{n/d}{t/d}^d / \binom{n}{t}$ times the best average complexity to solve $\mathsf{SD}(1, \mathbf{H}, \mathbf{s}, t)$. SDitH measures the difficulty of the d-split decoding problem with this lower bound on the complexity together with the complexity of the best known attack on $\mathsf{SD}(1, \mathbf{H}, \mathbf{s}, t)$. However, this bound is not tight and gives optimistic security levels. Indeed, it is considered here that we are only looking for a particular solution; the number of solutions to the problem is not taken into account. But recall that if there are many solutions, we just want to find one of them. We therefore state the following theorem that gives a more precise lower bound on the complexity we can expect to achieve:

Theorem 6.4. *Let $\mathbf{H}$ be drawn uniformly at random in $\mathbb{F}_q^{(n-k)\times n}$ and let $\mathbf{s} \in \mathbb{F}_q^n$. If an algorithm can solve $SD(d, \mathbf{H}, \mathbf{s}, t)$ in time T with probability p_d, then there is an algorithm that can solve $SD(1, \mathbf{H}, \mathbf{s}, t)$ in time T with probability p_1 with*

$$p_d \leqslant 1 - \left(1 - \frac{\binom{n}{t}}{\binom{n/d}{t/d}^d}\left(1 - (1-p_1)^{1/N_1}\right)\right)^{N_d} \approx \frac{\binom{n}{t}}{\binom{n/d}{t/d}^d}\frac{N_d}{N_1}p_1 \qquad (6.3)$$

where N_1 is the expected number of solutions to the problem $SD(1, \mathbf{H}, \mathbf{s}, t)$ and N_d is the expected number of solutions to the problem $SD(d, \mathbf{H}, \mathbf{s}, t)$.

Proof. Let $\mathscr{A}_d$ be an algorithm which finds a particular solution in $SD(d, \mathbf{H}, \mathbf{s}, t)$ in times T with probability ε_d. From Theorem 6.3, there exists an algorithm $\mathscr{A}_1$ which finds a particular solution in $SD(1, \mathbf{H}, \mathbf{s}, t)$ in times T with probability ε_1 with

$$1 - (1-\varepsilon_d)^{N_d} \leqslant 1 - \left(1 - \frac{\binom{n}{t}}{\binom{n/d}{t/d}^d}\varepsilon_1\right)^{N_d}$$

We end the proof by noticing that

$$p_d = 1 - (1-\varepsilon_d)^{N_d} \qquad \text{and} \qquad p_1 = 1 - (1-\varepsilon_1)^{N_1}$$

$\square$

In Theorem 6.4, since we address the d-split syndrome decoding problem where $\mathbf{s}$ is the syndrome of a d-split error vector of weight t, we have:

$$N_d = 1 + \frac{\binom{n/d}{t/d}^d(q-1)^t - 1}{q^{n-k}}. \qquad (6.4)$$

Moreover, the algorithm $\mathscr{A}_1$ consists essentially in repeating the algorithm $\mathscr{A}_d$ by permuting the code randomly so this algorithm solves the standard decoding problem where $\mathbf{s}$ is the syndrome of any t-weight error vector. So we have:

$$N_1 = 1 + \frac{\binom{n}{t}^d(q-1)^t - 1}{q^{n-k}}. \qquad (6.5)$$

Remark 6.5. Note that when t is smaller than the Gilbert-Varshamov distance, then the only solution to $SD(1, \mathbf{H}, \mathbf{s}, t)$ is the injected solution and has a probability $\binom{n/d}{t/d}^d / \binom{n}{t}$ to be a solution for $SD(d, \mathbf{H}, \mathbf{s}, t)$. So we get the same lower bound as in SDitH since $p_1 \approx \varepsilon_1$ and $p_d \approx \varepsilon_d$. On the contrary, if t is such that we have many solutions, then the injected solution has little impact and so we only have $p_d \leqslant p_1(1 + o(1))$. Note that when the number of solutions is large, p_d is close to p_1 because it is simpler to find a particular solution to the d-split decoding problem but there are also less solutions in proportion.

Adapting the Projective Stern Algorithm for d-Split. Theorem 6.4 induces a lower bound on the complexity of d-split decoding, but we cannot guarantee that it is actually possible to reach this bound. It is possible to give an actual algorithm to solve the d-split decoding problem. Indeed, we can apply the reduction of Sect. 4 and adapt our projective Stern algorithm to take into account the regularity of the weight of the solution we are looking for. More precisely, at each iteration of Algorithm 2, one can choose the information set as

$$I \stackrel{\text{def}}{=} I_1 \cup \ldots \cup I_d \tag{6.6}$$

where each I_i is a subset of $[\![(i-1)\frac{n}{d}+1, i\frac{n}{d}]\!]$ of size $\frac{k}{d}$. At each iteration, we bet that at least one sought solution $\mathbf{e}$ is such that for all $i \in [\![1, d]\!]$, $|\mathbf{e}_{I_i}| = \frac{p}{d}$.

Note that, in the context of SDitH, when adapting projective Stern to d-split, the optimal parameter p increases: it goes from 1 to 2. So the cost to produce the lists $\mathscr{L}_1$ and $\mathscr{L}_2$ increases quadratically. Consequently, the Gaussian elimination step becomes negligible, especially if we factorize it. It follows that the Canteaut-Chabaud technique is not relevant because it increases the number of iterations but it does not substantially reduce their cost. This is why finally, for $d > 1$, we do not use the Canteaut-Chabaud's trick. Appendix C, gives the formulas for the 2-split projective Stern algorithm.

7   Application to SDitH

In this section, we analyze the security of SDitH and we compare our results with those given in the SDitH specifications document [AMFG+23]. In the context of the NIST competition[5], the authors tried to reach different security levels:

- **category I:** at least 143 bits of security ($\approx$ AES-128);
- **category III:** at least 207 bits of security ($\approx$ AES-192);
- **category V:** at least 272 bits of security ($\approx$ AES-256).

Table 1 summarizes the parameters proposed in the NIST submission [AMFG+23] of SDitH to achieve the above security levels.

In the SDitH specifications, it is considered that the best algorithm to solve the decoding problem is Peters' version of Stern's algorithm of Sect. 3. However, there is a mistake in SDitH v1.0: it is considered that there is only one solution to the syndrome decoding problem when in fact there are several hundred for the parameters that have been chosen. Moreover, Theorem 6.3 which lower bounds the complexity of solving the d-split is not tight when there are many solutions. In Table 2 we give (i) the results claimed in the specifications of SDitH v1.0, (ii) the lower bound on the security when considering the multiple solutions and a tighter lower bound obtained from Theorem 6.4, (iii) the lower bound on the security we achieve with our projective Stern decoding used in conjunction with Theorem 6.4 and (iv) the security we achieve with the actual d-split Stern's

---

[5] https://csrc.nist.gov/projects/post-quantum-cryptography.

Table 1. Parameters of SDitH v1.0 for various security levels.

Parameter sets	NIST recommendations		d-split SD parameters				
	category	target security	q	n	k	t	d
SDitH_L1_gf256_v1.0	I	143 bits	256	230	126	79	1
SDitH_L1_gf251_v1.0	I	143 bits	251	230	126	79	1
SDitH_L3_gf256_v1.0	III	207 bits	256	352	193	120	2
SDitH_L3_gf251_v1.0	III	207 bits	251	352	193	120	2
SDitH_L5_gf256_v1.0	V	272 bits	256	480	278	150	2
SDitH_L5_gf251_v1.0	V	272 bits	251	480	278	150	2

algorithm described at the end of Sect. 6. The security is expressed in number of bits. Note that the last column corresponds to an actual attack on the scheme. Comparing (ii) and (iii), we can see in particular that the projective method is responsible for the loss of around 5 bits of security. In summary:

- even by improving the lower bound of [AMFG+23], this methodology for proving the security fails to meet the NIST requirements by around 11–14 bits, (column (iii))
- there is an actual attack on the scheme showing that its complexity is below the NIST requirements by around 9–14 bits, (column (iv)).

Table 2. Security level of SDitH v1.0.

Parameter sets	(1) Claimed in the specification document			(ii) Correction from Sect. 3 and Theorem 6.4			(iii) Projective Stern and Theorem 6.4				(iv) d-split projective Stern		
	p	ℓ	security	p	ℓ	security	p	ℓ	c	security	p	ℓ	security
SDitH_L1_gf256_v1.0	1	2	⩾143.46	1	2	⩾135.29	1	2	1	⩾129.23	1	2	129.23
SDitH_L1_gf251_v1.0	1	2	⩾143.45	1	2	⩾134.58	1	2	1	⩾128.52	1	2	128.52
SDitH_L3_gf256_v1.0	2	5	⩾207.67	2	5	⩾202.43	1	2	1	⩾196.76	2	4	199.30
SDitH_L3_gf251_v1.0	2	5	⩾207.61	2	5	⩾201.30	1	2	1	⩾195.68	2	4	198.19
SDitH_L5_gf256_v1.0	2	5	⩾272.35	2	5	⩾267.40	1	2	1	⩾262.63	2	4	264.30
SDitH_L5_gf251_v1.0	2	5	⩾272.29	2	5	⩾265.91	1	2	1	⩾261.19	2	4	262.84

Recently, after we communicated preliminary results in [CTH23], the SDitH designers proposed a new version 1.1 in https://groups.google.com/a/list.nist.gov/g/pqc-forum/c/OOnB655mCN8/m/rL4bPD20AAAJ with updated parameters. Table 3 presents the new parameters. Then, Table 4 compares the security claimed in SDitH v1.1 and our projective Stern decoder on the updated parameters. Our projective Stern's algorithm is around 2^5 times faster than the complexity claimed in SDitH v1.1. However, the SDitH designers took a margin of error of 4 bits compared to the NIST recommendations and therefore our attack

Table 3. Parameters of the d-split decoding problem in SDitH v1.1 for various security levels.

Parameter sets	NIST recommendations		d-split SD parameters				
	category	target security	q	n	k	t	d
SDitH_L1_gf256_v1.1	I	143 bits	256	242	126	87	1
SDitH_L1_gf251_v1.1	I	143 bits	251	242	126	87	1
SDitH_L3_gf256_v1.1	III	207 bits	256	376	220	114	2
SDitH_L3_gf251_v1.1	III	207 bits	251	376	220	114	2
SDitH_L5_gf256_v1.1	V	272 bits	256	494	282	156	2
SDitH_L5_gf251_v1.1	V	272 bits	251	494	282	156	2

is only one bit under the NIST recommendations for the category I parameters. For the other parameters, the lower bound methodology of [AMFG+23] (even after improvement) fails to meet the NIST criterion by about one bit in all cases (column (iii)). It remains to see whether the attack on the d-split version can be improved (this is used in category III and V parameters) because our corresponding attack (column (iv)) is just one bit above the required security level. The SageMath program which made it possible to compute the results is available on https://github.com/kevin-carrier/SDitH_security.

Table 4. Security level of SDitH v1.1.

Parameter sets	Target security	(i–ii) Claimed in the specification document			(iii) Projective Stern and Theorem 6.4				(iv) d-split projective Stern		
		p	ℓ	security	p	ℓ	c	security	p	ℓ	security
SDitH_L1_gf256_v1.1	143	1	2	$\geqslant$147.73	1	2	1	$\geqslant$141.54	1	2	**141.54**
SDitH_L1_gf251_v1.1	143	1	2	$\geqslant$147.72	1	2	1	$\geqslant$141.54	1	2	**141.54**
SDitH_L3_gf256_v1.1	207	2	5	$\geqslant$211.05	1	2	1	$\geqslant$205.59	2	4	**207.90**
SDitH_L3_gf251_v1.1	207	2	5	$\geqslant$210.99	1	2	1	$\geqslant$205.59	2	4	**207.86**
SDitH_L5_gf256_v1.1	272	2	5	$\geqslant$276.33	1	2	1	$\geqslant$271.69	2	4	**273.26**
SDitH_L5_gf251_v1.1	272	2	5	$\geqslant$276.28	1	2	1	$\geqslant$271.68	2	4	**273.23**

A   Proof of Theorem 4.1

Let us recall Theorem 4.1:

Theorem 4.1. *Let a code $\mathcal{C}$ be the right kernel of a parity-check matrix $\mathbf{H} \in \mathbb{F}_q^{(n-k) \times n}$ and let $\mathbf{s} \in \{\mathbf{H}\widetilde{\mathbf{e}} : |\widetilde{\mathbf{e}}| = t\}$ for $t \in [\![0, n]\!]$. Let $\mathcal{C}' \stackrel{\text{def}}{=} \langle \mathcal{C}, \mathbf{z} \rangle$ be the code generated by the codewords in $\mathcal{C}$ and any word $\mathbf{z} \in \mathbb{F}_q^n$ such that $\mathbf{Hz} = \mathbf{s}$. We denote by $\mathbf{H}'$ a parity-check matrix of this augmented code. Then we can solve the decoding problem $\mathsf{SD}(\mathbf{H}, \mathbf{s}, t)$ by solving, on average over $\mathbf{H}$, at most $\frac{q}{q-1}$ low weight codeword searches $\mathsf{SD}(\mathbf{H}', \mathbf{0}, t)$.*

Proof. First, by construction of $\mathbf{s}$ and $\mathbf{z}$, we know there exists a codeword $\mathbf{c} \in \mathcal{C}$ and an error vector $\tilde{\mathbf{e}} \in \mathbb{F}_q^n$ of weight t such that $\mathbf{z} = \mathbf{c} + \tilde{\mathbf{e}}$. So we have $\langle \mathcal{C}, \mathbf{z} \rangle = \langle \mathcal{C}, \tilde{\mathbf{e}} \rangle$ and $\mathbf{s} = \mathbf{H}\tilde{\mathbf{e}}$.

Let $\mathbf{e}$ be any solution of the low weight codeword search problem $\mathsf{SD}(\mathbf{H}', \mathbf{0}, t)$. Then, as said before, $\mathbf{e}$ is an error vector of weight t such that $\mathbf{He} = \alpha\mathbf{s}$ for a scalar $\alpha \in \mathbb{F}_q$, and $\mathbf{e}$ induces a solution of the original decoding problem if and only if $\alpha \neq 0$. On average over $\mathbf{H}$ and for $\mathbf{e}$ drawn uniformly at random in the solutions of $\mathsf{SD}(\mathbf{H}', \mathbf{0}, t)$, the probability that $\alpha = 0$ is

$$\mathbb{P}_{\mathbf{H},\mathbf{e}} \left(\alpha = 0 \right) = \frac{\mathbb{E}_{\mathbf{H}} \left(|\mathcal{C}(t)| \right)}{\mathbb{E}_{\mathbf{H}} \left(|\mathcal{C}'(t)| \right)}$$

where

$$\mathcal{C}(t) \stackrel{\text{def}}{=} \{\mathbf{e} \in \mathcal{C} : |\mathbf{e}| = t\}$$
$$\mathcal{C}'(t) \stackrel{\text{def}}{=} \{\mathbf{e} \in \mathcal{C}' : |\mathbf{e}| = t\}$$

We already know that

$$\mathbb{E}_{\mathbf{H}} \left(|\mathcal{C}(t)| \right) = \frac{\binom{n}{t}(q-1)^t}{q^{n-k}}.$$

Let us count $\mathcal{C}'(t)$. We remark that $\mathcal{C}'$ is the disjoint union of the cosets $\mathcal{C} + \alpha\tilde{\mathbf{e}}$ for all the $\alpha \in \mathbb{F}_q$. So

$$\mathbb{E}_{\mathbf{H}} \left(|\mathcal{C}'(t)| \right) = \sum_{\alpha \in \mathbb{F}_q} \mathbb{E}_{\mathbf{H}} \left(|\mathcal{C}'_\alpha(t)| \right)$$

where

$$\mathcal{C}'_\alpha(t) \stackrel{\text{def}}{=} \{\mathbf{e} + \alpha\tilde{\mathbf{e}} : \mathbf{e} \in \mathcal{C} \text{ and } |\mathbf{e} + \alpha\tilde{\mathbf{e}}| = t\}.$$

On one hand, we have that $\mathcal{C}'_0(t) = \mathcal{C}(t)$. On another hand, for all non-zero $\alpha, \alpha' \in \mathbb{F}_q^*$, the map $\mathbf{x} \longmapsto \alpha^{-1}\alpha'\mathbf{x}$ is a bijection from $\mathcal{C}'_\alpha(t)$ to $\mathcal{C}'_{\alpha'}(t)$; so for all $\alpha \in \mathbb{F}_q^*$, $|\mathcal{C}'_\alpha(t)| = |\mathcal{C}'_1(t)|$. Thus, we have

$$\mathbb{E}_{\mathbf{H}} \left(|\mathcal{C}'(t)| \right) = \mathbb{E}_{\mathbf{H}} \left(|\mathcal{C}(t)| \right) + (q-1)\mathbb{E}_{\mathbf{H}} \left(|\mathcal{C}'_1(t)| \right)$$

By doing a calculation similar to that of the Eq. (3.6), we can show that

$$\mathbb{E}_{\mathbf{H}} \left(|\mathcal{C}'_1(t)| \right) = 1 + \frac{\binom{n}{t}(q-1)^t - 1}{q^{n-k}}$$
$$= 1 - \frac{1}{q^{n-k}} + \mathbb{E}_{\mathbf{H}} \left(|\mathcal{C}(t)| \right).$$

and so

$$\mathbb{E}_{\mathbf{H}} \left(|\mathcal{C}'(t)| \right) = q\mathbb{E}_{\mathbf{H}} \left(|\mathcal{C}(t)| \right) + (q-1)\left(1 - \frac{1}{q^{n-k}}\right).$$

Finally, the probability that the reduction succeeds is

$$1 - \mathbb{P}_{\mathbf{H},\mathbf{e}} \left(\alpha = 0 \right) = 1 - \frac{1}{q + \frac{(q-1)(1-1/q^{n-k})}{\mathbb{E}_{\mathbf{H}}(|\mathcal{C}(t)|)}} \geqslant \frac{q-1}{q}.$$

$\square$

B   Proof of Theorem 5.4

Let us recall Theorem 5.4:

Theorem 5.4. *Let* $\tilde{e} \in \mathbb{F}_q^n$ *be such that* $|e| = t$. *On average over the choice of* $\mathbf{H}' \in \mathbb{F}_q^{(n-k-1) \times n}$ *that is such that* $\mathbf{H}'\tilde{e} = \mathbf{0}$, *we can solve the low weight codeword search problem* $\mathsf{SD}(\mathbf{H}', \mathbf{0}, t)$ *with a running time of order*

$$T_{\text{Stern-proj}} = N_{\text{out}} \left(T_{\text{Gauss}} + N_{\text{in}} \left(T_{\text{lists}} + T_{\text{check}} \right) \right) \tag{5.30}$$

where N_{out}, N_{in} *and* T_{Gauss} *are given by Eqs.* (5.28), (5.29) *and* (5.16), *and*

$$L_1 = \binom{\lfloor \frac{k+1}{2} \rfloor}{p} (q-1)^{p-1} \tag{5.31}$$

$$L_2 = \binom{k+1-\lfloor \frac{k+1}{2} \rfloor}{p} (q-1)^{p-1} \tag{5.32}$$

$$T_{\text{lists}} = \ell \left(k + 2p - 1 + 2\left(L_1 + L_2 \right) \right) \tag{5.33}$$

$$N_{\text{collisions}} = \frac{(q-1)L_1 L_2}{q^\ell} \tag{5.34}$$

$$T_{\text{check}} = \left(2p + \tfrac{q}{q-1}(t - 2p + 1)2p \left(1 + \tfrac{q-2}{q-1} \right) \right) \cdot N_{\text{collision}} \tag{5.35}$$

Proof. From the Subsect. 5.2, we have to iterate N_{out} times the outer loop which consists in a Gaussian elimination over c columns and N_{in} iterations of the inner loop. All that remains is to determine the cost of one iteration of the inner loop. To perform this iteration optimally, we will use Peters' implementation tricks [Pet10].

To build the lists $\mathscr{L}_1$ and $\mathscr{L}_2$, we need to define another representative of an equivalence class in $\mathbb{F}_q^{k+1}/\sim$. Let $\mathbf{x} \in \mathbb{F}_q^{k+1}$, we denote by $\hat{\mathbf{x}}$, the representative of $[\mathbf{x}]$ whose first non-zero symbol is 1. Thus, for $\mathscr{L}_1$, we produce successively the representatives $\widehat{\mathbf{x}_1}$ that have a weight p on the first half and zero elsewhere using exactly the same trick as Peters (except we fix the first non-zero symbol to 1 and that there is no syndrome to add). So we can compute successively $\mathbf{P}'\widehat{\mathbf{x}_1}$ by only adding one column or two consecutive columns (except for the first element that needs $2p - 2$ column additions). The single column additions allow to browse all the vectors of a same support and the two columns additions allow to move from one support to another. The two columns additions can actually be replaced by single column additions if we pre-compute all the sums of two consecutive columns in $\mathbf{P}'$. This costs $k + 1$ column additions. By fixing the first non zero symbol to one, we browse only one representative per equivalence class. However, it is not the good representative that we defined in Definition 5.2. But it is quite easy to find the factor $\alpha \in \mathbb{F}_q^*$ such that $\overline{\mathbf{x}_1} = \alpha\widehat{\mathbf{x}_1}$ by multiplying one column by a scalar. Then, we do not compute $\overline{\mathbf{x}_1}$ but we save the pair $(\alpha, \widehat{\mathbf{x}_1})$ instead. We proceed similarly for the list $\mathscr{L}_2$. So finally, the cost of producing $\mathscr{L}_1$ and $\mathscr{L}_2$ is

$$T_{\text{lists}} = \ell(k+1) + \ell(2p-2) + 2\ell\left(\binom{\lfloor\frac{k+1}{2}\rfloor}{p} + \binom{k+1-\lfloor\frac{k+1}{2}\rfloor}{p}\right)(q-1)^{p-1} \quad \text{(B.1)}$$

$$= \ell\left(k+2p-1+2\left(\binom{\lfloor\frac{k+1}{2}\rfloor}{p} + \binom{k+1-\lfloor\frac{k+1}{2}\rfloor}{p}\right)\right)(q-1)^{p-1} \quad \text{(B.2)}$$

To deal with the collisions we first need to count them. On average, there are

$$N_{\text{collision}} = \frac{\binom{\lfloor\frac{k+1}{2}\rfloor}{p}\binom{k+1-\lfloor\frac{k+1}{2}\rfloor}{p}(q-1)^{2p-2}}{1+(q^\ell-1)/(q-1)} \quad \text{(B.3)}$$

$$\cdot((q-1)\mathbb{P}\left(\mathbf{P}'\overline{\mathbf{x_1}} = \mathbf{0}\right) + \mathbb{P}\left(\mathbf{P}'\overline{\mathbf{x_1}} \neq \mathbf{0}\right)) \quad \text{(B.4)}$$

$$= \frac{\binom{\lfloor\frac{k+1}{2}\rfloor}{p}\binom{k+1-\lfloor\frac{k+1}{2}\rfloor}{p}(q-1)^{2p-2}}{1+(q^\ell-1)/(q-1)} \cdot \left(\frac{q-1}{q^\ell} + 1 - \frac{1}{q^\ell}\right) \quad \text{(B.5)}$$

$$= \frac{\binom{\lfloor\frac{k+1}{2}\rfloor}{p}\binom{k+1-\lfloor\frac{k+1}{2}\rfloor}{p}(q-1)^{2p-1}}{q^\ell} \quad \text{(B.6)}$$

For each collision, we must first apply the scalar multiplication to change the representative of the equivalence class. This costs $2p$ multiplications. Then we can apply the same trick as Peters and check for only $\frac{q}{q-1}(t-2p+1)$ rows on average. The cost to treat a row is $2p$ additions and $2p\frac{q-2}{q-1}$ multiplications. So the cost to check all the candidates (each coming from a collision) is

$$T_{\text{check}} = \left(2p + \frac{q}{q-1}(t-2p+1)2p\left(1+\frac{q-2}{q-1}\right)\right) \cdot N_{\text{collision}}. \quad \text{(B.7)}$$

$\square$

C Formulas for the 2-Split Projective Stern Algorithm

Here we address the 2-split decoding problem which is one of the instances of SDitH. In Sect. 6, we explained how to adapt our projective Stern's algorithm to d-split by splitting the support of the error into d equal parts and looking for an error $\mathbf{e}$ of weight t/d on each of the part.

We just give the formulas which differ from those we presented for the standard version 1-split in Sect. 5. In particular, for the 2-split version of our projective Stern's algorithm, Eqs. (5.12), (5.25), (5.16) (5.27), (5.31) and (5.32) become respectively:

$$q_{\text{in}} = \frac{\binom{\lfloor(k+1)/4\rfloor}{\lfloor p/2\rfloor}\binom{\lfloor(k+1)/2\rfloor-\lfloor(k+1)/4\rfloor}{p-\lfloor p/2\rfloor}}{\binom{\lfloor(k+1)/2\rfloor}{p}}$$
$$\cdot \frac{\binom{\lfloor(k+1)/2\rfloor-\lfloor(k+1)/4\rfloor}{\lfloor p/2\rfloor}\binom{k+1-2\lfloor(k+1)/2\rfloor+\lfloor(k+1)/4\rfloor}{p-\lfloor p/2\rfloor}}{\binom{k+1-\lfloor(k+1)/2\rfloor}{p}}$$
$$\cdot \frac{\binom{\lfloor(n-k-1)/2\rfloor-\lfloor\ell/2\rfloor}{t/2-p}\binom{n-k-1-\lfloor(n-k-1)/2\rfloor-\ell+\lfloor\ell/2\rfloor}{t/2-p}}{\binom{\lfloor(n-k-1)/2\rfloor}{t/2-p}\binom{n-k-1-\lfloor(n-k-1)/2\rfloor}{t/2-p}} \quad \text{(C.1)}$$

$$N_{\text{out}}^{\text{tmp}} = \frac{\left(\binom{\lfloor n/2 \rfloor}{\lfloor t/2 \rfloor}\right)^2}{\binom{\lfloor (k+1)/2 \rfloor}{p}\binom{k+1-\lfloor (k+1)/2 \rfloor}{p}\binom{\lfloor (n-k-1)/2 \rfloor}{t/2-p}\binom{n-k-1-\lfloor (n-k-1)/2 \rfloor}{t/2-p}} \tag{C.2}$$

$$T_{\text{Gauss}} = 2(n-k-1)\sum_{i=1}^{n-k-1}(n-i+1) = (n-k-1)^2(n+k+2) \tag{C.3}$$

$$N_{\text{sol}} = 1 + \frac{\binom{n/2}{t/2}^2(q-1)^{t-1}-1}{q^{n-k-1}} \tag{C.4}$$

$$L_1 = \binom{\lfloor (k+1)/4 \rfloor}{\lfloor p/2 \rfloor}\binom{\lfloor (k+1)/2 \rfloor-\lfloor (k+1)/4 \rfloor}{p-\lfloor p/2 \rfloor}(q-1)^{p-1} \tag{C.5}$$

$$L_2 = \binom{\lfloor (k+1)/2 \rfloor-\lfloor (k+1)/4 \rfloor}{\lfloor p/2 \rfloor}\binom{k+1-2\lfloor (k+1)/2 \rfloor+\lfloor (k+1)/4 \rfloor}{p-\lfloor p/2 \rfloor}(q-1)^{p-1} \tag{C.6}$$

References

[AAB+22] Melchor, C.A., et al.: BIKE. Round 4 Submission to the NIST Post-Quantum Cryptography Call, v. 5.1, October 2022

[ABC+22] Albrecht, M., et al.: Classic McEliece (merger of Classic McEliece and NTS-KEM). https://classic.mceliece.org. Fourth round finalist of the NIST post-quantum cryptography call, November 2022

[AMFG+23] Melchor, C.A., et al.: SDitH. Round 1 Additional Signatures to the NIST Post-Quantum Cryptography: Digital Signature Schemes Call, May 2023

[BCC+23] Banegas, G., et al.: Wave. Round 1 Additional Signatures to the NIST Post-Quantum Cryptography: Digital Signature Schemes Call, June 2023

[Ber10] Bernstein, D.J.: Grover vs. McEliece. In: Sendrier, N. (ed.) PQCrypto 2010. LNCS, vol. 6061, pp. 73–80. Springer, Heidelberg (2010). https://doi.org/10.1007/978-3-642-12929-2_6

[BJMM12] Becker, A., Joux, A., May, A., Meurer, A.: Decoding random binary linear codes in $2^{n/20}$: how 1+1=0 improves information set decoding. In: Pointcheval, D., Johansson, T. (eds.) EUROCRYPT 2012. LNCS, vol. 7237, pp. 520–536. Springer, Heidelberg (2012). https://doi.org/10.1007/978-3-642-29011-4_31

[BLP08] Bernstein, D.J., Lange, T., Peters, C.: Attacking and defending the McEliece cryptosystem. In: Buchmann, J., Ding, J. (eds.) PQCrypto 2008. LNCS, vol. 5299, pp. 31–46. Springer, Heidelberg (2008). https://doi.org/10.1007/978-3-540-88403-3_3

[BLP10] Bernstein, D.J., Lange, T., Peters, C.: Wild McEliece. In: Biryukov, A., Gong, G., Stinson, D.R. (eds.) SAC 2010. LNCS, vol. 6544, pp. 143–158. Springer, Heidelberg (2011). https://doi.org/10.1007/978-3-642-19574-7_10

[BLP11] Bernstein, D.J., Lange, T., Peters, C.: Wild McEliece incognito. In: Yang, B.-Y. (ed.) PQCrypto 2011. LNCS, vol. 7071, pp. 244–254. Springer, Heidelberg (2011). https://doi.org/10.1007/978-3-642-25405-5_16

[BM17] Both, L., May, A.: Optimizing BJMM with nearest neighbors: full decoding in $2^{2/21n}$ and McEliece security. In: WCC Workshop on Coding and Cryptography, September 2017

[BM18] Both, L., May, A.: Decoding linear codes with high error rate and its impact for LPN security. In: Lange, T., Steinwandt, R. (eds.) PQCrypto 2018. LNCS, vol. 10786, pp. 25–46. Springer, Cham (2018). https://doi.org/10.1007/978-3-319-79063-3_2

[Can17] Torres, R.C.: Asymptotic analysis of ISD algorithms for the q–ary case. In: Proceedings of the Tenth International Workshop on Coding and Cryptography, WCC 2017, September 2017

[CC98] Canteaut, A., Chabaud, F.: A new algorithm for finding minimum-weight words in a linear code: application to McEliece's cryptosystem and to narrow-sense BCH codes of length 511. IEEE Trans. Inform. Theory **44**(1), 367–378 (1998)

[CDMT22] Carrier, K., Debris-Alazard, T., Meyer-Hilfiger, C., Tillich, J.-P.: Statistical decoding 2.0: reducing decoding to LPN. In: Agrawal, S., Lin, D. (eds.) ASIACRYPT 2022. LNCS, vol. 13794, pp. 477–507. Springer, Cham (2022). https://doi.org/10.1007/978-3-031-22972-5_17

[CTH23] Carrier, K., Tillich, J.-P., Hatey, V.: Security analysis of SDiTH. Slides of the one-day workshop on code-based cryptography, 20 November 2023. https://inria.hal.science/hal-0431126

[DST19] Debris-Alazard, T., Sendrier, N., Tillich, J.-P.: Wave: a new family of trapdoor one-way sampleable functions based on codes. In: Galbraith, S.D., Moriai, S. (eds.) ASIACRYPT 2019. LNCS, vol. 11921, pp. 21–51. Springer, Cham (2019). https://doi.org/10.1007/978-3-030-34578-5_2

[Dum91] Dumer, I.: On minimum distance decoding of linear codes. In: Proceedings of the 5th Joint Soviet-Swedish International Workshop on Information Theory, Moscow, pp. 50–52 (1991)

[FJR22] Feneuil, T., Joux, A., Rivain, M.: Syndrome decoding in the head: shorter signatures from zero-knowledge proofs. In: Dodis, Y., Shrimpton, T. (eds.) CRYPTO 2022. LNCS, vol. 13508, pp. 541–572. Springer, Cham (2022). https://doi.org/10.1007/978-3-031-15979-4_19

[IIJ10] Howgrave-Graham, N., Joux, A.: New generic algorithms for hard knapsacks. In: Gilbert, H. (ed.) EUROCRYPT 2010. LNCS, vol. 6110, pp. 235–256. Springer, Heidelberg (2010). https://doi.org/10.1007/978-3-642-13190-5_12

[KT17] Kachigar, G., Tillich, J.-P.: Quantum information set decoding algorithms. Preprint, arXiv:1703.00263 [cs.CR], February 2017

[Meu12] Meurer, A.: A Coding-Theoretic Approach to Cryptanalysis. Ph.D. thesis, Ruhr University Bochum, November 2012

[MMT11] May, A., Meurer, A., Thomae, E.: Decoding random linear codes in $\tilde{O}(2^{0.054n})$. In: Lee, D.H., Wang, X. (eds.) ASIACRYPT 2011. LNCS, vol. 7073, pp. 107–124. Springer, Heidelberg (2011). https://doi.org/10.1007/978-3-642-25385-0_6

[MO15] May, A., Ozerov, I.: On computing nearest neighbors with applications to decoding of binary linear codes. In: Oswald, E., Fischlin, M. (eds.) EUROCRYPT 2015. LNCS, vol. 9056, pp. 203–228. Springer, Heidelberg (2015). https://doi.org/10.1007/978-3-662-46800-5_9

[MS09] Minder, L., Sinclair, A.: The extended k-tree algorithm. In: Mathieu, C. (ed.) Proceedings of SODA 2009, pp. 586–595. SIAM (2009)

[NCBB10] Niebuhr, R., Cayrel, P.-L., Bulygin, S., Buchmann, J.: On lower bounds for information set decoding over $\mathbf{F}_q$. In: Cid, C., Faugere, J.-C. (eds.) Proceedings of the Second International Conference on Symbolic Computation and Cryptography, SCC 2010, pp. 143–157 (2010)

[NPC+17] Niebuhr, R., Persichetti, E., Cayrel, P.-L., Bulygin, S., Buchmann, J.: On lower bounds for information set decoding over $\mathbb{F}_q$ and on the effect of partial knowledge. Int. J. Inf. Coding Theory **4**(1), 47–78 (2017)

[Pet10] Peters, C.: Information-set decoding for linear codes over $\mathbf{F}_q$. In: Sendrier, N. (ed.) PQCrypto 2010. LNCS, vol. 6061, pp. 81–94. Springer, Heidelberg (2010). https://doi.org/10.1007/978-3-642-12929-2_7

[Pet11] Peters, C.: Curves, Codes, and Cryptography. Ph.D. thesis, Technische Universiteit Eindhoven (2011)

[Pra62] Prange, E.: The use of information sets in decoding cyclic codes. IRE Trans. Inf. Theory **8**(5), 5–9 (1962)

[Ste88] Stern, J.: A method for finding codewords of small weight. In: Cohen, G., Wolfmann, J. (eds.) Coding Theory 1988. LNCS, vol. 388, pp. 106–113. Springer, Heidelberg (1989). https://doi.org/10.1007/BFb0019850

SiMLA – Security in Machine Learning and its Applications

One Class to Test Them All: One-Class Classifier-Based ADS-B Location Spoofing Detection

Alessandro Brighente[ID], Mauro Conti[ID], Sitora Salaeva[✉][ID],
and Federico Turrin[ID]

University of Padua, Padua 35121, Italy
{abrighen,conti,salaeva,turrin}@math.unipd.it

Abstract. Automatic Dependent Surveillance-Broadcast (ADS-B) is an integral part of the Next Generation Air Transport System, providing an efficient and safe transport infrastructure by monitoring and managing congested airspace through advanced surveillance. It is designed to replace traditional radar-based communication with a reliable system that requires aircraft to periodically transmit their real-time positions to the air traffic control center and nearby planes. However, despite being a relatively new standard, it lacks security measures. The absence of encryption and authentication leaves it vulnerable to various attacks, including spoofing (message injection or modification), deletion, jamming, and eavesdropping. While eavesdropping may not have immediate consequences, message spoofing can lead to severe traffic disruptions and potential aircraft collisions. Although authentication may mitigate the issue, it is incompatible with existing infrastructure and requires modifications to the current ADS-B protocol.

In this paper, we propose Hexa-ML, a novel one-class classifier-based approach to detect location spoofing attacks without requiring ADS-B protocol modifications. We focus on an attacker sending ADS-B signals with a location report that does not match its current location, and we aim to identify such attempts. Our method leverages the idea that a specific location should be associated with a physical signal with specific characteristics. To this aim, we divide the space with a hexagonal tessellation and train a one-class classifier for each hexagon with physical layer features of messages received within the hexagon. These features include power, as well as statistical characteristics of magnitude and power spectrum. The idea is that, if during detection the message does not generate from within a hexagon, its associated one-class classifier should reject it. To validate our approach, we deployed a testbed to collect real ADS-B signals from real airplanes during their cruise. Our experimental results consistently demonstrate that the Isolation Forest (IF) algorithm, implemented in both libraries, performs better than One-class SVM (OCSVM) (macro average F1-score 89%) and achieves an average F1-score of 93% within geospatial hexagonal cells.

Keywords: Automatic Dependent Surveillance-Broadcast · Location spoofing attack · Vehicle Security · Wireless Security

© The Author(s), under exclusive license to Springer Nature Switzerland AG 2024
M. Andreoni (Ed.): ACNS 2024 Workshops, LNCS 14587, pp. 55–74, 2024.
https://doi.org/10.1007/978-3-031-61489-7_4

1   Introduction

Cyber-Physical System (CPS) emerged as a new paradigm for monitoring inter-connected devices in various applications [23]. In the transportation sector, which includes air, sea, and ground modes, CPS offer unique opportunities to enhance performance through information technologies [14]. However, the increasing reliance on CPS-managed systems raises concerns about the vulnerability of critical infrastructure to network attacks. Aviation safety is of particular concern among transportation modes, especially as the aviation sector becomes more digital and dependent on wireless technologies, making it an attractive target for cyberattacks [22]. By exploiting vulnerabilities in inter-connected devices and systems, as well as design flaws, attackers can compromise aircraft electronic systems even while in flight. For instance, an expert demonstrated the ability to penetrate a Boeing 757 control system remotely and the possibility of hacking the in-flight entertainment system [2,13]. Additionally, the introduction of Automatic Dependent Surveillance-Broadcast (ADS-B) as a new surveillance technology [16,19] in the aviation industry opened up new vulnerabilities and attack vectors. Indeed, while offering numerous benefits, ADS-B broadcasts aircraft information without encryption or authentication, creating opportunities for eavesdropping, spoofing, message tampering, injection, deletion, and jamming [29]. These vulnerabilities can result in substantial damage, leading to severe disruptions in air traffic monitoring and potentially aircraft collisions [26]. Furthermore, the accessibility of inexpensive Software-Defined Radios (SDRs) exacerbates these security risks, as research has demonstrated that even moderately skilled attackers can execute such attacks using readily available SDRs [29]. For example, Ground-based attackers can leverage SDRs, while airborne attackers can involve malicious aircraft or drones equipped with ADS-B transponders. In both scenarios, the attacker's objectives are introducing a ghost aircraft into the system or obscuring the actual location of the malicious aircraft. The motivations of the attacker can range from unauthorized use of airspace to the concealment of an aircraft engaged in illegal activities.

The openness of ADS-B communications is a fundamental characteristic of the system and ADS-B security improvement solutions should allow seamless integration into the existing system without requiring any infrastructure modifications. However, most of the proposed security solutions for ADS-B require protocol modification [22]. Solutions that do not require protocol modifications do not involve scenarios involving airborne attackers or necessitate the use of multiple receivers for location verification. Aditionally, research involving physical layer features does not validate the detection of location spoofing using real ADS-B data.

In this paper, we propose Hcxa-ML, the first one-class classifier-based location spoofing detector for ADS-B. The idea behind one-class classification is that a detector cannot assume knowledge of the spoofed data, and should hence only be trained with legitimate data. Our method leverages both the physical characteristics of ADS-B signals and hexagonal spatial data to effectively identify and detect location spoofing attacks without modification of the ADS-B protocol or using multiple receivers. The idea behind our proposal is that the physical-layer properties of the signal are more difficult to modify consistently and without leaving a footprint [28], making them optimal indicators to identify spoofing attempts. We hence divide the ground space according to a hexagonal tessellation method and train a one-class classifier for each hexagon with physical layer features of legitimate signals. At the detection phase, upon receiving a new message, the detector feeds it to the one-class classifier associated with the hexagon that the ADS-B claimed location belongs to. If the one-class classifier rejects it, we deem it as a spoofing attempt. To verify the validity of our assumption, we developed a real-life testbed to collect aircraft data and extract real-world physical layer features. To assess the best set of features for spoofing detection, we evaluate their information gain, correlation, and feature importance. Our results show that analyzing the statistical physical layer attributes of ADS-B location messages within a specific small geographic area can be employed for anomaly detection in ADS-B communication. Our experimental results consistently demonstrate that the Isolation Forest (IF) algorithm performs better than One-class SVM (OCSVM) (F1-score 89%) and achieves an average F1-score of 93% within geospatial hexagonal cells.

Contributions. We can summarize our contributions as follows.

- We propose Hexa-ML, a one-class classifier-based system able to detect ADS-B location spoofing attacks leveraging the physical layer features of the signal received by a ground station. We create a hexagonal tessellation of the space and train a classifier for each hexagon. We test the legitimacy of the location claim of the received signal by providing its physical layer features as input to the hexagon to which the claimed location belongs to.
- We developed a real-life testbed thanks to which we collected real aircraft signals. We extract multiple physical layer features from these signals and thoroughly evaluate their importance via information gain in identifying location spoofing attacks.
- We test different implementations of one-class classifiers and evaluate their ability to identify location spoofing attacks. Our results show that our approach can identify location spoofing attacks with an average F1 score of 89% for One-Class Support Vector Machine and 93% for Isolation Forest.

Organization. The paper is organized as follows: Sect. 2 describes existing research and literature related to the security of ADS-B. In Sect. 3, we outline the system and threat models under consideration accordingly. In Sect. 4, we detail the setup of our experiments and explain the methodology employed in our research. Section 5 presents the results of our work, while Sect. 6 engages in discussions surrounding our findings. The paper concludes in Sect. 7, and discusses potential future research directions.

2 Related Works

In the last decade, researchers have proposed various methods to enhance the security of ADS-B transmissions. These methods can be classified into two main categories: secure broadcast authentication and secure location verification.

Secure broadcast authentication involves the use of cryptographic techniques, including symmetric and public key encryption [6,19,25,27]. However, implementing these cryptographic primitives would require modifications to the existing ADS-B protocol, making them incompatible with the currently deployed infrastructure [22]. Non-cryptographic methods at the physical layer, such as software-based and hardware-based fingerprinting, have also been explored, but they are also not suitable for ADS-B due to hardware similarity among airline operators and the dynamic nature of long-distance ADS-B networks [26]. For example, Strohmeier et al. [21] studied the transmission time interval of ADS-B messages in commercial aircraft and found different patterns for distinct types of ADS-B transponders and their implementation. However, the attacker with an SDR-based spoofer can fully control time intervals between message transmissions and mimic those transmission patterns, effectively evading detection. Furthermore, a malicious aircraft has the capability to impersonate another aircraft equipped with an ADS-B transponder of analogous implementation, such as one from the same manufacturer, as a means to elude detection [29].

For secure location verification, Multilateration (MLAT) is one of the possible surveillance technologies [26]. This method typically necessitates four or more receivers for validation and can be used for ADS-B message verification as shown by Dave et al. [2] and even without time synchronization among base stations [8]. Since the area covered by four sensors is too limited for message reception, Strohmeier et al. demonstrated a lightweight location verification approach as an improvement of MLAT [20]. This approach calculates the difference in Time of Arrival (TDoA) at different points in a two-dimensional grid and then compares it to the received TDoA. Even though this strategy expands the coverage area for message verification and requires only two receiving sensors, it is not sufficient for reliable message verification, nor is it applicable to air-to-air communication scenarios. Group verification is another approach where group members verify the position declarations of non-group members in air-to-air communication scenarios [17]. However, managing secure authentication for new group members, establishing trust within the group, and preventing malicious aircraft pose significant challenges [26]. Kalman filtering [7], a standard method for location verification, improves accuracy by combining measurements with predictions and filtering out noise and false messages. Different solutions have been proposed for ADS-B location verification based on the Kalman filtering method [9,10]. However, it is vulnerable to attacks such as the "frog-boiling attack" and denial of service attacks [22]. To address aircraft trajectory spoofing attacks, Ghose and Lazos introduced *PHY-layer* verification approach that exploits the RF characteristics of ADS-B transmissions, specifically the Doppler spread phenomenon, to estimate the real velocity and position of the aircraft with the claimed one. This approach does not require any modifications to the ADS-B protocol. However, it does not take into account airborne attack scenarios [4]. Ying et al. developed *SODA*, a spoofing detector for ADS-B, using a two-stage Deep Neural Network (DNN) approach that contains an aircraft and a message classifier. By analyzing *PHY-layer* functions such as samples and IQ phases, $SODA$ allows ground stations to evaluate incoming messages and identify potentially suspicious ones [29].

We propose a secure location verification approach that requires no protocol modification; instead, it can be seamlessly integrated into an existing system as a software deployment. This method leverages one or more receivers in the target area and relies on the physical layer attributes of the signal, which are challenging to modify without leaving a detectable footprint. Differently from previous works, we employed real-time collected data for the analysis and validation of our approach.

3   System and Threat Model

In this section, we describe the system and threat model depicted in Fig. 1. We describe the system settings in Sect. 3.1, and the attacker's aim and capabilities in Sect. 3.2.

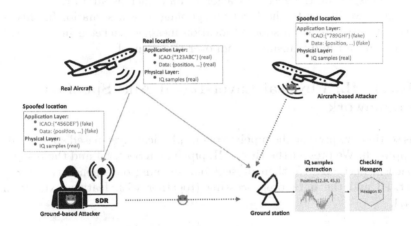

Fig. 1. Illustration of location spoofing attack.

3.1   System Model

The ADS-B standard envisions aircraft sending broadcast messages to the ground control station leveraging a pulse position modulation on a 1090 MHz carrier [1]. Due to the broadcast and cleartext transmission, receivers able to receive and decode ADS-B signals can retrieve the information sent by the transmitting aircraft. In this paper, we consider a system for data collection and analysis using one or more ground stations placed in different regions or areas. Ground stations serve both to receive air traffic information via ADS-B messages and to extract raw IQ data, i.e., in-phase (I) and quadrature (Q) components [11]) from the received signal. We assume that each ground station has sufficient resources to store and process ADS-B messages.

Ground stations then provide the received messages to the traffic control center, which manages the air traffic accordingly. To avoid safety issues related to location spoofing attacks, the ground stations should be able to identify legitimate and malicious messages. However, the current ADS-B standard does not envision such security measures.

3.2 Threat Model

We assume an attacker aiming at spoofing the location of an aircraft. To this aim, the attacker sends ADS-B messages including location reports different from the real source's location. We do not restrict the attacker to be inside an aircraft, but we also consider them sending ADS-B messages from a ground device leveraging e.g., an SDR. We consider the attacker to be able to consistently modify the content of the packets, but not the physical characteristics of the transmitted (and consequently, received) signal. In both scenarios, the attacker's goal is to influence traffic control by either introducing a ghost aircraft into the system or hiding and disguising the actual location of its malicious aircraft.

In Fig. 1, we illustrate the location spoofing attack scenario. In this situation, the attacker creates a spoofed location message packet using signals from legitimate aircraft and transmits them over the channel.

4   Hexa-ML: Physical Layer-Based Anti-Spoofing Framework

In this section, we present the pipeline of our physical layer-based spoofing detection approach. We present the Hexa-ML pipeline in Sect. 4.1 and the tessellation approach in Sect. 4.2. We then present our spoofing data generation approach in Sect. 4.3 and the data preprocessing (together with feature extraction) in Sect. 4.4.

4.1   Hexa-ML Pipeline

The main idea behind our proposal is that the physical characteristics of signals should be representative of the location of the transmitter. We assume that the space is divided according to a hexagonal tessellation, as proposed by McDougall et al. [12]. We consider an initial secure phase, where we can collect data only from legitimate airplanes (i.e., no location spoofing occurs). We use the collected signal to train a one-class classifier for each hexagon. Each classifier is trained with a set of physical layer features that we manually extract from the received signal.

Figure 2 shows the pipeline of our proposed location spoofing detector after the training phase. We assume that a malicious airplane spoofs its location in a different hexagon ❶. The malicious sender broadcasts the message that is received by the ground station ❷, which extracts a set of physical layer features from it ❸. The extracted features are then provided as input to the one-class classifier trained with the physical layer features of the signals coming from the received signal's claimed location ❹. The one class-classifier provides as output the information on whether the claimed location and the physical layer features are compliant with the training data. In case they are not, the detectors identify the received packet as spoofed.

4.2   Geo Tessellation

Various geospatial indexing systems have been developed for spatial indexing and analysis. Our work utilizes the H3 Hexagonal Hierarchical Geospatial Indexing System developed by Uber Technologies Inc. This system divides the world into hexagonal cells and supports sixteen resolutions, enabling the segmentation of areas into smaller hexagons   [5]. We employ the H3 geospatial tessellation method to divide the antenna coverage area into hexagonal cells with different resolutions.

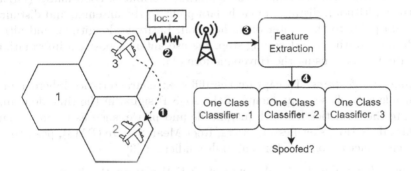

Fig. 2. Our physical layer-based spoofing detection pipeline.

The number of data points allocated to each hexagon depends on its resolution: higher resolutions yield smaller hexagons that cover more localized areas, resulting in a greater number of hexagons. Conversely, lower resolutions result in larger hexagons, fewer in number, with each hexagon covering a more extensive geographic area.

4.3   Spoofed Location Data Generation

To execute the location spoofing attack within the context of geo tessellation, we leverage the H3 library's capabilities to manipulate hexagonal cells and their geographic attributes. The process involves the following sequential steps:

1. *Define Target Hexagon:* Select the hexagon containing the highest sample count within its boundaries. This hexagon serves as the basis for the location spoofing attack.
2. *Determine Candidate Hexagon:* Randomly choose another hexagon. These chosen hexagons are candidates for spoofed samples.

3. *Generate Fake Coordinates:* Generate "new" coordinates for data points within the chosen candidate hexagons using the geographic coordinates of the chosen target hexagon while retaining original physical attributes, such as IQ samples.
4. *Update Hexagon Indexing:* Shift the hexagon indexing of data points from the chosen candidate hexagons to the selected target hexagon. This step transfers the spoofed data points to the target hexagon's area.

4.4   Data Preprocessing

Feature extraction. A wide range of features can be obtained from IQ samples. First, we compute the magnitude, phase, and power for each ADS-B message. Then, we use magnitude and phase information to extract additional features. These features can be categorized into spatial, time-domain, and frequency-domain functions.

Spatial features. will encompass the following attributes: coordinates (latitude, longitude, altitude), distance of each data point to the antenna, and distance of each data point to the center of its hexagon. Latitude, longitude, and altitude are obtained during the decoding step. We use antenna position information to calculate distances using the Haversine formula.

Time-domain features. To capture the different characteristics inherent in the magnitude and phase components of the ADS-B signal in the time domain, we calculate the statistics for both magnitude and phase, such as mean, variance, standard deviation, skewness, kurtosis, Root Mean Square (RMS), peak-to-peak value, crest factor, form factor, and pulse indicator [3].

Frequency-domain features. We extract statistics from the frequency domain using the Fast Fourier Transform (FFT) to convert the raw IQ samples from the time domain to the frequency domain. Subsequently, we calculate various statistics from the obtained power spectra, such as maxim value, sum, mean, variance, skewness, and kurtosis.

In total, we derive 31 features available for model training.

Feature selection. For feature selection, we employ two specific statistical methods: information gain and correlation coefficient, in addition to the embedded method of random forest. Statistical methods hold an advantage in computational efficiency compared to embedded methods. While random forest is commonly used as a machine learning technique, it can also serve as a feature selection tool.

4.5   Model Training

Train and Test sets. To apply machine learning models, we split the dataset of each hexagon into training and test sets using a split ratio of 80% for training and 20% for testing. To evaluate the model's ability to detect anomaly samples, the training set only contains normal (real) samples, while the test set will consist of both normal and anomalous (spoofed) data.

Anomaly Detection Models and Libraries. Anomaly Detection is used to detect abnormal events called anomalies. Anomalies refer to data points that deviate from an established pattern or behaviour. It plays a key role in many applications, especially in real-time, where the ability to detect anomalies is crucial, such as critical infrastructure, healthcare, and security [18]. Several anomaly detection algorithms are available, but we specifically focus on the well-known models due to their simplicity and effectiveness: OCSVM and IF. We conduct experiments with anomaly detection algorithms from the widely used scikit-learn library and the specialized PyOD outlier detection library [15,30]. We consistently apply both models from the two libraries using the same set of training parameters. Subsequently, we identify optimal parameters for each model, seeking configurations that yield the best results.

Performance Metrics. Given the imbalanced nature of our classes, we employ standard metrics to assess model performance, such as the F1-score and the macro-average F1-score for the final model evaluation.

5   Evaluation

In this section, we describe and discuss the results obtained from our experiment.

Device setup. To collect data from the airspace we assembled a testbed as shown in Fig. 3 with the following main components:

- ADS-B 1090 MHz outdoor antenna (installed on the roof of the building);
- SDR (RTL2832U) with a maximum sampling rate of 3.2MS/s;
  1090 MHz bandpass filter;
- Raspberry Pi.

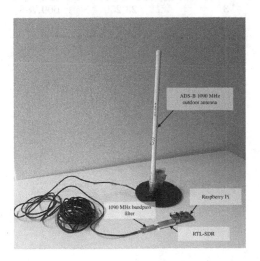

Fig. 3. Testbed for ADS-B Data Collection

Data collection and decoding. we employed an antenna and RTL-SDR equipment tuned to 1090 MHz to acquire data and perform real-time demodulation. We utilized the RTL Reader module from the open-source Python library pyModeS [24]. The RTL-SDR was configured with a gain of 49.6 and a sample rate of 2 MHz. In order to tailor the acquisition and demodulation process to our specific requirements, we have made slight modifications to the RTL Reader module. This modification allowed the extraction of IQ samples for each ADS-B message and focused solely on capturing location-related ADS-B messages. We utilized the pyModeS library to decode the location messages.

The data collection process was carried out over ten days, with each day including a continuous duration of six hours. In total, we collected 38,809 ADS-B location messages from 4,472 aircraft.

We retrieved the following data from IQ samples of each ADS-B message: the date and time when the message was received, the ICAO code (a unique aircraft identifier), type code, IQ samples, binary format of the message, hexadecimal format of the message, latitude, longitude, and altitude. Then, using raw IQ samples, we calculated the magnitude, phase, and signal power for each message.

Hexagon size. For the experiment, we analyzed 1, 2, 3, 4 and 5 as resolutions of the hexagon (Fig. 4). Table 1 shows the number of hexagons and maximum samples per resolution, respectively. We can notice that as the size of the hexagon increases, the number of hexagons increases, and the number of samples in the hexagon decreases.

Table 1. Resolutions for Hexagons

Hex size	Number of Hex	Max samples	Avg Hex Area(km^2) [5]
1	3	23,250	609,788
2	11	18,919	86,802
3	46	3,745	12,393
4	252	1,096	1,770
5	1,413	242	253

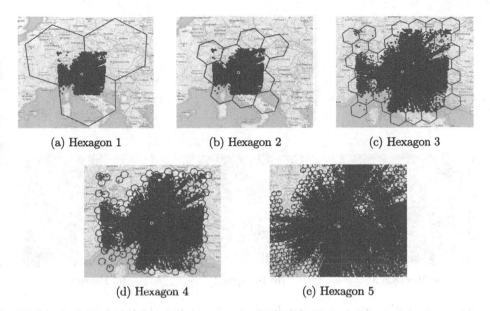

(a) Hexagon 1   (b) Hexagon 2   (c) Hexagon 3

(d) Hexagon 4   (e) Hexagon 5

Fig. 4. Hexagon tessellation on the map in different sizes. Blue dots: location coordinates, yellow circle: antenna location (Color figure online)

Although resolutions 1 and 2 encompass more data points within the hexagon, we chose hexagon resolutions where hexagons cover a smaller area for our experiment. In contrast, a hexagon with resolution 5 offers a large number of hexagons, allowing efficient analysis of data points. Even though the limited number of samples might not suffice for applying machine learning techniques, we also try to use this resolution in our experiment. Considering the range of hexagon sizes, we have chosen to proceed with resolutions 3, 4, and 5. For each resolution, our approach involves selecting one hexagon with the highest data point counts.

Results of Spoofed Locations. We created spoofed locations using the data-shifting method described in 4.3. Given our assumption that signal characteristics depend on the area and may vary, we specifically chose distant hexagons as potential candidates for generating spoofed samples in our experiment to validate this hypothesis. In Fig. 5, at the top, we denoted the target hexagon with green dots and the selected remote hexagons used to create spoofed samples with red dots for each chosen hexagon. At the bottom of the figure, we represented the spoofed locations in red, demonstrating the result of data point shifting. We marked the location of the receiving antenna with a yellow circle on the map.

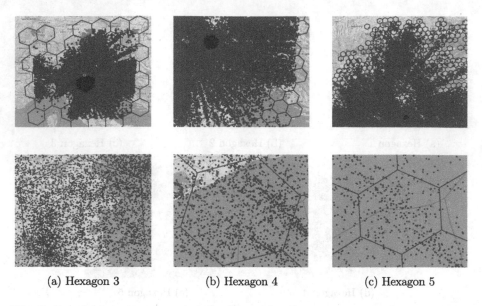

(a) Hexagon 3   (b) Hexagon 4   (c) Hexagon 5

Fig. 5. Spoofed locations in various hexagons: At the top, the target hexagon: green dots, red dots: selected hexagons used to generate spoofed samples. At the bottom, the result of data point shifting is showcased with the spoofed locations in red (Color figure online)

Results of feature selection. We conducted feature selection using two filter methods: information gain and correlation coefficient, along with one embedded method known as random forest. The results of the feature selection process are presented in terms of information gain in Fig. 6, and feature importance in Fig. 7. In Appendix A we also show the correlation existing among different physical layer features.

From the results, we can notice that features derived from the magnitude and power spectrum show greater significance compared to phase-derived features. While the random forest feature selection process identifies altitude as a significant feature, the information gain and correlation matrix analyses do not confirm this importance.

We selected the following ten features based on their high importance, information gain, and correlation score: power, mean of magnitude, RMS of magnitude, standard deviation of the magnitude, peak-to-peak range of magnitude, variance of magnitude, maximum value of the power spectrum, sum of all values in the power spectrum, mean of the power spectrum and variance of the power spectrum.

We initiate our experiment by employing anomaly detection algorithms from both libraries. This process is conducted separately for each hexagon of the chosen size. At the end of the experiment, we performed post-processing. In the post-processing step, we examine misclassified data points to analyze errors

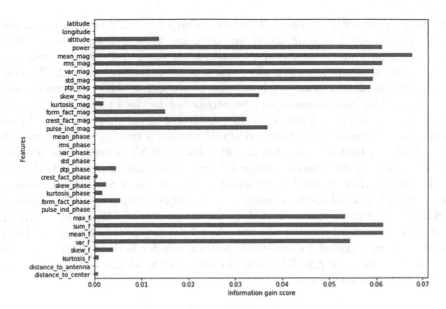

Fig. 6. Feature selection with information gain.

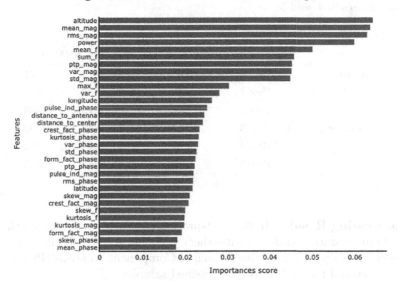

Fig. 7. Feature importance with random forest

in machine learning models, aiming to understand the models' weaknesses and identify potential improvements.

Results for Model Training. Table 2 displays the model performance metrics for Hexagons with resolution 3, 4 and 5 using the scikit-learn and PyOD libraries.

The hexagon with resolution 3 includes a larger number of data points and provides a diverse range of signal propagation characteristics. The OCSVM achieved an 83% macro-averaged F1 score using the PyOD library, similar to IF. However, IF demonstrates a more stable performance across both libraries.

Algorithms demonstrate a significant improvement in performance with Hexagon 4. This improvement can be attributed to the smaller hexagon size, leading to a more focused dataset with less diverse signal characteristics. In our evaluation, IF consistently delivered stable results, achieving a macro-average score of 93% for both libraries. On the other hand, OCSVM reached its best performance with an 89% macro-average F1 score when implemented with PyOD.

Hexagon 5, characterized by its smaller size and less diverse signal propagation, yielded improved results in comparison to larger hexagons, such as Hexagon 3. However, the performance is slightly lower than that of Hexagon 4, primarily due to the limited number of available data points within hexagon. The IF algorithm demonstrated a more stable performance for both libraries, achieving its best 85% macro-average F1 score. On the other hand, the OCSVM attained an 82% macro-average F1 score.

Table 2. Performance results of models using scikit-learn and PyOD libraries across Hexagons of sizes 3, 4, and 5

Metrics	Hexagon size	scikit-learn		PyOD	
		OC-SVM	IF	OC-SVM	IF
F1-score	Hex 3	0.62	0.71	0.71	0.71
	Hex 4	0.78	0.88	0.82	0.88
	Hex 5	0.75	0.81	0.79	0.83
Macro avg F1-score	Hex 3	0.77	0.82	0.83	0.83
	Hex 4	0.87	0.93	0.89	0.93
	Hex 5	0.79	0.84	0.82	0.85

Post-processing Results. In the post-processing phase, we leveraged the outcomes obtained during training with the PyOD library. We visually analyzed misclassified data points, applying Principal Component Analysis (PCA) to the entire test set and to a subset of misclassified samples.

Figures 8, 9, and 10 illustrate the two-dimensional PCA projection of the features for hexagon with resolutions 3, 4 and 5, respectively. In Fig. 11 we also illustrated the two-dimensional PCA projection of misclassified samples for all hexagons. These visualizations help to understand why models struggle to correctly classify samples and provide insights for future research directions, which we discuss in the Discussion and Conclusion sections.

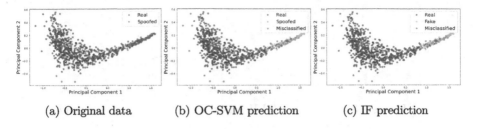

(a) Original data   (b) OC-SVM prediction   (c) IF prediction

Fig. 8. PCA 2D Projections for Hexagon 3

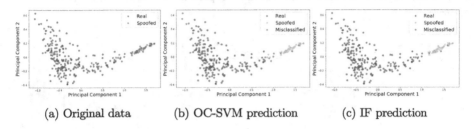

(a) Original data   (b) OC-SVM prediction   (c) IF prediction

Fig. 9. PCA 2D Projections for Hexagon 4

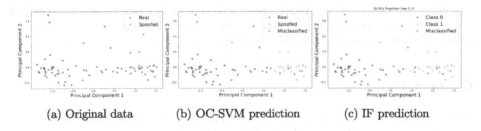

(a) Original data   (b) OC-SVM prediction   (c) IF prediction

Fig. 10. PCA 2D Projections for Hexagon 5

We assume that the receiver does not have a signal power amplifier. Consequently, the signal strength is expected to increase as the aircraft approaches the receiver. The strength of the transmitted signal depends on the movement in space, and when the aircraft is close to the receiver, the signal does not need to travel as far, resulting in a stronger received signal with more power. Conversely, when the aircraft is further away from the receiver, the signal can travel a greater distance, and this may result in reduced signal strength. Since we used data points from the farthest hexagonal cells when creating spoofed locations, we assume that the power of these signals tends to be lower than the signal power of the target hexagon that is closer to the receiving antenna. Figure 12 displays the distribution of power, including correctly classified and misclassified normal and anomaly samples.

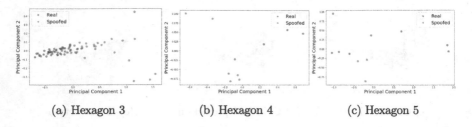

(a) Hexagon 3   (b) Hexagon 4   (c) Hexagon 5

Fig. 11. PCA 2D Projections of Misclassified Samples for Different Hexagons. Violet dots represent real samples, while red dots represent spoofed samples (Color figure online)

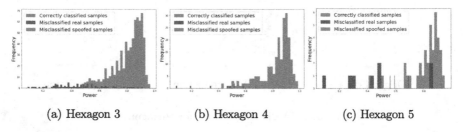

(a) Hexagon 3   (b) Hexagon 4   (c) Hexagon 5

Fig. 12. Distribution of the "power" feature for correctly classified and misclassified samples. Green: correctly classified samples, blue: misclassified real samples, red: misclassified spoofed samples (Color figure online)

6 Discussion

Analyzing the results of both anomaly detection models across different hexagon sizes, it becomes evident that IF tends to perform better in most cases, particularly in its ability to identify anomalies (class 1). Both models exhibit their best performance with Hexagon size 4, achieving macro-averaged F1-scores of 87% (scikit-learn) and 89% (PyOD) for OCSVM, and macro-averaged F1-scores of 93% (scikit-learn) and 93% (PyOD) for IF. In terms of Python tools for anomaly detection, PyOD consistently outperforms the traditional scikit-learn machine learning library. In both tools, IF performs well in detecting abnormal samples.

It is worth noting that the larger Hexagon 3 may encompass diverse signal propagation characteristics due to its larger area coverage. Contrarily, the smaller hexagon may have similar signal propagation characteristics due to its smaller coverage area. However, in our dataset, we have a limited number of samples to fully explore this assumption. Additionally, we observed that with a larger dataset of flight trajectories, OCSVM and IF exhibited more similar results for Hexagon 5 (Fig. 13a). In this context, we can assume that a comprehensive analysis of both flight trajectory and signal propagation within the hexagon could prove valuable in the detection of location spoofing attacks.

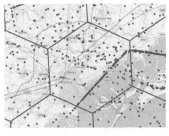

Metrics	OC-SVM	IF
F1-score	0.86	0.87
Macro avg F1-score	0.90	0.90

(a) Hexagon 5 on the map   (b) The models' performance

Fig. 13. Hexagon 5 and models performance with PyOD library

During post-processing, we found that distinguishing between normal and anomaly samples can be challenging for machine learning models. Nevertheless, further analysis using PCA on misclassified samples revealed that normal and anomaly samples can indeed be differentiated. However, due to the inherent non-linearity in the data, machine learning models may struggle to make this discrimination accurately.

Furthermore, an analysis of the power distribution among correctly classified and misclassified samples reveals that the signal strength of distant aircraft can sometimes be higher than that of aircraft close to the receiver. This case may be influenced by signal propagation characteristics or the transponder hardware of the aircraft.

7   Conclusions

In this paper, we proposed a one-class classifier-based ADS-B location spoofing detector. We tested various hexagon cell resolutions and employed H3 tools to generate spoofed locations. For each resolution, we trained well-known anomaly detection models, such as OCSVM and IF. In addition, we compared the performance of the traditional scikit-learn library with a PyOD library specifically designed for outlier detection. We also analyzed misclassified samples using PCA. Our results indicate better anomaly detection results using IF and the PyOD library, achieving an average F1 score of 93%. Performance with "Hexagon 4" demonstrated higher results in terms of accuracy, precision, recall, and F1-score for both libraries and models.

Overall, we find that monitoring and analyzing physical attributes of signal and spatial data within divided areas using hexagonal tessellation can assist in the detection of location spoofing attacks in the ADS-B system. As part of future work, we propose exploring the use of deep learning models for anomaly detection, leveraging both spatial data (including flight trajectory) and physical layer features of ADS-B signals. We believe that the statistical features we derived from IQ samples do not provide sufficient information for effective use in spoofed location detection. Therefore, feature engineering and the extraction of more informative features, including automated feature selection from the signal data, will be necessary.

A   Appendix

Figure 14 shows the correlation matrix of the different physical layer features we selected in our tests.

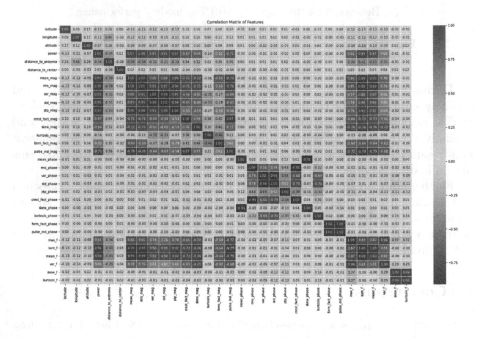

Fig. 14. Correlation matrix of the features.

References

1. Abdulaziz, A., Yaro, A.S., Adam, A.A., Kabir, M.T., Salau, H.B.: Optimum receiver for decoding automatic dependent surveillance-broadcast (ADS-B) signals. Am. J. Sig. Process. **5**(2), 23–31 (2015)
2. Dave, G., Choudhary, G., Sihag, V., You, I., Choo, K.K.R.: Cyber security challenges in aviation communication, navigation, and surveillance. Comput. Secur. 102516 (2022). https://doi.org/10.1016/j.cose.2021.102516
3. Gambera, M.: How to extract features from signals (2023). https://matteogambera. medium.com/how-to-extract-features-from-signals-15e7db225c15
4. Ghose, N., Lazos, L.: Verifying ads-b navigation information through doppler shift measurements. In: 2015 IEEE/AIAA 34th Digital Avionics Systems Conference (DASC), pp. 4A2–1–4A2–11 (2015).https://doi.org/10.1109/DASC.2015.7311412

5. H3 documentation: documentation of hexagonal hierarchical geospatial indexing system (2023). https://h3geo.org/docs/
6. He, D., Kumar, N., Choo, K.K.R., Wu, W.: Efficient hierarchical identity-based signature with batch verification for automatic dependent surveillance-broadcast system. IEEE Trans. Inf. Forensics Secur. **12**(2), 454–464 (2017). https://doi.org/10.1109/TIFS.2016.2622682
7. Kalman, R.E.: Others: a new approach to linear filtering and prediction problems. J. Basic Eng. **82**(1), 35–45 (1960)
8. Kim, S., Chong, J.: An efficient TDOA-based localization algorithm without synchronization between base stations. Int. J. Distrib. Sens. Netw. **2015**, 1–6 (2015). https://doi.org/10.1155/2015/832351
9. Kovell, B., Mellish, B.P., Newman, T.: Comparative analysis of ADS-B verification techniques (2012). https://api.semanticscholar.org/CorpusID:15440644
10. Krozel, J., Andrisani, D., Ayoubi, M., Hoshizaki, T., Schwalm, C.: Aircraft ADS-B data integrity check, November 2004. https://doi.org/10.2514/6.2004-6263
11. Lichtman, M.: IQ sampling (2023). https://pysdr.org/content/sampling.html
12. McDougall, J.A., Brighente, A., Großmann, W., McDougall, B.A., Stock, J., Federrath, H.: Love is in the air – location verification of ADS-B signals using distributed public sensors (2023)
13. Metwally, E.A., Mohammed, H.T.: Hacking an aircraft: Hacking the inflight entertainment system. Adv. Netw. **10**(1), 7–14 (2022). https://www.sciencepublishinggroup.com/article/10.11648/j.net.20221001.12
14. Möller, D.P., Vakilzadian, H.: Cyber-physical systems in smart transportation. In: 2016 IEEE International Conference on Electro Information Technology (EIT), pp. 0776–0781 (2016). https://doi.org/10.1109/EIT.2016.7535338
15. Pedregosa, F., et al.: Scikit-learn: Machine learning in Python. J. Mach. Learn. Res. **12**, 2825–2830 (2011)
16. RTCA: RTCA - DO-260C CHG 1: minimum operational performance standards for 1090 mhz extended squitter automatic dependent surveillance-broadcast (ADS-B) and traffic information services - broadcast (TIS-B). Technical Report, 25 January 2022
17. Sampigethaya, K., Poovendran, R.: Security and privacy of future aircraft wireless communications with offboard systems. In: 2011 Third International Conference on Communication Systems and Networks (COMSNETS 2011), pp. 1–6 (2011). https://api.semanticscholar.org/CorpusID:16150836
18. Schneider, P., Xhafa, F.: Chapter 3 - anomaly detection: Concepts and methods. In: Schneider, P., Xhafa, F. (eds.) Anomaly Detection and Complex Event Processing over IoT Data Streams, pp. 49–66. Academic Press (2022). https://doi.org/10.1016/B978-0-12-823818-9.00013-4
19. Strohmeier, M., Lenders, V., Martinovic, I.: Security of ADS-B: State of the Art and Beyond. ArXiv (2013), abs/1307.3664
20. Strohmeier, M., Lenders, V., Martinovic, I.: Lightweight location verification in air traffic surveillance networks. CPSS 2015 - Proceedings of the 1st ACM Workshop on Cyber-Physical System Security, Part of ASIACCS 2015, pp. 49–60, April 2015. https://doi.org/10.1145/2732198.2732202
21. Strohmeier, M., Martinovic, I.: On passive data link layer fingerprinting of aircraft transponders. In: Proceedings of the First ACM Workshop on Cyber-Physical Systems-Security and/or PrivaCy, CPS-SPC 2015, pp. 1-9. Association for Computing Machinery, New York, NY, USA (2015). https://doi.org/10.1145/2808705.2808712

22. Strohmeier, M., Martinovic, I., Lenders, V.: Securing the air–ground link in aviation. In: Keupp, M.M. (ed.) The Security of Critical Infrastructures. ISORMS, vol. 288, pp. 131–154. Springer, Cham (2020). https://doi.org/10.1007/978-3-030-41826-7_9

23. Sturaro, A., Silvestri, S., Conti, M., Das, S.K.: A realistic model for failure propagation in interdependent cyber-physical systems. IEEE Trans. Netw. Sci. Eng. 7(2), 817–831 (2020). https://doi.org/10.1109/TNSE.2018.2872034

24. Sun, J.: pymodes: an open source python library for mode s message decoding. https://github.com/junzis/pyModeS

25. Wesson, K.D., Humphreys, T.E., Evans, B.L.: Can cryptography secure next generation air traffic surveillance? (2014). https://api.semanticscholar.org/CorpusID: 21207906

26. Wu, Z., Shang, T., Guo, A.: Security issues in automatic dependent surveillance-broadcast (ADS-B): a survey. IEEE Access 8, 122147–122167 (2020). https://doi.org/10.1109/ACCESS.2020.3007182

27. Yang, A., Tan, X., Baek, J., Wong, D.S.: A new ADS-B authentication framework based on efficient hierarchical identity-based signature with batch verification. IEEE Trans. Serv. Comput. 10(2), 165–175 (2017). https://doi.org/10.1109/TSC.2015.2459709

28. Yılmaz, M.H., Arslan, H.: A survey: Spoofing attacks in physical layer security. In: 2015 IEEE 40th Local Computer Networks Conference Workshops (LCN Workshops), pp. 812–817. IEEE (2015)

29. Ying, X., Mazer, J., Bernieri, G., Conti, M., Bushnell, L., Poovendran, R.: Detecting ADS-B spoofing attacks using deep neural networks. In: 2019 IEEE Conference on Communications and Network Security (CNS), pp. 187–195 (2019)

30. Zhao, Y., Nasrullah, Z., Li, Z.: Pyod: a python toolbox for scalable outlier detection. arXiv preprint arXiv:1901.01588 (2019)

Model Extraction Attack Without Natural Images

Kota Yoshida$^{(\boxtimes)}$ and Takeshi Fujino

Ritsumeikan University, Nojihigashi 1-1-1,Kusatsu, Shiga, Japan
y0sh1d4@fc.ritsumei.ac.jp, fujino@se.ritsumei.ac.jp

Abstract. Model extraction attacks are one of the threats to machine learning as a service (MLaaS). An adversary's objective is to steal the ML model provided on the MLaaS through application programming interfaces (APIs). The adversary is motivated because the attack avoids various costs for training deep neural networks (DNNs) and infringes on the competitive features of the services. It is important to clarify possible attacks on these systems. Model extraction attacks have faced trade-offs between the domain knowledge in the extraction image sets and the query efficiency. This paper introduces a formula-driven model extraction attack that does NOT use natural images. Our extraction image sets consist of fractal images that represent patterns effectively on natural objects and scenes around us and are generated using mathematical formulas from fractal geometry. We expect the fractal image sets to reduce costs for acquiring images for attack and effectively extract features from the target DNN model.

Keywords: Deep neural networks · Formula-driven supervised learning · Model extraction attack

1 Introduction

Machine Learning as a Service (MLaaS) offers access to DNN models via application programming interfaces (APIs). In MLaaS, users submit queries and receive the DNN outputs. It enables adversaries to execute attacks by analyzing malicious queries and responses. Model extraction attack is a significant threat to MLaaS. An objective for adversaries is to steal DNN models provided on MLaaS. Trained DNN models are crucial intellectual property, necessitating extensive training datasets and expertise. These attacks allow adversaries to avoid these costs, compromising the competitive edge of the MLaaS.

So far, various model extraction attacks have been assessed to grasp the threat of attacks. Juuti et al. [3] performed a distillation-like model extraction attack against DNNs on MLaaS through prediction APIs. An adversary collects query and response pairs within budget limits through prediction APIs and trains substitute models using these. It is currently one of the most typical attack frameworks. Correia-Silva et al. [9] found that out-of-domain data could steal information on decision boundaries through queries. With the reinforcement

M. Andreoni (Ed.): ACNS 2024 Workshops, LNCS 14587, pp. 75–83, 2024.
https://doi.org/10.1007/978-3-031-61489-7_5

learning-based strategy, Orekondy et al. [6] improved extraction efficiency by querying images from the out-of-domain large natural image sets. Truong et al. [11] proposed model extraction attacks with generated images. The overall attack setup is similar to generative adversarial networks (GAN) [2]. A generator generates images for queries, and a student (substitute) model (equivalent to a discriminator in a GAN) classifies the generated images. The attack liberates the adversary from the limitations of collecting extraction image sets that consist of natural images.

So far, model extraction attacks face trade-offs between the domain knowledge in the extraction image sets and the query efficiency. It has been suggested that model extraction attacks using out-of-domain data work well by using a large number of natural images collected using large-scale public datasets and web scraping. However, the attack may not work well in the task in which the images are in a minor distribution (e.g. medical images) [6]. It is expected that methods utilizing generated data may effectively work regardless of the target domain. However, a large number of queries are consumed before the generative model is capable of generating appropriate queries [11].

In this paper, we introduce a formula-driven model extraction attack that does not use natural images. Our extraction image sets consist of the fractal image dataset proposed by Kataoka et al. [4]. A fractal image is generated in accordance with mathematical formulas from fractal geometry and is expected to represent patterns effectively on natural objects and scenes existing around us. It avoids consuming a large number of queries to obtain appropriate representation for generative models and expects to work well on miner domains.

Our contribution is summarized as follows:

- We found that fractal images are suitable for extracting knowledge through prediction APIs. The attack does NOT require large natural image sets and domain knowledge of the target DNN model.
- We demonstrate a formula-driven model extraction attack in grayscale image classification tasks, MNIST, and Fashion-MNIST[1]. We evaluated the substitute model's accuracy and budget efficiency. Substitute models extracted with fractal images achieved equivalent accuracy to the victim model with better efficiency than other domain-knowledge-less methods.
- We analyze the similarity of the victim and substitute models by adversarial examples (AEs) transferability. We expect that the transferability of the AEs between these models represents the similarity of the decision boundary of each model. Substitute models extracted with fractal images achieved the highest transferability against the victim model.

2   Fractal Database

Kataoka et al. [4] proposed fractal databases (FractalDB) to replace human-annotated datasets in DNN pre-training techniques. The FractalDB consists of

---

[1] Codes are available at https://github.com/y0sh1d4/model_extraction_attack_without_natural_images.

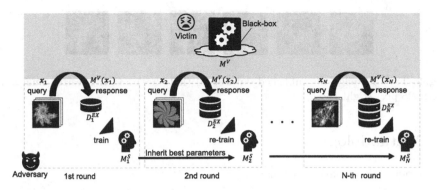

Fig. 1. Overview of formula-driven model extraction attack with "random-querying strategy"

images and corresponding labels that are automatically generated in accordance with the fractals. The fractal images are expected to represent various natural patterns in the real world and enable the pre-trained model that acquires features to recognize natural images on later tasks through fine-tuning. Various tasks are expected to benefit from pre-training with the FractalDB without being affected by problems that natural image datasets face.

Fractal images are rendered with an iterated function system (IFS) [1]. The fractal images are constructed in 2D Euclidean space $\chi = \mathbb{R}^2$ and the IFS is defined on the space χ by;

$$IFS = \{\chi; w_1, w_2, \cdots, w_N; p_1, p_2, \cdots, p_N\} \tag{1}$$

where $w_i; \chi \rightarrow \chi$ are transformation functions, p_i are probabilities that the corresponding w_i are performed, and N is the number of transformations. The IFS is defined on a 2D complete metric space χ and transformation w_i is assumed to be an Affine transformation as follows;

$$w_i(\mathbf{x}; \theta_i) = \begin{bmatrix} a_i & b_i \\ c_i & d_i \end{bmatrix} \mathbf{x} + \begin{bmatrix} e_i \\ f_i \end{bmatrix} \tag{2}$$

where the parameters θ_i represent rotations and shifting.

A fractal image is rendered by drawing dots on a black background in accordance with the random iteration algorithm. The algorithm repeats the following two steps for $t = 0, 1, 2, \cdots$ from an initial point $\mathbf{x}_0$;

1. Select a transformation w^* from $w_1, \cdots, w_N$ with pre-defined corresponding probabilities p to determine the i-th transformation.
2. Draw a new point $\mathbf{x}_{t+1} = w^*(\mathbf{x}_t)$.

In FractalDB, image category is associated to the fractal parameters a to f. Kataoka et al. [4] generated FractalDB-60 and 1k that consist of 60 and 1,000 different categories of fractal images, respectively, and published them. In this paper, we sample queries from FractalDB.

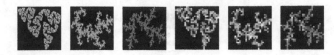

Fig. 2. Fractal images in published dataset [4] (left thee) and the resized images (28 pix × 28 pix) (right three).

3 Methodology

We denote the scenarios as follows:

- **Victim (MLaaS provider):** The MLaaS provides an image classification service. They train a victim DNN model with a secret training set. They provide access to the victim model through prediction APIs. The prediction APIs receive image queries from users and return the prediction results that represent the probability that the queried images belong to each class. They receive payments from users on the basis of the number of queries (e.g., $1 per 1k queries).
- **Adversary (MLaaS user):** The objective of the adversary is to obtain a substitute model that is "functionally-equivalent" to the victim model. The adversary knows the image size of the query and the number of classes through the prediction APIs. The adversary attempts to make the attack successful with a smaller budget (i.e. smaller number of queries).

Figure 1 represents an overview of the attack procedure. It basically follows the typical framework for extracting neural network models through prediction APIs presented in [3] similar to later studies [6,11]. We adopt a "random-querying strategy" in this paper.

The adversary prepares images $\mathbf{X}$ to query the victim model M^V. The adversary performs the following procedure for each round. In the n-th round, the adversary queries $\mathbf{x_n}$ sampled from $\mathbf{X}$ by uniform random sampling without replacement and collects responses $p(c|x_n) = M^V(\mathbf{x_n})$, where $p(c|x_n)$ represents conditional probability that x_n belongs to certain class c. The adversary adds the query and response pairs to the extraction dataset D_n^{EX}; where $D_0^{EX} = \phi$ and $D_{n+1}^{EX} = \{\mathbf{x_n}, \mathbf{M^V}(\mathbf{x_n})\} \cup D_{n-1}^{EX}$. The adversary trains the substitute model M_n^S using the extraction dataset; note that the model inherits the best parameters from the previous model parameters as an initial parameter. The objective of the training process is to minimize the distance between the probability distribution from the victim and substitute models. We use Kullback-Leibler (KL) divergence for the loss function. The adversary repeats the round until the substitute model achieves sufficient accuracy or the budget reaches the limit.

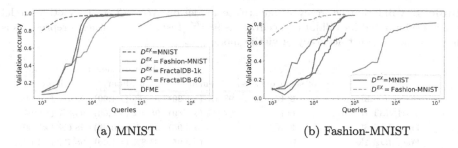

(a) MNIST   (b) Fashion-MNIST

Fig. 3. Validation accuracy through model extraction attack. The victim model is trained using each dataset. The dashed line results from the model extraction attack with the same dataset as victim model training.

4   Experiments

4.1   Datasets and Model Architectures

We evaluated the formula-driven model extraction attack on grayscale image classification tasks (MNIST [5] and Fashion-MNIST [12]) due to the fractal images being represented as grayscale images. We assumed the MLaaS provides APIs that charge every 1k queries, so the adversary queries 1k images at each round in this experiment.

We used the fractal images from FractalDB-60 and 1k that were created and published by Kataoka et al. [4], which contain 60 categories by 1,000 images (total of 60,000 images) and 1,000 categories by 1,000 images (total of 1,000,000 images), respectively. The fractal images were scaled linearly into 28×28 as shown in Fig. 2. We sampled images for the query in each round by uniform random sampling without replacement regardless of the categories. We set the maximum number of queries (i.e., adversary's budget) to 55,000 (the same as the number of images in the dataset) for FractalDB-60 and 100,000 (to evaluate a large number of queries than FractalDB-60) for FractalDB-1k.

We prepared three models, small, medium, and large to evaluate the difference in results between substitute model sizes. They are constructed from one convolution (Conv.) and fully connected (FC) layer, two Conv. and one FC layer, and three Conv. and two FC layers, respectively. The victim model architecture is the medium size.

For comparison, we prepared three additional attacks. First, we constructed an extraction dataset from images in the training dataset (55,000 images) for the victim model as the most ideal condition. For example, when the victim model is trained by the MNIST training dataset, the adversary queries images from it. This comparative scenario assumes the most advantageous scenario in which the adversary has full access to images (except labels) in the training dataset of the victim model. The maximum number of queries is set to 55,000 (the same as the number of images in the dataset).

Table 1. Validation accuracy of substitute model on **MNIST** task. Victim model size is medium and its validation accuracy is 98.8%. Inside of parentheses represents is magnification against accuracy of victim model.

D^{EX}	# of spent queries	substitute model		
		small	medium	large
MNIST (train)	60K	98.4% (×1.00)	98.8% (×1.00)	99.1% (×1.00)
Fashion-MNIST (train)	60K	87.9% (×0.89)	98.4% (×1.00)	94.3% (×0.95)
FractalDB-60	60K	94.2% (×0.95)	98.3% (×0.99)	98.6% (×1.00)
FractalDB-1k	100K	94.3% (×0.95)	98.8% (×1.00)	98.7% (×1.00)
DFME	2M	88.4% (×0.89)	98.3% (×0.99)	97.4% (×0.99)

Table 2. Validation accuracy of substitute model on **Fashion-MNIST** task. Victim model size is medium and its validation accuracy is 90.0%. Inside of parentheses represents is magnification against accuracy of victim model.

D^{EX}	# of spent queries	substitute model		
		small	medium	large
MNIST (train)	60K	59.7% (×0.66)	78.1% (×0.87)	45.9% (×0.51)
Fashion-MNIST (train)	60K	90.2% (×1.00)	90.1% (×1.00)	90.3% (×1.00)
FractalDB-60	60K	81.6% (×0.91)	88.6% (×0.98)	73.9% (×0.82)
FractalDB-1k	100K	82.5% (×0.92)	89.5% (×0.99)	83.5% (×0.93)
DFME	10M	42.7% (×0.47)	81.6% (×0.91)	76.4% (×0.85)

Second, we constructed an extraction dataset from images in the other training dataset from the victim model. For example, when the victim model is trained by the MNIST training dataset, the adversary queries images from the Fashion-MNIST training dataset. The settings from previous works inspire this scenario [3,6] but note that there are differences due to the following limitations.

- Our target tasks are grayscale and small resolution images.
- There are NO overlaps in sampling distribution in MNIST and Fashion-MNIST.
- These datasets are NOT large-scale and comprehensive.

We adopt a random strategy; that is, we sampled images for the query in each round by uniform random sampling without replacement regardless of the categories. The maximum number of queries is the same as above.

Finally, we prepared the data-free model extraction (DFME) attack [11] by modifying the author's public implementation a little. This requires a huge query budget, so we set the maximum number of queries (query budget) to 2,000,000 (this technique requires a huge number of queries than others). The unit of queries is 1,792 for each iteration according to the reference implementation, so we assume that the adversary queries 1,792 images at once.

4.2 Extraction Efficiency

Except for DFME, we trained a substitute model for 30 epochs in each round. We set training parameters, batch size to 128, optimizer to AMSGrad [8], and initial learning rate to 0.001. In DFME, we changed training parameters from published implementation, initial learning rate of substitute model training to 0.02 (MNIST) and 0.005 (Fashion-MNIST), student model architecture, and image size of generator output to 28 pix × 28 pix (grayscale).

Figure 3 shows the validation accuracy curve through the model extraction attack against the MNIST and Fashion-MNIST trained victim models. Understandably, the validation accuracy of the substitute model attacked by the same dataset as the victim model improved most efficiently. Fractal datasets were the next best efficiency. As suggested in the previous works [3,6], natural images that were sampled from different distributions than the victim task also extracted knowledge through queries. The DFME attack [11] succeeded in extracting knowledge from the victim model but it spent huge query budgets.

Tables 1 and 2 list the validation accuracy of the substitute model in each attack and model size against the MNIST and Fashion-MNIST trained victim models, respectively. There were few differences between attack methods in the MNIST task; most of the attacks achieved equivalent accuracy to the victim model. The model extraction attack with fractal images achieved more than ×0.95 accuracy against the victim model. Whereas, the results had several differences between attack methods and model architectures in the Fashion-MNIST task. Model extraction attacks with fractal images achieved the closest accuracy to the victim model than other methods without domain knowledge in most cases. The attacks achieved ×0.98 (FractalDB-60) and ×0.99 (FractalDB-1k) accuracy against the victim model when the substitute model has the same architecture as the victim one. The accuracy decreased when the substitute model architecture was different from the victim one.

4.3 Transferability of Adversarial Examples

We evaluate the transferability of AEs against the victim model generated by the substitute model. This belongs to black-box scenarios with the substitute model. AEs were discovered by Szegedy [10] as intriguing properties of DNNs. The AEs are created by adding perturbations that are barely perceptible to humans to images and cause misclassification of the victim model. The adversary not only steals the victim model but also confuses the MLaaS by deceiving the model. There are several studies to create AEs in black-box scenarios through the substitute model. Papernot et al. [7] proposed techniques to train a substitute model that approximated the decision boundary with a small number of domain images. Juuti et al. [3] evaluated the transferability of AEs generated from the substitute model against the victim model. We expect that the evaluation of the transferability of AEs from the substitute to victim model reveals the threat of the diversion of model extraction attacks to other attacks.

Table 3. Success rate (SR) and transferability (Trans.) on *MNIST* task ($\epsilon = 24/255.0$).Victim model size is medium and its SR is 84.3%.

		substitute model					
		small		medium		large	
D^{EX}	#queries	SR	Trans.	SR	Trans.	SR	Trans.
MNIST (train)	60K	99.7%	4.1%	90.5%	30.3%	30.8%	33.8%
Fashion-MNIST	60K	99.9%	4.9%	86.5%	69.6%	87.5%	24.7%
FractalDB-60	60K	98.8%	8.2%	86.4%	77.0%	83.7%	96.0%
FractalDB-1k	100K	99.0%	13.7%	84.3%	99.6%	83.1%	96.7%
DFME	2M	83.0%	15.8%	81.6%	78.1%	87.8%	69.6%

Table 4. Success rate (SR) and transferability (Trans.) on *Fashion-MNIST* task ($\epsilon = 24/255.0$).Victim model size is medium and its SR is 100.0%.

		substitute model					
		small		medium		large	
D^{EX}	#queries	SR	Trans.	SR	Trans.	SR	Trans.
MNIST	60K	100.0%	47.2%	100.0%	71.2%	99.8%	39.7%
Fashion-MNIST (train)	60K	100.0%	77.6%	100.0%	86.6%	99.9%	78.7%
FractalDB-60	60K	100.0%	83.8%	100.0%	99.5%	100.0%	80.0%
FractalDB-1k	100K	100.0%	90.2%	100.0%	99.9%	100.0%	95.6%
DFME	10M	99.5%	72.0%	100.0%	93.5%	99.8%	94.8%

We evaluate the success rate (SR) and transferability for each pair of victim and substitute models. The SR is the percentage of AEs created for the substitute model that can successfully fool it. The transferability is the percentage of AEs samples created for the substitute model that can successfully fool the victim model. In this paper, we set attack parameters, $\alpha = 1/255$ and $\epsilon = 24/255$. The purpose of this evaluation is to measure the similarity of the decision boundaries between two models based on the transferability of AEs. Therefore, large perturbations are selected to ensure the differences in transferability.

Tables 3 and 4 show the SR and transferability in each attack method and substitute model size ($\epsilon = 24/255.0$). Substitute models extracted with fractal images achieved a similar SR to the victim one and higher transferability in most cases. There are trends that the substitute model that has the same architecture as the victim one achieves relatively high transferability. DFME also achieved high transferability but it spent huge query budgets for the attack.

5   Conclusion

We evaluated a formula-driven model extraction attack in this work. The attack does NOT require any natural images and domain knowledge of the victim's task because it uses fractal images generated by a formula.

Substitute models extracted with fractal images achieved equivalent accuracy (up to ×1.0) to the victim model with smaller queries than other attacks without domain knowledge (DFME). In addition, it achieved the highest transferability (up to 99.9%) against the victim model. This indicates that the substitute model effectively approximated the decision boundary of the victim one.

These results show that the formula-driven model extraction attack can extract the victim model with smaller query budgets and high similarity without domain knowledge and image collection. Note that our findings are limited to low-resolution and gray-scale image classification tasks. We are currently working on expanding it to large-scale and color images.

Acknowledgement. This work was supported by JSPS Grant-in-Aid for Early-Career Scientists Grant Number 23K16910.

References

1. Barnsley, M.F.: Fractals Everywhere. Academic Press (2014)
2. Goodfellow, I., et al.: Generative adversarial nets. In: Advances in Neural Information Processing Systems, vol. 27 (2014)
3. Juuti, M., Szyller, S., Marchal, S., Asokan, N.: PRADA: protecting against DNN model stealing attacks. In: 2019 IEEE European Symposium on Security and Privacy (EuroS&P), pp. 512–527. IEEE (2019)
4. Kataoka, H., et al.: Pre-training without natural images. In: Asian Conference on Computer Vision (ACCV) (2020)
5. LeCun, Y., Cortes, C., Burges, C.: MNIST handwritten digit database. ATT Labs **2** (2010). http://yann.lecun.com/exdb/mnist
6. Orekondy, T., Schiele, B., Fritz, M.: Knockoff nets: stealing functionality of black-box models. In: Proceedings of the IEEE/CVF Conference on Computer Vision and Pattern Recognition, pp. 4954–4963 (2019)
7. Papernot, N., McDaniel, P., Goodfellow, I., Jha, S., Celik, Z.B., Swami, A.: Practical black-box attacks against machine learning. In: Proceedings of the 2017 ACM on Asia conference on computer and Communications Security, pp. 506–519 (2017)
8. Reddi, S.J., Kale, S., Kumar, S.: On the convergence of Adam and beyond. arXiv preprint arXiv:1904.09237 (2019)
9. da Silva, J.R.C., Berriel, R.F., Badue, C., de Souza, A.F., Oliveira-Santos, T.: Copycat CNN: stealing knowledge by persuading confession with random non-labeled data. CoRR abs/1806.05476 (2018). http://arxiv.org/abs/1806.05476
10. Szegedy, C., et al.: Intriguing properties of neural networks. arXiv preprint arXiv:1312.6199 (2013)
11. Truong, J.B., Maini, P., Walls, R.J., Papernot, N.: Data-free model extraction. In: Proceedings of the IEEE/CVF Conference on Computer Vision and Pattern Recognition, pp. 4771–4780 (2021)
12. Xiao, H., Rasul, K., Vollgraf, R.: Fashion-MNIST: a novel image dataset for benchmarking machine learning algorithms. CoRR abs/1708.07747 (2017). http://arxiv.org/abs/1708.07747

Privacy-Preserving Sentiment Analysis Using Homomorphic Encryption and Attention Mechanisms

Amirhossein Ebrahimi Moghaddam, Buvana Ganesh[✉], and Paolo Palmieri

School of Computer Science and IT, University College Cork, Cork, Ireland
{a.ebrahimimodhaddam,b.ganesh,p.palmieri}@cs.ucc.ie

Abstract. Homomorphic encryption (HE) is a promising approach to preserving the privacy of data used in machine learning by allowing computations to be performed on ciphertext and exploring ways to achieve faster encrypted neural networks with HE. This paper presents a privacy-preserving sentiment analysis method employing Cheon-Kim-Kim-Song (CKKS) homomorphic encryption [4] on a pre-trained deep learning model. The model is bifurcated into a client-side attention mechanism and a server-side prediction head. The attention mechanism at the client end encrypts pivotal data before transmission, thereby preserving privacy while reducing the computational burden on the server. The server handles this encrypted data with a simplified RNN layer and linear activation function, ensuring computational efficiency without compromising on data privacy. Finally, the client decrypts the server's encrypted output and applies a sigmoid function to obtain the sentiment score. We demonstrated the efficacy of this approach using the IMDb database [17], achieving an accuracy of 70.73%. This approach maintains a balance between privacy preservation and computational efficiency, showcasing a viable solution for secure and efficient machine learning applications.

Keywords: Privacy Preserving Neural Networks · Homomorphic Encryption · Attention Mechanisms · Accelerations · Recurrent Neural Networks

1 Introduction

In recent years, there has been a massive increase in data generation through various channels such as social networks, web browsing, and geolocation services. This has driven the need for advanced machine learning (ML) techniques to process and extract meaningful insights from the available data.

Neural Networks (NNs) are widely used for tasks, such as image classification, natural language processing, speech recognition, etc. However, as the use of ML becomes

Amirhossein Ebrahimi is supported by a PhD scholarship funded by the Science Foundation Ireland under Grant No. 18/CRT/6222

Buvana Ganesh is supported by a PhD scholarship funded by the Science Foundation Ireland under Grant No. 18/CRT/6223

P. Palmieri—This work is also supported by Science Foundation Ireland under Grant No. SFI/12/RC/2289_P2

P. Palmieri—The first two authors contributed equally to the paper.

M. Andreoni (Ed.): ACNS 2024 Workshops, LNCS 14587, pp. 84–100, 2024.
https://doi.org/10.1007/978-3-031-61489-7_6

more widespread, concerns about the privacy of the data also increase. When using cloud-based ML models, the privacy of both the data and the corresponding model should be considered. Sensitive data such as medical, census, or government data, may be subject to legal restrictions and cannot be shared.

Data outsourcing involves sending data to external or untrusted parties for improved storage and computational capacity and can pose risks to privacy if the data is not properly handled. Similarly, data sharing, where parties share data for purposes such as analysis and distribution can cause privacy violations if the owner does not impose proper access control and policies. To address these concerns, several methods can be employed, including differential privacy, homomorphic encryption, and secret sharing schemes or trusted execution environments [20].

Privacy-preserving prediction on ML models plays an important role with the aim of protecting the model from the client who queries the model and the client's evaluation data from the service provider. This approach allows organizations to leverage the computational resources of cloud service providers to perform ML tasks, while still maintaining control over their data and models.

One of the solutions to protect privacy is to use homomorphic encryption (HE) to run neural networks or any computation on encrypted data. While HE has been used for the inference phase in neural network models, the computations on HE data can be computationally intensive, making it difficult to perform complex computations in real time. Therefore, enhancing the efficiency of HE algorithms remains an active area of research.

1.1 Motivation and Contribution

In recent years, there has been a substantial increase in the deployment of ML algorithms to glean insights from the large datasets generated daily. While these developments have unlocked considerable value, they have equally amplified concerns surrounding data privacy.

The principle motivation behind our research lies in addressing these privacy concerns through the lens of homomorphic encryption, utilizing CKKS homomorphic encryption [4], a popular choice in privacy-preserving mechanisms. However, our approach seeks to reduce computational complexity while safeguarding data privacy. Our contributions are as follows:

- **Simplified Activation Function for RNN Layer:** Our strategy is to incorporate a linear activation function, delineated as $f(x) = x$ in the RNN layer, significantly easing the computational demands ordinarily involved in handling encrypted data. Moreover, by choosing this activation function the server doesn't need to do bootstrapping and have lots of communication with the client.
- **Client-Server Model with Segmented Responsibilities:** Our model splits the computations between the client and the server, where the client handles the attention mechanism while the server manages the prediction through the RNN layer with the simplified activation function. This bifurcation ensures not just efficiency but a higher level of privacy preservation, given that the server operates solely on encrypted data.

- **Attention Mechanism to Enhance Shallow Networks:** We integrated an attention mechanism with shallow networks to focus selectively on critical data during the inference process, retaining essential information and enhancing the network's performance without escalating the computational demands excessively.
- **Real-World Application and Validation:** Our methodology is empirically validated using the IMDb comment database for sentiment analysis, demonstrating its efficacy in real-world applications. Then we compare our work with the state of the art [21,22] to showcase the performance.

While this straightforward approach currently yields a performance metric of 70% accuracy—a decrease when compared to the results achieved in the existing literature—it opens up a novel pathway in privacy-preserving ML by demonstrating that satisfactory results can still be attained with markedly lesser computational resources, presenting a foundation upon which further optimizations can be built. By underlining a straightforward activation function in the framework, this research endeavors to foster advancements in privacy-preserving machine learning (PPML), steering it towards a more efficient PPML cloud service.

1.2 Related Work

Privacy and Security in Data Processing. When dealing with data, it is important to consider both the privacy and the security of the data as they satisfy different requirements [8]. Anonymity and obfuscation are achievable with privacy mechanisms like Differential Privacy (DP), multi-party computation, etc., which do not guarantee provable security. To achieve confidentiality and integrity, cryptographic primitives like encryption schemes and signature schemes come into play. We first explore the literature on privacy and move to secure schemes.

Secure Multi-Party Computation (SMPC) is also a very popular tool to execute ML operations as discussed in an early survey from Shokri et al. [25]. SecureML [19] has two non-colluding servers for linear and logistic regression with garbled circuits for an approximated linear logistic curve. MiniONN [15] uses secure two-party computation techniques with HE for oblivious inference. SecureNN [27], using a customized 3-Party SMPC for CNN with multiple servers. SMPC may be less attractive to cloud providers as it requires them to share part of the model with the client.

The earliest works on Privacy Preserving Neural Networks (PPNN) with provable security started with Barni et al. [2] using additive HE and garbled circuits. After the introduction of Fully Homomorphic Encryption (FHE) [9], the Cryptonets [10] framework was introduced covering all possible ML and NN algorithms using HE through the SEAL library [24] and parallel computations. Another framework, ML Confidential [11] uses Magma and executes classification algorithms with division-free integer polynomial approximation. Some surveys on PPNN [18,20,26] detail the security primitives, the different ways these can be combined and provide comparisons for all the methods.

Acceleration. In the context of machine learning and artificial intelligence, certain operations such as matrix multiplication, vectorization, and activation functions with non-linear operations can be challenging to perform directly on encrypted data. This can result in reduced performance when using privacy-preserving techniques. Solutions to the challenges of performing machine learning on encrypted data often involve trade-offs between privacy and accuracy. A common approach is to use polynomial machine learning, which approximates an algorithm as a polynomial of a given degree.

Some ways to perform polynomial approximation [13,22] are by Taylor's series, Chebyshev interpolation, and more numerical analysis methods. Chimera [3] uses the Vandermonde matrix to bridge the encoding techniques in BFV[1] [7] and TFHE[2] [5] by forming a torus-based scheme. This is especially helpful as the neural network can switch between BFV[3] [7] which does faster arithmetic operations and TFHE, which can perform non-linear operations faster. Glyph [16] achieves the same process with BGV and TFHE and is faster than the BFV approach.

With CryptoDL, Hesamifard et al. [13] focused on training and evaluating polynomial CNNs on both plaintext and homomorphically encrypted data. CryptoNN [28] utilizes functional encryption for logistic Regression on the iDASH data set [14] using polynomial approximation and data batching using the popular BFV cryptosystem.

Zhang et al. [29] used a CNN to perform encrypted speech recognition, with the final part of the network matching the output to the actual text being performed on the client side. Liu et al. [15] transformed a regular long short-term memory (LSTM) into a privacy-preserving LSTM by replacing activation functions with approximations, which were evaluated by the client. However, this leaked some information about the model to the client.

The RHODE framework [23] enables privacy-preserving training and prediction on RNNs with federated learning by relying on multiparty HE. However, most of these approaches are focused only on CNNs and do not work for RNNs. Keeping these shortcomings in mind, our approach uses approximation techniques on activation functions for RNNs, using only FHE as the cryptographic primitive and the HELib library [12]. None of the other works consider attention mechanisms or separating client-server computations in the way described in our work.

1.3 Outline

In the following sections, we will detail the foundations and implementations central to our research. Section 2 introduces the core principles of neural networks and homomorphic encryptions, alongside a discussion on threats and attacks pertinent to neural networks. Section 3 delineates our methodology and the specifics of our implementation, which is centered on a simplistic activation function in the RNN layer. Our findings are then presented and analyzed in Sect. 5. We conclude the paper in Sect. 6, offering final remarks and potential directions for future work in this area.

2 Preliminaries

In this section, we cover various types and operations in neural networks and homomorphic encryption (Sect. 2.1), accelerating homomorphic encryption and the components for efficiency, and how to use them to improve the security and functionality of encrypted data.

---

[1] Brakerski-Gentry-Vaikuntanathan.

[2] Fast Fully Homomorphic Encryption over the Torus.

[3] Brakerski-Fan-Vercauteren.

2.1 Homomorphic Encryption and Neural Networks

Fullu Homomorphic Encryption [9] is a secure solution to execute neural networks, as it allows extensive computations on encrypted data, preserving the privacy of the model and the data. One challenge of using HE for neural networks is the computational intensity, making real-time complex computations difficult. This arises from the many non-linear operations in various steps of a neural network.

Currently, backpropagation cannot be performed on homomorphically encrypted data, as it involves performing partial differentiations. As operations like exponentiations, tangents, etc., are hard to execute already, such partial differential equations and matrix multiplications become a computational burden. This only allows shallow neural networks, which do not perform well, in terms of accuracy. For activation layers, there is a need to identify an alternative function that only involves linear arithmetic operations.

Pre-processing or cleaning the encrypted data before it is fed to a neural network also has high overheads because of the large amount of input data and linear search. Though this step is not highly useful for deep learning's black-box approach, it saves a lot of computation power. Therefore, it is possible to only perform the inference phase using HE currently.

The CKKS homomorphic encryption scheme [4] supports approximate operations on real and complex numbers with predefined precision and is secure under the Ring Learning with Errors (RLWE) problem. The coefficient encoding, real number base, and the approximate nature of CKKS make it a suitable candidate for deep learning operations to be performed with higher accuracy. We use CKKS in our approach to increase the efficiency of the neural network.

Homomorphic encryption libraries, such as Microsoft SEAL [24] and HELib [12], are openly available and enable computations on encrypted data without the need for decryption. [6] compares the performance of the different homomorphic encryption schemes for implementing a secure neural network.

2.2 Efficient Activation Functions

Activation functions are non-linear functions that are applied to the output of a layer in a neural network to introduce non-linearity and enable the learning of complex patterns. However, activation functions are challenging to evaluate homomorphically, as they require high-degree polynomials or expensive operations such as exponentiation or logarithms.

Following the implementation in CryptoDL [13], Bakshi and Last [1] require the client to compute the activations on plaintext, but only considers shallow networks and short inputs. In Podschwadt and Takabi [22], the client was not involved in computation but was involved in noise removal.

Approximate activation functions can be expressed as low-degree polynomials or piecewise linear functions, such as the square function, sine function, the ReLU function, etc. Pre-trained activation functions can be stored as lookup tables and accessed homomorphically, such as the sigmoid function, the tanh function, the softmax function, etc. We use this approach to linearize the tanh activation function and use it in a recurrent neural network. Then the results are compared with the works of [21, 22].

3   Methodology

In this section, we expand on the methodology adopted in our study to develop a privacy-preserving sentiment analysis system leveraging CKKS homomorphic encryption and attention mechanisms in shallow neural networks. The methodology discusses the proposed method, outlining the architectural nuances of our model, the attention mechanism, and how we went about the training of the model, followed by a brief on the dataset utilized for this study. Figure 1 represents a schematic of our method.

3.1   Proposed Method

Our approach involves dividing the neural network model operations between client-side and server-side, based on the CKKS scheme. Here, we detail their specific functions:

- **Client-side Component:** On the client side, the initial layers of the neural network model, up to and including the attention mechanism, are deployed. After the attention mechanism, a dense layer and a reshape layer are utilized to compress the essential information into a compact format, which is structured as a $(None, 32, 32)$ matrix in our research. This compression is crucial as it facilitates a reduction in the computational load during the server-side processing, and enables the encapsulation of pertinent information. Then, the CKKS scheme encrypts this compact data, ensuring the preservation of privacy while transmitting the data to the server for further processing.
- **Server-side Component:** The server-side receives the encrypted data and processes it through the latter portion of the neural network model, which includes a SimpleRNN layer with a linear activation function ($f(x) = x$) followed by a dense layer. The choice of a linear activation function is strategic to minimize the computational demand since it involves fewer operations compared to other activation functions, hence avoiding the necessity for bootstrapping. This part of the model is structured to perform operations directly on the encrypted data, thus maintaining the confidentiality of the client's information. After processing the data, it remains encrypted and is sent back to the client for decryption and applying the *sigmoid* operation for final analysis.

Model Architecture. The architecture of the proposed neural network model is orchestrated to function optimally in a privacy-preserving environment, using the CKKS scheme. The architecture can be visualized as a sequence of layers, each designed with specific functionalities, as described below:

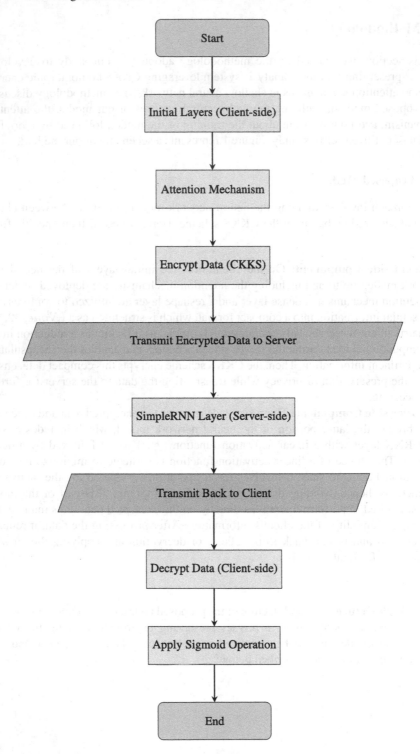

Fig. 1. Simplified Schematic Diagram of the Client-Server Privacy-Preserving Neural Network

– **Input Layer:** The initial layer receives input data in the shape of (None, n_{input}), facilitating the entry point for the dataset to flow through the network. It is really important to notice that the number of n_{input} is determined by the *padding* value that we use for our data and this *padding* has a strong impact on the accuracy of the machine, which will be discussed more on Sect. 5.
– **Embedding Layer:** Following the input layer is the embedding layer configured with dimensionality d_{emb}, transforming the input data to a higher dimensional space and facilitating the learning of more complex patterns.
– **Bidirectional Layer:** To enhance the learning capacity of the model, a bidirectional layer with n_{bi} units is employed, enabling the network to learn from both past (backward) and future (forward) data, enhancing the context awareness of the network.
– **Attention Mechanism:** Introduced to weigh the importance of different parts of the input, the attention mechanism operates in tandem with the bidirectional layer, enhancing the model's focus on pertinent features.
– **Concatenate and Flatten Layers:** Post the attention mechanism, the bidirectional and attention outputs are concatenated, followed by a flattening layer, preparing the data for further processing.
– **Dense Layer:** A dense layer featuring n_{dense} units is employed here, introducing non-linearity to the system and aiding in learning complex patterns from the flattened data as well as compacting the output information before sending it to the server.
– **Reshape Layer:** The dense layer output undergoes reshaping to a (n_{r1}, n_{r2}) matrix, setting the stage for the subsequent SimpleRNN layer.
– **Batch Normalization Layer:** Situated after the reshape layer, this layer normalizes the activations of the neurons in the current batch, which can potentially foster more favorable conditions for the linear activation function applied in the subsequent SimpleRNN layer. We will talk with more details about it in Sect. 4.
– **SimpleRNN Layer:** This layer houses n_{Simple} units and employs a linear activation function, a strategic choice aimed at reducing computational intensity during the homomorphic encryption operations.
– **Output Dense Layer:** The final layer in the architecture is a dense layer with a single unit, tasked with outputting the prediction score pre-activation, paving the path for further client-side operations post-encryption.

This architecture is crafted with an attention mechanism to the delegation into server and client parts, each playing a pivotal role in the privacy-preserving inference process, while also focusing on maintaining a lightweight computational footprint to work seamlessly with encrypted data. Figure 2 can represent the architecture we use with more detail.

3.2 Training and Inference

Training. In the training phase, the Keras framework was used to build and train the neural network on unencrypted data, enabling the precise determination of the weights for each layer.

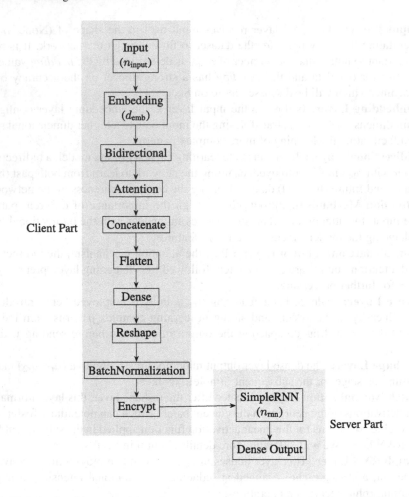

Fig. 2. High-level architecture of the privacy-preserving machine learning system, delineating the client and server components.

The data was preprocessed using Python and the NLTK library, which helped in cleaning and filtering out irrelevant content such as stopwords and non-alphabetic tokens, focusing on words with more than two characters. The Keras Tokenizer function then converted the cleaned data into sequences of integers, setting the stage for the next steps in the training process.

The embedding layer was configured to use GloVe with 50-dimensional pre-trained vectors, which facilitated understanding the relationships between words through the conversion of word integers into dense vectors.

To compile the model, the Adam optimizer was utilized, a popular choice for training deep neural networks owing to its efficiency. The binary cross-entropy loss function was chosen to compute the loss between the actual and the predicted values, as the task is binary classification (positive or negative sentiment). The accuracy metric was employed to evaluate the performance of the model during the training process.

Inference Phase. The inference phase, which is undertaken post-training, introduces an additional step to enhance data security. After the attention mechanism processes the data, it is encrypted and then sent to the server for further processing. The server, equipped with the pre-trained weights from the training phase, uses a simple RNN layer and a dense layer to process this encrypted data.

After server-side processing, the data is sent back to the client. Here, the output from the server is decrypted, and a sigmoid function is applied to the data to arrive at the final sentiment analysis result. This ensures the confidentiality of the data while leveraging the computational resources of the server for processing, embodying a secure and efficient framework for sentiment analysis.

Dataset Description. The dataset utilized in this research is sourced from the large movie review dataset, often referred to as the IMDb dataset. It is a well-established dataset for sentiment analysis containing a substantial number of movie reviews labeled with either positive or negative sentiments. The training subset of the dataset comprises 25,000 reviews, evenly distributed with 12,500 positive and 12,500 negative reviews. This large volume of data aids in training the model to discern intricate patterns and understandings of both positive and negative sentiments expressed in the reviews.

Given the computational and memory constraints invoked by utilizing the CKKS scheme to encrypt numerous plaintexts into a single ciphertext, the test subset was restricted to 200 samples per run. Specifically, increasing the test size necessitates expanding the number of slots in the CKKS encryption process, which in turn escalates the memory requirements exponentially, leading to memory issues. To mitigate the restriction imposed by this limitation and to achieve a comprehensive assessment of the model's performance, the testing was reiterated 50 times with different samples, each containing 200 reviews randomly chosen from the dataset.

In further sections, we will discuss more about the implementation of our method and the results we obtained by doing this.

4   Implementation

In this section, we detail the specific implementation steps undertaken to develop our privacy-preserving sentiment analysis system.

4.1   Hardware and Software Setup

In this section, we outline the critical hardware and software configurations employed during different stages of our project. The setup delineated below plays a quintessential role in both the training and inference phases.

Training. The training process was conducted using Python 3.8 and leveraging the Keras library, with the computational resources of Google Colab. The training parameters were chosen with a deliberate strategy to foster a robust neural network model. The detailed layer specifics are as follows:

- $n_{input} = 413$: specifying the dimension of the input layer.
- $d_{emb} = 50$: denoting the output shape of the embedding layer.
- $n_{bi} = 128$: the output dimension of the bidirectional layer.
- $n_{dense} = 1024$: defining the first dense layer's output dimension.
- $(n_{r1}, n_{r2}) = 32 \times 32$: illustrating the reshape layer dimensions.
- $n_{Simple} = 64$: indicating the SimpleRNN layer's output dimension.

The L2 regularization parameter was set to 0.001 to prevent overfitting, and the model was trained over 40 epochs. The activation functions used were ReLU for the first dense layer, $f(x) = x$ for the SimpleRNN layer, and a sigmoid function for the final dense layer.

Inference. During the inference stage, our system was implemented server-side utilizing C++ integrated with the CryptoDL library [13] to operate homomorphic encryption efficiently. This library, utilized for deep learning operations in encrypted space, has been a cornerstone in our implementation, working adeptly with the HElib library [12] for CKKS encryption[4]

4.2 Impact of Padding Number on the Implementation

A critical aspect of data preparation for both training and inference is the establishment of a consistent sequence length through padding. Given that our dataset comprises IMDb movie comments with lengths that exhibit a wide variability, it is imperative to carefully select an appropriate padding number that does not detrimentally affect the accuracy and decryption processes on the client side.

We noted that the longest comment in our dataset stretched to 1317 tokens. Setting the padding number to this maximum value would mean subjecting most comments to extensive zero-padding. This approach, however, is fraught with issues, primarily impacting the decryption stage preceding the sigmoid function application on the client side. Remarkably, a high padding number converges the decrypted values towards zero, essentially nullifying the output as it invariably turns out to be zero.

To mitigate this, we find an optimal padding number that would serve a dual purpose: retaining a high percentage of the original comment data while ensuring that the decrypted values remain meaningful for subsequent processing. Our first step was establishing an upper bound padding number, encapsulating at least 95% of the comments without truncation. This process yielded 620 as the suitable upper bound.

Subsequently, we embarked on a series of experimental procedures to pinpoint the optimal padding number, settling eventually on 413, which covers 75% of the length of

---

[4] More details can be found in https://github.com/inspire-lab/CryptoDL..

the comment without truncation. This value demonstrated the highest accuracy, recording a promising rate of 70.73%. Figure 3 visually encapsulates the comment length distribution, providing a vivid representation of the length variations and aiding in understanding the rationale behind the chosen padding number.

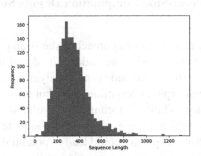

Fig. 3. Distribution of comment lengths in the dataset

In conclusion, the careful selection of a padding number is pivotal in maintaining a balance between accuracy and effective decryption, ensuring the reliability of the final outputs.

4.3 Rationale for Selecting a Linear Activation Function

To achieve an efficient privacy-preserving sentiment analysis, we have to find a very optimized way to represent the tanh activation function in the SimpleRNN layer. For this, we evaluated the feasibility of approximating it with a linear function. Prior research in this domain predominantly utilized Chebyshev approximation owing to its precision over large intervals [13,22]. Nonetheless, given the composition of our network where the output from the embedding layer does not directly feed into the SimpleRNN layer and is instead preceded by several layers including a BatchNormalization layer, a different approach was warranted.

The Batch Normalization layer could centralize the data distribution around zero, characterized by a relatively small standard deviation, thus allowing for a linear approximation to be a viable alternative. Positioned after the reshape layer, this layer works to normalize the activations of the neurons in the current batch, aiming to maintain a mean activation close to 0 and a standard deviation close to 1. While it doesn't necessarily guarantee a zero-centered distribution for the succeeding SimpleRNN layer with linear activation function, The pre-processing layers work diligently to condition the data, shaping and centralizing the inputs so that by the time they reach the SimpleRNN layer, they exist within a confined range where the tanh function's output doesn't vary significantly from a linear function. Essentially, within this operational sphere, the tanh function tends to behave almost linearly, thus creating a window of opportunity for a linear function to approximate the tanh function effectively.

This outcome reflected an effective approximation of the tanh function within the defined interval, leveraging the benefits of simplicity and computational efficiency. We believe that this linear approximation holds potential in enhancing the network's performance, and aligns well with the operational dynamics induced by the preceding network layers.

4.4 Justification for Server-Side Computation Despite Simplified Activation Function

An important aspect to consider in our approach is the strategic distribution of computational tasks between the client and server sides. The decision to employ a simplified linear activation function on the server side is not solely driven by the desire for computational efficiency in homomorphic encryption (HE), but also by the necessity to protect the server's model integrity. While it's technically feasible to execute the entire model on the client side, this would require exposing the complete model architecture and parameters to the client. Such exposure could lead to potential security risks, including the unauthorized replication or reverse-engineering of the server's proprietary model.

Our approach strategically partitions the model, where the client only possesses a portion of it. This partitioning is crucial in preserving the confidentiality of the server's model. The server retains a significant portion of the computational process, particularly the aspects that are pivotal for maintaining the model's proprietary nature. By processing encrypted data server-side, even with a simplified linear transformation, we add a layer of security against model theft or unauthorized access.

Moreover, the server-side computation takes into consideration the potential for enhanced memory and processing capabilities of the server compared to the client. This differential in computational resources allows the server to handle more complex operations on encrypted data, contributing to an overall more secure and efficient privacy-preserving machine learning (PPML) framework. Our proposed method demonstrates that it's not necessary for the server to conduct all computations to maintain effective PPML. By finding an optimal balance, we can leverage both the server's resource capabilities and the security benefits of keeping critical parts of the model undisclosed, thus ensuring a robust and efficient PPML system without the need for extensive bootstrapping or large memory requirements.

5   Results

In the field of cryptography, particularly under resource-constrained scenarios, achieving an optimal balance between computational efficiency, memory usage, and security is crucial. In this regard, our work introduces an innovative approach that distinctly stands out from previous methods. Here, we delineate the notable differences and benefits of our technique compared to two preceding works - one using interactive approach [21] and the other non-interactive [22].

Podschwadt et al. [21] have leveraged parallel structures, necessitating multiple cores and substantial RAM, while [22] employed bootstrapping for noise reduction, a process known to be time-consuming. In contrast, Our approach, by eschewing a parallel structure, demonstrates its viability in environments with limited RAM. This makes it particularly advantageous for scenarios where high computational resources are not feasible. In [22], the speed comes at the cost of higher RAM usage and a more complex server layer. Our work endeavors to find a middle ground by proposing a solution that is both time-efficient and less taxing on memory resources, without escalating the server layer's complexity.

One of the striking features of our work is the application of a reduced multiplicative depth (MD) of $2t$ in the CKKS scheme, whereas the referenced works employ a depth of $4t$. This reduction showcases our commitment to enhancing efficiency without compromising the integrity of the security protocols. Table 1 highlights the comparative advantages of our approach, especially in terms of lower RAM requirements, demonstrating its feasibility in resource-limited settings.

Table 1. Comparison of our work with previous approaches

Metric	Our Work	[22]	[21]
Use Bootstrapping	No	No	Yes
RAM Usage (GB)	12	215 - Cloud	32
Multiplicative Depth	$2t$	$4t$	$4t$
Activation Degree	1	3	3
Server Layer Complexity	Simple RNN	Parallel-Simple RNN	Simple RNN
Client Network Insight	Yes	No	No

Our method carefully navigates the delicate landscape of transparency and security, offering a strategy that maintains the crucial privacy of ML service providers while showcasing the benefits of client-server cooperation. By sharing selected layers and not the pivotal final ones, such as the SimpleRNN and prediction head, with the client, we ensure that the core functionalities remain secure and undisclosed. This approach essentially creates a buffer that protects the primary attributes of the server's ML model.

At the same time, this strategy presents an opportunity to enhance efficiency by offloading some computational tasks to the client-side. This means that the server can preserve resources and potentially offer faster services, carving out a pathway for more dynamic and responsive cryptographic solutions. It showcases that a smart distribution of tasks between the server and client can lead to a more streamlined and efficient service, heralding a promising avenue in the cryptographic landscape characterized by cooperative computation.

To further safeguard privacy while pursuing this cooperative approach, one strategy could be the development of secure multi-party computation techniques that would allow inputs from multiple parties to be integrated securely and privately. Although this might introduce a trade-off in terms of computational efficiency and potentially a slight dip in accuracy, it ensures a fortified security framework that holds a steadfast guard over the privacy of server operations, establishing a win-win scenario where both parties can reap the benefits of efficient computation without compromising on essential privacy norms.

In conclusion, our study demonstrates a practical and efficient solution in PPML, particularly under memory-restricted conditions. This approach not only encourages collaboration but also ensures feasibility in environments with limited computational resources. While this approach encourages working together, we recognize that there are small issues to fix to reach a solution that is both fast and safe. Looking ahead, we hope future research will take what we have started here and find ways to use even less memory without losing accuracy, and create a strong safety net that maintains a level of openness but protects important data.

6   Conclusion and Future Works

In summary, this work delves into strategies for enhancing the speed of encrypted neural networks that use FHE. Acknowledging the computational intensity of non-linear operations within HE, the paper introduces an innovative approach to approximating activation functions, particularly the tanh function. This approach notably curtails the computational intricacies of implementing Recurrent Neural Networks (RNN) on data encrypted through the CKKS cryptosystem. Through experiments conducted on the IMDb database for sentiment analysis, the findings underscore the substantial advancement in computational efficiency achieved by our method. Remarkably, this efficiency boost is achieved without compromising the data's privacy.

Some ways in which secure neural networks can be deployed are by making end-to-end security feasible. The pipeline of pre-processing, training, and inference should all be possible on encrypted data. Secure pre-processing can be achieved with private set intersection, bloom filters, or other such primitives that allow secure search, updations, and deletions on encrypted data. While FHE is a powerful tool, deployable solutions would have to combine it with other primitives like SMPC, FL, or DP for unlocking different functionalities efficiently.

References

1. Bakshi, M., Last, M.: CryptoRNN - privacy-preserving recurrent neural networks using homomorphic encryption. In: Dolev, S., Kolesnikov, V., Lodha, S., Weiss, G. (eds.) CSCML 2020. LNCS, vol. 12161, pp. 245–253. Springer, Cham (2020). https://doi.org/10.1007/978-3-030-49785-9_16
2. Barni, M., Orlandi, C., Piva, A.: A privacy-preserving protocol for neural-network-based computation. In: Proceedings of the 8th workshop on Multimedia & Security, MM&Sec 2006, Geneva, Switzerland, 26–27 September 2006, pp. 146–151. ACM (2006)
3. Boura, C., Gama, N., Georgieva, M., Jetchev, D.: CHIMERA: combining ring-LWE-based fully homomorphic encryption schemes. J. Math. Cryptol. **14**(1), 316–338 (2020)
4. Cheon, J.H., Kim, A., Kim, M., Song, Y.: Homomorphic encryption for arithmetic of approximate numbers. In: Takagi, T., Peyrin, T. (eds.) ASIACRYPT 2017. LNCS, vol. 10624, pp. 409–437. Springer, Cham (2017). https://doi.org/10.1007/978-3-319-70694-8_15
5. Chillotti, I., Gama, N., Georgieva, M., Izabachène, M.: TFHE: fast fully homomorphic encryption over the torus. J. Cryptol. **33**(1), 34–91 (2020)
6. Clet, P.-E., Stan, O., Zuber, M.: BFV, CKKS, TFHE: which one is the best for a secure neural network evaluation in the cloud? In: Zhou, J., et al. (eds.) ACNS 2021. LNCS, vol. 12809, pp. 279–300. Springer, Cham (2021). https://doi.org/10.1007/978-3-030-81645-2_16
7. Fan, J., Vercauteren, F.: Somewhat practical fully homomorphic encryption. IACR Cryptol. ePrint Arch. 144 (2012)

8. Ganesh, B., Palmieri, P.: Secure search over multi-key homomorphically encrypted data. In: 7th International Conference on Cryptography, Security and Privacy, CSP 2023, Tianjin, China, 21–23 April 2023, pp. 145–151. IEEE (2023). https://doi.org/10.1109/CSP58884. 2023.00031

9. Gentry, C.: A fully homomorphic encryption scheme. Ph.D. thesis, Stanford University, USA (2009). https://searchworks.stanford.edu/view/8493082

10. Gilad-Bachrach, R., Dowlin, N., Laine, K., Lauter, K.E., Naehrig, M., Wernsing, J.: CryptoNets: applying neural networks to encrypted data with high throughput and accuracy. In: Proceedings of the 33nd International Conference on Machine Learning, ICML 2016, New York City, NY, USA, 19–24 June 2016. JMLR Workshop and Conference Proceedings, vol. 48, pp. 201–210. JMLR.org (2016)

11. Graepel, T., Lauter, K., Naehrig, M.: ML confidential: machine learning on encrypted data. In: Kwon, T., Lee, M.-K., Kwon, D. (eds.) ICISC 2012. LNCS, vol. 7839, pp. 1–21. Springer, Heidelberg (2013). https://doi.org/10.1007/978-3-642-37682-5_1

12. Halevi, S., Shoup, V.: Algorithms in HElib. In: Garay, J.A., Gennaro, R. (eds.) CRYPTO 2014. LNCS, vol. 8616, pp. 554–571. Springer, Heidelberg (2014). https://doi.org/10.1007/978-3-662-44371-2_31

13. Hesamifard, E., Takabi, H., Ghasemi, M.: CryptoDL: deep neural networks over encrypted data. CoRR abs/1711.05189 (2017)

14. Kim, A., Song, Y., Kim, M., Lee, K., Cheon, J.H.: Logistic regression model training based on the approximate homomorphic encryption. IACR Cryptol. ePrint Arch. **2018**, 254 (2018)

15. Liu, J., Juuti, M., Lu, Y., Asokan, N.: Oblivious neural network predictions via MiniONN transformations. In: Proceedings of the 2017 ACM SIGSAC Conference on Computer and Communications Security, CCS 2017, Dallas, TX, USA, 30 October–03 November 2017, pp. 619–631. ACM (2017)

16. Lou, Q., Feng, B., Fox, G.C., Jiang, L.: Glyph: fast and accurately training deep neural networks on encrypted data. In: Advances in Neural Information Processing Systems 33: Annual Conference on Neural Information Processing Systems 2020, NeurIPS 2020, 6–12 December 2020, Virtual (2020)

17. Maas, A.L., Daly, R.E., Pham, P.T., Huang, D., Ng, A.Y., Potts, C.: Learning word vectors for sentiment analysis. In: Proceedings of the 49th Annual Meeting of the Association for Computational Linguistics: Human Language Technologies, pp. 142–150. Association for Computational Linguistics, Portland (2011). http://www.aclweb.org/anthology/P11-1015

18. Mann, Z.Á., Weinert, C., Chabal, D., Bos, J.W.: Towards practical secure neural network inference: the journey so far and the road ahead. IACR Cryptol. ePrint Arch. 1483 (2022)

19. Mohassel, P., Zhang, Y.: SecureML: a system for scalable privacy-preserving machine learning. In: 2017 IEEE Symposium on Security and Privacy, SP 2017, San Jose, CA, USA, 22–26 May 2017, pp. 19–38. IEEE Computer Society (2017)

20. Ng, L.L., Chow, S.M.: SoK: cryptographic neural-network computation. In: 2023 2023 IEEE Symposium on Security and Privacy (SP), pp. 497–514. IEEE Computer Society, Los Alamitos (2023)

21. Podschwadt, R., Takabi, D.: Classification of encrypted word embeddings using recurrent neural networks. In: PrivateNLP@ WSDM, pp. 27–31 (2020)

22. Podschwadt, R., Takabi, D.: Non-interactive privacy preserving recurrent neural network prediction with homomorphic encryption. In: 14th IEEE International Conference on Cloud Computing, CLOUD 2021, Chicago, IL, USA, 5–10 September 2021, pp. 65–70. IEEE (2021)

23. Sav, S., Diaa, A., Pyrgelis, A., Bossuat, J., Hubaux, J.: Privacy-preserving federated recurrent neural networks. CoRR abs/2207.13947 (2022)

24. Microsoft SEAL (release 3.5) (2020). https://github.com/Microsoft/SEAL. Microsoft Research, Redmond, WA

25. Shokri, R., Shmatikov, V.: Privacy-preserving deep learning. In: Proceedings of the 22nd ACM SIGSAC Conference on Computer and Communications Security, Denver, CO, USA, 12–16 October 2015, pp. 1310–1321. ACM (2015)
26. Tanuwidjaja, H.C., Choi, R., Kim, K.: A survey on deep learning techniques for privacy-preserving. In: Chen, X., Huang, X., Zhang, J. (eds.) ML4CS 2019. LNCS, vol. 11806, pp. 29–46. Springer, Cham (2019). https://doi.org/10.1007/978-3-030-30619-9_4
27. Wagh, S., Gupta, D., Chandran, N.: SecureNN: 3-party secure computation for neural network training. Proc. Priv. Enhanc. Technol. **2019**(3), 26–49 (2019)
28. Xu, R., Joshi, J.B.D., Li, C.: CryptoNN: training neural networks over encrypted data. In: 39th IEEE International Conference on Distributed Computing Systems, ICDCS 2019, Dallas, TX, USA, 7–10 July 2019, pp. 1199–1209. IEEE (2019)
29. Zhang, Q., Xin, C., Wu, H.: GALA: greedy computation for linear algebra in privacy-preserved neural networks. In: 28th Annual Network and Distributed System Security Symposium, NDSS 2021, Virtually, 21–25 February 2021. The Internet Society (2021)

Differential Privacy with Selected Privacy Budget ϵ in a Cyber Physical System Using Machine Learning

Ruilin Wang[✉] and Chuadhry Mujeeb Ahmed

School of Computing, University of Newcastle upon Tyne, Urban Sciences Building,
1 Science Square, Newcastle upon Tyne NE4 5TG, UK
wangruilin981021@163.com, mujeeb.ahmed@newcastle.ac.uk

Abstract. In contemporary data management practices, the adoption of Differential Privacy has emerged as a prevailing trend, offering an effective means to thwart an escalating array of query attacks. However, the implementation of Differential Privacy (DP) poses a nuanced challenge in determining the optimal privacy budget denoted by ϵ. A small ϵ imparts formidable privacy fortification to the dataset, albeit rendering it scarcely utilizable and thus prone to abandonment due to severely compromised data utility. Conversely, an excessively large ϵ renders the dataset amenable for use, albeit at the cost of heightened susceptibility to privacy breaches via rudimentary attacks. Against this backdrop, the pivotal task becomes the judicious selection of an appropriate privacy budget value, one that harmonizes the imperatives of robust privacy protection and substantive data utility. This study endeavors to leverage the stochastic gradient descent (SGD) algorithm as a strategic approach to navigate this problem, aspiring to yield optimal resolutions to the presented challenge. A case study on real-world CPS testbed SWaT is conducted to demonstrate the feasibility of DP-enabled data privacy in time series data in a Historian server.

Keywords: Privacy in CPS · Machine Learning and Privacy · Differential Privacy · privacy budget selection · stochastic gradient descent algorithm

1 Introduction

Cyber-physical systems (CPS) are composed of cyber and physical layers that interact to achieve automation in a range of processes. A few examples of CPS are industrial processes, utilities e.g., water treatment [1] and smart grid systems [2], and medical CPS e.g., pacemakers and insulin injectors [3]. In the last two decades, researchers started paying attention to the security and privacy of Cyber-Physical Systems (CPSs) [4–6]. The pervasive deployment of CPSs in our daily lives results in the generation, transmission, and collection of considerable volumes of privacy-sensitive data. For example, a recent work studied

M. Andreoni (Ed.): ACNS 2024 Workshops, LNCS 14587, pp. 101–116, 2024.
https://doi.org/10.1007/978-3-031-61489-7_7

information leakage attacks on a surgical robot potentially leaking the identity information of a patient [7]. Consequently, the escalating frequency of passive attacks targeting the privacy of this data underscores the imperative to fortify privacy safeguards within CPSs [8].

In response to this pressing concern, a privacy protection paradigm emerged concurrently with the conceptualization of CPSs. This approach, known as Differential Privacy [9], offers a methodological recourse by introducing controlled noise injection into datasets. Widely recognized as a judicious solution, Differential Privacy stands as a pivotal mechanism to safeguard the privacy of sensitive data within the realm of CPSs. In this project, the main aim is to justify the performance of Differential Privacy with selected privacy budget ϵ in the CPSs. To summarise, the following are the contributions of this study:

- Optimal epsilon value selection: We have used a machine learning-based approach to select the optimal epsilon value based on the distinguishability of the data by varying the epsilon value.
- Quantify the protection level of the privacy-sensitive data in a CPS after noise addition: We executed the mimic inquiry attacks to access the privacy-sensitive data and the attack outcome is analyzed.
- Usability of the dataset depends on the accuracy of the classification model after noise addition: The expression for measurement is $\Pr(\max f \in F | F(D) - F'(D)| \leq \alpha) > 1 - \beta$ where α and β are the accuracy parameter, for these, the results are analyzed. According to Vujovic et al. [10], if $|F(D) - F'(D)|$ is less than 0.2, it means the accuracy of the model has not been affected too much and the dataset will be considered as excellent to use [11]. We make similar observations in this work when applied to an example CPS testbed dataset.

Organization: Section 2 provides sufficient background information and related work in this area. Section 3 shows how to design the approach, including the algorithm and the tools the approach used, and some test results for analysis. Section 4 presents the results of experiments on CPS data and a discussion around the obtained results. Section 5 concludes the work and points out the potential future work.

2   Background

2.1   Differential Privacy

The concept of Differential Privacy was introduced by Dwork in 2006 [9]. Differential Privacy aims to prevent adversaries from leveraging information obtained through queries to discern specific details about individuals within a dataset. Several key components contribute to achieving this goal [12]. The foremost element is the privacy budget, conventionally denoted by ϵ. This budget regulates the efficacy of privacy, with smaller values of ϵ implying stronger privacy.

Typically, ϵ is set to 1 or even smaller. The second critical component is sensitivity, which determines the perturbation within differentially private mechanisms. Sensitivity is categorized into global and local sensitivity, although local sensitivity is often not considered due to its indirect applicability in mechanisms. The theorem governing global sensitivity is presented below [12].

Theorem 1. *For a query f, and the dataset D and its Neighboring dataset D', when f: D → R, the global sensitivity △ FGS will be calculated as*

$$\triangle FGS = \max D, D' \| f(D) - f(D') \| \tag{1}$$

After considering the privacy budget and sensitivity, the next component will be the incorporation of noise mechanisms. Presently, two widely utilized mechanisms are the Laplace mechanism and the Gaussian mechanism. First of all, the Laplace mechanism uses the Laplacian function to calculate the noise, the calculation will use the global sensitivity $\triangle F$ and the privacy budget ϵ, and the theorem is as below [12],

Theorem 2. *For a query f, and the dataset D, when f: D → R, the mechanism M will be calculated as*

$$M(D) = f(D) + Lap(\triangle F/\epsilon) \tag{2}$$

Similar to the Laplace mechanism, the Gaussian mechanism will need to use a function called Gaussian distribution, it requires to calculate a new global sensitivity $\triangle F_2$, the sensitivity will be calculated using L2 norm, the formula is $\triangle FGS = \max_{D, D'} \| f(D) - f(D') \|$, meanwhile, a new parameter σ which means the Gaussian perturbation will be added, the calculation method is $\sigma = \triangle F_2 \sqrt{2 ln(2/\sigma)})/\epsilon$, σ here represents any available number which is bigger than 0, the mechanism is defined as below [12],

Theorem 3. *For a query f, and the dataset D, when f: D → R, with the noise value N (0, σ^2), t the mechanism M will be calculated as*

$$M(D) = f(D) + N(0, \sigma^2) \tag{3}$$

Finally, after all the component has been calculated and set, the Differential Privacy method can be achieved, the theorem is as below, [12]

Theorem 4. *For a mechanism M and its output S, and for any dataset D and its Neighboring dataset D, if M satisfies*

$$Pr[M(D) \in S] \leq exp(\epsilon).Pr[M(D') \in S] + \sigma \tag{4}$$

In this occasion, if σ equals to 0, it is called pure Differential Privacy, if σ is over 0, it is called approximate Differential Privacy [13].

Types of Differential Privacy: In Differential Privacy, two main types are distinguished: Local Differential Privacy (LDP) and Central Differential Privacy (CDP), each characterized by unique features. The concept of Local Differential

Privacy (LDP) was first introduced by Duchi et al. [14]. LDP is tailored for data providers who lack trust in the statistician collecting data. It employs the randomized response concept to determine the value of ϵ [15]. In a typical LDP model, there is no centralized database [16], meaning that data providers handle tasks such as privacy budget generation and data perturbation, and there are no neighboring datasets.

Central Differential Privacy (CDP) is a commonly used model in Differential Privacy. Its mechanisms align with the standard Differential Privacy method mentioned earlier. In contrast to Local Differential Privacy, when users trust the server, the perturbation function is provided by the server [17]. This perturbation ensures that the new output is indistinguishable [18].

2.2 IoT Healthcare Data and DP

As per Alex Krall et al. [19], the researchers have not only devised a Differential Privacy method for securing IoT-based healthcare data with high accuracy but have also enhanced the method. They introduced a gradient perturbation mechanism to mitigate the risk of model inversion attacks, wherein an adversary can use the trained model and target data to infer the current dataset and glean sensitive patient information. Given that mini-batch gradient descent enhances the efficiency of distributed learning [20], the researchers posit that the improved Differential Privacy method applies to decentralized IoT-based healthcare data. This approach is anticipated to boost the adaptive learning rate, thereby accelerating convergence speed to thwart potential attacks. Transitioning to the newly designed algorithm, the inputs comprise a privacy budget ϵ, a regularization parameter λ, an initial learning rate $\eta=0$, the number of epochs K, and the batch size b. The output is the approximate noisy minimizer ω. The detailed process is outlined in the algorithm below.

Algorithm 1. Gradient perturbation algorithm [19]

Input: Data D, parameters $\epsilon, \lambda, \eta = 0$,K,b
Output: Approximate noisy minimizer $\overline{\omega}$
  1: Initialize $\omega^{(1)}, \tau = 1$, k = 1, $\tau_0 = \frac{1}{\lambda\eta_0}$
  2: Distribute D into a set of batches B, each of size b
  3: **while** $k \leq K$ **do**
  4:    **for** each j = 1, ... , $|B|$ **do**
  5:       Set $\eta^\tau = \frac{1}{\lambda(\tau_0 + \tau_{-1})}$
  6:       Draw a vector $\mathbf{Z}^\tau$ which used for Lap $\left(\frac{2\eta^{(\tau)}}{b\epsilon}\right)$
  7:       Set $\omega^{(\tau+1)} = \omega^{(\tau)} - \eta^{(\tau)}(\nabla j\left(\omega^{(\tau)}, B_j\right) + \frac{1}{b}\mathbf{Z}^{(\tau)})$
  8:       Set $\tau = \tau + 1$
  9:    **end for**
10:    Set $k = k + 1$
11: **end while**
12: Let $\overline{\omega} = \omega^{(\tau)}$

After implementing the algorithm it is found from Fig. 1 that when the ϵ decreases, the attack accuracy will drop significantly, while the model accuracy will only drop a little bit, when $\epsilon = 10^{-4}$, the attack accuracy will drop to 0, meanwhile, the model accuracy is very steady and almost has no difference with the baseline model accuracy.

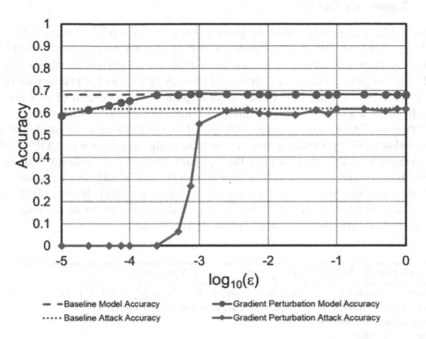

Fig. 1. Experiment result of the approach [19] (The blue solid and dash lines compare the accuracy of baseline and gradient perturbation model in original states, the red solid and dash lines compare the accuracy of baseline and gradient perturbation model when they are under attack) (Color figure online)

Analyzing the entire approach and its outcomes reveals its notable advantages. Firstly, it aligns closely with the conditions of Differential Privacy, making it highly suitable for integration with Differential Privacy methods and enhancing their performance. Additionally, experimental results demonstrate a significant reduction in the risk of model inversion attacks, with the potential for accuracy to approach zero. Furthermore, the accuracy of the new model remains consistently high and stable as the ϵ value changes, exhibiting minimal deviation from the initial model accuracy. Lastly, the accelerated convergence process contributes to an overall improvement in the efficiency of Differential Privacy. However, this approach is not without its drawbacks. The ϵ value is set too low during its operation, intensifying privacy protection but raising concerns about the usability of the current dataset [21]. Despite the model's steady accuracy, it experiences an approximately 10 percent drop when the ϵ value decreases, complicating the determination of the most feasible ϵ value for optimal model performance.

3   Design and Implementation

3.1   Approach Design

In Sect. 2.1, a comprehensive comparison between Central Differential Privacy (CDP) and Local Differential Privacy (LDP) has been undertaken, elucidating their respective advantages and drawbacks. Following a detailed feature analysis, preference is given to Central Differential Privacy (CDP) as the primary methodology for this research. This choice is underpinned by the origin of all collected data from a CPS system, which is managed and stored on a trusted server known as Historian. The presence of this centralized server facilitates the establishment of global sensitivity, creating an environment highly conducive to CDP. Within the domain of CDP, determining the optimal ϵ value and training models for CPSs involves the utilization of a gradient optimizer algorithm. Presently, two distinct optimizer versions are available: stochastic gradient descent (SGD) and Adam [22]. For this work, SGD is the preferred option due to its demonstrated superior performance in training compared to Adam.

Algorithm 2. Differentially private SGD (Outline)[23]

Input: Examples $\{x_1, ..., x_N\}$, loss function $L(\theta) = \frac{1}{N}\sum_i L(\theta, x_i)$. Parameters: learning rate η_t, noise scale σ, group size L, gradient norm bound C.
    Initialize θ_0 randomly
    for $t \in [T]$ **do**
        Take a random sample$L_t$with sampling probability L/N
        Compute gradient
        For each $i \in L_t$, compute $g_t(x_i) \leftarrow \nabla_{\theta_t} L(\theta_t, x_i)$
        Clip gradient
        $\bar{g}_t(X_i) \leftarrow g_t(x_i)/\max(1, \frac{\|g_t(x_i)\|_2}{C})$
        Add noise
        $\bar{g}_t \leftarrow \frac{1}{L}(\sum_i \bar{g}_t(X_i) + N(0, \sigma^2 C^2 I))$
        Descent
        $\theta(t+1) \leftarrow \theta_t - \eta_t \bar{g}_t$
Output: $\theta_T$and compute the overall privacy cost (ϵ, δ) using a privacy accounting method.
    end for

In this work, there will be some differences from the traditional SGD optimizer. Instead of calculating the privacy cost of the model, the primary objective is to select the most suitable ϵ value. Logistic regression modeling is used before implementing the SGD optimizer. The accuracy value from logistic regression serves as a benchmark for evaluating the model's accuracy post the SGD optimizer application. To gauge the level of privacy protection, mimic attacks will precede the evaluation phase. These attacks, primarily consisting of inquiry attacks, simulate scenarios where attackers have already breached the system. The attackers attempt to access data in the centralized database using specific conditions. A counter tallies whether the attackers successfully obtain the desired data. The entire process is evaluated using privacy metrics established in previous studies [24]. These metrics encompass two main components: the adversary's input and the output measurement.

The adversary's input includes two aspects: the adversary's estimate, representing the output data the adversary predicts in an ideal situation, and the adversary's resources, signifying the current information the adversary possesses. The output measurement comprises three properties: error, indicating the differences between the current output and the adversary's estimate; time, denoting the duration the mechanism takes to confuse the adversary (if the attack is successful, time is not recorded); and the adversary's success rate. Each attack is repeated 50 times, and if the success rate is below 10 percent [25], it means the attackers find it very difficult to implement the inquiry attack. The recorded results of these properties form a table, summarizing the privacy evaluation process.

3.2   Project Implementation

We set up our study around sensitive industrial chemical processes and used the dataset from a water treatment system known as SWaT [26]. SWaT is chosen as the datasets are publicly available and it is a time-sensitive critical process. We set up a scenario by exploiting the temporal variation in the sensor data. For example, morning water consumption and quality data can leak consumers' usage patterns resulting in privacy breaches. We created classes to test whether a classifier can uniquely identify those classes or not and report their accuracy. Next, we figure out data distinguishability accuracy without Differential Privacy parameters (we call this baseline). Further, accuracy is measured after introducing noise in the data to preserve privacy, and a trade-off is established by measuring the accuracy.

Given that the datasets encompass various data types collected by diverse sensors, such as pH value and conductivity, the initial plan was to assign distinct ϵ values to each data type to prevent potential alteration of data features. However, after extensive investigation, it was established that the privacy budget typically needs to be set to less than 1 to ensure robust privacy guarantees [27]. In this project, a privacy budget smaller than 1 does not affect the dataset's property features. Consequently, all ϵ values are selected from values ≤ 1, and all properties share the same ϵ value for enhanced model efficiency.

To determine the most suitable ϵ value, the gradient descent's value is utilized to predict the current accuracy after adding noise determined by sensitivity and ϵ value. Subsequently, a graph is generated, where the y-axis represents the model's accuracy, and the x-axis depicts the change in ϵ value. The ϵ value corresponding to the peak accuracy is considered the most suitable privacy budget for the model. Refer to Fig. 2 for a detailed illustration of the process. Figure 2, shows the classification accuracy after adding noise by using varying ϵ, we can see that the classification accuracy change of the model according to the change of ϵ value between [0,1], in this figure, when the ϵ equals to 0.6, the model has the best accuracy which is more than 97 %).

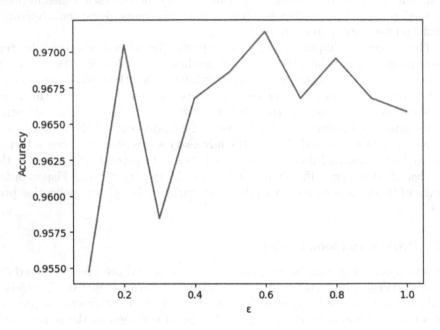

Fig. 2. Experiment result (The classification accuracy for varying ϵ.)

To simulate an inquiry attack, the initial step involves assuming that adversaries have successfully infiltrated the system and gained access to specific data within the dataset, such as the pH value and conductivity of a chemical process which can lead to either consumer privacy or leaking of intellectual property. However, these are the only details known to the adversaries. Subsequently, they attempt to utilize this limited data to identify the specific private information about the plant from which it was collected. In this context, an inquiry attack count is employed. If the output of the count falls within the range [0,1], it signifies that, based on the available information, the adversaries have successfully identified the particular process they sought, and the privacy of that process plant is compromised. Conversely, if the output is a positive number greater than 1, it implies that the adversaries have identified multiple different processes using the available data but have not pinpointed the exact process they intended. In this scenario, the privacy of the process is preserved. In an exceptional case where the output is a negative number, it indicates a simulation issue, rendering the result unusable. The attack simulation is then re-executed until a result ≥ 0 is achieved.

4   Results and Discussion

4.1   SGD Function and ϵ Value Selection

In the SGD function test, a set of 8 diverse datasets collected from the SWaT system will be utilized. These datasets were collected over the period of two days, specifically from the 23rd to 24th of June 2021. For each dataset, a series of 4 tests will be iterated under identical conditions. The primary objective of this repetition is to ensure the robust functionality of the model. With an ample number of samples to scrutinize, any potential model issues can be promptly identified and addressed. The secondary objective involves the strategic repetition of tests. This abundance of attempts aids in determining the most suitable ϵ value more robustly. Through these tests, the ϵ value delivering optimal performance can be discerned and chosen for subsequent applications.

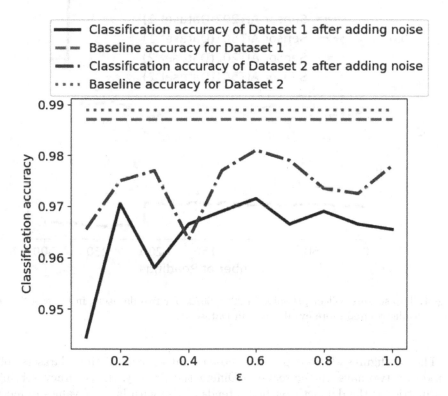

Fig. 3. Classification accuracy change for datasets under varying ϵ value selected from the two example datasets collected in 2021/06/23, the classification accuracy is higher for higher values of ϵ but at the cost of reduced privacy.

As discussed earlier, we have divided datasets based on temporal patterns to create different classes for identification. In the example below we mention two sets of data, dataset 1(AM data), dataset 2 (PM data). Figure 3, shows classification accuracy results under varying ϵ. We can see that for the two datasets we have an upper limit for accuracy without any noise addition and we call it baseline accuracy. It could be seen that for higher values of ϵ we have higher accuracy but at the cost of reduction in privacy preservation. To understand the variation of accuracy within both datasets, we need to see examples of a couple of sensors that are used in this classifier. Figure 4, shows the example data from for sensors from dataset 1 and 2. Dataset 2 being more smooth values and containing little variations resulted in higher classification accuracy.

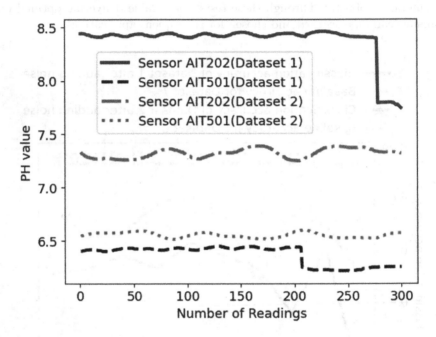

Fig. 4. Two sensors collect pH value in 2021/06/23 for two datasets, in Dataset 2, the data was distributed more evenly than in Dataset 1.

The two figures above depict the chosen ϵ values for 8 distinct datasets collected over two days. In the realm of Differential Privacy, the accuracy, serving as a metric for the dataset's usability, tends to rise with larger ϵ values in most instances. This phenomenon substantiates that the model adheres to the stipulated conditions of Differential Privacy. Conversely, when the ϵ value is very small, the model's accuracy diminishes significantly.

4.2 Inquiry Attack Simulation

Before the evaluation process, the first thing that needs to be done is to implement the potential attack, and in the program, there is a counter has been added, the result means how much data can the attackers find out according to the inquiry they insert, if the output of the counter equals to 1, this means the adversaries can find out the exact data they want, and the attack will be considered as successful, if the output is 3, it means during the attack, the adversaries has find out data which contains similar attributes to the data that the attackers wants to find out, and these data are unable to be distinguished, so the attack is failed, the maximum output equals the number of data in the dataset, for example, if there are 3600 data in the dataset, then the maximum output of the counter will be 3600. To evaluate the results of the simulated inquiry attack, the privacy evaluation table which has been introduced in Sect. 3.1 will be used, it is a standard metric that includes the following information, the adversary's estimate, the adversary's resources, average error, average time and the success rate. The adversary's estimate means the result that the attackers expect to have, in this approach, the attackers will expect the output of the attack simulation to be 1. The adversary's resource here means some information of the data that the attackers already know about, such as the pH value or the Conductivity, according to the resource, the attacks have been divided into 4 kinds and each kind will be repeatedly attacked 50 times. The average error means after 50 repeated attacks, the average differences between the true average output value of the counter and the output value of the counter which the attackers expect to have, for example, after 50 attacks, the average value of the output of the counter is 3.674, since the output of the counter that the attackers expect is 1, so there has a distance between the actual output and the expected output, it is remarked as the average error and the value is 2.674, similar to the condition of the output, the bigger the value of average error is, the better the protection will be. In addition, the average time represents how fast this approach will be executed to make the attackers feel confused, the less average time it takes, the better the protection will be, and the best condition is when the average execution time is under 0.1 s [24]. Finally, the adversary's success rate means that during the 50 attacks for each kind of attack, how many times will the attackers successfully reach their estimation, and if all 50 attacks fail, then the success rate will be 0 percent. After the attack has been finished, all the information that the privacy evaluation table needs will be recorded, in this evaluation table, if the average error is bigger than 0, then it means the defense is successful and the attackers will find more than 1 result in one attack and the defense is successful, and the average time and success rate shows how fast the program will be executed and how good the protection is, and the final privacy evaluation tables are presented below.

Table 1. Privacy evaluation table for 2021/06/23 (day1), the output that the attacker expects to have is 1, and the attackers assume to have some pH value data collected from different sensors and then begin their attack, the average differences between the output that the attackers suppose to have and the actual output are 2.674,2.841,3.722,2.963, the average execution time of the defense are all under 0.1 s and for each kind of attacks, none of these 50 attacks will be successful.

	Attack 1	Attack 2	Attack 3	Attack 4
adversary's estimate	The attacker wants the output value from the counter is 1	The attacker wants the output value from the counter is 1	The attacker wants the output value from the counter is 1	The attacker wants the output value from the counter is 1
adversary's resources	The pH value data collect from sensor 'AIT 501' and 'AIT 201'	The pH value data collect from sensor 'AIT 502' and 'AIT 202'	The pH value data collect from sensor 'AIT 503' and 'AIT 203'	The pH value data collect from sensor 'AIT 501' and 'AIT 201'
average error	2.674	2.841	3.722	2.983
average time	0.023 s	0.031 s	0.052 s	0.084 s
adversary's success rate	0 %	0 %	0 %	0 %

Table 2. Privacy evaluation table for 2021/06/24 (day 2), the output that the attacker expects to have is 1, and the attackers assume to have the pH value data collected from the same sensors as Table 1 shows and then begin their attack, the average differences between the output that the attackers suppose to have and the actual output are 3.731,4.022,4.482,3.328, the average execution time of the defense are all under 0.1 s and for each kind of attacks as well, only in attack kind 2, the attackers will be successful for 2 times and all other attacks are failed, and this result is acceptable.

	Attack 1	Attack 2	Attack 3	Attack 4
adversary's estimate	The attacker wants the output value from the counter is 1	The attacker wants the output value from the counter is 1	The attacker wants the output value from the counter is 1	The attacker wants the output value from the counter is 1
adversary's resources	The pH value data collect from sensor 'AIT 501' and 'AIT 201'	ThepH value data collect from sensor 'AIT 502' and 'AIT 202'	The pH value data collect from sensor 'AIT 503' and 'AIT 203'	The pH value data collect from sensor 'AIT 501' and 'AIT 201'
average error	3.731	4.022	4.482	3.328
average time	0.028 s	0.025 s	0.035 s	0.047 s
adversary's success rate	0 %	4 %	0 %	0 %

According to the privacy evaluation tables, for most of the inquiry attacks, after using the recommend ϵ value and the global sensitivity to implement the Differential Privacy function, these attacks are nearly impossible to succeed even though they have already got access to some data in the dataset. Meanwhile, the distance between the estimation and the final output is large enough to make the adversaries unable to find the data as they expected. Meanwhile, the execution time is very short which means it will only take a very short time to make the adversaries confused. All these clues have shown that the privacy of the dataset has been protected very well (Table 2).

4.3 Discussion

The primary aim of this work is to determine the most appropriate ϵ value for each dataset using the SGD function model. This objective has been accomplished, considering that each dataset now has its unique ϵ value, and the processes differ based on the output graph of the model. Moving to the second contribution, which is to verify whether the implemented Differential Privacy method, using the selected ϵ values, effectively safeguards the privacy of the datasets. According to the investigation corresponding to the privacy evaluation table in Sect. 4.2, it is concluded that the privacy of all datasets is well-protected.

For the third contribution, the assessment involves checking whether the usability of the current dataset remains satisfactory after applying the selected ϵ value. Post the ϵ value selection, the accuracy of the model, representing usability, has been graphically presented. For all datasets, the accuracy loss falls within the range of 0.15 after introducing Differential Privacy noise, which is smaller than the standard range of 0.2. Consequently, this indicates that the current datasets maintain good usability, satisfying the formulated hypothesis. With all objectives successfully achieved, the final goal is to validate the performance of Differential Privacy with the selected ϵ values in the CPS system. Based on the attained objectives, the Differential Privacy model not only offers robust privacy protection but also preserves high data usability. Thus, the performance of this method aligns perfectly with the requirements of the CPS system.

5   Conclusions and Future Work

This work aims to assess the performance of the Differential Privacy method with an optimal privacy budget in a CPS system. To achieve this, the SGD algorithm's functionality has been chosen as a viable solution, and various experiments have been meticulously designed and executed. As a fundamental model in machine learning, logistic regression has been applied. The accuracy of the logistic regression model is employed as a benchmark against the output model's accuracy after implementing Differential Privacy, demonstrating minimal functional loss. The simulation of inquiry attacks, utilizing selected data as adversary resources, reveals that the chosen ϵ value renders attackers unable to access desired information, inducing confusion in a short time. Moreover, it highlights that, with an appropriate ϵ value, a perfect balance between data usability and dataset privacy protection can be achieved, reaching peak performance.

However, despite the accomplishment of objectives and the main aim, certain limitations arise from factors such as abnormal data, the use of datasets not originally from the CPS system, tool capability constraints, and a lack of diverse model testing. Addressing these issues is crucial for effective project implementation and further study to identify optimal solutions that rectify challenges without compromising the model's current performance.

For future endeavors, the initial focus should be on finding efficient solutions for handling abnormal data, potentially employing cleaning algorithms [28]. These algorithms can detect and cleanse potential abnormal data without adversely affecting other normal data in the datasets. Additionally, exploring the integration of various machine learning methods with Differential Privacy is imperative to identify the most suitable method for optimal Differential Privacy performance. Additionally, the generalization of the proposed scheme can be tested by using different datasets, e.g., including water distribution process [29]. Lastly, attention should be directed towards devising an algorithm applicable to Local Differential Privacy (LDP). Despite LDP utilizing a random response mechanism to determine perturbation, the selection of the privacy budget remains essential. Therefore, an algorithm aiding in privacy budget selection for LDP needs exploration [30].

References

1. Ahmed, C.M., Murguia, C., Ruths, J.: Model-based attack detection scheme for smart water distribution networks. In: Proceedings of the 2017 ACM on Asia Conference on Computer and Communications Security, ASIA CCS 2017, pp. 101–113. Association for Computing Machinery, New York (2017)
2. Ahmed, C.M., Kandasamy, N.K.: A comprehensive dataset from a smart grid testbed for machine learning based CPS security research. In: Abie, H., et al. (eds.) CPS4CIP 2020. LNCS, vol. 12618, pp. 123–135. Springer, Cham (2021). https://doi.org/10.1007/978-3-030-69781-5_9
3. Greer, C., Burns, M., Wollman, D., Griffor, E.: Cyber-physical systems and Internet of Things (2019)
4. Lee, E.: The past, present and future of cyber-physical systems: a focus on models. Sensors (Basel, Switzerland) **15**, 4837–4869 (2015)
5. Ahmed, C.M., Zhou, J.: Challenges and opportunities in cyberphysical systems security: a physics-based perspective. IEEE Secur. Privacy **18**(6), 14–22 (2020)
6. Ahmed, C.M., Gauthama Raman, M.R., Mathur, A.P.: Challenges in machine learning based approaches for real-time anomaly detection in industrial control systems. In: Proceedings of the 6th ACM on Cyber-Physical System Security Workshop, CPSS 2020, pp. 23–29. Association for Computing Machinery, New York (2020)
7. Shah, R., Ahmed, C.M., Nagaraja, S.: Can you still see me?: identifying robot operations over end-to-end encrypted channels. In: Proceedings of the 15th ACM Conference on Security and Privacy in Wireless and Mobile Networks, WiSec 2022, pp. 298–300. Association for Computing Machinery, New York (2022)

8. Bhattacharjee, A., Badsha, S., Hossain, Md.T., Konstantinou, C., Liang, X.: Vulnerability characterization and privacy quantification for cyber-physical systems. In: 2021 IEEE International Conferences on Internet of Things (iThings) and IEEE Green Computing & Communications (GreenCom) and IEEE Cyber, Physical & Social Computing (CPSCom) and IEEE Smart Data (SmartData) and IEEE Congress on Cybermatics (Cybermatics), pp. 217–223 (2021)
9. Dwork, C.: Differential privacy. In: Bugliesi, M., Preneel, B., Sassone, V., Wegener, I. (eds.) ICALP 2006. LNCS, vol. 4052, pp. 1–12. Springer, Heidelberg (2006). https://doi.org/10.1007/11787006_1
10. Vujovic, Z.: Classification model evaluation metrics. Int. J. Adv. Comput. Sci. Appl. **12**(599–606), 07 (2021)
11. Liu, J., Hu, Y., Guo, X., Liang, T., Jin, W.: Differential privacy performance evaluation under the condition of non-uniform noise distribution. J. Inf. Secur. Appl. **71**, 103366 (2022)
12. Zhu, T., Li, G., Zhou, W., Yu, P.S.: Preliminary of differential privacy. In: Zhu, T., Li, G., Zhou, W., Yu, P.S. (eds.) Differential Privacy and Applications. AIS, vol. 69, pp. 7–16. Springer, Cham (2017). https://doi.org/10.1007/978-3-319-62004-6_2
13. Beimel, A., Nissim, K., Stemmer, U.: Private learning and sanitization: pure vs. approximate differential privacy. In: Raghavendra, P., Raskhodnikova, S., Jansen, K., Rolim, J.D.P. (eds.) APPROX/RANDOM 2013. LNCS, vol. 8096, pp. 363–378. Springer, Heidelberg (2013). https://doi.org/10.1007/978-3-642-40328-6_26
14. Duchi, J.C., Jordan, M.I., Wainwright, M.J.: Local privacy and statistical minimax rates. In: 2013 51st Annual Allerton Conference on Communication, Control, and Computing (Allerton), p. 1592 (2013)
15. Erlingsson, Ú., Pihur, V., Korolova, A.: Rappor: randomized aggregatable privacy-preserving ordinal response. In: Proceedings of the 2014 ACM SIGSAC Conference on Computer and Communications Security, CCS 2014, pp. 1054–1067. Association for Computing Machinery, New York (2014)
16. Bebensee, B.: Local differential privacy: a tutorial (2019)
17. Bernau, D., Robl, J., Grassal, P.W., Schneider, S., Kerschbaum, F.: Comparing local and central differential privacy using membership inference attacks. In: Barker, K., Ghazinour, K. (eds.) DBSec 2021. LNCS, vol. 12840, pp. 22–42. Springer, Cham (2021). https://doi.org/10.1007/978-3-030-81242-3_2
18. Naseri, M., Hayes, J., De Cristofaro, E.: Local and central differential privacy for robustness and privacy in federated learning (2022)
19. Krall, A., Finke, D., Yang, H.: Gradient mechanism to preserve differential privacy and deter against model inversion attacks in healthcare analytics. In: 2020 42nd Annual International Conference of the IEEE Engineering in Medicine & Biology Society (EMBC), pp. 5714–5717 (2020)
20. Song, S., Chaudhuri, K., Sarwate, A.D.: Stochastic gradient descent with differentially private updates. In: 2013 IEEE Global Conference on Signal and Information Processing, pp. 245–248 (2013)
21. Lee, J., Clifton, C.: How much is enough? Choosing ϵ for differential privacy. In: Lai, X., Zhou, J., Li, H. (eds.) ISC 2011. LNCS, vol. 7001, pp. 325–340. Springer, Heidelberg (2011). https://doi.org/10.1007/978-3-642-24861-0_22
22. Kingma, D.P., Ba, J.: Adam: a method for stochastic optimization. arXiv preprint arXiv:1412.6980 (2014)
23. Abadi, M., et al.: Deep learning with differential privacy. In: Proceedings of the 2016 ACM SIGSAC Conference on Computer and Communications Security, CCS 2016, pp. 308–318. Association for Computing Machinery, New York (2016)

24. Wagner, I., Eckhoff, D.: Technical privacy metrics: a systematic survey. ACM Comput. Surv. **51**(3) (2018)
25. Lan, Y., Liu, S.-P., Lin, L., Ma, Y.-Y.: Effectiveness evaluation on cyberspace security defense system. In: 2015 International Conference on Network and Information Systems for Computers, pp. 576–579 (2015)
26. Ahmed, C.M., et al.: Noiseprint: attack detection using sensor and process noise fingerprint in cyber physical systems. In: Proceedings of the 2018 on Asia Conference on Computer and Communications Security, ASIACCS 2018, pp. 483–497. Association for Computing Machinery, New York (2018)
27. Rosenblatt, L., Allen, J., Stoyanovich, J.: Spending privacy budget fairly and wisely (2022)
28. Shen, X., Fu, X., Zhou, C.: A combined algorithm for cleaning abnormal data of wind turbine power curve based on change point grouping algorithm and quartile algorithm. IEEE Trans. Sustain. Energy **10**, 46–54 (2018)
29. Ahmed, C.M., Palleti, V.R., Mathur, A.P.: Wadi: a water distribution testbed for research in the design of secure cyber physical systems. In: Proceedings of the 3rd International Workshop on Cyber-Physical Systems for Smart Water Networks, CySWATER 2017, pp. 25–28. Association for Computing Machinery, New York (2017)
30. Zhao, Y., et al.: Local differential privacy-based federated learning for Internet of Things. IEEE Internet Things J. **8**(11), 8836–8853 (2021)

LEE – Low-Latency Encryption

Construction of 4×4 Lightweight Low-Latency Involutory MDS Matrices

Zheng Zhao[1,3], Qun Liu[1,3], Yanhong Fan[1,2,3](✉), and Meiqin Wang[1,2,3]

[1] School of Cyber Science and Technology, Shandong University, Qingdao, China
{zhaozheng,qunliu}@mail.sdu.edu.cn, {yanhongfan,mqwang}@sdu.edu.cn
[2] Quan Cheng Laboratory, Jinan, China
[3] Key Laboratory of Cryptologic Technology and Information Security, Ministry of Education, Shandong University, Jinan, China

Abstract. As the demand for lightweight cryptographic solutions continues to rise, the need for cryptography applications on devices with limited resources becomes increasingly crucial. In this context, low-area and low-latency implementations of linear layers have emerged as critical factors in the field of lightweight cryptography. Maximal Distance Separable (MDS) matrices, due to their ability to provide maximum branch number and effectively resist differential and linear cryptanalysis, have been widely used in the design of linear diffusion layers in block ciphers. In this paper, we propose an efficient search framework to search for the 4×4 low-latency involutory MDS matrices over $\mathbb{F}_{2^4}$ and then find lightweight ones among them.

With the assistance of this framework, we have discovered 4 involutory MDS matrices that require only 42 XOR gates to be implemented with a circuit depth of 3, resulting in one XOR gate saved compared to the previous best result. Then we have constructed 32×32 binary involutory MDS matrices with 84 XOR gates, which are also the best-known results. The 32×32 matrices with 84 XORs are trivially obtained from the 42-XOR matrices using the subfield construction. Moreover, we conduct a partial search over $\mathbb{F}_{2^8}$ and investigate the impact of the number of identity matrices among 16 entries of a 4×4 involutory MDS matrix on the implementation cost.

Keywords: Lightweight cryptography · MDS matrix · Low latency · Involutory matrix

1 Introduction

The linear diffusion layer plays a crucial role in symmetric-key cryptography by providing resistance against differential and linear cryptanalysis. A matrix possessing optimal diffusion properties is referred to as a Maximum Distance Separable (MDS) matrix. One of its typical applications is used in the MixColumns operation of AES [12]. Additionally, MDS matrices are extensively employed in

© The Author(s), under exclusive license to Springer Nature Switzerland AG 2024
M. Andreoni (Ed.): ACNS 2024 Workshops, LNCS 14587, pp. 119–140, 2024.
https://doi.org/10.1007/978-3-031-61489-7_8

various other ciphers, including hash functions (Maelstrom [1], PHOTON [14]), and stream ciphers (MUGI [26]).

However, the search for lightweight MDS matrices is a very challenging task, and the use of MDS matrices might be luxury in resource-constrained devices. In such cases, designers often resort to almost MDS matrices [2,3], utilizing linear operations achieved through multiple bitwise XORs [5], or even employing bit-level permutations through appropriate wiring [7]. Nonetheless, these design strategies frequently result in increased number of rounds and might complicate the security analysis. Hence, it is an important endeavor to construct lightweight MDS matrices. Notably, the pursuit of lightweight involutory MDS matrices becomes even more compelling as it allows the reuse of the same circuit when the inverse matrix is required.

As an important criterion, latency has been attracting more and more attention in the design of cryptographic primitives. Many of the applications require low latency, including automobiles, robots, or mission-critical computation applications. This is because latency impacts the throughput of encryption/decryption and plays an important role in the low-energy consideration of ciphers [3]. In CHES 2021, Leander *et al.* propose a new cipher SPEEDY [18], which explores a low-latency architecture. Usually, the circuit depth can be used as an approximation for latency. The depth is the critical path length of the circuit. The low-latency optimization for linear layers is formulated as the Shortest Linear Program problem with the minimum Depth (SLPD).

Regarding the optimization of low-latency implementations for matrices, currently, there are two most effective heuristic methods: *forward search* and *backward search*. For the forward search algorithm, Li *et al.* first proposed a method to add depth constraints to Boyar-Peralta (BP) algorithm (referred to as LSL algorithm according to the initials of all authors) [20], where the BP algorithm is given in [9]. Subsequently, Banik *et al.* [4] improved the LSL algorithm by considering the influence of different permutations on matrices. The backward search algorithm was introduced by Liu *et al.* in [22]. In [23], to further optimize the low-latency implementation of linear layers, Liu *et al.* proposed a new general search framework, which incorporates division optimization and extending base techniques. In terms of the number of XOR gates and search time, this new search framework outperforms previous heuristic algorithms, including forward search and backward search algorithms. By applying the general search framework on the previous results, they get the lightest low-latency implementations of 4×4 involutory matrices both in $M_4(GL(4, \mathbb{F}_2))$ and $M_4(GL(8, \mathbb{F}_2))$ with the restriction that the depth is 3, which need 43 XOR and 85 XOR respectively.

1.1   Our Contributions

In this paper, our main objective is to find lightweight involutory MDS matrices with minimum circuit depth. More specifically, in low-latency scenarios, we find new involutory MDS matrices with low hardware costs in a larger search space than previous works. To this end, we propose a search algorithm that can search for all involutory MDS matrices for one specific representation of the field $\mathbb{F}_{2^4}$

and design a three-layer processing framework to pick lightweight ones. Along this way, the matrices and implementations that we found can be applied to future work for designing lightweight ciphers. In addition, we search for matrices on words and estimate the implementation cost on bits.

We first propose a novel low-latency involutory MDS matrix search framework, which consists of a search algorithm to obtain all candidate involutory MDS matrices that can be implemented at optimal depth and a new three-layer processing framework to find low-latency implementations of candidate matrices. Our search algorithm enables us to obtain a typical class of all 4×4 involutory MDS matrices over $\mathbb{F}_{2^4}$ that can be implemented optimally in terms of depth. Subsequently, utilizing advanced heuristic algorithms suitable for low-latency scenarios, we design a three-layer processing framework to efficiently handle all obtained candidate matrices and explore their lightweight low-latency implementations. Our three-layer processing framework adopts a hierarchical processing approach and fully considers the characteristics of the three heuristic algorithms in terms of processing speed and optimization effectiveness. This enables a well-balanced trade-off between processing efficiency and search space exploration. Applying our novel search framework, we discover the lightest 16×16 low-latency involutory MDS matrix with implementation depth of 3 to date, which can be implemented using 42 XOR gates, surpassing the previous best result requiring 43 XOR gates. Even without the restriction that the MDS matrix must be involutory, the results we have obtained for 42 XORs are the best so far.

Furthermore, we extend our investigation to construct 32×32 low-latency involutory MDS matrices. Leveraging the obtained 16×16 MDS matrices, we employ two construction methods to construct 32×32 binary involutory MDS matrices with an implementation cost of 84 XOR gates in the limitation of circuit depth 3, outperforming the previously known best 32×32 MDS matrix which required 85 XOR gates [23]. Additionally, by imposing restrictions on candidate MDS matrices in $M_4(GL(8, \mathbb{F}_2))$, we conduct a partial search over $\mathbb{F}_{2^8}$ and classify all obtained candidate matrices based on the number of identity matrices among their 16 entries. Subsequently, each matrix class undergoes both forward and backward search algorithms to investigate the impact of the number of identity matrices on the matrix implementation cost in our search for low-latency involutory MDS matrices. We observe that for a 4×4 involutory MDS matrix constructed over a given field, the quantity of identity matrices in its entries does not exhibit a clear linear relationship with its implementation cost.

The main results and comparison with some best-known matrices are shown in Table 1. In this paper, all the results of XOR gate counts correspond to the general-XOR (g-XOR) metric.

1.2   Organization

In Sect. 2, we give some basic notations and metrics, and briefly introduce some state-of-the-art heuristics involved in matrix processing in this paper. Our new low-latency involutory MDS matrix search framework is introduced in Sect. 3. We then show how to construct MDS Matrices in $M_4(GL(8, \mathbb{F}_2))$ in Sect. 4. Finally, we conclude and propose future research directions in Sect. 5.

Table 1. Comparison of the cost for minimum latency implementations of MDS matrices.

Entries	Size	Matrix type	XOR count	Minimum depth	Optimization
$GL(4, \mathbb{F}_2)$	16	Involutory	35	✗	[28]
$GL(4, \mathbb{F}_2)$	16	Hadamard-non-involutory	35	✗	[28]
$GL(4, \mathbb{F}_2)$	16	Circulant	43	✓	[4]
$GL(4, \mathbb{F}_2)$	16	Toeplitz	43	✓	[4]
$GL(4, \mathbb{F}_2)$	16	Involutory	43	✓	[23]
$GL(4, \mathbb{F}_2)$	16	Involutory	**42**	✓	Sect. 3
$GL(8, \mathbb{F}_2)$	32	Non-involutory	67	✗	[13]
$GL(8, \mathbb{F}_2)$	32	Involutory	70	✗	[28]
$GL(8, \mathbb{F}_2)$	32	Involutory	88	✓	[20]
$GL(8, \mathbb{F}_2)$	32	Involutory	86	✓	[22]
$GL(8, \mathbb{F}_2)$	32	Involutory	85	✓	[23]
$GL(8, \mathbb{F}_2)$	32	Involutory	**84**	✓	Sect. 4

2   Preliminaries

Let $M_n(\mathbb{R})$ be the set of all $n \times n$ matrices whose entries are taken from a ring $\mathbb{R}$. Then, $n \times n$ matrices over $\mathbb{F}_{2^m}$ can be denoted as $M_n(\mathbb{F}_{2^m})$ and the $n \times n$ matrices whose entries are $m \times m$ invertible binary matrices can be denoted as $M_n(GL(m, \mathbb{F}_2))$, where $GL(m, \mathbb{F}_2)$ is a general linear group. Besides, each matrix both in $M_n(\mathbb{F}_{2^m})$ and $M_n(GL(m, \mathbb{F}_2))$ can be represented as an $mn \times mn$ binary matrix.

2.1   MDS Matrices

Let x be an input vector and $y = L \cdot x$ be an output vector, where $x \in \mathbb{F}_{2^m}^n$, and L is an $n \times n$ matrix over $\mathbb{F}_{2^m}$. The definitions of its differential branch number and linear branch number are given as follows.

Definition 1 ([12]). *The differential branch number of a matrix L can be defined as*

$$\mathcal{B}_d(L) = \min_{x \in \mathbb{F}_{2^m}^n, x \neq 0} \{wt(x) + wt(L \cdot x)\}$$

where $L \in M_n(\mathbb{F}_{2^m})$ and $wt(x)$ denotes the number of nonzero entries of the vector x.

Definition 2 ([12]). *The linear branch number of a matrix L can be defined as*

$$\mathcal{B}_l(L) = \min_{x \in \mathbb{F}_{2^m}^n, x \neq 0} \{wt(x) + wt(L^{\mathsf{T}} \cdot x)\}$$

where $L \in M_n(\mathbb{F}_{2^m})$ and L^{T} is the transpose of L.

We call L a maximum distance separable (MDS) matrix if both $\mathcal{B}_d(L)$ and $\mathcal{B}_l(L)$ reach the maximum value $n + 1$. In this paper, instead of verifying the original definitions, we use the following theorem to check the MDS property.

Theorem 1 ([6,21]). *Let L be an $n \times n$ square matrix. Then, L is an MDS matrix if and only if all square sub-matrices of L are non-singular.*

Note that the MDS matrix definition and Theorem 1 can also be generalized to cases where $\mathbb{R}$ is not a field, such as the case when $\mathbb{R} = GL(m, \mathbb{F}_2)$. But in this paper, we only consider the matrices over $\mathbb{F}_{2^m}$.

2.2 Metrics

To estimate the hardware cost of a given matrix, we count the number of bit XORs required in its implementation. In this paper, we mainly discuss the following two metrics.

Definition 3 ([16]). *(d-XOR) Let L be an $n \times n$ invertible binary matrix. The d-XOR count of L is defined as the sum of nonzero elements in each row minus the order n. Namely, it can be expressed as $wt(L) - n$, where $wt(L)$ is the Hamming weight of L.*

Definition 4 ([27]). *(g-XOR) Given an $m \times n$ binary matrix A over $\mathbb{F}_2$, the implementation of A can be viewed as a sequence of XOR operations $x_i = x_{j_1} \oplus x_{j_2}$ where $0 < x_{j_1}, x_{j_2} < i$ and $i = n, n+1, ..., t-1$. The general-XOR (g-XOR) count is defined as the minimal number of operations $x_i = x_{j_1} \oplus x_{j_2}$ that compute the m outputs completely.*

Besides the circuit area (measured by the number of XOR gates required for an implementation), another important metric of an implementation is the latency, which imposes constraint on the clock frequency at which the circuit can operate. The latency of an implementation can be characterized by its depth.

Definition 5 ([20]). *Let M be an $m \times m$ binary matrix. Then the function $f_M : x \in \mathbb{F}_2^m \to Mx \in \mathbb{F}_2^m$ can be implemented with a finite number of XOR gates. The critical path of such an implementation is defined as the path between an input and output involving the maximum number of XOR gates, and the depth of the implementation is the number of XOR gates involved in the critical path.*

2.3 The State-of-the-Art Global Optimization Tools for Low-Latency Scenarios

The Shortest Linear Program (SLP) problem is to minimize the number of linear operations necessary to compute a set of linear forms. More specifically, in this scenario, the SLP problem is defined as follows:

Definition 6. *Given a matrix $A_{m \times n}$ over $\mathbb{F}_2$, where each row $y_i, 0 \le i \le m$, represents an output node. The goal is to find an implementation of A that involves only XOR gates and uses the least number of XOR gates.*

The SLP problem has been proven to be NP-hard over a finite field [8]. To address this challenge, various heuristic algorithms have been proposed to search for implementations with a reduced number of XOR gates.

In addition, if one considers building a minimum latency implementation, then the problem of shortest linear programming with minimum depth limit (SLPD) arises, where the goal is to find the minimum latency implementation of the target matrix using the minimum number of XOR gates [23].

The purpose of this paper is to find low-latency lightweight involutory MDS matrices. Since in the process of finding lightweight matrices, we need to calculate the implementation of each matrix, it is important to choose an effective optimization tool. Next, we will briefly introduce some heuristics involved in matrix processing in this paper.

Paar's Algorithm. In 1997, Paar [24] proposed two algorithms for exploring bit-level optimal implementations. For an $n \times n$ binary matrix, let $x = (x_0, x_1, x_2, ..., x_{n-1}) \in \mathbb{F}_2^n$ be the input vector, and the output vector y can be expressed by n linear combinations of $x_i, i = 0, 1, 2, ..., n - 1$. The basic idea is to sort the frequencies of XOR pairs appearing in the output and replace the highest-frequency pair with a new variable. Thus, the maximum number of $x_i \oplus x_j$ with $i \neq j$ in vector y will be replaced by a new variable x_n. This process is repeated until all XOR pairs in the output vector have been replaced. When multiple XOR pairs occur with the same highest frequency, the first one encountered is selected in the algorithm.

It is worth noting that Paar's algorithm is cancellation-free, meaning that the same component cannot appear in both variables of an XOR operation, which somewhat affects the optimization effectiveness. Furthermore, the algorithm require additional registers to store intermediate variables. Although Paar's heuristic is not sufficient for optimizing matrices to the best possible extent, Paar's algorithm is easy to implement and offers significant advantages in terms of processing speed compared to other heuristic algorithms.

BP Algorithm with Circuit Depth Awareness. The BP algorithm was introduced by Boyar and Peralta in 2010 [10]. Although this algorithm is much slower than Paar's algorithm and is not suitable for large-sized matrices due to its exhaustive search nature for distance vectors, it often generates more efficient circuits. The overall idea of BP is to find a common path among as many targets as possible. Therefore, at each step, the next gate is chosen to minimize the distance to the maximum number of objectives.

In [20], a improved BP algorithm with circuit depth awareness was proposed, which allows the depth of the output circuit to be limited. The goal of the original BP algorithm is to minimize the number of XOR gates in an implementation, regardless of the circuit depth, which is not suitable for low-latency scenarios. Therefore, in [20], modifications were made to the BP algorithm by selecting only signals that do not exceed a certain depth limit and introducing a new distance concept that takes circuit depth into account. The improved BP algorithm can handle the optimization of MDS matrix implementations at the optimal depth. Li *et al.* used this algorithm to search for low-latency MDS matrices in a certain space and achieved a minimum cost of 88 XOR gates with a circuit depth of 3.

Backward Search. In [22], Liu *et al.* proposed a novel backward search algorithm for low-latency scenarios. The algorithm aims to iteratively split each output (dividing it into two XOR operations) until all inputs appear. By imposing a restriction on the splitting time, the algorithm can discover a suboptimal solution with a minimal circuit depth.

Applying the proposed backward search algorithm from the paper, an implementation of the AES MixColumns matrix with a depth of 3 and 103 XOR gates is obtained, which represents one of the best hardware implementations for the AES linear layer. The advantage of the backward search method lies in its backward framework, which ensures that each node reaches the minimum depth, a feature that holds true for all matrices. In contrast, forward algorithms lack this characteristic, which affects whether a node can be used to generate new nodes. As a result, for certain matrices, this algorithm can cover a greater number of implementations with minimum depth within a limited time compared to previous algorithms.

The General Search Framework. In [23], in order to further optimize the implementation of the linear layer, Liu *et al.* proposed a new general search framework, which incorporates two additional techniques: *division optimization* and *extending base*. In terms of the number of XOR gates and search time, the new search framework outperforms previous heuristic algorithms, including forward and backward search algorithms.

For forward search algorithms (such as BP algorithm) and backward search algorithms, many good candidate implementations are discarded due to the significant reduction in the search space during the search process. The new search framework with the two optimization techniques introduced by Liu *et al.* partially addresses this issue. The framework partitions the given circuit, extends the base, and progressively optimizes the parallel circuits, enabling the optimization of the entire circuit based on the results of any heuristic algorithm. Specifically, the framework does not optimize the complete matrix, but only considers a portion of the circuit and extends additional bases for the heuristic algorithm. More details about this algorithm can be found in [23].

3 A New Low-Latency Involutory MDS Matrix Search Framework

Much of the previous work has focused on constructing matrices with entries that can be implemented efficiently, i.e., local optimization [11,15,19,21,25]. However, since the entries that can be implemented efficiently do not guarantee that the overall matrix is optimal in implementation, this construction method may leave out lighter matrices. In recent years, many global optimization tools have been proposed, and it has been proved that global optimization tools are superior to local optimization methods for the implementation of the whole matrix in most cases [17].

In this section, we consider searching for matrices in a larger space and using the heuristics described in the previous section to optimize the matrices. Our main goal is to construct lightweight low-latency involutory MDS matrices in $M_4(GL(4, \mathbb{F}_2))$. We use a matrix search method to find the candidate 4×4 involutory MDS matrices over $\mathbb{F}_{2^4}$. We then design a three-layer processing framework that uses the heuristics mentioned in Sect. 2.3 to process all the candidate matrices to find the matrices with the lowest cost. Using our framework, we have obtained the lowest-cost low-latency involutory MDS matrices in $M_4(GL(4, \mathbb{F}_2))$ to date, requiring only 42 XOR gates for its implementation.

3.1 Searching for Low-Latency 4×4 Involutory MDS Matrices

In the process of searching for 4×4 involutory MDS matrices over $\mathbb{F}_{2^4}$ with minimum depth, the entries can be represented by elements over $\mathbb{F}_{2^4}$ generated by the irreducible polynomial $x^4 + x + 1$ or by invertible binary matrices over $GL(4, \mathbb{F}_2)$,and the matrices can be represented as follows

$$M = \begin{pmatrix} A^{\epsilon_{11}} & A^{\epsilon_{12}} & A^{\epsilon_{13}} & A^{\epsilon_{14}} \\ A^{\epsilon_{21}} & A^{\epsilon_{22}} & A^{\epsilon_{23}} & A^{\epsilon_{24}} \\ A^{\epsilon_{31}} & A^{\epsilon_{32}} & A^{\epsilon_{33}} & A^{\epsilon_{34}} \\ A^{\epsilon_{41}} & A^{\epsilon_{42}} & A^{\epsilon_{43}} & A^{\epsilon_{44}} \end{pmatrix} \tag{1}$$

with $A^{\epsilon_{ij}} \in GL(4, \mathbb{F}_2)$, where A is a 4×4 binary matrix satisfying $A^4 + A + I = 0$, and ϵ_{ij} are integers between 0 and 14 for $1 \le i, j \le 4$. At this stage, A is the companion matrix of the generated polynomial $x^4 + x + 1$

$$A = \begin{pmatrix} 0 & 1 & 0 & 0 \\ 0 & 0 & 1 & 0 \\ 0 & 0 & 0 & 1 \\ 1 & 1 & 0 & 0 \end{pmatrix}.$$

In the process of searching for MDS matrices, we can indeed have each entry of the matrix traverse all the elements in the field $\mathbb{F}_{2^4}$ and then check the matrix, but this will cause the search space to become extremely large. Therefore, given the involutory property of our target matrices, we can apply the following theorem to reduce the search space.

Theorem 2 ([28]). *Let* $A = \begin{pmatrix} A_1 & A_2 \\ A_3 & A_4 \end{pmatrix}$ *be a* $2n \times 2n$ *involutory matrix over* $\mathbb{F}_{2^m}$ *where* $A_1, A_2, A_3, A_4 \in M_n(\mathbb{F}_{2^m})$. *If the entries of* A_1, A_2 *are given and the matrix* A_2 *is non-singular, then* A_3 *and* A_4 *can be uniquely determined.*

See [28] for the proof of the theorem.

We investigate the construction of involutory matrices in $M_n (\mathbb{F}_{2^4})$ whose multiplication is defined by irreducible polynomials $x^4 + x + 1$. According to Theorem 2, when n = 2, we have

$$A = \begin{pmatrix} A_1 & A_2 \\ A_3 & A_4 \end{pmatrix},$$

where A_1, A_2, A_3, A_4 are 2×2 matrices over $\mathbb{F}_{2^4}$. If A_1 and A_2 are given, and A_2 is an invertible matrix, then the remaining unknown entries can be uniquely determined. The calculation formula of A_3 and A_4 can be derived as follows

$$A_3 = A_2^{-1}(A_1^2 + I), \tag{2}$$

$$A_4 = A_2^{-1}A_1A_2. \tag{3}$$

One of our requirements for the target matrices is low latency, which means that the matrices can be implemented at optimal depth. In [20], Li et al. proved that for an MDS matrix in $M_4(GL(8, \mathbb{F}_2))$, the circuit depth is at least 3. We take a similar approach to arrive at the following theorem.

Theorem 3. *The circuit depth of an MDS matrix $A \in M_4(GL(4, \mathbb{F}_2))$ is at least 3.*

Proof. Let

$$A = \begin{pmatrix} A_{1,1} & A_{1,2} & A_{1,3} & A_{1,4} \\ A_{2,1} & A_{2,2} & A_{2,3} & A_{2,4} \\ A_{3,1} & A_{3,2} & A_{3,3} & A_{3,4} \\ A_{4,1} & A_{4,2} & A_{4,3} & A_{4,4} \end{pmatrix} \text{ with } A_{i,j} \in GL(4, \mathbb{F}_2) \tag{4}$$

be an MDS matrix with a circuit depth of 2 in $M_4(GL(4, \mathbb{F}_2))$, indicating that each of its $4 \times 4 = 16$ rows contains at most four 1's. Therefore, the Hamming weight of each row in a 4×4 submatrix is 1. Otherwise, if there were a row in some submatrix $A_{i,j}$ with a Hamming weight of 0, it would contradict the assumption that A is an MDS matrix. Then, we can deduce that each column of $A_{i,j}$ contains exactly one 1. Hence, $A_{i,j}$ is a permutation matrix. Now, consider the submatrix A' of Eq. (4) defined as follows:

$$A' = \begin{pmatrix} A_{1,1} & A_{1,2} \\ A_{2,1} & A_{2,2} \end{pmatrix}.$$

In this case, both the rows and columns of A' have Hamming weights of 2. Consequently, the sum of the $2 \times 4 = 8$ rows of A' results in a zero vector, indicating that A' is not a matrix of full rank, which means that A is not invertible. This directly contradicts the MDS property of A. $\qquad\square$

Our search algorithm adopts a similar idea as the search algorithm in [28], but adds a restriction on the depth based on it, which can search all low-latency involutory MDS matrices over $\mathbb{F}_{2^4}$ for one specific representation. Our search algorithm follows the logic described below. First, we let the entries of A_1 and A_2 traverse the elements of $\mathbb{F}_{2^4}$. We calculate A_3 and A_4 based on Eq. (2), Eq. (3) and concatenate them to form the complete $M_4(GL(4, \mathbb{F}_2))$ matrix. Subsequently, we design 3 functions to assist in the selection of candidate matrices: CheckMDS4(), CheckInvolutory(), and CheckDepth(). The principles and functionalities of these three functions are implemented as follows:

- CheckMDS4():
  Principle: This function checks whether the input matrix satisfies the MDS property.
  Functionality: It verifies if every $1 \times 1, 2 \times 2, 3 \times 3$ submatrix of the given matrix and the whole 4×4 matrix has full rank, indicating the matrix's MDS property.
- CheckInvolutory():
  Principle: This function examines if the matrix is involutory, i.e., it satisfies the property $A^2 = I$, where A is the matrix and I is the identity matrix.
  Functionality: It checks whether the matrix multiplied by itself results in the identity matrix.
- CheckDepth():
  Principle: This function evaluates whether the given matrix can be implemented at depth 3.
  Functionality: It determines the depth of the matrix by calculating whether the number of 1 in each row of the matrix is less than 8. If the matrix does not satisfy this condition, then it cannot be implemented at depth 3.

These functions play a crucial role in screening out the candidate matrices that do not meet the desired properties of being MDS, involutory, or having the required depth.

Furthermore, Theorem 2 requires the matrix A_2 to be non-singular. Since all square submatrices of an MDS matrix are invertible, an MDS matrix must satisfy $|A_2| \neq 0$. Therefore, any involutory MDS matrix with minimal depth that can be represented in this form can be found using our search program. We obtained approximately 500,000 involutory MDS matrices with a depth of 3 in $M_4(\mathbb{F}_{2^4})$. Our approach employs an exhaustive search for involutory MDS matrices of one specific representation over $\mathbb{F}_{2^4}$, but compared to a straightforward search strategy, our search strategy overcomes the computational burden by applying Theorem 2 and screening functions. This significantly reduces the search space.

It is imperative to clarify that, in our perspective, neither this paper nor the method proposed in [28] for identifying 4×4 low-latency involutory MDS matrices in $\mathbb{F}_{2^4}$ is deemed exhaustive. This discrepancy arises from the fact that none of our algorithms account for the diverse representations of the finite field $\mathbb{F}_{2^4}$. When defining matrix A in Eq. (1), our restriction confines A to be the companion matrix of $x^4 + x + 1$. Nevertheless, A can take on any other matrix associated with the minimal polynomial $x^4 + x + 1$ (i.e., any matrix in the form $P^{-1}C_{x^4+x+1}P$, where P is an arbitrarily invertible 4×4 binary matrix and C_{x^4+x+1} is the companion matrix of $x^4 + x + 1$). This allows for alternative representations of the field $\mathbb{F}_{2^4}$, resulting in representation-specific XOR counts.

Consequently, we explicitly acknowledge that our exhaustive search is confined to a specific representation of the finite field.

Additionally, it is necessary to note that our search algorithm is equally applicable to other fields. However, as the number of elements within a field increases, the search space may become excessively large. Hence, when deploying our search algorithm within larger fields, additional constraints might be required to manage the expanded search space effectively.

For specific details of our search algorithm, see Algorithm 1.

Algorithm 1. Our Search Algorithm

1: **Input:** the set of elements of a specific representation of the field $\mathbb{F}_{2^4}$ $\mathcal{F}$
2: **Output:** the set of all involutory MDS matrices that can be implemented at a circuit depth of 3 $\mathcal{M}$
3: Initialize matrix M as a 4×4 zero matrix
4: Initialize 4 submatrices A_1, A_2, A_3 and A_4 of matrix M as 2×2 zero matrices
5: **for** each entry in A_1 and A_2 **do**
6:     Traverse all elements in $\mathcal{F}$
7:     Compute submatrices A_1 and A_2 based on the 8 entries obtained by the traversal
8:     Compute submatrices A_3 and A_4 based on Eq. (2), Eq. (3)
9:     Construct matrix M using A_1, A_2, A_3, and A_4
10:     **if** M is involutory, M is an MDS matrix and the circuit depth of M is 3 **then**
        ▷ Judge by the three functions mentioned above
11:         $\mathcal{M} \leftarrow \mathcal{M} \cup \{M\}$ ▷ Find the involutory MDS matrix and put it in $\mathcal{M}$
12:     **end if**
13: **end for**
14: **return** $\mathcal{M}$

3.2   Three-Layer Processing Framework for Candidate Matrices

In this subsection, we provide a detailed explanation of our approach for processing all candidate matrices obtained in the previous section and formalize our three-layer processing framework. Our three-layer processing framework adopts a hierarchical processing approach and fully considers the characteristics of the three heuristic algorithms in terms of processing speed and optimization effectiveness. In other works on MDS matrix search, such as [28] and [20], they only consider using one optimization tool to obtain the implementation cost of the matrix. In contrast, our framework combines three state-of-the-art heuristics suitable for low-latency scenarios, which enables a well-balanced trade-off between processing efficiency and search space.

We first use the BP algorithm with circuit depth awareness proposed by [20], which is later called LSL algorithm, to carry out the first-layer processing of all candidates. The LSL algorithm demonstrates superior processing speed compared to backward search algorithm and the general search framework attaching the *division optimization* and *extending base* techniques. Therefore, we choose LSL algorithm as the tool of the initial processing step for the candidate matrices, selecting matrices with lower costs for further optimization in the subsequent layers. Table 2 presents the statistical results of matrices with XOR counts ranging from 43 to 60 after applying the LSL algorithm. To investigate the effectiveness of the Paar algorithm screening in our scenario, we compare the results obtained with and without the Paar algorithm screening before the LSL algorithm. For further processing, we choose matrices with XOR counts between 43 and 49, whose number is 5463.

In Yang *et al.*'s work [28], due to a larger number of candidate matrices and considerations regarding implementation efficiency, they adopted Paar algorithm screening strategy to process all candidate matrices. This strategy is based on the assumption that the matrix processed by Paar algorithm with high cost cannot be implemented efficiently by other heuristic algorithms. However, it should be noted that the Paar algorithm provides an inaccurate estimation. Therefore, although the screening strategy significantly improves processing efficiency, it may overlook the lightest matrices in our specific scenario due to the limitations of the Paar algorithm. Additionally, with the introduction of depth restrictions, the number of candidate matrices generated in our search process is significantly fewer compared to [28]. Therefore, we considered excluding the use of the Paar algorithm to avoid missing potential lightest matrices.

Table 2. Comparison of the processing results of LSL algorithm screened by Paar algorithm and not screened by Paar algorithm.

Screened by Paar		No Screened	
XOR count	Number of matrices	XOR count	Number of matrices
43	3	43	3
44	45	44	45
45	150	45	155
46	353	46	397
47	702	47	878
48	806	48	1238
49	1524	49	2747
50	2334	50	5847
51	2438	51	10533
52	2441	52	18696
53	1820	53	29580
54	1239	54	43375
55	786	55	55988
56	362	56	67423
57	113	57	70270
58	57	58	67106
59	29	59	58284
60	5	60	42323

For the second layer, we adopted the backward search algorithm proposed in [22] to process the remaining matrices after the first-layer processing. The backward search algorithm exhibits significant advantages in low-latency matrix implementations. Hence, we further processed the 5463 candidates selected from the previous layer using this heuristic algorithm. Subsequently, we calculated the minimal XOR MDS matrices, resulting in a cost of 42 XOR gates, saving one XOR gate compared to the best results reported in the literature.

To further optimize the obtained 42-XOR optimal MDS implementation, we applied the general search framework codes proposed in [23] for the third-layer processing. From the perspective of low-latency metrics, this framework helps find better implementations based on the given implementation. We utilized our 42-XOR circuit obtained through backward search as input and attempted further optimization using the general search framework codes. As the algorithm involves random selection operations, it continuously attempted optimizations once initiated. Referring to the settings provided in [23], we set the algorithm's running time to 5 days of CPU time. Upon completion of the algorithm, no results smaller than 42 XOR gates were obtained. Although we did not obtain better results for the corresponding MDS matrices, the third-layer processing covered a broader range of possible implementations, ensuring the superiority of our results.

In summary, we can formalize our three-layer processing framework as shown in Fig. 1. By applying our search framework, we performed three steps on the more than 500,000 low-latency involutory MDS matrices obtained from the previous section.

Step 1: Initial screening of candidate matrices using a faster heuristic algorithm, namely the LSL algorithm, for the preliminary selection of candidate matrices. After this step, we selected matrices with XOR counts ranging from 43 to 49 for further processing, resulting in 5463 matrices.

Step 2: Processing the remaining 5463 matrices using the backward search algorithm. We obtained four optimal depth-3 involutory MDS matrices with the lightest cost of 42 XOR gates.

Step 3: Applying the general search framework, incorporating division optimization and extending base techniques, to attempt further optimization on the obtained optimal implementations. The algorithm was set to run for 5 days of CPU time. Upon completion, no results smaller than 42 XOR gates were obtained.

Through our three-layer processing framework, we obtained four lightest depth-3 involutory MDS matrices with a cost of 42 XOR gates, while the previous best results required 43 XOR gates. The specific forms of the four matrices can be found in Table 3. We noted that they actually belong to a permutation-equivalence class. One implementation of the MDS matrix with 42 XOR gates is provided in Table 4, which corresponds to the first matrix of Table 3.

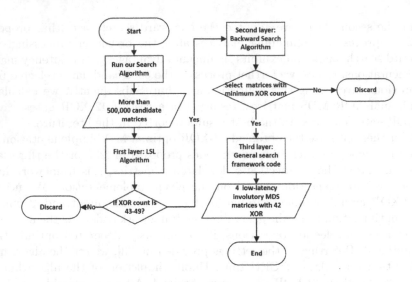

Fig. 1. Diagram of our three-layer processing framework

Table 3. All MDS matrices with cost of 42 XOR gates.

No.	Matrices	No.	Matrices
1	$\begin{pmatrix} A^{13} & I & I & I \\ A^2 & A^{13} & I & A^2 \\ A & A^{14} & A^{13} & A^2 \\ A^{14} & A^{14} & I & A^{13} \end{pmatrix}$	2	$\begin{pmatrix} A^{13} & A^2 & A^{14} & A \\ I & A^{13} & A^{14} & A^{14} \\ I & A^2 & A^{13} & A^2 \\ I & I & I & A^{13} \end{pmatrix}$
3	$\begin{pmatrix} A^{13} & I & I & I \\ A & A^{13} & A^2 & A^{14} \\ A^{14} & I & A^{13} & A^{14} \\ A^2 & I & A^2 & A^{13} \end{pmatrix}$	4	$\begin{pmatrix} A^{13} & A & A^2 & A^{14} \\ I & A^{13} & I & I \\ I & A^{14} & A^{13} & A^{14} \\ I & A^2 & A^2 & A^{13} \end{pmatrix}$

4 Constructing MDS Matrices in $M_4(GL(8, \mathbb{F}_2))$

In this section, we attempt to construct low-latency involutory matrices in $M_4(GL(8, \mathbb{F}_2))$ from two aspects. On the one hand, we build matrices in $M_4(GL(8, \mathbb{F}_2))$ based on two constructions using previously obtained MDS matrices in $M_4(GL(4, \mathbb{F}_2))$. On the other hand, to further achieve lower implementation costs for MDS matrices, we conduct a partial search for 4×4 MDS matrices over $\mathbb{F}_{2^8}$ and process the candidate matrices using the LSL algorithm and backward search algorithm. Through our approach, we obtain the currently best low-latency implementations of involutory MDS matrices in $M_4(GL(8, \mathbb{F}_2))$, requiring only 84 XOR gates. Additionally, we analyze the impact of the number of identity matrices (I) among the 16 entries of the matrix on its optimized implementation cost.

Table 4. An implementation of our matrices with 42 XOR gates.

No.	Operation	Depth	No.	Operation	Depth
1	$t_{16} = t_2 + t_6$	1	22	$t_{37} = t_{33} + t_{36}$	2
2	$t_{17} = t_7 + t_{15}$	1	23	$t_{38} = t_0 + t_4$	1
3	$t_{18} = t_5 + t_{13}$	1	24	$t_{39} = t_{38} + t_{28}$	2
4	$t_{19} = t_0 + t_9$	1	25	$t_{40} = t_{39} + t_{29}//y_{13}$	3
5	$t_{20} = t_{19} + t_{18}$	2	26	$t_{41} = t_4 + t_8$	1
6	$t_{21} = t_1 + t_{11}$	1	27	$t_{42} = t_7 + t_{14}$	1
7	$t_{22} = t_{21} + t_{17}//y_{15}$	2	28	$t_{43} = t_{41} + t_{42}$	2
8	$t_{23} = t_{10} + t_{21}$	2	29	$t_{44} = t_{16} + t_{43}//y_4$	3
9	$t_{24} = t_1 + t_5$	1	30	$t_{45} = t_{43} + t_{23}//y_7$	3
10	$t_{25} = t_6 + t_{14}$	1	31	$t_{46} = t_{43} + t_{37}//y_{12}$	3
11	$t_{26} = t_{24} + t_{25}$	2	32	$t_{47} = t_2 + t_{15}$	1
12	$t_{27} = t_{20} + t_{26}//y_2$	3	33	$t_{48} = t_{41} + t_{47}$	2
13	$t_{28} = t_{10} + t_{12}$	1	34	$t_{49} = t_{11} + t_{48}//y_8$	3
14	$t_{29} = t_{24} + t_{28}//y_{10}$	2	35	$t_{50} = t_{48} + t_{37}//y_{14}$	3
15	$t_{30} = t_{11} + t_{13}$	1	36	$t_{51} = t_0 + t_{10}$	1
16	$t_{31} = t_{30} + t_{16}//y_9$	2	37	$t_{52} = t_{51} + t_{25}//y_3$	2
17	$t_{32} = t_{26} + t_{31}//y_1$	3	38	$t_{53} = t_4 + t_9$	1
18	$t_{33} = t_3 + t_{12}$	1	39	$t_{54} = t_3 + t_{53}$	2
19	$t_{34} = t_{33} + t_8$	2	40	$t_{55} = t_{17} + t_{54}//y_0$	3
20	$t_{35} = t_{18} + t_{34}//y_{11}$	3	41	$t_{56} = t_{39} + t_{54}//y_5$	3
21	$t_{36} = t_0 + t_{15}$	1	42	$t_{57} = t_{54} + t_{37}//y_6$	3

4.1 Construction for Obtaining MDS Matrices in $M_4(GL(8, \mathbb{F}_2))$ from Matrices in $M_4(GL(4, \mathbb{F}_2))$

In this subsection, based on our obtained lightweight MDS matrices in $M_4(GL(4, \mathbb{F}_2))$, we use two constructions to get the MDS matrices in $M_4(GL(8, \mathbb{F}_2))$.

We take one of the lightest involutory MDS matrices we've found as an example. Each of its entries can be represented by an element on $\mathbb{F}_{2^4}$ generated by $x^4 + x + 1$ or by an invertible binary matrix over $GL(4, \mathbb{F}_2)$

$$ L = \begin{pmatrix} A^3 + A^2 + I_4 & I_4 & I_4 & I_4 \\ A^2 & A^3 + A^2 + I_4 & I_4 & A^2 \\ A & A^3 + I_4 & A^3 + A^2 + I_4 & A^2 \\ A^3 + I_4 & A^3 + I_4 & I_4 & A^3 + A^2 + I_4 \end{pmatrix}. $$

We apply the subfield construction in [16,20] as **Construction 1**. Using this construction method, we can obtain a 32×32 binary matrix C_1 in $M_4(M_2(GL(4, \mathbb{F}_2)))$

$$
C_1 = \begin{pmatrix}
(A^3 + A^2 + I_4)' & I_8 & I_8 & I_8 \\
(A^2)' & (A^3 + A^2 + I_4)' & I_8 & (A^2)' \\
A' & (A^3 + I_4)' & (A^3 + A^2 + I_4)' & (A^2)' \\
(A^3 + I_4)' & (A^3 + I_4)' & I_8 & (A^3 + A^2 + I_4)'
\end{pmatrix},
$$

where A' is defined as the matrix $\begin{pmatrix} A & 0 \\ 0 & A \end{pmatrix}$.

Proposition 1 ([17]). *If the matrix L needs m XOR gates in its implementation, then the matrix $L' = subfield(L)$ can be implemented with $2m$ XOR gates.*

The implementation of L' can be regarded as two multiplications by L, each of which operates on half of the input bits and utilizes an equal number of XOR gates. Therefore, the implementation cost of L' is twice that of L, and the implementation circuit of L' can be derived from the implementation circuit of L. Utilizing this property, we can construct a 32×32 matrix from a 16×16 matrix that requires 42 XOR gates, resulting in a 32×32 matrix that requires 84 XOR gates to implement. After verification, the obtained matrix retains the properties of being MDS and involutory, just like the previous matrix, while satisfying the constraint of a circuit depth of 3. In Table 5, we show the implementation of C_1 with 84 XOR gates.

In order to construct a matrix with lower cost, we explored an alternative method of field extension called **Construction 2** [13]. We select an 8×8 binary matrix B, satisfying the equation $B^8 + B^2 + I_8 = (B^4 + B + I_8)^2 = 0$. It can be deduced that: $(B^2)^4 + B^2 + I_8 = 0$. Thus, we chose to construct the involutory MDS matrix in $M_4(GL(8, \mathbb{F}_2))$ using the companion matrix of the polynomial $x^8 + x^2 + 1$. The entries of matrix L can be expressed as polynomials of the matrix B^2. As a result, we obtain a 32×32 binary matrix

$$
C_2 = \begin{pmatrix}
B^6 + B^4 + I_8 & I_8 & I_8 & I_8 \\
B^4 & B^6 + B^4 + I_8 & I_8 & B^4 \\
B^2 & B^6 + I_8 & B^6 + B^4 + I_8 & B^4 \\
B^6 + I_8 & B^6 + I_8 & I_8 & B^6 + B^4 + I_8
\end{pmatrix},
$$

where

$$
B = \begin{pmatrix}
0 & 0 & 0 & 0 & 0 & 0 & 0 & 1 \\
1 & 0 & 0 & 0 & 0 & 0 & 0 & 0 \\
0 & 1 & 0 & 0 & 0 & 0 & 0 & 1 \\
0 & 0 & 1 & 0 & 0 & 0 & 0 & 0 \\
0 & 0 & 0 & 1 & 0 & 0 & 0 & 0 \\
0 & 0 & 0 & 0 & 1 & 0 & 0 & 0 \\
0 & 0 & 0 & 0 & 0 & 1 & 0 & 0 \\
0 & 0 & 0 & 0 & 0 & 0 & 1 & 0
\end{pmatrix}.
$$

Table 5. An implementation of C_1 with 84 XOR gates.

No.	Operation	Depth	No.	Operation	Depth	No.	Operation	Depth
1	$t_{32} = t_2 + t_{10}$	1	30	$t_{61} = t_{59} + t_{39}//y_{11}$	3	59	$t_{90} = t_{84} + t_{89}//y_5$	3
2	$t_{33} = t_{11} + t_{27}$	1	31	$t_{62} = t_{59} + t_{53}//y_{24}$	3	60	$t_{91} = t_7 + t_{28}$	1
3	$t_{34} = t_9 + t_{25}$	1	32	$t_{63} = t_2 + t_{27}$	1	61	$t_{92} = t_{91} + t_{20}$	2
4	$t_{35} = t_0 + t_{17}$	1	33	$t_{64} = t_{57} + t_{63}$	2	62	$t_{93} = t_{76} + t_{92}//y_{23}$	3
5	$t_{36} = t_{35} + t_{34}$	2	34	$t_{65} = t_{19} + t_{64}//y_{16}$	3	63	$t_{94} = t_4 + t_{31}$	1
6	$t_{37} = t_1 + t_{19}$	1	35	$t_{66} = t_{64} + t_{53}//y_{26}$	3	64	$t_{95} = t_{91} + t_{94}$	2
7	$t_{38} = t_{37} + t_{33}//y_{27}$	2	36	$t_{67} = t_0 + t_{18}$	1	65	$t_{96} = t_4 + t_{12}$	1
8	$t_{39} = t_{18} + t_{37}$	2	37	$t_{68} = t_{67} + t_{41}//y_3$	2	66	$t_{97} = t_{96} + t_{76}$	2
9	$t_{40} = t_1 + t_9$	1	38	$t_{69} = t_8 + t_{17}$	1	67	$t_{98} = t_{97} + t_{87}//y_{29}$	3
10	$t_{41} = t_{10} + t_{26}$	1	39	$t_{70} = t_3 + t_{69}$	2	68	$t_{99} = t_{12} + t_{20}$	1
11	$t_{42} = t_{40} + t_{41}$	2	40	$t_{71} = t_{33} + t_{70}//y_0$	3	69	$t_{100} = t_{15} + t_{30}$	1
12	$t_{43} = t_{36} + t_{42}//y_2$	3	41	$t_{72} = t_{55} + t_{70}//y_9$	3	70	$t_{101} = t_{99} + t_{100}$	2
13	$t_{44} = t_{18} + t_{24}$	1	42	$t_{73} = t_{70} + t_{53}//y_{10}$	3	71	$t_{102} = t_{74} + t_{101}//y_{12}$	3
14	$t_{45} = t_{40} + t_{44}//y_{18}$	2	43	$t_{74} = t_6 + t_{14}$	1	72	$t_{103} = t_{101} + t_{81}//y_{15}$	3
15	$t_{46} = t_{19} + t_{25}$	1	44	$t_{75} = t_{15} + t_{31}$	1	73	$t_{104} = t_{101} + t_{95}//y_{28}$	3
16	$t_{47} = t_{46} + t_{32}//y_{17}$	2	45	$t_{76} = t_{13} + t_{29}$	1	74	$t_{105} = t_6 + t_{31}$	1
17	$t_{48} = t_{42} + t_{47}//y_1$	3	46	$t_{77} = t_4 + t_{21}$	1	75	$t_{106} = t_{99} + t_{105}$	2
18	$t_{49} = t_3 + t_{24}$	1	47	$t_{78} = t_{77} + t_{76}$	2	76	$t_{107} = t_{23} + t_{106}//y_{20}$	3
19	$t_{50} = t_{49} + t_{16}$	2	48	$t_{79} = t_5 + t_{23}$	1	77	$t_{108} = t_{106} + t_{95}//y_{28}$	3
20	$t_{51} = t_{34} + t_{50}//y_{19}$	3	49	$t_{80} = t_{79} + t_{75}//y_{31}$	2	78	$t_{109} = t_4 + t_{22}$	2
21	$t_{52} = t_0 + t_{27}$	1	50	$t_{81} = t_{22} + t_{79}$	2	79	$t_{110} = t_{109} + t_{83}//y_7$	2
22	$t_{53} = t_{49} + t_{52}$	2	51	$t_{82} = t_5 + t_{13}$	1	80	$t_{111} = t_{12} + t_{21}$	1
23	$t_{54} = t_0 + t_8$	1	52	$t_{83} = t_{14} + t_{30}$	1	81	$t_{112} = t_7 + t_{111}$	2
24	$t_{55} = t_{54} + t_{34}$	2	53	$t_{84} = t_{82} + t_{83}$	2	82	$t_{113} = t_{75} + t_{112}//y_4$	3
25	$t_{56} = t_{55} + t_{45}//y_{25}$	3	54	$t_{85} = t_{78} + t_{84}//y_6$	3	83	$t_{114} = t_{97} + t_{112}//y_{13}$	3
26	$t_{57} = t_8 + t_{16}//y_2$	1	55	$t_{86} = t_{22} + t_{28}$	1	84	$t_{115} = t_{112} + t_{95}//y_{14}$	3
27	$t_{58} = t_{11} + t_{26}$	1	56	$t_{87} = t_{82} + t_{86}//y_{22}$	2			
28	$t_{59} = t_{57} + t_{58}$	2	57	$t_{88} = t_{23} + t_{29}$	1			
29	$t_{60} = t_{32} + t_{59}//y_8$	3	58	$t_{89} = t_{88} + t_{74}//y_{21}$	2			

Optimized by our three-layer processing framework in Sect. 3.2, matrix C_2 and other matrices constructed by **Construction 2** can be implemented with at least 86 XOR gates limited to a circuit depth of 3. Although we extended the processing time of this implementation in the third layer framework code, we never found an implementation with a smaller XOR number.

4.2 Partial Search for 4 × 4 MDS Matrices over $\mathbb{F}_{2^8}$

Our method by **Construction 2** in the previous section did not achieve the same result as **Construction 1**, as we obtained low-latency involutory MDS matrices with only 84 XORs by **Construction 1**. Therefore, we consider applying the search algorithm from Sect. 3 to find more MDS matrices in $M_4(GL(8, \mathbb{F}_2))$ and apply the LSL algorithm and backward search algorithm to process the candidate matrices. However, due to the increased computational complexity, we can only perform a partial search by adding restrictions on the candidate matrices.

During the search process, we impose the following restriction on the candidate MDS matrices: among the 16 entries, we constrain the diagonal to be $B^6 + B^4 + I_8$, while leaving the other positions unconstrained. We use Algorithm 1 to search for all depth-3 involutory MDS matrices and classify the obtained matrices based on the number of identity matrices I among the 16 entries. The results of this processing are presented in Table 6. We perform this classification for two main purposes: first, to facilitate the parallel processing of matrices and improve the algorithm's efficiency; second, to explore the impact of the number of identity matrices I on the matrix processing performance, thereby providing valuable insights for future MDS matrix construction and the design of linear layer components in algorithms.

For the obtained 1878 candidate matrices, we applied both the LSL algorithm and the backward search algorithm to obtain their implementations. The results can be seen in Table 7. Although we did not obtain a low-latency involutory MDS matrix with a lower implementation cost, we can observe the following phenomenon from our statistical results: In low-latency scenarios, for 4×4 involutory MDS matrices in $M_4(\mathbb{F}_{2^8})$, the number of I in 16 entries of the MDS matrix with minimum implementation circuit is 5. Moreover, the average implementation cost of all candidate matrices satisfying this condition is significantly reduced compared to other candidate matrices. This phenomenon is also consistent with the form of the 42-XOR matrices we obtained in $M_4(\mathbb{F}_{2^4})$, where the number of I among its 16 entries is also 5. From the results shown in Table 7 and Fig. 2, the following inferences can be drawn: the quantity of I within the matrix entries does not exhibit a clear linear relationship with its implementation cost. Categorizing the count of I in MDS matrix entries might reveal a phenomenon where a certain category of matrices consistently has a smaller implementation cost compared to other categories. Furthermore, within this category of matrices, it may be easier to identify a matrix with the smallest implementation cost across the entire set of matrices.

Table 6. All depth-3 involutory MDS matrices under our limitation.

I Count	Number of Matrices
3	1248
4	498
5	72
6	60
7	0
Sum	1878

Table 7. Results for all candidate matrices in $M_4(\mathbb{F}_{2^8})$.

Algorithm	I Count	Min	Average
LSL	3	91	114.6
	4	90	119.3
	5	88	94.1
	6	96	109.4
Backward Search	3	89	108.2
	4	91	119.8
	5	**86**	**92.1**
	6	102	111.0

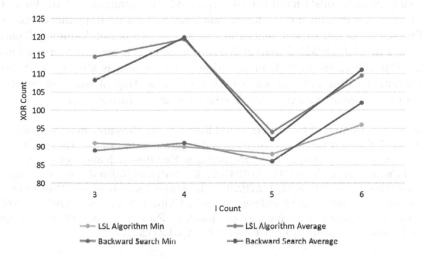

Fig. 2. Comparison of the implementation costs obtained by the two algorithms for MDS matrices with different I counts, including minimum and average.

Subsequently, we take the smallest circuit obtained from the aforementioned process, achievable using 86 XORs, and subject it to further processing using general search framework codes(the algorithm employed in the third layer of the three-layer processing framework in Sect. 3) with the aim of achieving a smaller implementation circuit. Following this processing, we attained an implementation circuit requiring only 85 XORs. While this outcome is larger than the 84 XORs achieved using **Construction 1**, it aligns with the smallest results documented in previous literature (presented in [23]).

5 Conclusion

In this paper, we introduced a new search framework to find lightweight involutory MDS matrices in low-latency scenarios. An efficient search algorithm for involutory MDS matrices which can be implemented in optimal circuit depth was proposed. By this method, we can obtain all 4×4 involutory MDS matrices over $\mathbb{F}_{2^4}$ for one specific representation. To find the lightweight ones, we designed a three-layer processing framework, which enables us to find so far the lightest involutory MDS matrices in $M_4(GL(4, \mathbb{F}_2))$ whose implementation requires only 42 XOR gates. With these lightweight results, we constructed involutory MDS matrices in $M_4(GL(8, \mathbb{F}_2))$ with 84 XOR gates, which are also the best known results. Moreover, as an attempt to construct a matrix with lower cost, we conduct a partial search added additional restrictions for matrices over $\mathbb{F}_{2^8}$ and classify all obtained candidate matrices based on the number of identity matrices among their 16 entries. We investigate the impact of the number of identity matrices on the matrix implementation cost and find that for a 4×4 involutory MDS matrix constructed over a given field, the quantity of I in the matrix entries does not exhibit a clear linear relationship with its implementation cost.

The results of our experiments show when the number of I among 16 entries of a 4×4 involutory MDS matrix is 5, we usually can get a better implementation. But the theoretical demonstration of the reason is still open. It would be interesting to further explore the effect of the setting of some entries in the matrix on the optimization result. We leave it as our future work.

Acknowledgements. The authors would like to thank the anonymous reviewers and the shepherd for their valuable comments and suggestions to improve the quality of the paper. This research is supported by the National Key Research and Development Program of China (Grant No. 2018YFA0704702), the National Natural Science Foundation of China (Grant No. 62032014, U2336207), the Major Basic Research Project of Natural Science Foundation of Shandong Province, China (Grant No. ZR202010220025), Department of Science & Technology of Shandong Province (No. SYS202201), Quan Cheng Laboratory (Grant No. QCLZD202301, QCLZD202306).

References

1. AlTawy, R., Youssef, A.M.: Preimage analysis of the maelstrom-0 hash function. In: Chakraborty, R.S., Schwabe, P., Solworth, J. (eds.) SPACE 2015. LNCS, vol. 9354, pp. 113–126. Springer, Cham (2015). https://doi.org/10.1007/978-3-319-24126-5_7
2. Avanzi, R.: The QARMA block cipher family. Almost MDS matrices over rings with zero divisors, nearly symmetric even-Mansour constructions with non-involutory central rounds, and search heuristics for low-latency s-boxes. IACR Trans. Symmetric Cryptol. **2017**(1), 4–44 (2017). https://doi.org/10.13154/tosc.v2017.i1.4-44
3. Banik, S., Bogdanov, A., Isobe, T., Shibutani, K., Hiwatari, H., Akishita, T., Regazzoni, F.: Midori: a block cipher for low energy. In: Iwata, T., Cheon, J.H. (eds.) ASIACRYPT 2015, Part II. LNCS, vol. 9453, pp. 411–436. Springer, Heidelberg (2015). https://doi.org/10.1007/978-3-662-48800-3_17
4. Banik, S., Funabiki, Y., Isobe, T.: Further results on efficient implementations of block cipher linear layers. IEICE Trans. Fundam. Electron. Commun. Comput. Sci. **104-A**(1), 213–225 (2021). https://doi.org/10.1587/transfun.2020CIP0013

5. Beierle, C., et al.: The SKINNY family of block ciphers and its low-latency variant MANTIS. In: Robshaw, M., Katz, J. (eds.) CRYPTO 2016, Part II. LNCS, vol. 9815, pp. 123–153. Springer, Heidelberg (2016). https://doi.org/10.1007/978-3-662-53008-5_5

6. Blaum, M., Roth, R.: On lowest density MDS codes. IEEE Trans. Inf. Theory 45(1), 46–59 (1999). https://doi.org/10.1109/18.746771

7. Bogdanov, A., et al.: PRESENT: an ultra-lightweight block cipher. In: Paillier, P., Verbauwhede, I. (eds.) CHES 2007. LNCS, vol. 4727, pp. 450–466. Springer, Heidelberg (2007). https://doi.org/10.1007/978-3-540-74735-2_31

8. Boyar, J., Matthews, P., Peralta, R.: On the shortest linear straight-line program for computing linear forms. In: Ochmański, E., Tyszkiewicz, J. (eds.) MFCS 2008. LNCS, vol. 5162, pp. 168–179. Springer, Heidelberg (2008). https://doi.org/10.1007/978-3-540-85238-4_13

9. Boyar, J., Matthews, P., Peralta, R.: Logic minimization techniques with applications to cryptology. J. Cryptol. 26(2), 280–312 (2013). https://doi.org/10.1007/s00145-012-9124-7

10. Boyar, J., Peralta, R.: A new combinational logic minimization technique with applications to cryptology. In: Festa, P. (ed.) SEA 2010. LNCS, vol. 6049, pp. 178–189. Springer, Heidelberg (2010). https://doi.org/10.1007/978-3-642-13193-6_16

11. Chand Gupta, K., Ghosh Ray, I.: On constructions of involutory MDS matrices. In: Youssef, A., Nitaj, A., Hassanien, A.E. (eds.) AFRICACRYPT 2013. LNCS, vol. 7918, pp. 43–60. Springer, Heidelberg (2013). https://doi.org/10.1007/978-3-642-38553-7_3

12. Daemen, J., Rijmen, V.: The Design of Rijndael - The Advanced Encryption Standard (AES). Information Security and Cryptography, 2nd edn. Springer, Heidelberg (2020). https://doi.org/10.1007/978-3-662-60769-5

13. Duval, S., Leurent, G.: MDS matrices with lightweight circuits. IACR Trans. Symmetric Cryptol. 2018(2), 48–78 (2018). https://doi.org/10.13154/tosc.v2018.i2.48-78

14. Guo, J., Peyrin, T., Poschmann, A.: The PHOTON family of lightweight hash functions. In: Rogaway, P. (ed.) CRYPTO 2011. LNCS, vol. 6841, pp. 222–239. Springer, Heidelberg (2011). https://doi.org/10.1007/978-3-642-22792-9_13

15. Güzel, G.G., Sakallı, M.T., Akleylek, S., Rijmen, V., Çengellenmiş, Y.: A new matrix form to generate all 3×3 involutory MDS matrices over F2M. Inf. Process. Lett. 147, 61–68 (2019). https://doi.org/10.1016/j.ipl.2019.02.013

16. Khoo, K., Peyrin, T., Poschmann, A.Y., Yap, H.: FOAM: searching for hardware-optimal SPN structures and components with a fair comparison. In: Batina, L., Robshaw, M. (eds.) CHES 2014. LNCS, vol. 8731, pp. 433–450. Springer, Heidelberg (2014). https://doi.org/10.1007/978-3-662-44709-3_24

17. Kranz, T., Leander, G., Stoffelen, K., Wiemer, F.: Shorter linear straight-line programs for MDS matrices. IACR Trans. Symmetric Cryptol. 2017(4), 188–211 (2017). https://doi.org/10.13154/tosc.v2017.i4.188-211

18. Leander, G., Moos, T., Moradi, A., Rasoolzadeh, S.: The SPEEDY family of block ciphers engineering an ultra low-latency cipher from gate level for secure processor architectures. IACR Trans. Cryptogr. Hardw. Embed. Syst. 2021(4), 510–545 (2021). https://doi.org/10.46586/tches.v2021.i4.510-545

19. Li, Q., Wu, B., Liu, Z.: Direct constructions of (involutory) MDS matrices from block Vandermonde and Cauchy-like matrices. In: Budaghyan, L., Rodríguez-Henríquez, F. (eds.) WAIFI 2018. LNCS, vol. 11321, pp. 275–290. Springer, Cham (2018). https://doi.org/10.1007/978-3-030-05153-2_16

20. Li, S., Sun, S., Li, C., Wei, Z., Hu, L.: Constructing low-latency involutory MDS matrices with lightweight circuits. IACR Trans. Symmetric Cryptol. **2019**(1), 84–117 (2019). https://doi.org/10.13154/tosc.v2019.i1.84-117
21. Li, Y., Wang, M.: On the construction of lightweight circulant involutory MDS matrices. In: Peyrin, T. (ed.) FSE 2016. LNCS, vol. 9783, pp. 121–139. Springer, Heidelberg (2016). https://doi.org/10.1007/978-3-662-52993-5_7
22. Liu, Q., Wang, W., Fan, Y., Wu, L., Sun, L., Wang, M.: Towards low-latency implementation of linear layers. IACR Trans. Symmetric Cryptol. **2022**(1), 158–182 (2022). https://doi.org/10.46586/tosc.v2022.i1.158-182
23. Liu, Q., Zhao, Z., Wang, M.: Improved heuristics for low-latency implementations of linear layers. In: Rosulek, M. (ed.) CT-RSA 2023. LNCS, vol. 13871, pp. 524–550. Springer, Cham (2023). https://doi.org/10.1007/978-3-031-30872-7_20
24. Paar, C.: Optimized arithmetic for reed-Solomon encoders. In: Proceedings of IEEE International Symposium on Information Theory, p. 250. IEEE (1997)
25. Sajadieh, M., Dakhilalian, M., Mala, H., Omoomi, B.: On construction of involutory MDS matrices from Vandermonde matrices in GF (2 q). Des. Codes Crypt. **64**, 287–308 (2012)
26. Watanabe, D., Furuya, S., Yoshida, H., Takaragi, K., Preneel, B.: A new keystream generator MUGI. In: Daemen, J., Rijmen, V. (eds.) FSE 2002. LNCS, vol. 2365, pp. 179–194. Springer, Heidelberg (2002). https://doi.org/10.1007/3-540-45661-9_14
27. Xiang, Z., Zeng, X., Lin, D., Bao, Z., Zhang, S.: Optimizing implementations of linear layers. IACR Trans. Symmetric Cryptol. **2020**(2), 120–145 (2020). https://doi.org/10.13154/tosc.v2020.i2.120-145
28. Yang, Y., Zeng, X., Wang, S.: Construction of lightweight involutory MDS matrices. Des. Codes Cryptogr. **89**(7), 1453–1483 (2021). https://doi.org/10.1007/s10623-021-00879-3

CIMSS – Critical Infrastructure and Manufacturing System Security

Guidelines for Cyber Risk Management in Autonomous Shipping

Meixuan Li[✉][iD], Awais Yousaf[iD], Mark Goh[iD], Jianying Zhou[iD], and Sudipta Chattopadhyay[iD]

iTrust, Singapore University of Technology and Design, Singapore, Singapore
{li_meixuan,awais_yousaf,mark_goh,jianying_zhou,
sudipta_chattopadhyay}@sutd.edu.sg

Abstract. The emergence of autonomous ships represents a significant advancement in maritime technology, promising enhanced efficiency, reduced operating costs and reducing or even completely removing crews from hazardous environments. However, the progress is accompanied by a burgeoning concern on the cyber security of these autonomous ships due to their exposure to the "connected world". The four key systems investigated in this study are: 1) Shore Control Centre (SCC); 2) Communication System; 3) Autonomous Ship Controller (ASC), and 4) Autonomous Navigation System (ANS). The paper highlights specific operational technology (OT) risks associated with MASS (Maritime Autonomous Surface Ship). For completeness, the study also drills down to cyber risks and impacts associated with sub-systems of these major OT systems. A comprehensive cyber risk assessment methodology employing the MITRE framework is provided to evaluate the severity of risks. Recommended mitigations include defence-in-depth cybersecurity protections for all systems, security-by-design approaches, personnel training and redundancy in certain critical systems (The full version of guidelines is accessible through this link for further reference). Taking into account all aspects, this paper functions as a case study examining cyber risks of the OT system of autonomous ships.

Keywords: Autonomous ship · Ship systems · Maritime operations · Cyber risk · Cybersecurity · Risk analysis

1 Introduction

A significant transformation in terms of advancements in technology, shifts in customer behaviours and changes in the competitive landscape is in underway with the emergence of autonomous ships [1]. The International Maritime Organisation (IMO) defines MASS as "a ship which, to a varying degree, can operate independent of human interaction" [2]. Four degrees of automation are listed by IMO - *Degree one*: Ship with automated processes and decision support. Seafarers are on board to operate and control shipboard systems and functions. Some operations may be automated and at times be unsupervised but with seafarers on board ready to take control; *Degree two*: Remotely controlled ship with seafarers on board. The ship is controlled and operated from another location. Seafarers are available on board to take control and to operate the shipboard systems and functions; *Degree three*: Remotely controlled ship without seafarers on board: The ship is controlled and operated from another location. There are no seafarers on board; *Degree four*: Fully autonomous ship. The OS of the ship is able to make decisions and determine actions by itself.

This study focuses on Degree 3 MASS because it strikes a balance between automation and human involvement. The prevailing academic literature and established guidelines within the autonomous shipping domain prioritize the notion of 'remotely controlled' over 'completely autonomous'. Human operators will continue to be essential for ensuring the safety, security, and widespread acceptance of autonomous ships in the foreseeable future [3,4]. Degree 3 autonomy is favoured in this study due to its potential for unmanned or minimally manned operations. A Degree 3 autonomous ship possesses the ability to perceive its surroundings, chart optimal collision-free routes in compliance with maritime regulations, and regulate propulsion systems to adhere to planned trajectories while avoiding potential hazards. It solicits human input solely when faced with unprecedented circumstances beyond its operational scope, activating alerts in case of anomalies. The envisaged autonomous and automation systems are designed to function robustly and securely for extended durations with minimal onshore supervision. However, the extensive reliance on the interconnected network connecting the ship to the SCC amplifies the vulnerability to cyber-attacks [5]. Notably, a critical limitation of Degree 3 systems lies in their incapacity to dynamically evaluate their competency and revert control to human operators when autonomy falters. Instead, they depend on operators to actively monitor for any arising issues. This constraint implies that autonomous ships at sea will likely necessitate ongoing vigilance from onshore personnel. Onboard systems are exposed to risks such as malware infections, and some AI-based models integrated into these systems are susceptible to adversarial attacks [6,7]. Furthermore, given that seamless connectivity between ship and shore infrastructures forms the cornerstone of autonomous and remotely controlled technologies, cybersecurity assumes a paramount role in ensuring the operational efficacy of these autonomous ships.

This research aims to precisely define the intended scope of autonomous ships, as cyber-attack surfaces are contingent upon the degree of autonomy [8]. The focus of this investigation is to mitigate the potential cyber risks faced by envisaged autonomous OT ship systems and to recommend appropriate cybersecurity measures so as to protect the ship's operation and data. Numerous shipping organisations such as the Lloyd's Register (LR), Det Norske Veritas (DNV), Bureau Veritas (BV), Maritime UK, China Classification Society (CCS), ClassNK, Russian Maritime Register of Shipping (RS), American Bureau of Shipping (ABS), and Korean Register (KR), primarily emphasise offering counsel concerning secure design and functional prerequisites in autonomous systems, encompassing certain facets of cybersecurity precautions. These publications duly recognise that autonomous ships necessitate an all-encompassing strategy consisting of risk assessment, technical dependability, operational safety, human factors, and cybersecurity throughout the complete lifecycle of the system [9–18]. Nevertheless, upon thorough examination of various autonomous ship projects, it is found that there is a gap in the understanding - and conversely the identification - of cyber threats, and viable mitigation strategies that can be promptly implemented by engineers, IT specialists, and vessel inspectors. Hence, this research aspires to bridge this gap and provide a comprehensive analysis, interpretation and implications of cybersecurity on OT systems within the maritime industry.

The remaining part of the paper is organised as follows: Sect. 2 summarizes some pertinent autonomous ship projects and associated research released by various classification societies and organizations. Section 3 describes the intended capabilities and operations of proposed autonomous ship systems found in a typical MASS. Section 4 categorizes the cybersecurity threats associated with these OT systems by breaking them down into potential attack scenarios, and describes various countermeasures intended to alleviate the identified cyber risks. Section 5 conducts an in-depth analysis of the vulnerabilities present in these OT systems, followed by highlighting the features of this guidelines compared to our earlier work. Conclusions are drawn in Sect. 6.

2   Literature Review

2.1   Related Projects

The advent of initiatives in MASS marks a paradigm shift in maritime technology, where navigational decision making is partially or entirely influenced by advanced algorithms, optimisation, machine learning and a combination of old and new technologies onboard. However, this transition to crewless ships present significant challenges, as sensor technologies, real-time data processing and effective communication are paramount in the absence of crew. The challenges notwithstanding, there are several notable MASS projects (Table 1) that have contributed to technological advancements and shaping of and preparing for the future of autonomous shipping. For example, MUNIN provided early insights into potential autonomous ship benefits like lower costs and improved safety [19]. Its concepts, findings, and prototypes laid groundwork for subsequent maritime automation progress. Though full autonomy remains unrealized, MUNIN was an influential early initiative.

It is evident from these MASS projects that the ships are jam-packed with technologies that facilitate varying degrees of automation and with them, cybersecurity challenges.

2.2   Related Work

Recognising the uncertainties around the operation of MASS, Lloyd's Register (LR), Det Norske Veritas (DNV), Bureau Veritas (BV), Maritime UK, China

Table 1. List of notable autonomous ship projects selected from different countries

Country	Name of MASS projects	Duration	Brief description	Ref.
Europe	Maritime Unmanned Navigation through Intelligence in Networks (MUNIN)	2012–2015	MUNIN was an ambitious European Commission-funded research project to conceptualize, develop, and validate an autonomous dry bulk carrier. The initiative made significant progress by prototyping key systems like autonomous navigation	[19,20]
	Mayflower Autonomous Ship (MAS)	2015–2020	The MAS was developed through a collaboration between ProMare research non-profit and IBM. Equipped with hybrid electric/solar propulsion for extended operation, this unmanned vessel achieved a key milestone in June 2022 by completing the first fully autonomous transatlantic voyage from Plymouth, UK to Plymouth, Massachusetts	
Japan	MEGURI2040	2020-ongoing	A Nippon Foundation-led initiative is underway to create a fully autonomous ship capable of operating without a crew or onboard support systems. This ambitious, long-term project is set to span the next two decades, with the primary objective of revolutionizing the shipping industry and mitigating its environmental footprint. Propelled by renewable energy sources, the autonomous ship serves as an eco-friendly alternative to conventional shipping methods	[21]
Singapore	Smart Maritime Autonomous Vessel (SMAV)	2019–2020	ST Engineering in Singapore completed initial sea trials in local waters for their pioneering autonomous tug project. The collision avoidance algorithm strictly followed COLREGS rules, especially regarding safe overtaking, head-on encounters, and vessel crossings	[22]
China	Zhi Fei	2021–2022	The Zhi Fei, meaning "flying wisdom," is an autonomous containership developed by Qingdao Shipyard. Its maiden voyage on April 22nd marked a key milestone. The state-of-the-art vessel can transition between manned, remote, and unmanned modes. Beginning sea trials in April 2021, the ship underwent comprehensive testing to evaluate its capabilities	[23]
Korea	Samsung Autonomous Ship (SAS)	2022 - ongoing	Samsung Heavy Industries signed an MOU to develop autonomous ship designs to support maritime digitalization, partnering with Kongsberg Maritime. Samsung's Autonomous Ship system processes data from radar, GPS, and AIS to identify nearby vessels and obstructions	[24]

Classification Society (CCS), ClassNK, Russian Maritime Register of Shipping (RS), IRCLASS - Indian Register of Shipping, American Bureau of Shipping (ABS) and Korean Register (KR) have published guidelines around the safe design, construction and operation - cyber or otherwise - of MASS (Table 2).

Seeking to gain wider perspective, this research has attempted to compare existing literature across several relevant dimension in a manner cognizant of our own limitations (See Fig. 1). Empty circle, filled circle, and half circle are used as visual indicators to represent different levels of completion or depth of information. Here's how they are defined:

1) *Empty Circle: An empty circle is used to indicate that a specific aspect or content element in the table is completely missing or not addressed at all.*
2) *Half Circle: A half circle (or a semicircle) is used to show partial completeness or depth. It signifies that there is some content present, but it's not exhaustive or complete.*
3) *Filled Circle: A filled circle is used to represent full or complete content in each category.*

Publishers / Features	KR	Maritime UK	ABS	IRCLASS	ClassNK	BV	CCS	DNV	LR	RS
Completeness in functional description of autonomous systems	◐	◐	●	◐	◐	●	●	◐	◐	●
Practicality and novelty in risk assessment approach	◐	○	◐	◐	●	◐	○	○	◐	◐
Details in cyber risk/hazards descriptions	◐	◐	◐	○	◐	◐	◐	◐	◐	◐
Examinations and discussions in regulation terms	○	●	●	◐	◐	●	◐	●	○	●
Precision and clarity in autonomy level / scope definition	●	●	○	○	○	●	○	●	○	○
Feasibility for autonomous ship concept design	●	◐	◐	●	●	◐	◐	◐	◐	◐

Fig. 1. Existing guidelines comparison

While existing works have made valuable contributions analyzing particular facets, it appears further efforts adopting an integrated perspective across more in-depth autonomous shipping dimensions remains an open research gap with opportunity for additional investigation. This study strives to provide targeted systems insights. As an evolving field, it is acknowledged that the analysis this paper can offer will undoubtedly improve with further understanding and additional research in this area will need to remain adaptable and reactive to arising progress and obstacles.

Table 2. List of significant research selected from different shipping organisations

Name of Publisher	Name of the Document	Year	Comments	Ref.
KR	Guidance for Autonomous Ships	2022	The Korea Register of Shipping's Guide for Autonomous Ships presents a 5-level cyber autonomy model, spanning from basic cyber access to full autonomy with no onboard presence. It details system configurations and ship traits for each level, along with a risk-based approval framework for remote and autonomous ship systems	[9]
Maritime UK	MASS UK Industry Conduct Principles and Code of Practice 2022 (V6)	2022	Maritime UK's 2022 voluntary Industry Code of Practice aims to establish best practices for designing, building, owning, operating and controlling autonomous vessels under 24 m in UK waters, aligning with technological, commercial and regulatory advancements	[10]
ABS	Guide for Autonomous and Remote Control Functions	2021	The ABS introduced Guide for Autonomous and Remote Control Functions providing guidance for applying risk-based approval process to autonomous and remote control features on marine vessels. It introduced notable aspects such as the AUTONOMOUS and REMOTE-CON notation and a distinct acknowledgment of remote-control functions	[11]
IRCLASS	Guidelines on Remotely Operated Vessels and Autonomous Surface Vessels	2021	The primary objective of this guidelines is to furnish a comprehensive framework, drawing from industry best practices, for stakeholders engaged in the design, construction, and testing phases of such vessels	[12]
ClassNK	Guidelines for Automated/Autonomous Operation on ships (Ver.1.0)	2020	ClassNK's guidelines present a scheme covering technical, operational, human factors and documentation requirements to evaluate safety of automated and autonomous ship systems	[13]
RS	Regulations for Classification of Maritime Autonomous And Remotely Controlled Surface Ships (MASS)	2020	The RS-published Regulations for the Classification of Maritime Autonomous and Remotely Controlled Surface Ships (MASS) encompass specifications for the electrical, automation, radio, and navigational equipment employed in autonomous ships. Additionally, it outlines a risk-oriented procedure aimed at maintaining a safety standard during the operation of MASS	[14]
BV	Guidelines for Autonomous Shipping	2019	BV's standards emphasize functional requirements for autonomous systems on ships. The guidelines provide technical standards and specifications for the design, performance, and integration of autonomous technologies like navigation, propulsion, and control systems on ships	[15]
CCS	Guidelines for Autonomous Cargo Ships	2018	Similar to BV guidelines, CCS's work provide a "safety and functionality-oriented" scheme to support autonomous shipping adoption	[16]
DNV	Remote-Controlled and Autonomous Ships	2018	DNV's study elaborates on the regulatory landscape and the compliance verification process that autonomous ships must undergo to meet international and industry standards. It also emphasizes the safety assurance management to ensure protection against cyber threats	[17]
LR	Cyber-enabled ships: ShipRight procedure - autonomous ships (First edition)	2016	It presents a specialized framework concentrating on cybersecurity, pivotal for the seamless functioning of autonomous ships that heavily depend on integrated digital systems. The guidelines maintain a continuous focus on cybersecurity aspects, integrating them comprehensively into the development and lifecycle of autonomous systems	[18]

3   Shipboard Autonomous OT Systems

The OT systems scoped in this paper for autonomous ships encompass key elements necessary to facilitate uncrewed operation, namely the Shore Control Centre (SCC), the Communication System, the Autonomous Ship Controller (ASC), and the Autonomous Navigation System (ANS) as illustrated in Fig. 2. This list is built upon the analysis of research projects and literature on autonomous ship systems. The primary OT systems deployed on autonomous vessels can be decomposed into various subsystems. This facilitates analysis of the distinct components and their complex intra- and inter-system interactions which cumulatively enable ship autonomy.

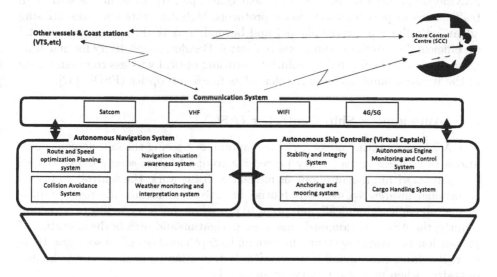

Fig. 2. System Overview of an Envisaged Autonomous Ship

3.1   Shore Control Centre (SCC)

The SCC refers to a land-based station and it is a backbone that enables the remote monitoring and control of autonomous ships from shore, and is considered an essential component in the foreseeable future for autonomous shipping in IMO's Degree Two and Three autonomy. The operators at SCC may initiate remote control for general oversight of the autonomous ship or to switch to the manual mode to handle specific hazardous or emergency situations that are beyond the ship's autonomous capabilities [16,25,26]. SCC requires a specific human-machine interface design and acts as a hub for human operators to supervise unmanned maritime operations through sensor data analysis, communications links, and active control interventions when required [27].

3.2   Communication System

The communication system on autonomous ships enables connectivity for monitoring, control, and coordination between the ship, other ships, and shoreside centres [28]. For ship-to-ship communication, AIS and VHF radio allow autonomous ship to enhance situational awareness and exchange vital information with other ships at sea [29]. Within the ship, networks and industrial protocols can be used to connect various onboard systems and components. Lastly, the communication system establish a reliable link between the autonomous ship and the SCC for the transmission of critical operational data. Long range satellite links enable consistent global coverage for monitoring and emergency situations with the shoreside operators. Higher bandwidth options like 4G and 5G cellular provide supplementary connectivity near coasts [30,31]. In scenarios with high traffic, such as port areas, IP-based protocols, high-data-rate networks utilising advanced cellular networks like 5G and beyond, and Wi-Fi systems are pivotal for efficient data exchange and remote control. Besides, connectivity for maritime networks is also facilitated by solutions utilising optical wireless communication in the infrared band, commonly referred as free space optics (FSOs) [32].

3.3   Autonomous Ship Controller (ASC)

The ASC assumes the role of a virtual captain, overseeing the autonomous operations of crewless ships [7]. By processing comprehensive sensor data from all subsystems within the autonomous navigation framework, the controller upholds situational awareness, averts potential hazards, and commands route adjustments, all while dynamically adapting to ever-changing sea conditions. Predominantly, the ASC autonomously manages navigation and directs the operation of propulsion and engine systems through an in-depth analysis of sensor data. However, it retains the capability to seamlessly transition control to remote human operators when unforeseen circumstances arise.

Autonomous Engine Monitoring and Control System (AEMCS)
The AEMCS is a key subsystem within the autonomous ship controller that is responsible for robust automation and control. It could integrate additional subsystems such as ANS, to ensure dependable propulsion power and provide feedback on the running condition [16]. Significant disparities in the power systems of conventional ships versus autonomous ships revolve around several key factors, including levels of automation and control, redundancy and safety measures, energy efficiency, and the integration of advanced sensor technologies [33]. Within this context, the AEMCS shall facilitate autonomous ships in maintaining uninterrupted propulsion and power supply, especially when adhering to voyage plans and executing collision avoidance manoeuvres.

Anchoring and Mooring System (AMS)
The AMS is a specialised sub-module within the autonomous ship controller. The goal is to guarantee the ship's safe arrival and departure at the dock, or anchoring and weighing anchor at designated anchorages, with effective securing

at the predetermined position [16]. Both the anchoring and mooring operations align with the signals and data detected and received on a real-time basis. AMS conducts continuous real-time assessments of the ship's positioning and conditions to determine the suitability of anchoring and mooring manoeuvres [16]. It may also on sensor data, environmental factors and navigational inputs to assist in making decisions.

Stability and Integrity System (SIS)
Since 2012, the emphasis on stability has remained steadfast in light of the heightened level of automation and collisions, groundings, and the subsequent water ingress leading to capsizing or sinking have consistently emerged as significant risk factors for ships [34]. The SIS, as a specialized subsystem within the autonomous ship controller responsible for providing ships' officers with clear and concise information regarding the ship's watertight subdivision together with the integrity of related equipment, is pivotal in proactively averting catastrophic accidents [35].

Cargo Handling System (CHS)
The CHS is an integral module within the autonomous ship controller. It is envisioned to task with overseeing essential cargo parameters such as real-time information on the status of cargo by means of sensors, and adeptly manage the loading and unloading sequences to ensure smooth operations [15]. It may involve interface with the ship's communication system to replay cargo operations and updates to the SCC as it provides visibility to shoreside operators. CHS operates seamlessly within the ASC, interacting with other subsystems like navigation, stability, and power management to ensure cargo operations align with overall ship control and decision-making.

3.4   Autonomous Navigation System (ANS)

An ANS refers to the integrated hardware and software responsible for operating a ship without constant human control or supervision. It utilises various sensors, processors, algorithms and actuation capabilities to sense the environment, analyse navigational complexities, plot collision-free routes, and manoeuvre the vessel accordingly. A more detailed hierarchical architecture of an autonomous cargo ship may include additional systems such as Positioning, Navigation and Timing System, Lights System and Dynamic Positioning System [36]. However, this study aims at a concise system structure and focuses mainly on the most relevant functionalities.

Navigation and Situational Awareness System (NSAS)
The NSAS is a specialised subsystem within the broader ANS responsible for localisation and comprehensive understanding of the operating environment. It integrates fusing data from navigational sensors such as RADARs, cameras, AIS receivers, GNSS receivers and LiDARs to construct a robust internal representation of the contextual factors surrounding the autonomous vessel [15, 16, 37]. Through sensor fusion and analytics, it detects, identifies, tracks and predicts

the behaviour of maritime entities and anomalies even in degraded visibility or adverse weather [38]. It serves as a critical input to other planning and decision-making subsystems, including collision avoidance, route optimisation, and SCC.

Route and Speed Optimization and Planning System (RSOPS)

The RSOPS, as a sub-system, refers to the algorithms and software responsible for charting the optimal navigational path and speed profile for an autonomous vessel to safely, adaptively and efficiently reach its destination. It processes inputs like the voyage plan, real-time environmental data, maritime traffic density, and control actions from the controller to generate multi-dimensional trajectory optimization objectives such as lowest fuel consumption, maximum operational efficiency and safety, and shortest arrival time [39]. This course is continuously revised at a regular interval with the most current obstacle information, prompting the motion planning module to revaluate the optimal path on each update [40]. Periodic re-planning ensures that obstacle data is refreshed to accommodate unforeseen alterations. It executes the trajectory in conjunction with other autonomous navigation subsystems, such as the collision avoidance system, to assess collision risks and securely guide the vessel [36].

Collision Avoidance System (CAS)

The CAS is a critical subsystem in the ANS that is responsible for detecting obstacles and planning collision-free manoeuvres in dynamic maritime environments. CAS operates within the framework of predefined Closest Point of Approach (CPA) and Time to Closest Point of Approach (TCPA) limits, adhering to the principles of COLREGs to determine the most appropriate avoidance strategy [15, 36]. In situations where potential collision risks arise, the CAS activates necessary measures, which may involve altering the vessel's course or adjusting its speed to proactively prevent accidents. It is also subject to human supervision from a SCC when it lacks a viable solution or operators within SCC disagree with the proposed solution [41].

Weather Monitoring and Interpretation System (WMIS)

Weather conditions have significantly impacted sea transportation and all maritime affairs, emphasizing the necessity of a WMIS in the context of crewless operation onboard [42]. The fundamental mission of WMIS is to monitor and interpret dynamic atmospheric and oceanographic conditions, ensuring the autonomous ship's responsiveness to ever-changing weather phenomena and its potential impact on ship operations. The WMIS aggregates real-time data from onboard sensors and equipment like anemometers and NAVTEX [36]. Weather analytics used to derive actionable insights such as detecting severe storms, are integrated with route planning, situational awareness, and collision avoidance functionalities to initiate appropriate navigational adaptations to avoid hazards or dangerous conditions.

4   Major Cyber Risks and Potential Countermeasures

Shipboard OT systems rely heavily on interconnected sensors, networks, and remote monitoring infrastructure. While this integrated systems-of-systems facilitate unmanned operations aboard autonomous ships, it significantly amplifies the vulnerability to cyber threats compared to conventional ships. The proliferation of cyber access points, coupled with low cyber hygiene and/or awareness, render essential OT systems susceptible to potential exploitation by malicious actors. The numerous entry points provide adversaries with avenues to infiltrate critical operational systems essential for ensuring safe navigation, thereby potentially causing threats to the ship and her crew. The severity of potential consequences underscores the crucial need for robust and comprehensive cybersecurity measures specifically tailored for autonomous ships. The identified potential cyber security risks and mitigations from the literature are consolidated in Table 3, drawing upon our prior research endeavors, which are currently in preparation for publication. These measures encompass a spectrum of strategies and across organisational levels, from network segmentation, vigilant monitoring, stringent access controls, and robust encryption to risk-informed policies and crew training. It is essential to emphasise the integration of cybersecurity measures at every layer of the OT infrastructure and associated workflows. Without such concerted efforts, autonomous ships remain at significant risk of intrusions and manipulations.

5   Cyber Risk Assessment

Having presented a list of attack vectors for the OT sub-systems, it is now imperative to scrutinise and classify these vectors to a cyber risk assessment. This section is dedicated to highlight the cyber risk assessment framework adopted for the identification and calculations of cyber risks associated with fundamental systems of an autonomous ship.

5.1   Methodology

There are many risk assessment frameworks used in the industry. Some of the popular and commonly used ones are risk-matrix based approach, Fault Tree Analysis (FTA), Process Hazard Analysis (PHA), Hazard Identification (HAZID), Hazard Analysis and Critical Control Points (HACCP), Failure Modes and Effects Analysis (FMEA), Failure Modes, Effects, and Criticality Analysis (FMECA). Most of these frameworks require expert opinions and judgments, therefore may contain some inherent biases. Improved and relatively less dependent on expert feedback and involvements are FMECA-ATT&CK framework and FMECA-ATT&CK-ATLAS(or "FAA" in short) framework [43–45]. For the identification and calculations of risks associated with OT sub-systems of an autonomous ship, we opted for FAA framework due to its simplicity and broad coverage of cyber threats not just for OT and IT systems but also for AI/ML systems. The FMECA, a widely embraced industry standard for risk analysis in sectors such as aerospace, automotive, and manufacturing, has paved the way for its successor, the FAA framework [46]. The FAA framework, building upon the established reputation and familiarity of its predecessor, appears poised to

Table 3. Cyber risks & Protections in Different Segments of Envisaged Future ships

OT System	Sub-system	Risks/Threat Scenarios/Vulnerabilities	Mitigation
SCC	N.A	Unauthorised access and intrusions; Insider threats; Social engineering; Data tampering and modification; Communication vulnerabilities; Supply chain attacks; Code & Malware injection;	Alarm systems; Tamper-resistant mechanisms; Multi-factor authentication; Physical protection; Regular training and monitoring Redundancy in certain aspects; Network segmentation strategy; Software patch installation;
Communication System (SATCOM /VHF/WiFi/4G /5G)	N.A	Data modification and corruption; VSAT software vulnerabilities; Eavesdropping; Hijacking; Spoofing; Jamming; Denial of Service (DoS);	Intrusion Detection System (IDS); Multiple frequency bands; Anti-jamming technology; Signal filtering; Security patch; Encryption algorithms; Integrity check on data; Redundancy mechanism; Incident response plan;
ASC	SIS	Data tampering; DoS attacks	Cross-checking diverse sensors; Encryption of transmitted data Sensor data validation
	AEMCS	DoS attacks; Outdated software; Unauthorised access and intrusions;	Specialised DoS migation services; Strict patch management; Regular vulnerability assessments; Principle of least privilege;
	AMS	Malware infections; Spoofed sensor data; Communication disruption	Antivirus software; Backup Equipment Suitable bandwidth Cryptographic techniques; Secure protocols; Synchronized timestamp;
	CHS	Unauthorised access and intrusions; Insider threats	Authentication scheme; IDS deployment ; Timeout policy; Principle of least privilege; Log activity monitoring
ANS	RSOPS	Algorithm undermined; False feedback; DoS attacks; Communication interception	Periodic audits; Data validation; Secure key management; Anomaly detection
	NSAS	GNSS spoofing; AIS spoofing; Sensor manipulation; Communication disruption Dos attacks Sensing equipment-related attacks	Real-time monitoring; Anti-jamming antennas; Verification of GNSS signals; Redundant and diverse sensors
	CAS	False data injection; Sensor manipulation; DoS attacks; Communication interception	Firewalls deployment; Strict access controls; Continuous integrity checks; Network traffic monitoring
	WMIS	Sensor jamming and spoofing; DoS attacks; Algorithm undermined	Secure code practices; Redundant and diverse sensors

inherit these advantages. Nevertheless, it is crucial to acknowledge that each risk assessment framework possesses its unique strengths and weaknesses. In our study, the selection of the FAA framework as the preferred choice is grounded in its alignment with the specific requirements and characteristics of the system under analysis. It would be particularly well-suited within the framework of autonomous ships, given its extensive utilisation of AI/ML. Furthermore, the choice of the FAA framework over alternative risk assessment methodologies is based on its strengths in quantitative analysis, structured methodology, and systematic decomposition of systems [47]. This selection is driven by the framework's ability to provide a more detailed and numerical understanding of risks, its organized approach that enhances repeatability, and its systematic breakdown of complex systems for a thorough examination. The main steps of FAA framework are depicted in Fig. 3. Please consult our joint efforts on the methodology for cyber risk assessment for more details [43].

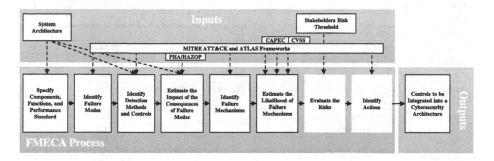

Fig. 3. Overview of the Proposed FMECA-based Approach [43]

Shore Control Centre is beyond the scope of this study's risk analysis. However, SCC plays a pivotal role in managing and controlling the operations of autonomous ships and they are central hubs for data management and communication. Such centralisation makes it attractive targets for cyberthreats seeking to exploit. Given these factors, this study assumes SCC to be categorised as high risk in the context of cybersecurity assessment for autonomous ship systems. The rest of the systems represent the major functional divisions of a typical autonomous ship, each responsible for a specific aspect of its operation. But the complexity doesn't stop there. Each of these systems is further subdivided into subsystems, each with its unique purpose and responsibilities. For instance, the ASC consists of four distinct subsystems: SIS, CHS, AMS, and AEMCS. These subsystems can further be subdivided into sub-subsystems. The AMS can have an AI Server, PLCs and a network switch. So, the risks are calculated for these sub-subsystems, which are at the lowest level in the hierarchical structure and summed up to get the risk value associated with AMS.

Table 4. Classifying system into different risk levels

Components	Number of Risks		
	Low	Medium	High
Navigation Situation Awareness System	427	32	2
Ballast Water Management System	33	10	1
Cranes	13	3	0
Autonomous Engine Monitoring and Control System - AI Server	460	1	0
Autonomous Engine Monitoring and Control System - PLCs	52	1	0
Engine	15	1	0
RADAR	604	0	0
Dynamic Positioning Controller	601	0	0
Cargo Handling System - AI Server	461	0	0
Stability and Integrity System - AI Server	460	0	0
Anchoring and Mooring System - AI Server	456	0	0
Route and Speed Optimization Planning System	454	0	0
Automatic Identification System	414	0	0
Main Data Historian	388	0	0
Satellite Router	123	0	0
VHF	123	0	0
Broadband Router	103	0	0
Stability and integrity System - Network Switch	83	0	0
Cargo Handling System - Network Switch	83	0	0
Anchoring and Mooring System - Network Switch	83	0	0
Autonomous Engine Monitoring and Control System - Network Switch	83	0	0
Perception System - Network Switch	83	0	0
Cargo Handling System - PLCs	53	0	0
Anchoring and Mooring System - PLCs	53	0	0
GNSS	27	0	0
Thrusters	16	0	0
PTZ Cameras	11	0	0
LiDAR	7	0	0
Sensor Fusion	7	0	0
Others	i=7	0	0

After applying the FAA framework to the entire autonomous ship, more than 5,000 risk values for autonomous ship systems were obtained. The risks were then classified as 'Low,' 'Medium,' and 'High,' and the number of risks against each component (subsystem) of the ship was counted. A glimpse of our risk analysis is tabulated in Table 4. Using the FAA framework, we found that the NSAS and Ballast Water Management System exhibit the highest levels of risk exposure compared to the other systems. Evidently, some systems (e.g., Cranes) have a minor number of low, medium and high risks compared to critical systems (e.g., RADAR) have large number of low risk but they have not medium and high risks associated with them. Therefore, components with medium and high-risk ratings are categorised as high-risk. Additionally, we have established a threshold of 600 as the point at which a high number of low-risk components are also classified as high risk. In this particular situation, RADAR and the dynamic positioning controller are exceptions and are placed in the high-risk category.

5.2   Risk Evaluation

To better manage complex systems such as interconnected components, a structured approach is crucial. Hierarchical management offers a clear and systematic framework for dealing with such intricacies. At its core, hierarchical management involves breaking down a complex system into a series of manageable subsystems and organising them in a hierarchical structure. Table 4 gives an overview of the OT systems of an autonomous ship that are considered in this study, and each is given a "tier colour", where red is associated with Tier T1 (highest urgency), yellow (Tier T2; medium urgency) and green (Tier T3; lowest urgency).

Vulnerabilities within high-risk systems present opportune targets for potential attackers, thereby posing a significant risk of financial loss to the organisation and disruption of ship operations. Medium-risk systems have relatively lower susceptibility to attacks; nevertheless, their compromise could lead to network unavailability and resource disruption. Systems categorised as low risk face diminished probabilities of being targeted compared to the other two groups. However, any compromise within these systems, despite the reduced risk, can still jeopardise the safety of the ship, its crew, and cargo.

5.3   Discussion of Features

In our earlier research, we incorporated viewpoints from conventional ship operations to discern the cybersecurity risks linked with OT systems [48]. This investigation has changed the target to be autonomous ships and further delivers a consolidation of OT system knowledge to advance MASS developments through disparate streams of research, projects, and classification documentation. Both studies prescribe comprehensive cybersecurity controls to mitigate associated threats and vulnerabilities per system. The differing factor lies in the methodology employed for the risk assessment. The former study condenses complex risk factors into a matrix which can lead to an oversimplified view of multidimensional risks. Nuances may get lost in generalisation and wide rating bands may undermine precise risk analysis. However, the method applied in this study - FAA works in top-down fashion and it keeps decomposing a big system into subsystems until fundamental building blocks are reached. At the granular level, it calculates the risk associated with each fundamental building block and then sum up all the risks associated with all the subsystem, for a system which is hierarchically at higher level of structure. Likelihood, impact and detectability of an attack are included in the risk equation and all the failure modes and mechanisms are deduced from MITRE ATT&CK and MITRE ATLAS tactics and techniques. Compared to risk matrices which can potentially introduce human bias, MITRE could have deeper expertise in risk management, responding to real-world cyber threats effectively.

6   Conclusion

The integration of Operational Technology (OT) systems in autonomous ships is a pivotal advancement that brings transformative potential to the maritime industry. However, this advancement is not without its challenges, and cybersecurity emerges as a critical concern. The overview of cyber risks underscores the vulnerability of interconnected OT systems to various malicious activities, including Denial-of-Service (DoS) attacks, spoofing, malware infiltration, and sensor manipulation. These risks, if realized, can jeopardize vessel safety, operational efficiency, and environmental integrity. To mitigate these threats effectively, a multi-faceted approach is essential. Implementing robust cybersecurity measures, such as network segmentation, access controls, encryption, and real-time monitoring, can fortify the autonomous ship's digital infrastructure against potential intrusions. A comprehensive understanding and systematic approach toward addressing cyber risks in autonomous ships are imperative for ensuring the successful, secure, and widespread adoption of this groundbreaking maritime technology.

Acknowledgments. First and foremost, the team wish to extend deepest thanks to Philip Kwa for his invaluable insights throughout the research process. The team are equally indebted to Dr Ahmed Amro from NTNU, whose expertise and collaborative efforts were fundamental in the risk assessment methodology. The team are also grateful to Dr Kimberly Tam from University of Plymouth, Dr Meriam Chaal and Dr Victor Bolbot both from Aalto University for their valuable discussions that enriched this research.

Disclosure of Interests. The authors declare no conflict of interest. This research is supported by the National Research foundation, Singapore (NRF), Maritime and Port Authority of Singapore (MPA) and Singapore Maritime Institute (SMI) under its Maritime transportation Programme (Project No. SMI-2022-MTP-04). Any opinions, finds and conclusions or recommendations expressed in this material are those of the author(s) and do not reflect the views of NRF, MPA and SMI.

References

1. Tijan, E., Jović, M., Aksentijević, S., Pucihar, A.: Digital transformation in the maritime transport sector. Technol. Forecast. Soc. Chang. **170**, 120879 (2021)
2. Annex 2 framework for the regulatory scoping exercise for the use of maritime autonomous surface ships (mass). https://maiif.org/wp-content/uploads/2019/06/MSC-100_20-Annex-20-1.pdf. Accessed 06 Nov 2023
3. Ahvenjärvi, S.: The human element and autonomous ships. TransNav: Int. J. Mar. Navig. Saf. Sea Transp. **10**(3), 517–521 (2016)
4. Mallam, S.C., Nazir, S., Sharma, A.: The human element in future maritime operations-perceived impact of autonomous shipping. Ergonomics **63**(3), 334–345 (2020)
5. Kavallieratos, G., Spathoulas, G., Katsikas, S.: Cyber risk propagation and optimal selection of cybersecurity controls for complex cyberphysical systems. Sensors **21**(5), 1691 (2021)
6. Bolbot, V., Theotokatos, G., Boulougouris, E., Vassalos, D.: Safety related cyber-attacks identification and assessment for autonomous inland ships. In: International Seminar on Safety and Security of Autonomous Vessels (ISSAV) (2019)

7. Yoo, J., Jo, Y.: Formulating cybersecurity requirements for autonomous ships using the square methodology. Sensors **23**(11), 5033 (2023)
8. Cho, S., Orye, E., Visky, G., Prates, V.: Cybersecurity considerations in autonomous ships. NATO Cooperative Cyber Defence Centre of Excellence: Tallinn, Estonia (2022)
9. Guidance for autonomous ships. http://krs.westus.cloudapp.azure.com/Files/KRRules/KRRules2022/data/data_other/ENGLISH/gc28e000.pdf. Accessed 06 Nov 2023
10. Mass uk industry conduct principles and code of practice 2022 (v6). https://www.maritimeuk.org/priorities/innovation/maritime-uk-autonomous-systems-regulatory-working-group/mass-uk-industry-conduct-principles-and-code-practice-2022-v6/. Accessed 06 Nov 2023
11. Autonomous and remote control functions. https://safety4sea.com/wp-content/uploads/2021/07/ABS-Autonomous-and-Remote-Control-Functions-2021_07.pdf. Accessed 06 Nov 2023
12. Guidelines on remotely operated vessels and autonomous surface vessels. http://www.irclass.org/media/5777/asv-guidelines_dec-2021_new.pdf. Accessed 06 Nov 2023
13. Guidelines for automated/autonomous operation on ships (ver.1.0). https://maritimecyprus.com/wp-content/uploads/2020/01/classnk-autonomous.pdf. Accessed 06 Nov 2023
14. Regulations for classification of maritime autonomous and remotely controlled surface ships (mass). https://lk.rs-class.org/regbook/getDocument2?type=rules3&d=7CA5D1FA-BD6A-4DB0-A826-BC26E4219555&f. Accessed 06 Nov 2023
15. Guidelines for autonomous shipping. https://erules.veristar.com/dy/data/bv/pdf/641-NI_2019-10.pdf. Accessed 06 Nov 2023
16. Guidelines for autonomous cargo ships. https://www.ccs.org.cn/ccswzen/articleDetail?id=201910000000003792. Accessed 06 Nov 2023
17. Autonomous and remotely-operated ships. https://www.dnv.com/maritime/publications/remote-controlled-autonomous-ships-paper-download.html. Accessed 06 Nov 2023
18. Cyber-enabled ships: Shipright procedure - autonomous ships. https://issuu.com/lr_marine/docs/lr_cyber-enabled_ships_shipright_pr. Accessed 06 Nov 2023
19. Final report summary-munin (maritime unmanned navigation through intelligence in networks). https://www.semanticscholar.org/paper/Final-Report-Summary-MUNIN-%28-Maritime-Unmanned-in-%29-Munin-Grant/5aebf0ce4f2da30bc665f4745b069a8f6b6729b1. Accessed 06 Nov 2023
20. The mayflower autonomous ship project. https://mas400.com. Accessed 06 Nov 2023
21. The nippon foundation meguri2040 fully autonomous ship program. https://www.nippon-foundation.or.jp/en/news/articles/2022/20220111-67000.html. Accessed 06 Nov 2023
22. Partnered with st engineering on sea trials of autonomous vessel technology on our harbour tug. https://posh.com.sg/partnered-with-st-engineering-on-sea-trials-of-autonomous-vessel-technology-on-our-harbour-tug-posh-harvest/. Accessed 06 Nov 2023
23. Vessel review | zhi fei - chinese-built 300teu boxship boasts autonomous navigation features. https://www.bairdmaritime.com/ship-world/boxship-world/vessel-review-zhi-fei-chinese-built-300teu-boxship-boasts-autonomous-navigation-features/. Accessed 06 Nov 2023

24. Samsung heavy industries succeeds autonomous vessel navigation. https://www.hellenicshippingnews.com/samsung-heavy-industries-succeeds-autonomous-vessel-navigation/. Accessed 06 Nov 2023

25. Porathe, T., Prison, J., Man, Y.: Situation awareness in remote control centres for unmanned ships. In: Proceedings of Human Factors in Ship Design & Operation, 26–27 February 2014, London, UK, p. 93 (2014)

26. Kim, M., Joung, T.H., Jeong, B., Park, H.S.: Autonomous shipping and its impact on regulations, technologies, and industries. J. Int. Marit. Saf. Environ. Aff. Shipp. 4(2), 17–25 (2020)

27. Veitch, E., Alsos, O.A.: A systematic review of human-AI interaction in autonomous ship systems. Saf. Sci. **152**, 105778 (2022)

28. Lynch, K.M., Banks, V.A., Roberts, A.P., Radcliffe, S., Plant, K.L.: What factors may influence decision-making in the operation of maritime autonomous surface ships? A systematic review. Theor. Issues Ergon. Sci. 1–36 (2022)

29. Höyhtyä, M., Martio, J.: Integrated satellite-terrestrial connectivity for autonomous ships: survey and future research directions. Remote Sens. **12**(15), 2507 (2020)

30. Xu, Y.: Quality of service provisions for maritime communications based on cellular networks. IEEE Access **5**, 23881–23890 (2017)

31. Höyhtyä, M., Huusko, J., Kiviranta, M., Solberg, K., Rokka, J.: Connectivity for autonomous ships: Architecture, use cases, and research challenges. In: 2017 International Conference on Information and Communication Technology Convergence (ICTC), pp. 345–350. IEEE (2017)

32. Alqurashi, F.S., Trichili, A., Saeed, N., Ooi, B.S., Alouini, M.S.: Maritime communications: a survey on enabling technologies, opportunities, and challenges. IEEE Internet Things J. (2022)

33. Jovanović, I., Perčić, M., Vladimir, N.: Identifying differences between power system of conventional and autonomous ship with respect to their safety assessment. In: 2023 18th Conference on Electrical Machines, Drives and Power Systems (ELMA), pp. 1–5. IEEE (2023)

34. King, T., Van Welter, C., Svensen, T.E.: Stability barrier management for large passenger ships. Ocean Eng. **125**, 342–348 (2016)

35. Ship design and stability. https://www.imo.org/en/OurWork/Safety/Pages/ShipDesignAndStability-default.aspx. Accessed 06 Nov 2023

36. Chaal, M., Banda, O.A.V., Glomsrud, J.A., Basnet, S., Hirdaris, S., Kujala, P.: A framework to model the STPA hierarchical control structure of an autonomous ship. Saf. Sci. **132**, 104939 (2020)

37. Thombre, S., et al.: Sensors and AI techniques for situational awareness in autonomous ships: a review. IEEE Trans. Intell. Transp. Syst. **23**(1), 64–83 (2020)

38. Wang, J., Xiao, Y., Li, T., Chen, C.P.: A survey of technologies for unmanned merchant ships. IEEE Access **8**, 224461–224486 (2020)

39. Ohn, S.W., Namgung, H.: Requirements for optimal local route planning of autonomous ships. J. Mar. Sci. Eng. **11**(1), 17 (2022)

40. Longo, G., Martelli, M., Russo, E., Zaccone, R., et al.: Collision-avoidance capabilities reduction after a cyber-attack to the navigation sensors. In: Conference Proceedings of the 2022 International Ship Control Systems Symposium (2022)

41. Ramos, M.A., Utne, I.B., Mosleh, A.: Collision avoidance on maritime autonomous surface ships: operators' tasks and human failure events. Saf. Sci. **116**, 33–44 (2019)

42. Wu, Y., Pelot, R.P., Hilliard, C.: The influence of weather conditions on the relative incident rate of fishing vessels. Risk Anal. Int. J. **29**(7), 985–999 (2009)

43. Amro, A., Gkioulos, V., Katsikas, S.: Assessing cyber risk in cyber-physical systems using the ATT&CK framework. ACM Trans. Priv. Secur. **26**(2), 1–33 (2023)
44. Amro, A., Gkioulos, V.: Cyber risk management for autonomous passenger ships using threat-informed defense-in-depth. Int. J. Inf. Secur. **22**(1), 249–288 (2023)
45. Yousaf, A., Amro, A., Kwa, P., Li, M., Zhou, J.: Cyber risk assessment of cyber-enabled autonomous cargo vessel. In submission
46. Jun, L., Huibin, X.: Reliability analysis of aircraft equipment based on FMECA method. Phys. Procedia **25**, 1816–1822 (2012). International Conference on Solid State Devices and Materials Science, April 1-2, 2012, Macao
47. Sulaman, S.M., Armin, B., Michael, F., Martin, H.: Comparison of the FMEA and STPA safety analysis methods-a case study. Softw. Qual. J. **27**, 349–387 (2019)
48. Rajaram, P., Goh, M., Zhou, J.: Guidelines for cyber risk management in shipboard operational technology systems. J. Phys. Conf. Ser. **2311**, 012002. IOP Publishing (2022)

Identity-Based Cluster Authentication and Key Exchange (ID-CAKE) Message Broadcasting and Batch Verification in VANETs

Apurva K. Vangujar[✉][iD], Alia Umrani[iD], and Paolo Palmieri[iD]

University College Cork, Cork, Ireland
{a.vangujar,a.umrani,p.palmieri}@cs.ucc.ie

Abstract. Vehicle Ad Hoc Networks (VANETs) play a pivotal role in intelligent transportation systems, offering dynamic communication between vehicles, road side units, and the internet. Given the open-access nature of VANETs and the associated threats, such as impersonation and privacy violations, ensuring the security of these communications is of utmost importance. This paper presents the Identity-based Cluster Authentication and Key Exchange (ID-CAKE) scheme, a new approach to address security challenges in VANETs. The ID-CAKE scheme integrates the Cluster Consensus Identity-based Identification (CCIBI) with Zero-Knowledge (ZK) proof and the Identity-based Multi-receiver Key Exchange Mechanism (ID-mKEM) signature scheme. This integration provides robust *authorization* via CCIBI, while the ID-mKEM signature ensures message *integrity*, and guarantees both *non-repudiation* and *unforgeability* through mKEM for message broadcasting. The scheme employs a novel three-party ZK proof for batch verification using mKEM, which significantly reduces computational burdens. Our scheme also ensures *anonymity* and *unlinkability* by introducing pseudo-identities to all users in the cluster. The rigorous security proof provided confirms the resilience of the ID-CAKE scheme against potential attacks, adhering to the different scenarios, against the hardness of the elliptic curve computational diffie-hellman under the random oracle model. The ID-CAKE scheme establishes a robust security framework for VANETs, and its introduction highlights potential pathways for future exploration in the realm of VANET security.

Keywords: Identity-based Identification · Key Exchange · Batch Verification · Zero-Knowledge · VANETs · Authentication Scheme · Signature Scheme

1 Introduction

Vehicle Ad Hoc Networks (VANETs), a key application of intelligent transportation systems, comprise vehicles, Road Side Units (RSUs), and internet servers. They facilitate Vehicle-to-Vehicle (V2V) and Vehicle-to-Infrastructure (V2I) communication,

Apurva K Vangujar and Alia Umrani are supported by PhD scholarships funded by the Science Foundation Ireland Centre under Grant number 18/CRT/6222. This research has also been supported by Science Foundation Ireland under Grant number 13/RC/2077_P2.

enhancing road safety through secure message broadcasting [24]. Thousands of people are injured and killed in traffic accidents every year all around the world, causing around 1.35 million deaths and currently ranking as the eighth leading cause of deaths. If no substantial measures are taken, road accidents are projected to become the seventh leading cause of death by 2030 [12]. Vehicles continuously communicate with each other using dedicated short-range communication protocols to update nearby vehicles about road conditions, traffic congestion, location and lane information, etc. Exchanging such information can improve traffic conditions, avoid collisions, and ensure safety. For example, in the case of traffic congestion, a vehicle broadcasts a message to the other vehicles to warn them about the traffic conditions and suggest they change routes.

However, due to the open-access environment, such communication is vulnerable to several attacks, such as impersonation and privacy violations [6,23]. For example, if a malicious vehicle appears on the network, it can generate a false emergency message to mislead other vehicles. Maintaining security in VANETs requires understanding potential attacks, which can range from impersonation, Sybil, modification, identity (ID) disclosure, location tracking, and replay to denial of service and bogus information attacks [5].

To address these concerns, VANETs largely depend on cryptographic schemes capable of identifying illegitimate nodes and fake messages. For example, an ID-based signature scheme provides message *integrity*, while the Key Exchange Mechanism (KEM) generates a symmetric key that ensures *non-repudiation*. Moreover, Zero-Knowledge (ZK) provides *authorization*, Pseudo-Identity (PID) techniques provide *anonymity* and *unlinkability*. In this paper, we present a novel ID-based authentication scheme designed for VANETs in cluster settings, where messages are broadcasted among vehicles. Our approach uses the ID-based Identification (IBI) scheme and Multi-receiver Key Exchange Mechanisms (mKEM) to ensure *authorization, non-repudiation*, and message *integrity*. To provide *anonymity*, each cluster member is assigned a PID. Moreover, we introduce a three-party ZK proof that ensures *authorization* and Batch Verification (BV). By combining IBI, mKEM, and ZK proof, we offer a comprehensive anonymous ID-based authentication and BV solution, well-suited for clustered VANET environments. This approach addresses the unique challenges posed by VANETs and provides an efficient and secure solution.

1.1   Related Work

ID-Based Authentication Schemes. Identity-based Cryptography (IBC), introduced by Shamir *et al.* [14], has since inspired various encryption and signature schemes and provides a certificate-free authentication framework crucial for VANETs, reducing overhead and enhancing efficiency and security. Sun *et al.* [17] proposed an IBC system using PID, ensuring vehicle privacy and traceability in VANETs. This method reduces storage and message overhead compared to Elliptic Curve (EC) cryptography-based Public Key Infrastructure (PKI) schemes. However, its scalability in dynamic environments needs further exploration and improvement. Bharadiya *et al.* [1] introduced an authentication with multiple levels of anonymity protocol that offers multi-level anonymity using an ID-based signature scheme along with PID and reduces message overhead compared to traditional PKI schemes. Kalmykov *et al.* [8] proposed ZK authentication protocol, reduced modular multiplicative operations time to minimize the disclosures of user authentication parameters while accessing the network. It reduces the authentication time and maximises the security level. Adopting IBC, we enhance authentication in Cluster Consensus IBI (CCIBI) scenarios to ensure *authorization* via ZK proof. Our method prioritises forming distinct clusters to boost security and efficiency in VANETs.

Key Exchange Schemes. Kim *et al.* [9] presented a scheme using group signatures for mutual identification and key exchange, with vehicles employing private keys for hashing and the group manager signing messages. This facilitates secure communication through ephemeral Diffie-Hellman (DH) exchanges. Palani *et al.* [13] proposed a V2V key exchange protocol that enables vehicles to verify the time-bounded validity of certificates and *integrity* of keys. It also performs key exchange in the Random Oracle (RO) model and proves it is secure using verification on the Tamarin tool. S.A. Chaudhary in [3] proposes a secure message exchange protocol for internet of vehicles communication with RSUs via wireless channels. The scheme uses symmetric encryption and hash functions to achieve mutual authentication, session key establishment, and message *integrity*. Umrani *et al.* [20] introduced an anonymous multi-receiver signcryption scheme using mKEM and data encapsulation mechanisms, applicable in VANETs. It provides secure communication with authentication, confidentiality, and *anonymity* based on EC Discrete Logarithm (ECDL) and EC Computational DH (ECCDH) assumptions, while ensuring *unlinkability*, *non-repudiation*, and forward secrecy. We propose an identity-based Cluster Authentication and Key Exchange (ID-CAKE) scheme where a KEM produces a symmetric key and a message signature guaranteeing both *non-repudiation, integrity*, and *unforgeability* among cluster vehicles and seamlessly integrates with ZK, adding an innovative touch to our approach. The same authors also presented a separate scheme for multi-receiver certificateless signcryption (MCLS) [19].

Batch Verification. The ID-based BV by Tzeng *et al.* [18] scheme ensures anonymous authentication, message *integrity*, privacy, and traceability with a low computational cost due to BV, requiring only a few Bilinear Pairing (BP) and point multiplication computations. However, this scheme involves a complex process of anonymous ID generation as well as message signing and verification. Zhang *et al.* [22] proposed an ID-based BV technique that enhances message verification efficiency by processing a large number of messages. It employs IBC to minimise communication overhead and ensure privacy with unique PIDs. However, it does not handle security attacks. In the ID-CAKE scheme, we use the ID-based BV technique for three parties in a cluster setting, which reduces the complexity drastically and guarantees *anonymity* and *unlinkability* via PID based algorithm.

1.2   Contribution

In this study, we construct the ID-CAKE scheme, a groundbreaking solution for VANET communications. At its core, ID-CAKE optimises the strength of the CCIBI scheme with ZK proof, based on the Boneh-Lynn-Shacham (BLS) [2] scheme, and thoughtfully incorporates the ID-mKEM signature scheme. This unique amalgamation offers not only a secure environment but also a paradigm shift in VANETs through its cluster-based approach. Further enhancing the privacy landscape of VANETs, we introduce a cluster-based PID generation algorithm. This algorithm ensures ID privacy for each vehicle, striking a delicate balance between *anonymity* and *unlinkability*. Alongside, our use of mKEM allows senders to generate cluster-based signatures, setting a new gold standard in message *integrity*, *unforgeability*, and *non-repudiation*. With BV using ZK proofs ensuring *authorization*, ID-CAKE dramatically reduces computational costs. Furthermore, its security robustness under the RO model with the ECCDH assumption shows its reliability and practicality in real-world VANET scenarios.

1.3 Organization

The paper is structured as follows: Sect. 2 introduces the notations and preliminaries used in the rest of the paper. Section 3 gives the construction of building blocks, which are used in the ID-CAKE scheme. Section 4 discusses the requirements, participants, system description, ID-CAKE definition, and security models. Section 5 provides a detailed construction of a novel ID-CAKE scheme. Section 6 gives the proof under the RO model for our ID-CAKE scheme, and in Sect. 7, we discuss the efficiency of this proposed scheme. Finally, Sect. 8 points out the conclusion, followed by the future work at last.

2 Preliminaries

2.1 Elliptic Curve Computational Diffie-Hellman

Definition 1. *The security assumption of ECCDH is according to [4]. The ECCDH assumption holds that given* $(P, aP, bP) \in \mathbb{G}$ *where* $a, b \in \mathbb{Z}_q^*$, *it is computationally infeasible for any Probabilistic Polynomial-Time (PPT) algorithm to compute* abP.

2.2 IBI Scheme

Definition 2. *The definition of the IBI scheme given by Kurosawa and Heng [10] has three PPT algorithms. IBI =* (KeyGen, Extract, Verification) *is defined as follows:*

1. KeyGen. *On input* 1^λ, *it outputs the public parameter* PP *and the master secret key* msk.
2. Extract. *It takes input as* (msk, ID) *and returns the private key* d.
3. Verification. *In this phase, the prover* P *and the verifier* V *communicate with each other.* P *takes input as* (PP, ID, d), *whereas* V *takes input as* (PP, ID). *P and* V *communicate with each other and give output in a boolean decision 0 (rejects) or 1 (accepts). The ZK protocol acts in four steps, as follows: (i) P sends commitment* CMT *to* V. *(ii) V provides challenge* CHA *which is randomly chosen. (iii) P calculates the response* RSP *to* V *as per challenge. (iv) V verifies* (param, ID, CMT, CH, RSP) *is DH tuple.*

2.3   The Multi-receiver Key Exchange Mechanism (mKEM)

Definition 3. *The notion of mKEM was first proposed by N.P. Smart [15] and has a KEM-like construction that takes multiple receivers. The mKEM consists of four algorithms* (Setup, KeyGen, mKEM.Encaps, mKEM.Decaps) *and is given as below:*

1. Setup. *On input the security parameter* 1^λ, *it outputs* PP.
2. KeyGen. *Taking* PP *as input, it outputs each user's public key* pk *and secret key* sk.
3. mKEM.Encaps. *On input* PP *and a set of receiver public keys* pk_{r_i} *where* $1 \leq i \leq t$, *it outputs a symmetric session key* K *for each receiver and an encapsulation* C_i *of* K.
4. mKEM.Decaps. *Taking* PP, *receiver's private key* sk_{r_i}, *and* C_i *as input, it outputs* K. *The correctness of mKEM holds if* $K = $ mKEM.Decaps(PP, sk_{r_i}, C_i).

3   Building Block for ID-CAKE Scheme

3.1   Cluster Consensus Identity-Based Identification (CCIBI) Scheme

In this section, we introduce a transformation of the BLS signature scheme [2] into a BLS IBI scheme as proposed by Kurosawa and Heng's [10]. We construct the CCIBI scheme under the ECCDH assumption as the building block for the new ID-CAKE scheme. For clarity, we use cluster C_i where $1 \leq i \leq m$ and $ID_{(i,j)}$ where $1 \leq j \leq n$ to represent the generic approach.

1. KeyGen. Trusted Authority (TA) takes an input 1^λ where λ is a security parameter, choosing an elliptic curve E and a generator $P \in \mathbb{G}$ of a prime order q. $\mathbb{G}$ is the cyclic group, and $H : \{0,1\}^* \times \mathbb{G} \to \mathbb{G}$ is the hashing function. TA outputs PP $= \{\mathbb{G}, q, E, P, H\}$. TA takes the input as PP and selects a random integer $x \in \mathbb{Z}_q^*$, generating mpk $= xP$ and msk $= x$. Next, for cluster manager CM_i of C_i, TA selects a random integer $y_i \in \mathbb{Z}_q^*$ and generates cluster public key $cpk_i = y_i P$ and cluster secret key $csk_i = y_i$.
2. Join. This algorithm allows new members to securely join the cluster. Assume $ID_{(i,j)}$ where $1 \leq i \leq m$ and $1 \leq j \leq n$ wants to join C_i and TA selects a random integer $\hat{x}_{(i,j)} \in \mathbb{Z}_q^*$ and generates user public key $upk_{(i,j)} = \hat{x}_{(i,j)} P$ and user secret key $usk_{(i,j)} = \hat{x}_{(i,j)}$. The cluster setting is $C_{IBI} = (C_1, C_2, \ldots, C_i, \ldots, C_m)$ where $1 \leq i \leq m$.
3. Extract. Consider $ID_{(i,j)}$ from C_i, takes an input $(ID_{(i,j)}, mpk, usk_{(i,j)})$ and calculates $Q_{ID_{(i,j)}} = H(ID_{(i,j)})$. It outputs the user secret key $d_{(i,j)} = \hat{x}_{(i,j)} Q_{ID_{(i,j)}}$.[1]
4. Verify. This algorithm is the communication between a P as a cluster member and a V as a CM. The ZK offers BV of the cluster IDs as follows:
   (a) CMT. P and selects a random number $r_{(i,j)} \in \mathbb{Z}_q^*$ for each $1 \leq j \leq n$ and calculates $R_{(i,j)} = r_{(i,j)} P$. P sends $R_{(i,j)}$ to V.
   (b) CHA. A random challenge $c \in \mathbb{Z}_q^*$ is generated by V and passed it to P.
   (c) RES. For each $1 \leq j \leq n$, P calculates a response $U_{(i,j)} = r_{(i,j)} + cd_{(i,j)}$ and sends all $U_{(i,j)}$ to V.

---

[1] d of all the identities for each available ID can be calculated with the same technique described in the Extract algorithm of the CCIBI scheme.

(d) If the equation $U_{(i,j)}P = R_{(i,j)} + \mathsf{upk}_{(i,j)}Q_{\mathsf{ID}_{(i,j)}}c$ holds by ECCDH assumption for all j, V accepts cluster identities. If it does not hold, V rejects cluster identities.

$$U_{(i,j)}P = R_{(i,j)} + \mathsf{upk}_{(i,j)}Q_{\mathsf{ID}_{(i,j)}}c$$
$$= r_{(i,j)}P + \hat{x}_{(i,j)}PQ_{\mathsf{ID}_{(i,j)}}c$$
$$= (r_{(i,j)} + \hat{x}_{(i,j)}Q_{\mathsf{ID}_{(i,j)}}c)P$$
$$= (r_{(i,j)} + \hat{x}_{(i,j)}\mathsf{d}_{(i,j)}c)P$$
$$U_{(i,j)} = r_{(i,j)} + \hat{x}_{(i,j)}\mathsf{d}_{(i,j)}c.$$

The CCIBI scheme's four PPT algorithms contribute to the establishment of a secure ID-CAKE scheme in VANETs.

3.2 Construction of ID-MKEM

This section introduces our ID-mKEM signature scheme, based on Definition 2.3. Adopting mKEM from [20], we upgraded the scheme by transforming from signcryption to signature. ID-mKEM signature scheme has four PPT algorithms described below and has n users where $\mathsf{ID}_n = (\mathsf{ID}_s, \{\mathsf{ID}_1, \ldots, \mathsf{ID}_{r_i}, \ldots, \mathsf{ID}_{r_t}\})$ where $1 \leq i \leq t$ and $t < n$. Assume a sender with anonymous ID_s sends a message m to t receivers denoted with anonymous ID_{r_i}.

1. KeyGen. Taking security parameter λ as input, TA chooses the cyclic group $\mathbb{G}$ of large prime order q, derived from an elliptic curve E. The TA selects a generator point $P \in \mathbb{G}$ and generates four hash functions. The first hash function is $H_0 : \{0,1\}^\ell \to \mathbb{G}$, where ℓ is a positive integer; $H_1 : \{0,1\}^* \times \mathbb{G} \to \mathbb{G}$; $H_2 : \mathbb{G} \to \{0,1\}^k$, where k is the plaintext box length; and $H_3 : \{0,1\}^* \times \mathbb{G} \times \mathbb{G} \times \mathbb{G} \to \mathbb{Z}_q^*$. The TA outputs the public parameters $\mathsf{PP} = \{\mathbb{G}, q, E, P, H_0, H_1, H_2, H_3\}$. Next, it randomly selects $x \in \mathbb{Z}_q^*$ as the msk is kept secret and calculates the mpk $= xP$. Subsequently, the Register Authority (RA) selects a random $y \in \mathbb{Z}_q^*$ as its secret key $\mathsf{sk}_{\mathsf{RA}}$ and calculates the public key $\mathsf{pk}_{\mathsf{RA}} = yP$. Each user vehicle randomly chooses $\bar{x} \in \mathbb{Z}_q^*$ as the secret key of vehicle sk_v and computes the public key of vehicle $\mathsf{pk}_v = \bar{x}P$. To compute PID, each user chooses a random real $\mathsf{ID} \in \{0,1\}^\ell$ and computes $R = \hat{x}P$ where $\hat{x} \in \mathbb{Z}_q^*$ is randomly chosen. Taking $(\mathsf{ID}, \hat{x})$ as input, it computes initial $\mathsf{PID}_1 = \mathsf{ID} \oplus H_0(\hat{x}\mathsf{pk}_{\mathsf{RA}})$ and sends (PID_1, R) to RA. RA Takes (PID_1, R) as input and verifies the $\mathsf{ID} = \mathsf{PID}_1 \oplus H_0(Ry)$. If ID is valid, the RA accepts the registration request from users and assigns $\mathsf{PID} = \mathsf{ID} \oplus H_0(\hat{x}\mathsf{pk}_{\mathsf{RA}})$ to the respective user.
2. Extract. For each PID in set $\mathsf{PID}_n = (\mathsf{PID}_s, \{\mathsf{PID}_1, \ldots, \mathsf{PID}_{r_i}, \ldots, \mathsf{PID}_{r_t}\})$, the TA takes mpk as input and generates user private key $\mathsf{d} = xQ_{\mathsf{PID}}$ where $Q_{\mathsf{PID}} = H_1(\mathsf{PID}\|\mathsf{mpk})$.
3. Sign. The sender with PID_s and sk_s runs following steps to sign a message m and sends signature σ_i to receivers PID_{r_i} using mKEM-Encaps. Each sender randomly chooses $r \in \mathbb{Z}_q^*$ and computes $U = rP$. Taking pk_{r_i} and $Q_{\mathsf{PID}_{r_i}}$ as input, computes $Z_{1_i} = \mathsf{d}_sQ_{\mathsf{PID}_{r_i}}$ and $Z_{2_i} = \bar{x}_s\mathsf{pk}_{r_i}$. It then computes $\psi_i = Z_{1_i}Z_{2_i}$, $K_i = H_2(\psi_i)$,

$f_i = H_3(m, \psi_i, \mathsf{PID_s}, \mathsf{PID_{r_i}}, \mathsf{pk_s}, \mathsf{pk_{r_i}})$, and $S_i = r^{-1}(f_i + wd_s\bar{x}_s)$ where $w = x_U$ mod q, which is the x-coordinate of U. The sender sets $C_{1_i} = (f_i, S_i)$ and outputs $\sigma_i = (C_{1_i}, K_i, m)$.

4. Verify. The designated receiver with $\mathsf{PID_{r_i}}$ takes $(\mathsf{sk_{r_i}}, \mathsf{pk_s})$ as input and runs the following phases to verify the σ_i:

   Phase-1 (mKEM-Decaps). Taking $\bar{x}_{r_i}$ and d_{r_i} as input, computes $Z_{1_i} = d_{r_i}Q_{\mathsf{PID_s}}$ and $Z_{2_i} = \mathsf{pk_s}\bar{x}_{r_i}$. Then computes $\psi_i = Z_{1_i}Z_{2_i}$ and $K_i = H_2(\psi_i)$. If $K_i = \perp$, the receiver aborts; otherwise, verifies the S_i as follows:

   Phase-2 (Ver). Taking C_{1_i}, m, and $\mathsf{pk_s}$ as input, we finally compute f' where $f_i' = H_3(m', \psi_i, \mathsf{PID_s}, \mathsf{PID_{r_i}}, \mathsf{pk_s}, \mathsf{pk_{r_i}})$. If $f_i' = f_i$, verify S_i by checking if $U = rP$ and $w' = x_U$ mod q. If $w' = w$, the receiver will accept the m otherwise, it returns $\perp$ and aborts.

For the construction of the ID-CAKE scheme, we take the Sign and Verify algorithms from the ID-mKEM.

4   Our ID-CAKE VANETs Scheme

4.1   VANETs Participants and Requirements

The ID-CAKE scheme is structured around three key entities: TA, RA, and clusters $(C_1, C_2, \ldots, C_i, \ldots, C_m)$. Within each cluster, there is a designated sender and multiple receivers. Assume $C_i = (\text{Sender} : \mathsf{ID_{s_i}}, \{\text{Receivers} : \mathsf{ID_{r_{(i,1)}}}, \mathsf{ID_{r_{(i,2)}}}, \ldots, \mathsf{ID_{r_{(i,j)}}}, \ldots, \mathsf{ID_{r_{(i,n)}}}\})$ where $1 \leq i \leq m$ and $1 \leq j \leq n$. Moreover, our ID-CAKE scheme meets the requirements in VANETs outlined in Table 1.

- **TA**. The TA is linked to the RA via a wired channel and serves as an administrator with greater storage and computational capabilities than the RA and vehicles. It generates keys and updates system parameters in the cluster.
- **RA**. It is positioned along roadsides or parking zones and has key duties in the cluster: offering internet to vehicles, amplifying VANETs' range by relaying messages, and reporting traffic updates and malicious activities. As semi-trusted entities, they generate their private key $\mathsf{sk_{RA}}$ and public key $\mathsf{pk_{RA}}$ and handle ID-based BV using ZK proofs and PID generation.
- **Sender Vehicle**. The sender with anynomous $\mathsf{PID_{s_i}}$ of $\mathsf{ID_{s_i}}$ for $1 \leq i \leq m$ signs message m using mKEM-Encaps and sends signature $\sigma_{(i,j)}$ to cluster receivers.
- **Receiver Vehicles**. Cluster receivers get the signed m from an RA-approved $\mathsf{PID_{s_i}}$. They use mKEM-Decaps to extract m. If the shared secret key K is mismatched, they report the $\mathsf{PID_{s_i}}$ to RA.

4.2   System Description

We integrate CCIBI and ID-mKEM schemes to offer cluster authentication and BV in VANETs' anonymous broadcasts. Our VANETs system has three phases:

Table 1. Requirements in VANETs

Requirements	Description	Techniques
Authorization	Verifying the validity of the sender ID_{s_i} prior to communication. In the ID-CAKE scheme, the V (RA) verifies the ID_{s_i} of the P (sender) using ZK. If the ID_{s_i} is valid, then the V authorises the P to communicate with receivers.	Verify- ZK
Anonymity	Each user is assigned a PID by the RA. The user signs the message m for multiple receivers using PID and keeps the real ID private.	Extract-PID
Unlinkability	We use randomness in PID where PID values are changing every session; attackers cannot associate m with the original cluster vehicle.	Extract-PID
Integrity	The ID-CAKE scheme uses collision hash functions in the Sign algorithm to avoid message modification.	Sign- Hash
Non-repudiation	We use mKEM to generate a symmetric key K by utilising sender and receiver's (sk, pk). If K is valid, communication takes place.	Sign, Verify- mKEM
Unforgeability	Our scheme signs m with the sender's sk using mKEM-Encaps, and receivers verify the signature σ using the sender's pk. Since only the sender knows its sk, no adversary can forge the σ.	Sign -mKEM-Encaps

1. **System Initialization**. The setup includes infrastructure establishment, security configuration, trust building, key distribution, and creating system parameters for secure VANETs. The KeyGen algorithm initializes keys for TA and RA in the cluster.
2. **Vehicle Joining and Registration**. New vehicles register with the cluster, generate keys, and establish secure communication with the RA using the Join and Extract algorithm. The RA creates PID for all the vehicles, forming a new anonymous cluster.
3. **Message Signing and Verification**. Vehicles broadcast message m, signing with ID-mKEM for authenticity using the Sign algorithm. RA verifies the PID_{s_i}, and, if valid, sends the signature $\sigma_{(i,j)}$ to receivers. Vehicles then authenticate the source, ensure message *integrity*, evaluate trust, and make decisions using the Verify algorithm.

4.3   Definition of ID-CAKE Scheme

The ID-CAKE scheme is built on Definition 2, the CCIBI 3.1, and the ID-mKEM 3.2 signature scheme and consists of the following five PPT algorithms:

1. KeyGen. With the security parameter 1^λ, the TA produces a public parameter PP. Then, the TA outputs a pair of master public and secret keys (mpk, msk). While the RA generates a pair of registry public and secret keys, (rpk, rsk).
2. Join. To add a new vehicle to the cluster, the RA executes the registration protocol and assigns a PID to the vehicle. *Phase-1*. Assuming a sender vehicle with identity

ID_{s_i}, it performs key setup and generates a pair of keys (pk_{s_i}, sk_{s_i}). The same technique is used for setting up keys for receiver vehicles, generating $(pk_{r_{(i,j)}}, sk_{r_{(i,j)}})$. Vehicles send their pk to RA for registration along with their real ID. *Phase-2*. Each vehicle generates an initial PID in the cluster using their ID. *Phase-3*. The RA verifies the initial PID and issues PID for all vehicles in the cluster.

3. Extract. The TA generates user private keys d for all vehicles in the cluster and d_{RA} for RA, using inputs (PID, msk).
4. Sign. The sender, using inputs $(PID_{s_i}, sk_{s_i}, m, d)$, runs the mKEM-Encaps algorithm and generates a signature σ_i to send to all receivers in the cluster.
5. Verify. This algorithm has two phases, facilitating communication between the sender, RA, and receivers via ZK and mKEM. *Phase-1*. The communication between the sender PID_{s_i} (as P) and the RA (as V) performs a ZK proof using (CMT, CHA, RES). If V accepts RES, the process forwards to the subsequent phase. *Phase-2*. Receiver vehicles compute an encapsulation key K using the mKEM-Decaps algorithm. If it holds, then it verifies the signature component with the Ver algorithm. If it is valid, each receiver in the cluster accepts the original message m.

4.4   Security Models

In our ID-CAKE scheme, we provide security using the RO model under the ECCDH assumption. The ID-CAKE scheme views the RA as semi-honest and focuses on the potential malicious behaviour of other communication entities.

Impersonator as a Sender. The ID-CAKE scheme guarantees *authorization, non-repudiation, unforgibility*, and *integrity* under the following scenarios:

1. Malicious TA as a sender. A malicious TA as sender ID_{s_i} creates a pair (pk_{s_i}, sk_{s_i}) and attempts impersonation using a new PID. The RA, however, verifies the real ID for each PID. Detecting a mismatch, which signals TA impersonation, the RA rejects the PID registration and removes it, ensuring VANETs' privacy and security.
2. Malicious RA as a sender. Malicious RA as a sender where malicious RA will not hold the PID of sender and it randomly generates the pair of (pk_{s_i}, sk_{s_i}). Malicious RA as sender tries to generate PID via honest RA, but it does not hold RA's rpk. Hence, the algorithm aborts.

Malicious TA as a RA. In this scenario, the ID-CAKE scheme ensures *anonymity* and *unlinkability*. Malicious TA as RA where malicious TA run the KeyGen and generates its own set of (rpk, rsk) along with d_{RA}. It can generate PIDs for each user; however, the initial PID_1 is verified using rsk, which cannot be verified by the malicious TA since it does not know the original rsk of RA.

There can be multiple scenarios, such as malicious sender, where the sender can be an inter-cluster identity, an intra-cluster identity, or an outsider identity for *non-repudiation, authorization*, and *unforgeability*. For this paper, we will be giving security proof only to the impersonator as the sender in Sect. 6. We will explain the rest of the proof in the extended version.

5 Proposed Identity-Based Cluster Authentication and Key Exchange

The ID-CAKE scheme offers unique authentication and BV for VANETs, integrating components from Sect. 3.1 and 2.3. In ID-CAKE, the RA employs an efficient ZK proof of IBI and mKEM for verifying sender authenticity. This ensures only verified vehicles broadcast in VANET clusters while preserving *anonymity* using a new PID generation algorithm. The cluster vehicle arrangement is shown in Fig. 1. For security, ID-CAKE operates under the RO model and is grounded on the ECCDH assumption from the base schemes. It has three phases, as mentioned in Sect. 4.2, all supported by the following PPT algorithms.

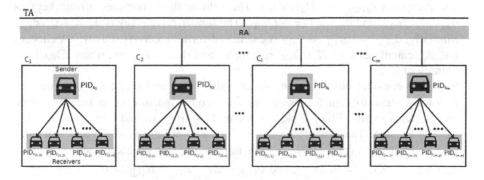

Fig. 1. Vehicles Arrangement for ID-CAKE Scheme

1. KeyGen. TA initialises the system by taking the security parameter λ as input. It selects a large prime order q and an elliptic curve E. It generates a cyclic additive $\mathbb{G}$ of a prime order q and selects a generator P of $\mathbb{G}$. TA defines four hash functions. $H_0 : \{0,1\}^\ell \rightarrow \mathbb{G}$ where ℓ is a positive integer, $H_1 : \{0,1\}^\ell \rightarrow \mathbb{G}$, $H_2 : \{0,1\}^* \rightarrow \{0,1\}^\ell$, and $H_3 : \{0,1\}^* \times \mathbb{G} \times \mathbb{G} \rightarrow \mathbb{G}$. TA generates $\mathsf{PP} = \{\mathbb{G}, q, E, P, H_0, H_1, H_2, H_3\}$. TA chooses $x \in \mathbb{Z}_q^*$ randomly as master secret key msk and computes master public key $\mathsf{mpk} = xP$. Next, RA chooses $y \in \mathbb{Z}_q^*$ randomly as RA's secret key rsk and computes RA's public key $\mathsf{rpk} = yP$ and sends rpk to TA.

2. Join. The Join ensures a secure process for admitting new vehicles into the cluster. Each cluster from $\mathsf{C} = (\mathsf{C}_1, \mathsf{C}_2, \ldots, \mathsf{C}_i, \ldots, \mathsf{C}_m)$, $\mathsf{C}_i = (\text{Sender} : \mathsf{ID}_{s_i}, \{\text{Receivers} : \mathsf{ID}_{r_{(i,1)}}, \mathsf{ID}_{r_{(i,2)}}, \ldots, \mathsf{ID}_{r_{(i,j)}}, \ldots, \mathsf{ID}_{r_{(i,n)}}\})$ where $1 \leq i \leq m$ and $1 \leq j \leq n$.
   Phase-1. Each vehicle generates an user public key and an user secret key pair themeselves. For sender, it chooses a random integer $\bar{x}_{s_i} \in \mathbb{Z}_q^*$ as sender secret key sk_{s_i} and computes sender public key $\mathsf{pk}_{s_i} = \bar{x}_{s_i} P$. For receivers, it generates the receiving vehicle public key $\mathsf{pk}_{r_{(i,j)}} = \bar{x}_{r_{(i,j)}} P$ and the vehicle secret key $\mathsf{sk}_{r_{(i,j)}} = \bar{x}_{r_{(i,j)}}$. Next, each vehicle sends their pk along with real ID to RA. *Phase-2.* In cluster C_i, each vehicle with ID generates the initial PID and ensures *anonymity*. For sender, we consider ID_{s_i} where $1 \leq i \leq m$ in the C_i. ID_{s_i} takes rpk as input,

chooses $\hat{x}_{s_i} \in \mathbb{Z}_q^*$ randomly, and calculates $R = \hat{x}_{s_i}P$. The sender computes initial $\text{PID}_{s_{i1}} = \text{ID}_{s_i} \oplus H_0(\hat{x}_{s_i}\text{rpk})$ and sends $(\text{PID}_{s_{i1}}, R)$ to RA. Similarly, receivers generate their own $\text{PID}_{r_{(i,j1)}} = \text{ID}_{r_{(i,j)}} \oplus H_0(\hat{x}_{r_{(i,j)}}\text{rpk})$ and send it to RA along with R. *Phase-3*. The RA takes registration requests and verifies initial PIDs from all vehicles in the cluster before assigning their PIDs. For sender, RA takes an input $(\text{PID}_{s_{i1}}, R)$, verifies $\text{ID}_{s_i} = \text{PID}_{s_{i1}} \oplus H_0(Ry)$, and calculates $\text{PID}_{s_i} = \text{ID}_{s_i} \oplus H_0(\hat{x}_{s_i}\text{rpk})$. If $\text{ID}_{s_i} = \text{PID}_{s_{i1}}$, RA accepts the registration request and assigns PID_{s_i}. Similarly, RA takes an input $(\text{PID}_{r_{(i,j1)}}, R)$ for receivers and assigns $\text{PID}_{(i,j)}$ for receivers. After verification, it creates an anonymous cluster $C_i = (\text{PID}_{s_i}, \{\text{PID}_{r_{(i,1)}}, \text{PID}_{r_{(i,2)}}, \ldots, \text{PID}_{r_{(i,j)}}, \ldots, \text{PID}_{r_{(i,n)}}\})$ where $1 \leq i \leq m$ and $1 \leq j \leq n$.

3. Extract. This algorithm extracts the private key associated with a specific PID from the cluster and ensures its authenticity. The sender takes $(\text{mpk}, \text{PID}_{s_i})$ as input and computes $Q_{\text{PID}_{s_i}} = H_1(\text{PID}_{s_i})$. The vehicle then computes private keys as $d_{s_{i1}} = xQ_{\text{PID}_{s_i}}$ and $d_{s_{i2}} = 1/x + Q_{\text{PID}_{s_i}}$. The sender private key is $d_{s_i} = (d_{s_{i1}}, d_{s_{i2}})$. Similarly, $d_{r_{(i,j)}} = (d_{r_{(i,j1)}}, d_{r_{(i,j2)}})$ is calculated for all receivers. Lastly, TA chooses $t \in \mathbb{Z}_q^*$, calculates $\alpha = H_1(\text{ID}_{\text{RA}}, \text{rpk}, \text{mpk})$, and $d_{\text{RA}} = t + x\alpha$, where ID_{RA} is an identity of RA.

4. Sign. We consider cluster C_i, the sender with PID_{s_i} and secret key sk_{s_i} runs the following steps to sign a message m and sends signature σ_i to receivers from the cluster C_i with $(\text{PID}_{r_{(i,j)}}, \text{pk}_{r_{(i,j)}})$ where $1 \leq i \leq m$ and $1 \leq j \leq n$ using mKEM-Encaps. The sender chooses PID_{s_i} randomly as $r_i \in \mathbb{Z}_q^*$ and computes $U_i = r_iP$. It takes $(\text{pk}_{r_{(i,j)}}, Q_{\text{PID}_{r_{(i,j)}}})$ as input, computes for each receiver $Z_{1_{(i,j)}} = d_{s_{i1}}Q_{\text{PID}_{r_{(i,j)}}}$, $Z_{2_{(i,j)}} = \bar{x}_{s_i}\text{pk}_{r_{(i,j)}}$, and $\psi_{(i,j)} = Z_{1_{(i,j)}}Z_{2_{(i,j)}}$, $K_{(i,j)} = H_2(\psi_{(i,j)})$, $f_{(i,j)} = H_3(m, \psi_{(i,j)}, \text{pk}_{s_i}, \text{pk}_{r_{(i,j)}})$, and $S_{(i,j)} = r_i^{-1}(f_{(i,j)} + w_i d_{s_i}\bar{x}_{s_i})$ where $w_i = x_{U_i} \mod q$ which is the x-coordinate of U_i. The sender then sets ciphertext $ct_{(i,j)} = (f_{(i,j)}, S_{(i,j)})$ and outputs $\sigma_{(i,j)} = (ct_{(i,j)}, m)$.

5. Verify. The algorithm has two phases: In the first, the sender's vehicle's identity is authenticated using a ZK proof with RA.

$$X_{s_i}P = V_{s_i} + \text{mpk}Q_{\text{PID}_{s_i}}c \tag{1}$$

In the second, receivers use the mKEM-Decaps algorithm to verify signatures and retrieve the message. This protocol ensures secure communication between the sender, RA, and receivers in the cluster.

Correctness Proof. RA calculates and accepts if the equation holds for each i is

$$X_{s_i}P = V_{s_i} + \text{mpk}Q_{\text{PID}_{s_i}}c$$
$$X_{s_i}P = \hat{r}_iP + xPQ_{\text{PID}_{s_i}}c$$
$$= (\hat{r}_i + xQ_{\text{PID}_{s_i}}c)P$$
$$= (\hat{r}_i + cd_{s_{i1}})P$$

The receiver accepts the message after signature The receiver accepts the message after signature $S_{(i,j)}$ verification by proving $U_i = r_iP$ if $u_1 = f_{(i,j)}P$ and $u_2 = w_i\text{pk}_{s_i}Z_{1_{(i,j)}}Q_{\text{PID}_{r_{(i,j)}}}^{-1}$, $U_i = S_{(i,j)}^{-1}(u_1+u_2) = S_{(i,j)}^{-1}(f_{(i,j)}P + w_i\text{pk}_{s_i}Z_{1_{(i,j)}}Q_{\text{PID}_{r_{(i,j)}}}^{-1}) =$

$$S_{(i,j)}^{-1}(f_{(i,j)}P + w_i \mathsf{pk}_{s_i} \mathsf{d}_{s_i} Q_{\mathsf{PID}_{r_{(i,j)}}} Q_{\mathsf{PID}_{r_{(i,j)}}}^{-1}) = S_{(i,j)}^{-1}(f_{(i,j)}P + w_i x_{s_i} P \mathsf{d}_{s_i}) =$$

$$\frac{f_{(i,j)}P + w x_{s_i} P \mathsf{d}_{s_i}}{S_{(i,j)}} = \frac{P(f_{(i,j)} + w_i x_{s_i} \mathsf{d}_{s_i})}{r^{-1}(f_{(i,j)} + w_i x_{s_i} \mathsf{d}_{s_i})} = \frac{P}{r_i^{-1}} = r_i P.$$

If $K_{(i,j)} = K'_{(i,j)}$, then receivers verify $S_{(i,j)}$. To further verify $S_{(i,j)}$, the receivers compute $f'_{(i,j)}$ and w'_i. If $f_{(i,j)} = f'_{(i,j)}$ and $w_i = w'_i$, then the receiver accepts the m; otherwise, it aborts and reports the corresponding PID_{s_i} along with $\sigma_{(i,j)}$ to the RA.

Identity Authentication and Signature Batch Verification using ZK Proof for VANETs

Sender	RA	Receivers
$(\mathsf{pk}_{s_i}, \mathsf{PID}_{s_i}, \mathsf{d}_{s_i}, \sigma_{(i,j)})$		$(\bar{x}_{r_{(i,j)}}, \mathsf{d}_{r_{(i,j)}}, \mathsf{pk}_{s_i})$
$\hat{r}_i \in \mathbb{Z}_q^*$		
$V_{s_i} = \hat{r}_i P$		
$\xrightarrow{\quad V_{s_i} \quad}$		
$\xrightarrow{\quad \sigma_{(i,j)} \quad}$		
$\xleftarrow{\quad c \quad}$	$c \in \mathbb{Z}_q^*$	
$X_{s_i} = \hat{r}_i + cd_{s_{i1}}$	$\xrightarrow{\quad X_{s_i} \quad}$ Verify Eq.1 $\xrightarrow{\dfrac{(\mathsf{PID}_{s_i}, \sigma_{(i,j)})}{\text{If accepts}}}$	Computes
		$Z1_{(i,j)} = \mathsf{d}_{r_{(i,j)}} Q_{\mathsf{PID}_{s_i}}$
		$Z2_{(i,j)} = \mathsf{pk}_{s_i} \bar{x}_{r_{(i,j)}}$
		$\psi_{(i,j)} = Z1_{(i,j)} Z2_{(i,j)}$
		$K'_{(i,j)} = H_2(\psi_{(i,j)})$
		$K_{(i,j)} = K'_{(i,j)} \text{accepts}^5, f'_{(i,j)} =$
		$H_3(m, \psi_{(i,j)}, \mathsf{pk}_{s_i}, \mathsf{pk}_{r_{(i,j)}})$
		$w'_i = x_{U_i} \mod q$
		$f_{(i,j)} = f'_{(i,j)}, w_i = w'_i$
		Verifies $S_{(i,j)}$
		If valid it accepts m
	$\xleftarrow{\dfrac{\sigma_{(i,j)}}{\text{Report}(\mathsf{PID}_{s_i})}}$	If not valid $\perp$

6 Security Analysis

In this section, we present the full security proof for the case of a malicious TA as a sender using the security model defined in Sect. 4.4. The scheme also guarantees security against a malicious TA as a sender and RA. Malicious TA as RA where ID-CAKE scheme ensure *anonymity* and *unlinkability*. Malicious TA as RA where malicious TA run the KeyGen and generates its own set of (rpk, rsk) along with d_{RA}. It can generate PIDs for each user however, the initial PID_1 is verified using rsk which cannot be verified by the malicious TA since it does not know the original rsk of RA. Since the following proof of the latter property largely follows from the proof of the former (below), with minor deviations, we only include it in the extended version.

6.1 Malicious TA as a Sender

Theorem 1. *The ID-CAKE scheme is secure against impersonation in the RO model if the ECCDH assumption holds. Impersonator I cannot distinguish the ECCDH assumption on a shared secret from a random element in $\mathbb{G}$ with a non-negligible advantage ϵ to ensure authorization, integrity, unforgeability, and non-repudiation.*

Proof. According to Definition 1, the challenger $\mathbb{C}$ interacts with the simulator S to ensure *unforgeability*, *integrity*, *authorization*, and *non-repudiation* by solving ECCDH as follows:

1. KeyGen. $\mathbb{C}$ generates PP $= (\mathbb{G}, q, E, P, H_0, H_1, H_2, H_3)$ by giving input 1^λ and passes PP. Again, it takes mpk $= \theta P$ by choosing a random integer θ and passing mpk to I. I selects a $ID_{s_i}^*$ as a target sender identity.
2. **Training Phase.** In the training phase, I aims to learn from the sender's responses. $\mathbb{C}$ maintains sender's responses in a list of hash queries oracle $\{L_0, \dots, L_3\}$. $\mathbb{C}$ maintains the list L_{pk} to store public and secret parameters. I can issue a series of q queries that are polynomially bounded.
   Case 1. $ID_{s_i} = ID_{s_i}^*$ where $ID_{s_i}^*$ is a targeted sender.
   (a) Join. I sends ID_{s_i} to $\mathbb{C}$ to get (pk_{s_i}, sk_{s_i}). $\mathbb{C}$ checks if $ID_{s_i} = ID_{s_i}^*$. If yes, the $\mathbb{C}$ aborts. So, both *unlinkability* and *anonymity* are protected, as shown by the Join algorithm, which stops making a new $PID_{s_i}^*$.
   (b) Extract. Upon receiving the H_1 query, if $PID_{s_i} = PID_{s_i}^*$, the $\mathbb{C}$ aborts. The $\mathbb{C}$ will still calculate d_{RA} for RA.
   (c) Sign. Upon receiving the H_2 query, $PID_{s_i} = PID_{s_i}^*$, the $\mathbb{C}$ aborts.
   (d) Verify. When a transcript is created, even if it has not yet been queried before as an Extract query. $PID_{s_i}^*$ as P participates in the transcript and adds to the set. RA will not be able to issue a transcript for the already malicious sender. Hence, upon receiving H_3, receivers in the cluster will not get $(PID_{s_i}, \sigma_{(i,j)})$ and game aborts. PID_{s_i} is a targeted ID, and RA needs to verify it. $PID_{s_i} = PID_{s_i}^*$, I acts as the cheater P, RA as the V, and $\mathbb{C}$ does not have the user secret key of $PID_{s_i}^*$, however, it needs to create it again to run ZK. When I tries to forge $PID_{s_i}^*$ then he should know sk_{s_i} and Verify aborts here. We can perform the transcript as many times as the number of queries does not exceed.

Case 2. $ID_{s_i} \neq ID_{s_i}^*$ is a targeted sender.

(a) Join. Given $ID_{s_i} \neq ID_{s_i}^*$, the I aims to participate as a cluster member by generating (q_{pk}, q_{sk}) and passes to $\mathbb{C}$. $\mathbb{C}$ randomly chooses γ as $sk_{s_i}^*$ and computes $pk_{s_i}^* = \gamma P$. $\mathbb{C}$ sends the $(pk_{s_i}^*, sk_{s_i}^*)$ to I and updates L_{pk}. I then attempts to extract PID from

RA. When the I sends a H_0 query, $\mathbb{C}$ checks if $(\mathsf{PID}^*_{s_{i1}}, \mathsf{ID}^*_{s_i}, R)$ is already listed in L_0. If found, $\mathbb{C}$ provides $\mathsf{PID}^*_{s_i}$ to I. Otherwise, the $\mathbb{C}$ computes $\mathsf{PID}^*_{s_i} = \mathsf{ID}^*_{s_i} \oplus H_0(\hat{x}_{s_i}\mathsf{rpk})$ and sends $\mathsf{PID}^*_{s_i}$ to I and updates L_0.

(b) Extract. Upon receiving $(\mathsf{q}_{d_{s_{i1}}}, \mathsf{q}_{d_{s_{i2}}})$ queries, if it exists in L_{pk}, the $\mathbb{C}$ returns it to I. Otherwise, it computes $Q^*_{\mathsf{PID}_{s_i}} = H_1(\mathsf{PID}^*_{s_i})$ and updates L_1. $\mathbb{C}$ selects a random integer β and returns $d^*_{s_{i1}} = \beta Q^*_{\mathsf{PID}_{s_i}}$ and using θ, $d^*_{s_{i2}} = \frac{1}{\theta + Q^*_{\mathsf{PID}_{s_i}}}$ and sends it to I. Also, $\mathbb{C}$ updates L_{pk} $(\mathsf{PID}^*_{s_i}, d^*_{s_{i1}}, d^*_{s_{i2}}, \mathsf{pk}^*_{s_i}, \mathsf{sk}^*_{s_i})$.

(c) Sign. Upon receiving the Sign query $\mathsf{q}_{\mathsf{Sign}.}$, the $\mathbb{C}$ performs normal Sign. operation as defined in Sect. 5. It fetches the list L_2 to get $\psi_{(i,j)}$, L_3 to get $f_{(i,j)}$ and L_{pk} to get values of $(U_{(i,j)}, Z_{1_{(i,j)}}, Z_{2_{(i,j)}}, S_{(i,j)}, ct_{(i,j)}, \sigma_{(i,j)})$ and passes the $S_{(i,j)}$ to I.

(d) Verify. If $\mathsf{PID}_{s_i} = \mathsf{PID}^*_{s_i}$, then $\mathbb{C}$ gets values $(\mathsf{pk}_{s_i}, \mathsf{PID}_{s_i}, d_{s_i}, \sigma_{(i,j)})$ from L_{pk} and does a regular Verify ZK proof between the malicious sender and RA. It then sends $(\mathsf{PID}_{s_i}, \sigma_{(i,j)})$ to all the receivers in the clusters.

3. **Challenge.** The I takes targeted $\mathsf{PID}^*_{s_i}$ chooses target plaintext m^* and forged $ct^*_{(i,j)} = (f^*_{(i,j)}, S^*_{(i,j)})$ along with $\sigma^*_i = (f^*_{(i,j)}, ct^*_{(i,j)}, m^*)$ which is the valid signature and is not the result of Sign oracle. I sends it to the $\mathbb{C}$. Moreover, the I can not ask for the sk_{s_i}. Also, I generates $(V^*_{s_i}, X^*_{s_i})$, updates in L_3, and passes to $\mathbb{C}$ which is a RA. $\mathbb{C}$ selects β_1 and returns $(V^*_{s_i}, X^*_{s_i})$. $\mathbb{C}$ verifies $X^*_{s_i}P = V^*_{s_i} + \mathsf{mpk}^*Q^*_{\mathsf{PID}_{s_i}}c$ and $\mathbb{C}$ aborts and $\sigma_{(i,j)}$ will be sent further to receivers.

4. **Breaking Phase.** In this phase, I acts as a cheating V and tries to convince $\mathbb{C}$ based on information gathered in the training Phase. I wins the game if it successfully convinces the $\mathbb{C}$ to accept with non-negligible probability. Taking the target sender's $\mathsf{PID}^*_{s_i}$ and the receiver's $\mathsf{PID}_{r_{(i,j)}}$, I outputs a forged $ct^*_{(i,j)} = (f^*_{(i,j)}, S^*_{(i,j)})$ along with $\sigma^*_{(i,j)}$ on m^* where $\sigma^*_{(i,j)} = (f^*_{(i,j)}, ct^*_{(i,j)}, m^*)$ which is the valid signature and is not the result of Sign oracle. Moreover, $\mathsf{PID}^*_{s_i}$ I outputs malicious values $(V^*_{s_i}, X^*_{s_i})$ which is the valid transcript for ZK and not the result of Verify oracle.

The $\mathbb{C}$ extracts L_{pk} for the record $(\mathsf{PID}^*_{s_i}, d^*_{s_{i1}}, d^*_{s_{i2}}, \mathsf{pk}^*_{s_i}, \mathsf{sk}^*_{s_i})$ and L_3 for the record $(m^*, \psi^*_{(i,j)}, f^*_{(i,j)}, V^*_{s_i}, X^*_{s_i})$. If $\mathsf{PID}_{s_i} = \mathsf{PID}^*_{s_i}$, the $\mathbb{C}$ takes $\mathsf{mpk} = \theta P$, and fetches L_{pk} to extract $d^*_{s_{i1}} = \beta Q^*_{\mathsf{PID}_{s_i}}$. The $\mathbb{C}$ will win by obtaining $\theta\beta P$ which is the solution to the ECCDH assumption, by evaluating $\frac{\theta Z_{1_{(i,j)}} - d_{r_{(i,j)}}r}{(d_{s_{i1}} - U_i)} = \theta\beta P$. The $\mathbb{C}$ takes $\mathsf{pk}^*_{s_i} = \gamma P$, and fetches L_{pk} to extract $d^*_{s_{i2}} = 1/\theta + Q^*_{\mathsf{PID}_{s_i}}$. The $\mathbb{C}$ will win by obtaining $d^*_{s_{i2}}\gamma bP$ which is the solution to the ECCDH assumption. We consider $Q^*_{\mathsf{PID}_{s_i}} = bP$, using $d^*_{s_{i2}}$ we can calculate $d^*_{s_{i2}}(xP + bP) = P$. If I can compute $d^*_{s_{i2}}bP$, call this value as θ, then I can compute $\theta\gamma = d^*_{s_{i2}}bP\gamma = d^*_{s_{i2}}\gamma bP$. Hence, $\mathbb{C}$ will win by obtaining $d^*_{s_{i2}}\gamma bP$ which is a solution to the ECCDH assumption.

For probability distribution to prove *zero-knowledgeness* for $\mathbb{C}$, it is winning the game after solving the ECCDH assumption. Event A denotes the success of solving the ECCDH assumption, while event B denotes not aborting the calculations. Joint probability $P(A|B)$ joint probability represents the conditional probability of event A occurring given that event B has occurred. The $\mathbb{C}$ is able to find $\theta\beta P$ and $d^*_{s_{i2}}\gamma bP$, which is the solution to the ECCDH assumption. Next, we analyse the advantage of the $\mathbb{C}$ in winning the game based on the occurrence of the events in which the game aborts as follows:

- The secret key q_{sk} query is where the game aborts for $ID_{s_i} = ID^*_{s_i}$. The probability is $Pr(q_{sk}) = 1/q_{sk}$. The game aborts when it guesses right $ID^*_{s_i}$, then the probability of the game stopping any random guess is 1 out of q_{sk}.
- In Extract, there is a queries $d_{s_{i1}}$ which query separately for $q_{d_{s_{i1}}}$ and $q_{d_{s_{i2}}}$. The probability of game abort is $Pr(q_{d_{s_{i1}}}) = 1/q_{d_{s_{i1}}}$ and $Pr(q_{d_{s_{i2}}}) = 1/q_{d_{s_{i2}}}$.
- Sign query where game due to fake m. The probability of aborting the game is q_{Sign} aborts $Pr(1/2^k)$ where 2^k is message space.
- $\mathbb{C}$ in the challenge phase aborts the game if I queries for $PID_{s_i} \neq PID^*_{s_i}$. The probability of aborting is $Pr(q_{H_3}) = (1 - 1/q_{H_3})$.

Next, the $\mathbb{C}$ takes the L_2 to fetch ψ_i and L_3 to fetch $(V_{s_i}, X_{s_i}, f_{(i,j)})$ and calculates $\theta\beta P$ and $d_{s_{i2}}\gamma bP$ having independent probability $(1/q_{H_2}, 1/q_{H_3})$. $\mathbb{C}$ winning the game with calculated inverse of each abort probability advantage ϵ' as follows:

$$\epsilon' \geq \epsilon \left(\frac{1}{q_{H_2}}\right) \left(\frac{1}{q_{H_3}}\right) \left(\frac{1}{q_{d_{s_i}}}\right) \left(1 - \frac{1}{q_{sk}}\right) \left(1 - \frac{q_{Sign}}{2^k}\right) \qquad (2)$$

7 Efficiency Analysis

In this section, we show the efficiency of existing VANET authentication schemes with the ID-CAKE scheme. Table 2 contrasts computational and communication costs for Sign and Verify algorithms against current authentication and BV schemes. In the Anonymous Authentication Scheme (AAAS) by [7], vehicles sign a message for authentication and compute its signature, using a random number. This message, along with signature is sent to RSU, which verifies it using three BP operations. The AAAS's communication cost is 304 bytes, with the complexity of both signing $\mathcal{O}(n) + \mathcal{O}(k^2) + \mathcal{O}(k^c) = \mathcal{O}(k^c)$ and verification being $\mathcal{O}(k^c)$, where k is the number of exponent bits and $c > 1$. Wang et al. [21] talk about the cost of computational and communication using the "MNT159" asymmetric group $\mathbb{G}_1$ with a 159-bit base field, focusing on how well it works in BV. We found that verifying n signatures at once takes scales as $\mathcal{O}(n \times k^{c-1})$ time compared to verifying a single signature, which takes $\mathcal{O}(k^c)$, which is 84 bytes. The byte cost in our table also accounts for the hash, which was overlooked in the original paper.

Liu et al. [11] exhibits a linear computing cost, $\mathcal{O}(k)$, which scales with group size, as shown in Table 2. While providing a generic security proof, the scheme does not clarify its assumption model. For communication, the scheme costs amount to 94 bytes, $\mathbb{G} = 256$ bits, $\mathbb{Z}^*_q = 160$ bits, and $T = 2.6$ s for each user. Therefore, the size would be $2 \times 256 + 3 \times 160 + 2.6 = 94$ bytes. The message size is not standardized as it varies with shared user information. Zhang et al. [22] has a total transmission overhead of $21 + 125n$ for the BLS and $21 + 42n$ for ID-based BV. The overhead scales linearly with the number of receivers, leading to $\mathcal{O}(k)$ complexity. Our ID-CAKE scheme has the least computation costs and communication cost for n signature in Sign is $\mathcal{O}(k) + \mathcal{O}(k) + \mathcal{O}(k) = \mathcal{O}(k)$ and Verify is $\mathcal{O}(k)$, overall combined cost is $\mathcal{O}(k)$, the estimated size would be $2 \times 20 + 2 \times 20 = 80$ bytes. Figure 2 shows a graphical comparison of communication costs, and it is evident that our scheme has the

Table 2. Comparison of the Computation Cost, Security, and Communication Costs

Paper	E	A	M	H	BP	Complexity	Security	Communication Cost	Byte
Jiang et al. [7]	6	0	6	2	3	$\mathcal{O}(k^c)$	SVO	$2|\mathbb{G}_1| + |\mathbb{Z}_q^*| + |TS| + |Exp|$	304
Wang et al. [21]	4	1	4	1	3	$\mathcal{O}(n \times k^{c-1})$	HSM	$3|\mathbb{Z}_q^*| + 2|Exp| + 1|H|$	90
Liu et al. [11]	0	1	2	1	6	$\mathcal{O}(k)$	Informal	$3|\mathbb{Z}_q^*| + 1|\mathbb{G}| + 1|T|$	92
Zhang et al. [22]	0	1	2	2	3	$\mathcal{O}(k)$	Informal	$4|\mathbb{Z}_q^*| + 2|\mathbb{G}| + 2|H|$	209
ID-CAKE	0	2	2	2	1	$\mathcal{O}(k)$	RO	$2|\mathbb{Z}_q^*| + 2|H|$	80

Legends: k number of bits in the exponent, c is greater than one, n is the number of signatures being batch verified. E is Exponentiation in $\mathbb{Z}_q^*$, A is Addition in $\mathbb{Z}_q^*$, M is a Multiplication $\mathbb{Z}_q^*$, P is BP operation, and H is hash operations.

Table 3. Comparison of the Security Requirements

Requirements	Jiang et al. [7]	Wang et al. [21]	Liu et al. [11]	Zhang et al. [22]	Our ID-CAKE
Authorization	✓	✓	✗	✗	✓
Anonymity	✓	✓	✓	✓	✓
Integrity	✗	✗	✗	✓	✓
Non-repudiation	✓	✓	✗	✗	✓
Unforgeability	✗	✗	✗	✓	✓
Unlinkability	✓	✗	✗	✓	✓

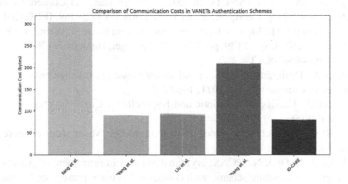

Fig. 2. Communication Cost Analysis

lowest communication cost compared with others. In Table 3, we present a comparative analysis of the security requirements between our scheme and existing authentication schemes. Our proposed scheme successfully achieves all security requirements, with higher efficiency with lower computational cost.[2]

---

[2] Communication cost refers to the total size of message transmitted. According to [16], for type A pairing with respect to 80 bit security level, the size of p is equal to 64 bytes, A point on the group of points $E(F_q)$ consists of x and y coordinates. This means that the size of each element in $\mathbb{G}_1$ is $64 \times 2 = 128$ bytes whilst that of each element in $\mathbb{G}_2$ is $20 \times 2 = 40$ bytes. In addition, the size for a general hash H function in $\mathbb{Z}_q^*$, a expiration, and a timestamp are considered to be 20 bytes, 4 bytes, and 4 bytes, respectively. As the basic configuration information is the same for above schemes, we ignore the size of message and only take into account the size of the signature on the message with the corresponding PID_{s_i}.

8   Conclusion and Future Work

In the face of rising security concerns in VANETs, this paper introduces the innovative ID-CAKE scheme under the ECCDH assumption. Using CCIBI with ZK proof and ID-mKEM, ID-CAKE proves a robust mechanism for VANETs authentication, ensuring identity *authorization, anonymity, integrity, unforgeability, non-repudiation*, and *unlinkability*. Its unique ability to create cluster-based signatures using the mKEM method and its fast BV through ZK proofs show that it could also help reduce the amount of work that needs to be done on computers. The ID-CAKE-CAKEme is proven secure under the RO model for different scenarios in VANETs. The ID-CAKE scheme enhances VANETs' security by blending *anonymity* with consensus transparency. Its integration into intelligent transportation systems can further elevate security. Future research may focus on optimising real-time performance and exploring lattice-based post-quantum cryptography.

References

1. Bhavesh, N.B., Maity, S., Hansdah, R.C.: A protocol for authentication with multiple levels of anonymity (AMLA) in VANETs. In: 2013 27th International Conference on Advanced Information Networking and Applications Workshops, pp. 462–469. IEEE (2013)
2. Boneh, D., Franklin, M.: Identity-based encryption from the weil pairing. In: Kilian, J. (ed.) CRYPTO 2001. LNCS, vol. 2139, pp. 213–229. Springer, Heidelberg (2001). https://doi.org/10.1007/3-540-44647-8_13
3. Chaudhry, S.A.: Designing an efficient and secure message exchange protocol for internet of vehicles. Secur. Commun. Netw. **2021**, 1–9 (2021)
4. Cohen, H., et al.: Handbook of Elliptic and Hyperelliptic Curve Cryptography. CRC Press, Boca Raton (2005)
5. Engoulou, R.G., Bellaïche, M., Pierre, S., Quintero, A.: Vanet security surveys. Comput. Commun. **44**, 1–13 (2014)
6. Gong, Z., Gao, T., Guo, N.: PCAS: cryptanalysis and improvement of pairing-free certificateless aggregate signature scheme with conditional privacy-preserving for vanets. Ad Hoc Netw. **144**, 103134 (2023)
7. Jiang, Y., Ge, S., Shen, X.: AAAS: an anonymous authentication scheme based on group signature in VANETs. IEEE Access **8**, 98986–98998 (2020)
8. Kalmykov, I.A., Olenev, A.A., Kalmykova, N.I., Dukhovnyj, D.V.: Using adaptive zero-knowledge authentication protocol in vanet automotive network. Information **14**(1), 27 (2022)
9. Kim, D., Choi, J., Jung, S.: Mutual identification and key exchange scheme in secure vanets based on group signature. In: 2010 7th IEEE Consumer Communications and Networking Conference, pp. 1–2. IEEE (2010)
10. Kurosawa, K., Heng, S.-H.: From digital signature to ID-based identification/signature. In: Bao, F., Deng, R., Zhou, J. (eds.) PKC 2004. LNCS, vol. 2947, pp. 248–261. Springer, Heidelberg (2004). https://doi.org/10.1007/978-3-540-24632-9_18
11. Liu, L., Wang, Y., Zhang, J., Yang, Q.: A secure and efficient group key agreement scheme for vanet. Sensors **19**(3), 482 (2019)
12. World Health Organization: Global status report on road safety: time for action (2021). https://www.afro.who.int/publications/global-status-report-road-safety-time-for-action

13. Palaniswamy, B., Camtepe, S., Foo, E., Simpson, L., Baee, M.A.R., Pieprzyk, J.: Continuous authentication for vanet. Veh. Commun. **25**, 100255 (2020)
14. Shamir, A.: Identity-based cryptosystems and signature schemes. In: Blakley, G.R., Chaum, D. (eds.) CRYPTO 1984. LNCS, vol. 196, pp. 47–53. Springer, Heidelberg (1985). https://doi.org/10.1007/3-540-39568-7_5
15. Smart, N.P.: Efficient key encapsulation to multiple parties. In: Blundo, C., Cimato, S. (eds.) SCN 2004. LNCS, vol. 3352, pp. 208–219. Springer, Heidelberg (2005). https://doi.org/10.1007/978-3-540-30598-9_15
16. Identity-Based Cryptography Standard: 1: Supersingular curve implementations of the BF and BB1 cryptosystems
17. Sun, J., Zhang, C., Zhang, Y., Fang, Y.: An identity-based security system for user privacy in vehicular ad hoc networks. IEEE Trans. Parallel Distrib. Syst. **21**(9), 1227–1239 (2010)
18. Tzeng, S.F., Horng, S.J., Li, T., Wang, X., Huang, P.H., Khan, M.K.: Enhancing security and privacy for identity-based batch verification scheme in vanets. IEEE Trans. Veh. Technol. **66**(4), 3235–3248 (2015)
19. Umrani, A., Vangujar, A.K., Palmieri, P.: A multi-receiver certificateless signcryption (MCLS) scheme. In: 8th International Conference on Cryptography, Security and Privacy, CSP 2024, Osaka, Japan, 20–22 April 2024 (2024)
20. Umrani, A., Vangujar, A.K., Palmieri, P.: Anonymous multi-receiver certificateless hybrid signcryption for broadcast communication. In: Proceedings of the 10th International Conference on Information Systems Security and Privacy, ICISSP 2024, Rome, Italy, 26–28 February 2024. SciTePress (2024)
21. Wang, Y., Zhong, H., Xu, Y., Cui, J., Wu, G.: Enhanced security identity-based privacy-preserving authentication scheme supporting revocation for vanets. IEEE Syst. J. **14**(4), 5373–5383 (2020)
22. Zhang, C., Lu, R., Lin, X., Ho, P.H., Shen, X.: An efficient identity-based batch verification scheme for vehicular sensor networks. In: IEEE INFOCOM 2008-The 27th Conference on Computer Communications, pp. 246–250. IEEE (2008)
23. Zhou, Y., Wang, Z., Qiao, Z., Yang, B., Zhang, M.: An efficient and provably secure identity authentication scheme for vanet. IEEE Internet Things J. (2023)
24. Zhu, F., Yi, X., Abuadbba, A., Khalil, I., Huang, X., Xu, F.: A security-enhanced certificateless conditional privacy-preserving authentication scheme for vehicular ad hoc networks. IEEE Trans. Intell. Transp. Syst. (2023)

Posters

Posters

One Time Chat – A Toy End-to-End Encrypted Web Messaging Service

Kamil Kaczyński(✉) ⓘ and Michał Glet ⓘ

Military University of Technology, Warsaw, Poland
kamil.kaczynski@wat.edu.pl

Abstract. In the digital age, instant messaging (IM) is a cornerstone of communication, necessitating secure and efficient platforms. The One Time Chat web application addresses this need through end-to-end encryption and a serverless design, ensuring user privacy. Emphasizing security without sacrificing usability, it offers ephemeral messaging through peer-to-peer connections. This paper introduces One Time Chat, a toy web app detailing its cryptographic foundations, key authentication, and user experience. With its open-source nature and publicly available deployment, One Time Chat not only serves as a messaging service but also as a basis for future secure communication tools.

Keywords: messaging · web app · web crypto · browser · end-to-end encryption

1 Introduction

In an era where communication is instantaneous and global, the need for efficient and secure instant messaging (IM) applications has never been greater. Instant messaging has revolutionized the way we interact, breaking down geographical barriers and enabling real-time collaboration and socialization. However, this ease of communication also brings forth significant challenges, particularly in the realms of privacy and data security.

The pervasive nature of IM apps means that they often hold vast amounts of personal information, from casual conversations to sensitive data shared in a professional context. This reality has been the impetus for a growing public concern about how this data is managed and protected [1]. High-profile data breaches and the misuse of personal information by third-party entities have only served to heighten these concerns [2].

In response, there is an increasing demand for messaging platforms that prioritize user privacy and data security without compromising on the user experience. In this paper, we proposed a toy chat web – One Time Chat which offers end-to-end encryption, ephemeral messaging, and a serverless architecture that ensures users can communicate with confidence that their conversations remain confidential and are not archived indefinitely.

M. Andreoni (Ed.): ACNS 2024 Workshops, LNCS 14587, pp. 183–187, 2024.
https://doi.org/10.1007/978-3-031-61489-7_11

2 App Design

The design of the One Time Chat web application is centered around three key pillars: cryptographic protocols available in the Web Cryptography API [3], authentication of keys to minimize the possibility of man-in-the-middle attacks, and a serverless architecture to enhance privacy and security.

2.1 Cryptographic Protocols

The choice of cryptographic protocols was limited by the ones available in Web Cryptography API. Our toy messaging service is a playground for future work and implementation of more sophisticated solutions; thus, our first choice was to use ECDH key exchange (with curve P-256) for deriving shared secret and AES-GCM for ensuring the confidentiality and integrity of messages.

- **ECDH Key Exchange**: The ECDH algorithm is used to securely exchange cryptographic keys between users over an insecure channel. Each user generates an ephemeral public-private key pair based on the elliptic curve, which underpins the security of the key exchange without requiring a pre-shared secret. A new keypair is generated whenever the user visits the website.
- **AES Message Encryption**: Once the shared secret is established via ECDH, it is used to generate a unique AES encryption key for the session. AES is a symmetric key algorithm that is widely recognized for its strength and speed, making it suitable for real-time messaging. Messages are encrypted and decrypted using this session key, ensuring that the content remains confidential and tamper-proof.

2.2 Key Authentication

Key authentication is a critical feature to minimize the possibility of man-in-the-middle (MITM) attacks, where an attacker could intercept the key exchange process. To mitigate this risk, we decided to use a combination of two techniques. First, we decided to use the hash of the chat host's public key as a room identifier. Second, the application implements a Short Authentication String (SAS) method.

After the ECDH key exchange, both parties compute a hash of the shared secret and convert it into a human-readable SAS. For generating user-readable strings we decided to use words from BIP39 [4], thus giving us a set of 2048 unique words. By comparing a simple representation of this hash (such as a pair of words) over a trusted channel, users can verify that they have derived the same encryption key, confirming the authenticity of the key exchange process.

2.3 Serverless Architecture

The application adopts a serverless P2P design, which has several advantages:

- **No Central Servers**: By not relying on central servers for message routing, the application ensures that there is no single point of collection for metadata or message content. This design inherently protects against mass surveillance and data mining practices.

- **Direct Communication**: Messages are sent directly from one user to another, reducing latency and eliminating the dependency on third-party servers, which could be a potential target for hackers.
- **Ephemeral Messaging**: The serverless nature allows for ephemeral messaging, where messages are not stored after the session ends. This aligns with the principle of data minimization, a key aspect of privacy-by-design.

3 Actual Implementation

The implementation of the one-time chat web application is the result of a careful selection of technologies and frameworks to create a toy app which can act as a basis for future projects. Our idea was to provide open-source code to allow wide contribution to the project, which utilises well-known technologies for the new use case. Below are the key components and methodologies employed in the development process.

3.1 Technology Stack

The front end of the application is built using Create React App [5], a widely adopted boilerplate that sets up a modern web application by running one command. It encapsulates the best practices in frontend development and provides a solid foundation with a well-defined structure, enabling rapid development and efficient maintenance. This choice allows developers to focus on writing the application-specific code rather than spending time on configuration.

For real-time communication, the application utilizes PeerJS [6], a wrapper library for WebRTC, which simplifies peer-to-peer data, video, and audio calls. PeerJS abstracts the complexity of WebRTC's connection management and provides a straightforward API for establishing direct browser-to-browser connections.

The application uses the default signalling server provided by PeerJS during the initial handshake. It is important to note that this server is only used for signalling purposes to establish the connection, and no message content passes through it, preserving the confidentiality of the communication. Users can decide to use a self-hosted signaling server, compatible with PeerJS.

Security is paramount in the application, and the Web Cryptography API is at the core of all cryptographic operations. This API allows the app to perform cryptographic operations such as hashing, key generation, and encryption securely and efficiently. Using the Web Cryptography API ensures that cryptographic practices are in line with current standards and are executed in a safe environment, resistant to common web vulnerabilities.

3.2 User Flow

Our toy app uses a simplified flow for creating the chat room. We have two users – host (H) and guest (G). To create a new chat room, H opens the web app, which generates unique link to be securely shared with G. Link consists of website URL, route join and query string parameter peerId, e.g. https://one-time-chat.pages.dev/join?peerId=77c

6646bd018a9d9c9d7421ff29d1cb0c282c77150e941556e003c59250c323d. The peerId value is equal to the SHA-256 hash of the H public key. G opens that url initiating key negotiation between users. First G sends its public key to H, and H sends its public key to G. G computes the hash of H's public key and compares it to the peerId, if it's equal, then both G and H are computing shared secret according to the ECDH. The generated shared secret is used as a key for the AES-GCM and used to encrypt and decrypt all the messages exchanged in the communication.

To further mitigate MitM attacks, we decided to use Short Authentication String (SAS) to allow H and G easy comparison of shared secrets. We compute the hash of the shared secret using SHA-256, and then we select the first 24 bits of the computed hash. The application then performs the following operations on these 24 bits:

- Bit Shifting: The 24-bit section is shifted 13 bits to the right. In binary, this is equivalent to moving the bits 13 places to the right, which effectively discards the last 13 bits.
- Bit Masking: After the shift, a bitwise AND operation with the number 0x7ff is performed. This operation masks the section to only keep the first 11 bits of the shifted value, resulting in *index1*.
- Index Calculation: The application also calculates a second index, *index2*, by performing a bitwise AND operation on the original 24-bit section with 0x7ff. This operation masks everything except for the last 11 bits, which become index2.
- Word Selection: The two indexes *index1* and *index2* are each used to select a word from the BIP39 word list, which as mentioned earlier, contains 2048 unique words. The indexes are effectively positioned in this list.

Both parties then verbally communicate this SAS over a trusted channel (like a phone call) and verify that they match. If they do, it confirms that the session is secure and that there is no man-in-the-middle attack. Now, both parties can securely exchange messages in that session.

3.3 Open Source and Availability

Adhering to the principles of transparency and community collaboration, the entire source code for the one-time chat application is made publicly available on the GitHub repository at https://github.com/kkaczynski/one-time-chat. This open-source approach allows for peer review, community contributions, and ensures that anyone interested can inspect, modify, and enhance the codebase.

Users have the flexibility to build and deploy their instance of the application or utilize the version already deployed at https://one-time-chat.pages.dev. The deployed version is a testament to the application's ease of use, providing an accessible platform for secure communication without the need for setup or configuration by the end user.

Through the combination of these tools and practices, the one-time chat web application stands as a robust solution for secure messaging, offering an accessible platform while not compromising on security and privacy.

4 Future Work

The current implementation of the one-time chat application presents a toy web app for secure text-based communication, utilizing established cryptographic protocols and peer-to-peer connections. Looking ahead, there are several avenues for enhancement and expansion to ensure the application remains at the forefront of secure communication technology. In future iterations could explore the integration of more sophisticated cryptographic protocols. This could include algorithms that not only ensure the confidentiality and integrity of the messages but also provide forward secrecy, ensuring that the compromise of long-term keys does not compromise past session keys. To achieve this, we will need to explore new ways of implementing cryptographic algorithms for web browsers, possibly using Web Assembly or other promising technologies.

We plan also to simplify key authentication to make it more user-friendly, thus allowing the reuse of our framework for other projects. The addition of features to support the exchange of media files, such as images and documents, would greatly enhance the usability of the application. Moreover, integrating voice and video call capabilities could be achieved by expanding the use of WebRTC, enabling users to have real-time conversations with the same level of privacy and security as their text-based communications.

In conclusion, the roadmap for the one-time chat application is filled with opportunities for growth and improvement. By embracing emerging technologies and focusing on the user experience, our toy application can create a framework for a secure and modern communication platform.

References

1. Kaczyński, K.: Security analysis of Signal Android database protection mechanisms. Int. J. Inf. Technol. Secur. **11**(4), 63–70 (2019). ISSN 1313-8251
2. Glet, M., Kaczyński, K.: Access logs – underestimated privacy risks. Int. J. Electron. Commun. **66**(3), 405–410 (2020). https://doi.org/10.24425/ijet.2020.131892
3. Web Cryptography API. https://www.w3.org/TR/WebCryptoAPI. Accessed 06 Nov 2023
4. BIP39. https://github.com/bitcoin/bips/blob/master/bip-0039.mediawiki. Accessed 06 Nov 2023
5. Create React App. https://create-react-app.dev. Accessed 06 Nov 2023
6. PeerJS. https://peerjs.com. Accessed 06 Nov 2023

Game Theoretic Modeling of Insider Threats in an Organization

K. C. Lalropuia[1]([✉])[ID], Sanjeev Goyal[2,3][ID], and Borja Garcia de Soto[1,4][ID]

[1] Center for Cyber Security and S.M.A.R.T. Construction Research Group, Division of Engineering, New York University Abu Dhabi (NYUAD), Experimental Research Building, Saadiyat Island, P.O. Box 129188, Abu Dhabi, United Arab Emirates
kc17487@nyu.edu
[2] Division of Social Sciences, New York University Abu Dhabi, Abu Dhabi, United Arab Emirates
sg6280@nyu.edu
[3] Faculty of Economics, University of Cambridge, Cambridge CB3 9DD, UK
[4] Department of Civil and Urban Engineering, Tandon School of Engineering, New York University (NYU), 6 MetroTech Center, Brooklyn, NY 11201, USA
garcia.de.soto@nyu.edu

Abstract. Insider threats have emerged as serious threats to organizations due to the rapid advancement and incorporation of communication technologies. Insider threats incurred significant costs to different organizations. Tackling these threats is a big challenge as insiders can misuse their privilege and their behavior is not known completely. Insiders are mainly motivated by financial gain, espionage, disgruntlement, etc. To address this issue, a great deal of research has been done in the literature on detection and mitigation of the threats. However, the existing work have not investigated properly the important problems such as how various types of people (i.e., honest and trained, honest but untrained in cybersecurity, malicious insiders) evolve in organizations, which type of people would be prevalent and which types would co-exist in the long run. Hence, we propose a novel evolutionary game model to address these problems. Based on the proposed model, we have insights into how malicious insiders and honest people would interact, survive or coexist in the organization.

Keywords: Insider threats · Security · Evolutionary game

1 Introduction

The rapid growth and adoption of communication technologies by organizations highly facilitate insiders to carry out adversarial attack and this poses serious

Supported by the Center for Cyber Security (CCS) at New York University Abu Dhabi, funded by Tamkeen under the NYUAD Research Institute Award G1104 in collaboration with the NYUAD Center for Interacting Urban Networks (CITIES), funded by Tamkeen under the NYUAD Research Institute Award CG001.

threats to different organizations. There are two types of insider threats, namely, intentional and unintentional insider threats [6]. Malicious insiders make use of their privilege to launch the intentional attacks, whereas occurrence of the unintentional attacks largely depends on the capability of insiders in cybersecurity and their carelessness as well. For instance, unintentional attack can take place by unwittingly clicking a phishing link. Generally, malicious insiders are motivated by financial gain, espionage and disgruntlement, etc. Furthermore, the consequences of insider attacks include data theft, leakage, tampering and sabotage.

2   Motivation

In a recent survey report, 20% of the respondents considered insider attacks to be the highest level threats in construction industry [13]. Moreover, it has been reported that 60% of all the attacks are launched from inside [3]. A number of research work have addressed insider threats by using various methods such as game theory [5,8,11,14]. Bayesian network [4], machine learning [2,7,10], etc. However, the current literature have not dealt with properly how various types of people (i.e., honest and trained, honest but untrained in cybersecurity, malicious insiders) evolve in organizations and who will survive in the long run. Moreover, the case of insider attack has increased exponentially and this trend will continue in the future [12]. Therefore, it is important to address insider threats to ensure organizations' information security, and in this work we tackle the threats by formulating a novel evolutionary game model. In addition, we obtain insightful information crucial to organizations' information security.

3   Proposed Model and the Main Results

We consider an organization where there are three types of people: (i) honest who are untrained (HU) in cybersecurity and unintentionally performs insider attack (ii) malicious insider (MI), who intentionally launches a cyberattack against the vulnerable HU (iii) honest who are trained in cybersecurity (HT) at the cost of $\omega > 0$ and are able to detect MI. The communications in the organization takes place between each pair of the types by means of some communication network such as intranets. Let $\alpha > 0$ denote the malicious insider's payoff due to the successful attack on HU. Moreover, HT gets α for detecting MI when confronted. Thus, the interactions among different types in the organization can be captured as a strategic form game:

Matrix 1

$$
\begin{array}{cccc}
 & HU & MI & HT \\
\begin{array}{c} HU \\ MI \\ HT \end{array} &
\left[\begin{array}{ccc}
\{1,\ 1\} & \{-\alpha,\ \alpha\} & \{1,\ 1-\omega\} \\
\{\alpha,\ -\alpha\} & \{0,\ 0\} & \{-\alpha, \alpha-\omega\} \\
\{1-\omega,\ 1\} & \{\alpha-\omega, -\alpha\} & \{1-\omega,\ 1-\omega\}
\end{array}\right]
\end{array}
$$

We analyze the interactions based on evolutionary game theory and obtain the main results:

Proposition 1. *(i) Honest and untrained HU is evolutionarily stable strategy (ESS) if and only if $0 < \alpha < 1$ and $0 < \omega$.*

(ii) Malicious insider MI is ESS if and only if $1 < \alpha < \omega$.

(iii). There is a stable mixed population that comprises malicious insider MI and honest and trained insider HT if $\alpha < \omega < \frac{2\alpha(1+\alpha)}{2\alpha+1}$. Moreover, the stable proportion of the types is given by $(0, 1+\alpha-\omega, \omega-\alpha)$, where $\omega-1 < \alpha < \omega$.

(iv) Apart from the stable strategies in (i), (ii) and (iii), there is no other stable strategies.

The stability regions for different strategies HU, MI, mixed population MI and HT are represented by blue, purple and red color, respectively as shown in Fig. 1. Moreover, the green color represents the region where both HU and mixed MI and HT are stable and the grey color indicates the region where there is no stable strategies.

Proposition 1 (i) implies that if MI's payoff is less than HU's payoff and if the training is not free of cost, the organization would contain only HU type. On the other hand, Proposition 1 (ii) states that when MI's payoff is greater than HU's payoff but less than the training cost, the organization would eventually be full of MI people. In addition, Proposition 1 (iii) shows that there is a stable mixed population of MI and HT in the organization. The stability region is represented by the red and green color in Fig. 1. Moreover, it can be noticed that there is a striking result in which HU overlaps the mixed population MI and HT in the green region (i.e., there are multiple ESS). This implies that in this region either HU or mixed MI and HT would survive in the organization in the long run.

The Proposed Model and Classical Games. Suppose that there are two types of people (a) HU and MI or (b) MI and HT in the organization. In scenario (a) if $\alpha > 1$ the game model can be considered as a Prisoner dilemma (PD) [9], whereas if $\alpha < 1$, it is not PD and it becomes a co-ordination game (CG) [9]. In scenario (b) if $1 < \omega < \alpha$, the game is a PD, whereas if $\alpha < \omega < \alpha+1$ and $\omega > 1$, the game is not a PD and it becomes a CG. Thus, all the results with respect to ESS in the two classical games PD and CG apply to the proposed model in the two scenarios [15]. In the PD scenario, MI is ESS and in the CG scenario, both honest HU/HT and MI are ESSs.

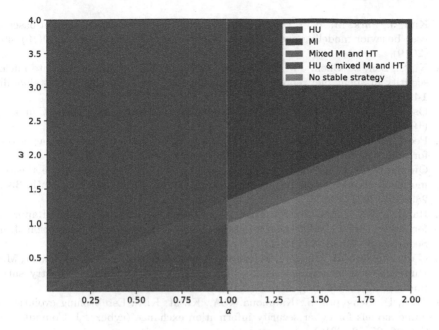

Fig. 1. Stable strategies corresponding to different values of α and ω

Acknowledgements. The first author (KC Lalropuia) acknowledges the support provided by the Center for Cyber Security (CCS) at New York University Abu Dhabi and the Center for Interacting Urban Networks (CITIES) at New York University Abu Dhabi.

References

1. Al-Shehari, T., Alsowail, R.A.: An insider data leakage detection using one-hot encoding, synthetic minority oversampling and machine learning techniques. Entropy **23**(10), 1258 (2021)
2. AlSlaiman, M., Salman, M.I., Saleh, M.M., Wang, B.: Enhancing false negative and positive rates for efficient insider threat detection. Comput. Secur. **126**, 103066 (2023)
3. Amiri-Zarandi, M., Karimipour, H., Dara, R.A.: A federated and explainable approach for insider threat detection in IoT. Internet Things **24**, 100965 (2023)
4. d'Ambrosio, N., Perrone, G., Romano, S.P.: Including insider threats into risk management through Bayesian threat graph networks. Comput. Secur. **133**, 103410 (2023)
5. Elmrabit, N., Yang, S.H., Yang, L., Zhou, H.: Insider threat risk prediction based on Bayesian network. Comput. Secur. **96**, 101908 (2020)
6. Homoliak, I., Toffalini, F., Guarnizo, J., Elovici, Y., Ochoa, M.: Insight into insiders and it: a survey of insider threat taxonomies, analysis, modeling, and countermeasures. ACM Comput. Surv.(CSUR) **52**(2), 1–40 (2019)

7. Kim, J., Park, M., Kim, H., Cho, S., Kang, P.: Insider threat detection based on user behavior modeling and anomaly detection algorithms. Appl. Sci. **9**(19), 4018 (2019)

8. Ni, S., Zou, S., Chen, J.: Evolutionary game model of internal threats to nuclear security in spent fuel reprocessing plants based on RDEU theory. Sustainability **14**(4), 2163 (2022)

9. Osborne, M.J., Rubinstein, A.: A Course in Game Theory. MIT Press, Cambridge (1994)

10. Peccatiello, R.B., Gondim, J.J.C., Garcia, L.P.F.: Applying one-class algorithms for data stream-based insider threat detection. IEEE Access (2023)

11. Quinteros, M.J., Villena, M.J., Villena, M.G.: An evolutionary game theoretic model of whistleblowing behaviour in organizations. IMA J. Manag. Math. **33**(2), 289–314 (2021)

12. Randive, K., Mohan, R., Sivakrishna, A.M.: An efficient pattern-based approach for insider threat classification using the image-based feature representation. J. Inf. Secur. Appl. **73**, 103434 (2023)

13. García de Soto, B., Turk, Ž., Maciel, A., Mantha, B., Georgescu, A., Sonkor, M.S.: Understanding the significance of cybersecurity in the construction industry: survey findings. J. Constr. Eng. Manag. **148**(9), 04022095 (2022)

14. Tosh, D., Sengupta, S., Kamhoua, C.A., Kwiat, K.A.: Establishing evolutionary game models for cyber security information exchange (cybex). J. Comput. Syst. Sci. **98**, 27–52 (2018)

15. Weibull, J.W.: Evolutionary Game Theory. MIT Press, Cambridge (1997)

Smart Appliance Abnormal Electrical Power Consumption Detection

Rajesh Nayak$^{(\boxtimes)}$ (ID) and C. D. Jaidhar

Department of Information Technology, National Institute of Technology
Karnataka Surathkal, Mangaluru 575025, Karnataka, India
rajeshnayak.207it003@nitk.edu.in

Abstract. Potential cyber threats now have an immensely larger attack surface due to the widespread use of smart devices and smart environments. Smart home appliances build a network of linked objects that exchange information and communicate with each other. Detecting abnormal electrical power consumption becomes a first line of protection for bolstering the security of smart homes. Using Machine Learning (ML), anomalous electrical power consumption of the Smart Appliance can be identified. This work proposes an ML-based anomalous electrical power consumption detection to identify the security breach of the Smart Appliances. SimDataset is used for anomalous power consumption detection as a proof of concept for experimentation, and results depicted that Random Forest (RF) classifier outperformed other ML-based classifiers while detecting the abnormal electrical power usage.

Keywords: Anomaly Detection · Cyber Attacks · Machine Learning · Micro-moment

1 Introduction

Smart houses with smart/Internet of Things (IoT) devices have become a necessary component of modern lifestyles in the age of networked living. These intelligent surroundings promise unprecedented efficiency and ease. Smart meters which is a key component of smart grid, installed in houses to track and optimize energy use are essential to this endeavor. Identifying anomalous power usage reveals a layer of security issues critical to protecting the privacy and integrity of smart home ecosystems and holds the secret to energy efficiency.

The main goals of cyber attacks are the loss of data privacy on smart grid/power grid networks and to disturb normal operation of the computing environment. Losing data privacy is, therefore, incredibly costly and eventually detrimental to the country's economy [1]. Compromising smart meter security allows attackers to inject false data and hack smart devices in the smart home environment. Even though every component in a smart home environment is operating effectively if one of the components somehow acquired false information as a result of external interference or data corruption in the communication line, this false information could also cause the component to take needless

M. Andreoni (Ed.): ACNS 2024 Workshops, LNCS 14587, pp. 193–197, 2024.
https://doi.org/10.1007/978-3-031-61489-7_13

actions that could be extremely dangerous for the entire community connected to that power network [2]. These false data injections and hacked appliances will impact the power consumption patterns. It will alter the regular power consumption pattern to some irregular pattern, which can be called anomalous power consumption. Finding unusual power usage is a critical component of the smart home security.

The primary motivation for this work is, as the consumer will not know about these attacks, one way to make them aware of such a situation is to have a model that performs anomalous power consumption detection and alert the consumer about such irregularities. This work proposes the anomalous power consumption detection based on appliance power consumption data.

The significant contributions are mentioned as follows:

- Security issues and the necessity of anomalous power consumption detection are effectively discussed.
- An appliance power consumption dataset (SimDataset) is utilized to detect anomalous power utilization.
- Different ML-based models are trained and tested to effectively identify anomalous power utilization.
- To the best of our knowledge, proposed work is the first work to detect anomalous power consumption with ML classifiers using an appliance-wise dataset generated from SimDataset.

2   Related Work

Various authors have proposed different approaches for securing the smart meter system, smart grid environment, and to identify anomalous power consumption. A few of them are discussed in this section. The authors of [1] examined and emphasized the aspects of smart meters utilized in various applications. They concentrate on the vulnerabilities in smart meters and use eleven trust models for smart meter security. These are some of the widely used approaches for obtaining and protecting the data privacy that the smart meter observes.

The authors in [2], presented three methods for injecting fake data into the smart grid that are independent of network architecture. These methods include linear regression, linear regression with a time stamp, and delta thresholds. In [3], researchers presented a plan known as "STDL" for effectively gathering power consumption data in advanced metering infrastructure networks while protecting users' privacy by employing deep learning to deliver spoof broadcasts. Using the Change and Transmit method, they first created a dataset for transmission patterns using a clustering algorithm and actual power usage values. Next, an attacker model based on deep learning was trained.

The following two works are related to anomalous power consumption detection using SimDataset. The authors of [4] described a deep learning-based method to identify anomalous power consumption. Deep Neural Networks was used for classification. The author of [5] has proposed an Improved K-Nearest

Neighbors (IKNN) model to categorize unusual power use. They have used unsupervised outlier identification methods and supervised anomaly detection methods that use micro-moments.

3 Proposed Methodology

In the smart home environment, the cyber attacker can access the smart meter through a cyber attack, hack the household smart appliances, and inject false data into the smart meter. Anomalous power consumption detection module is part of the smart meter inside the smart home. The proposed approach (shown in Fig. 1) represents the implementation of the anomalous power consumption detection module where the SimDataset [6] (see Table 1) is used, and the dataset is divided based on the Appliance_ID after removing highly correlated redundant feature. After dividing the dataset, each appliance dataset is divided into 80% training and 20% testing datasets and five classifiers, namely Random Forest (RF), Support Vector Machine (SVM), KNN, Naive Bayes (NB), and Decision Tree(DT). The performance is evaluated using standard performance metrics: accuracy, precision, recall, and F1-Score.

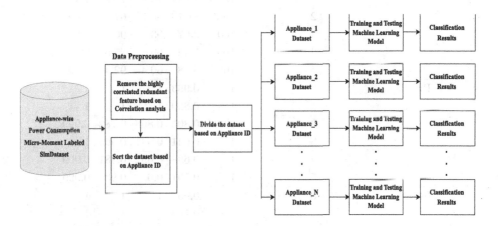

Fig. 1. Proposed Smart Appliance Abnormal Electrical Power Consumption Detection Model

4 Results and Discussion

Experiments are conducted by dividing the SimDataset based on the Appliance_ID feature after removing redundant feature. Using Sklearn library, five ML classifiers are configured and used for the experiments. The hyperparameters of the model kelp as default just by changing the RF criterion to entropy because the dataset utilized in this study is imbalanced, and the Gini criterion is inappropriate. The Table 2 shows the performance results of the experiments

Table 1. Appliance-wise details of SimDataset.

Appliance_ID	Number of Instances					
	Class 0	Class 1	Class 2	Class 3	Class 4	Total
0	11068	1455	1455	0	3542	17520
1	11122	1454	1453	0	3491	17520
2	10427	1406	1405	910	3372	17520
3	11210	1965	1964	1116	1265	17520
4	8405	1039	1041	1818	5217	17520
5	7193	461	461	2499	6906	17520

Class 0-Good usage, Class 1-Turn on, Class 2-Turn off, Class 3-Excessive consumption, and Class 4-consumption while outside

Table 2. Performance of ML classifiers on six appliance datasets

Performance Metric	Appliance_ID	RF	SVM	KNN	NB	DT
Accuracy(%)	0	100	96	100	100	100
	1	100	79.2	100	100	100
	2	99.7	81.1	80.7	67.8	99.9
	3	100	93.7	93.3	96.1	100
	4	100	70.3	69.3	75.5	99.9
	5	100	59.8	60.4	92.4	99.9
Precision	0	1	0.963	1	1	1
	1	1	0.899	1	1	1
	2	0.997	0.805	0.808	0.782	0.999
	3	1	0.941	0.931	0.965	1
	4	1	0.688	0.692	0.881	0.999
	5	1	0.591	0.6	0.93	0.999
Recall	0	1	0.96	1	1	1
	1	1	0.792	1	1	1
	2	0.997	0.811	0.807	0.678	0.999
	3	1	0.937	0.933	0.961	1
	4	1	0.703	0.693	0.755	0.999
	5	1	0.598	0.604	0.924	0.999
F1-Score	0	1	0.959	1	1	1
	1	1	0.808	1	1	1
	2	0.997	0.808	0.808	0.682	0.999
	3	1	0.939	0.932	0.962	1
	4	1	0.691	0.692	0.778	0.999
	5	1	0.593	0.602	0.922	0.999

performed appliance-wise. Results clearly depicts for Appliance_ID 0 and 1 all models except SVM (due to its dependency on scale of the feature values) performed well. Overall it can be concluded that RF classifier outperformed all other classifiers in all appliance datasets.

5   Conclusion

As the inclusion of smart meters presents many advantages in monitoring power consumption and device behavior, it also involves security risk as it becomes a source for attackers to hack the devices and perform false data injection attacks, leading to abnormal power consumption patterns. This work proposed an ML-based classifier using SimDataset as proof of concept to detect these abnormal power consumption because proper false data injected datasets are unavailable. Results depicted that on the SimDataset, RF classifier has produced the best results on all appliance datasets. One of the limitations of this work is that the dataset has power consumption data for only six appliances. Future studies can include using more smart appliance power consumption data and performing false data injection, identifying anomalous power, and alerting consumers about security threats.

References

1. Abdalzaher, M.S., Fouda, M.M., Ibrahem, M.I.: Data privacy preservation and security in smart metering systems. Energes **15**(19) (2022)
2. Nawaz, R., Akhtar, R., Shahid, M.A., Qureshi, I.M., Mahmood, M.H.: Machine learning based false data injection in smart grid. Int. J. Electi. Power Energy Syst. **130** (2021)
3. Ibrahem, M.I., Mahmoud, M., Fouda, M.M., Alsolami, F., Alasmary, W., Shen, X.: Privacy preserving and efficient data collection scheme for ami networks using deep learning. IEEE Internet Things J. **8**(23), 17131–17146 (2021)
4. Himeur, Y., Alsalcmi, A., Bensaali, F., Amira, A.: A novel approach for detecting anomalous energy consumption based on micro-moments and deep neural networks. Cogn. Comput. **12**, 1381–1401 (2020). https://doi.org/10.1007/s12559-020-09764-y
5. Himeur, Y., Alsalemi, A., Bensaali, F., Amira, A.: Smart power consumption abnormality detection in buildings using micro-moments and improved K-nearest neighbors. Int. J. Intell. Syst. **36**, 2865–2894 (2021). https://doi.org/10.1002/int.22404
6. Alsalemi, A., et al.: Endorsing domestic energy saving behavior using micro-moment classification. Appl. Energy **250**, 1302–1311 (2019). https://doi.org/10.1016/j.apenergy.2019.05.089

Towards Secure 5G Infrastructures for Production Systems

Martin Henze[1,2(✉)], Maximilian Ortmann[3], Thomas Vogt[1], Osman Ugus[4],
Kai Hermann[5], Svenja Nohr[6], Zeren Lu[4], Sotiris Michaelides[1],
Angela Massonet[3], and Robert H. Schmitt[1,3]

[1] RWTH Aachen University, Aachen, Germany
henze@spice.rwth-aachen.de
[2] Fraunhofer FKIE, Wachtberg, Germany
[3] Fraunhofer IPT, Aachen, Germany
[4] Swissbit Germany AG, Berlin, Germany
[5] Utimaco IS GmbH, Aachen, Germany
[6] oculavis GmbH, Aachen, Germany

Abstract. To meet the requirements of modern production, industrial communication increasingly shifts from wired fieldbus to wireless 5G communication. Besides tremendous benefits, this shift introduces severe novel risks, ranging from limited reliability over new security vulnerabilities to a lack of accountability. To address these risks, we present approaches to (i) prevent attacks through authentication and redundant communication, (ii) detect anomalies and jamming, and (iii) respond to detected attacks through device exclusion and accountability measures.

Keywords: 5G · Network Security · Industrial Networks · Wireless Networks

1 Introduction

The digital transformation of production requires a change from conventional to flexible and networked systems such as the Industrial Internet of Things (IIoT) [6,8,11]. 5G communication offers the opportunity to advance the networking of production and thus plays a key role in the digitization of production. Yet, deploying 5G as the communication technology in industrial settings introduces new cybersecurity risks for manufacturing companies.

These risks mainly result from the introduction of wireless communication into previously wired industrial networks as illustrated in Fig. 1 [3]. The first concern involves the *limited reliability of systems*. Current production systems are designed with high-reliable fieldbuses, optimized for specific use cases, posing a challenge to replicate in wireless 5G environments. Second, by breaking up local fieldbus systems through the introduction of 5G, *new security vulnerabilities* are emerging on the safety-critical production shop floor. Finally, the integration of 5G systems into production increases the number of companies

© The Author(s), under exclusive license to Springer Nature Switzerland AG 2024
M. Andreoni (Ed.): ACNS 2024 Workshops, LNCS 14587, pp. 198–203, 2024.
https://doi.org/10.1007/978-3-031-61489-7_14

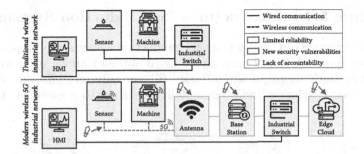

Fig. 1. Moving from wired to wireless industrial communication introduces novel risks: limited reliability, new security vulnerabilities, and lack of accountability. (Color figure online)

involved, leading to a *lack of accountability*. Consequently, to capitalize on the promisingly significant benefits of 5G and wireless communication, it is requires to address the risks, especially w.r.t. security.

Related Work. Several works study the challenges resulting from switching to 5G communication in general (not specific to production) [1,13]. Similarly, separate research focuses on securing industrial and IIoT networks without considering 5G [6,11,14]. However, a systematic and holistic approach to securely deploy 5G in real-world production systems is missing.

Contributions. We report on our ongoing work to secure industrial 5G communication. Our overarching goal is to design, implement, and validate a comprehensive toolbox of solutions for the prevention, detection, and response to the risks associated with using 5G for industrial communication.

2   5G in Industrial Communication

Wireless communication is a key component of future smart factories, facilitating comprehensive automation, optimization, and flexibility through the scalable, networked operation of sensors and actuators, the integration of large computing resources, and the incorporation of IIoT devices on the shop floor.

Operating Technologies (OT) in manufacturing require communication technology to ensure reliability, availability, and real-time capability. 5G non-public networks are gaining attention for meeting these demands, offering superior performance and security compared to WiFi, Bluetooth, or LTE [4]. With capabilities like Massive Machine Type Communication (mMTC), and Ultra-Reliable Low-Latency Communication (URLLC), 5G addresses diverse scenarios, including IIoT needs for low latency and reliable communication.

However, the transition from wired, vendor-specific industrial solutions to multi-vendor wireless networks introduces new risks, such as insufficient integrability into existing IT infrastructures, new security vulnerabilities, and a lack of accountability. Therefore, a widespread adoption of 5G in production is challenging due to security and legal related uncertainties in such diverse architectures.

3   Secure 5G Infrastructures for Production Systems

To realize secure 5G infrastructures for production systems, we propose a comprehensive approach (Fig. 2) encompassing (i) authentication, authenticity, and redundancy methods to *prevent* attacks, (ii) anomaly and jamming *detection*, and (iii) device exclusion and accountability measures to *respond* to attacks.

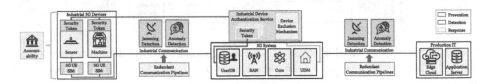

Fig. 2. Our secure 5G infrastructure for production systems provides mechanisms to prevent, detect, and respond to attacks. (Color figure online)

3.1   Prevention

To secure industrial devices in 5G networks, we provide measures to mitigate threats such as impersonation, physical compromise, and machine-in-the-middle.

Industrial Device Authentication. To mutually authenticate industrial devices, we develop a hardware security token-based industrial device authentication (IDA) service, independent of the network, with a 5G system interface for device exclusion (cf. Sect. 3.3). The IDA service periodically authenticates all industrial 5G devices using a challenge-response-based mutual entity authentication protocol. A hardware security token stores cryptographic material, and keys are provided by a certificate authority through the X.509 PKI standard. Certificates can be requested and revoked via REST, EST, CMP, SCEP, or ACME. The validity status of each certificate is saved at an OCSP responder and verified via OCSP [10] or a revocation list. Furthermore, our key establishment method based on the IDA service and secure tokens addresses threats that cannot be solved by device authentication alone, e.g., by providing keys for security protocols supporting pre-shared keys, such as TLS. By combining identifiers, i.e., device identity and SIM, with mutual authentication between IDA service and devices, unauthenticated devices can be detected and excluded.

Redundant Communication. To enable industrial real-time applications, we develop a deterministic 5G Time-Sensitive Networking (TSN) infrastructure with redundant, hardware-separated communication pipelines. As TSN operates at the OSI MAC layer (Layer 2), higher-level security mechanisms offer no protection to TSN data [12]. Hence, we must implement security at Layer 2 or below to mitigate TSN-specific security risks, and satisfy low latency and high performance requirements. MACsec [7] safeguards authenticity and optionally confidentiality in TSN-based communication. We obtain MACsec keys from the key establishment mechanism of the IDA service to transfer the trust and security gained from device authentication into a TSN-based redundant communication.

3.2   Detection

We propose complementary approaches to detect any remaining anomalies in industrial 5G communication as well as jamming attacks on the physical layer.

Anomaly Detection. Unlike intrusion detection in office networks and data centers, anomaly detection in industrial networks leverages the predictability and determinism of industrial communication. It is proven effective in identifying subtle anomalies in timing, order of communication, or recognizing invalid physical states [2,5,14]. However, when considering wireless communication, unique challenges prevent the adoption of existing anomaly detection for industrial networks. Most notably, inherent wireless characteristics such as the use of a shared medium result in less predictable communication patterns. Likewise, the use of wireless communication further demands for encrypted communication, preventing detection approaches relying on deep packet inspection [14].

To address these issues, we develop a method for detecting anomalies in industrial 5G by incorporating wireless characteristics, such as packet drops and retransmissions, to existing timing- and sequence-based solutions. Concretely, we extend the IPAL framework for industrial intrusion detection [14] to realize anomaly detection for less predictable wireless communication. To optionally also allow for the inclusion of process state information despite the use of encrypted communication, we further extend the IPAL framework to decrypt TLS.

Jamming Detection. Denial of service attacks on the physical layer of 5G through radio jamming pose a major threat to highly connected production systems. Easily accessible jamming devices can be used to disrupt the connectivity of assets, resulting in machine downtime or, in the worst case, causing harm to humans. To counter corresponding threats, we develop a jamming detection and localization framework using software-defined radios tested in a realistic shop floor environment. The framework will enable the development of mitigation and response strategies tailored to industrial environments.

3.3   Response

Supplementing prevention and detection, response mechanisms include technical approaches such as device exclusion as well as legal accountability guidelines.

Device Exclusion. Compared to information technology, OT systems prioritize aspects such as performance, resource limitations, and availability in relation to potential system failures. Therefore, two device exclusion mechanisms will be examined: (i) a PKI-based devices exclusion mechanisms executed by the IDA service when the authenticity of an industrial device cannot be verified and (ii) a 5G-based device exclusion approach that blocks SIM cards in case of detected malicious activities. As PKI-based response, we can suspend and/or revoke the certificate of the malicious industrial device using corresponding PKI APIs. However, as the industrial device still remains integrated into the 5G network, this strategy requires entities to validate certificates via the OCSP responder for secure certificate-based communication whenever connecting with an industrial device. To lift this requirement, a 5G-based response allows to block the SIM responsible for linking the malicious industrial device to the 5G network, e.g., by utilizing the 5G API to remove the corresponding subscriber from the 5G core network. The device's credentials, such as the SUPI, are made available to the IDA service for this purpose.

Accountability. To address legal questions of responsibility and accountability for production failures due to vulnerabilities in 5G communication infrastructures, multi-vendor architectures, and networked production facilities, a legal assessment of the developed approaches complements our ongoing work. This includes considerations for legal requirements in cybersecurity, the strengthened powers of supervisory authorities, and questions regarding the use of communication data under civil and data protection law. Furthermore, the impact of planned regulations such as the European NIS2 Directive, the European Data Act, and the European Cyber Resilience Act is also covered.

4 Outlook and Conclusion

Our collaborative effort between industry and academia aims to comprehensively address cyberattacks on 5G communication in industrial production by developing, implementing, and integrating preventive, detection, and response measures. We evaluate these approaches in industry-driven use cases, focusing on machine monitoring and remote maintenance within the 5G-Industry Campus Europe [9], covering a machine hall and $1\,km^2$ of outdoor space. This enables us to research and develop 5G technologies for complex industrial applications and validate them in practical settings to ensure that our solutions are practical and adaptable to new use cases and environments.

Acknowledgments. This work has been funded by the German Federal Office for Information Security (BSI) under project funding reference numbers 01MO23016A, 01MO23016B, 01MO23016C, 01MO23016D, and 01MO23016G (5G-Sierra). The authors are responsible for the content of this publication.

References

1. Ahmad, I., et al.: 5G security: analysis of threats and solutions. In: CSCN (2017)
2. Aoudi, W., Iturbe, M., Almgren, M.: Truth will out: departure-based process-level detection of stealthy attacks on control systems. In: ACM CCS (2018)
3. Bodenhausen, J., et al.: Securing wireless communication in critical infrastructure: challenges and opportunities. In: MobiQuitous (2023)
4. Caro, J.B., et al.: Empirical study on 5G NR cochannel coexistence. vol. 11 (2022)
5. Choi, H., et al.: Detecting attacks against robotic vehicles: a control invariant approach. In: ACM CCS (2018)
6. Dahlmanns, M., et al.: Missed opportunities: measuring the untapped TLS support in the industrial internet of things. In: ACM ASIA CCS (2022)
7. IEEE: IEEE standard for local and metropolitan area networks-media access control (MAC) security. In: IEEE Std 802.1AE-2018 (2018)

8. Kehl, P., et al.: Comparison of 5G enabled control loops for production. In: IEEE PIMRC (2020)
9. König, N., Kehl, P.: 5G-industry campus Europe (2022)
10. Santesson, S., et al.: X.509 internet public key infrastructure online certificate status protocol - OCSP. In: RFC 6960, June 2013
11. Serror, M., et al.: Challenges and opportunities in securing the industrial internet of things. IEEE Trans. Ind. Inf. **17**(5), 2985–2996 (2021)
12. Watson, V., Ruland, C., Waedt, K.: MAC-layer security for time-sensitive switched ethernet networks. In: GI INFORMATIK (2020)
13. Wen, M., et al.: Private 5G networks: concepts, architectures, and research landscape, vol. 16 (2022)
14. Wolsing, K., et al.: IPAL: breaking up silos of protocol-dependent and domain-specific industrial intrusion detection systems. In: RAID (2022)

Cybersecurity Awareness Education: Just as Useful for Technical Users

Daniel Köhler(✉)📧, Michael Büßemeyer, and Christoph Meinel

Hasso Plattner Institute, University of Potsdam, Potsdam, Germany
daniel.koehler@hpi.de, michael.buessemeyer@student.hpi.de

Abstract. Cybersecurity education is often perceived as necessary particularly for laypersons, as experts in the field are usually expected to be aware of the risks posed by human-centered attacks such as phishing. In a lab study with 48 participants from IT-related study programs, we studied their phishing investigation behavior using an eye tracker across three email classification sessions. Between the first two sessions, participants received additional training on detecting phishing attacks. The third session, one week later served to measure retention of performance. Exposure to the teaching material particularly showed to decrease investigation time required for the classification. Further, it helped participants focus on the important indicators inside the phishing emails.

Keywords: Phishing · Education · Experts · Eye Tracking

1 Introduction

Cybersecurity attacks are still a dominant part of everyday life. With increased digital exposure, more and more people become potential targets for cybercriminals. Phishing, a threat from the social engineering category, has become a significant threat to people, having been used as a vector of initial access in more than 90% of data breaches as reported by Cisco [3].

The threat of email phishing can generally be accounted for by either technical controls such as email filters and sandboxes or by employing organizational measures such as education. Educational measures for phishing have been of great interest since the early years of phishing research. Much relevant work has been published by authors such as *Kumaraguru et al.* who investigated (game-based) educational measures to collect insights on participant perception and recall of phishing education [6,7]. Further significant work has been aggregated by various researchers investigating which cues in emails particularly resonate with users and how users behave around phishing emails [4,9].

Various previous publications, as analyzed in the comparative literature review by *Jampen et al.* [5] point out that the technicality of a target impacts their susceptibility to fall victim to a phishing attack. Therefore, phishing education is often aimed at laypersons to get them on par with their more technically advanced peers to achieve an appropriate level of protection amongst, for example, employees in a company.

Our manuscript provides a preliminary insight into an in-lab study with 48 rather technical participants, each categorizing a total of 30 emails for being phishing or legitimate across three study sessions. During the sessions, participant behavior was tracked by an eye tracker to ensure that the categorization performance and the decision process could be analyzed. From the data collected during our study, we present one preliminary contribution:

While educational material has not increased the classification performance of participants, it reduced the time required for the classification activity and increased the relative time of focus on phishing indicators inside the emails.

2   Methodology

Our in-lab study featured a multi-stage design as presented in Fig. 1. In two sessions per participant, participants performed three email classification tasks. In between, they were exposed to different teaching materials[1] and a break of one week to measure retention. During the conceptualization of our study, we prepared three sets of emails with ten emails each. To ensure an internally valid study design, these were distributed among participants so that each sequence of email sets was studied with eight participants (48 participants and six variations of the sequence of the email sets). Further, we designed our emails to be of similar difficulty across the three sets. To achieve this, each email set contained six phishing emails of differing difficulty (2 easy, 2 medium, 2 difficult) and four legitimate emails. Emails were designed based on vectors reported by previous research such as being *Loss-*, or *Reward-Based* [2], containing *images and logos* [10], a *personal salutation* and targeting psychological vectors such as *urgency* or *fear* [8].

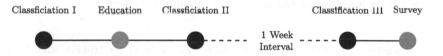

Classficiation I   Education   Classficiation II   Classification III   Survey

1 Week
Interval

Fig. 1. Overview of the study design featuring three email classification sessions, intervened with an education session and a one-week study interception.

During the classification tasks, participants were recorded by an eye tracker, which allowed later analysis of behavior on top of classification performance. Our participants were students recruited from the Bachelor and Master programs in Digital Engineering at the Hasso Plattner Institute. Therefore, all participants

---

[1] The analysis of this work towards the impact of the different types of teaching materials has not yet been completed. Hence, this poster omits the differentiation between the four styles of teaching material and solely presents overarching results.

have a relatively high affinity towards IT systems. In the survey, participants further reported their self-perceived cybersecurity knowledge on a scale from 1 (*No Knowledge*) to 5 (*Expert Knowledge*). Most participants rated their knowledge level 2 (N = 20) or 3 (N = 17), confirming the assumption of a relatively coherent skill level among participants.

3 Study Results

Across the three classification tasks in the three stages of the study, the performance in terms of correct classifications did not significantly change. The performance across all the stages averaged at 84.01% correct classifications ($P_{S1} = 84.38\%, P_{S2} = 83.75\%, P_{S3} = 83.91\%$). As the classification performance was neither affected by the study material nor by the interval of one week between stages two and three, we investigated other measures of behavior.

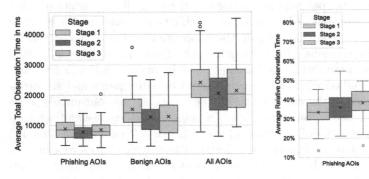

(a) **Absolute** observation time   (b) **Relative** observation time

Fig. 2. Email view time throughout the different stages of the study. Aggregated average view times for phishing and benign AOIs in phishing emails.

One measure we could investigate based on the used eye tracker was the time a participant spent on their classification tasks. Figure 2a presents an overview of averaged **absolute email observation** times. We categorized all areas of interest (AOIs) inside the emails into either phishing or benign. Viewing phishing AOIs should induce suspiciousness, but viewing benign areas should increase the trustworthiness of an email. As Fig. 2a shows, after consuming the teaching material, the absolute view time of emails increases in the test for retention in stage three. We could not observe statistically significant differences in the absolute view times of the phishing or benign indicators.

Due to the overall email view time change, Fig. 2b presents the averaged **relative viewtime** of phishing and benign indicators. Visually observable is that throughout the three stages, even after the one-week intervention, the average relative time spent investigating phishing indicators increases from 33.44% in stage one to 38.22% in stage three. This difference is significant, as confirmed with a t-test with $p = 0.0018$, assuming $\alpha = 0.05$ as the threshold for significance.

Figure 3 presents additional detailed information on the phishing indicators viewed and investigated by participants. We observe the consistent increase of relative view time for the indicators surrounding the *sender address (suspicious part)* and *domain*. Therefore, participants now focus more on the email addresses and corresponding domains used in the phishing emails. Such behavior can properly help detect various forms of sender obfuscation currently observed in the wild, such as attackers using additional top-level domains to obfuscate their phishing attempts (e.g., *amazon.supportsite.com* instead of *amazon.com* to imitate a supposed helpdesk).

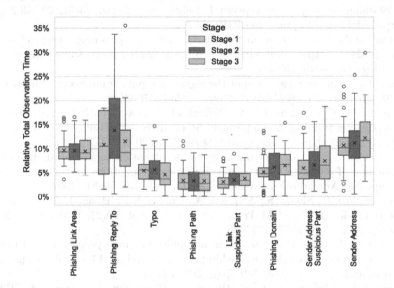

Fig. 3. Overview of the averaged relative view time of phishing and benign AOIs.

4   Discussion and Conclusion

This work shall open up discussions on whom to target with phishing education. Further, we appreciate the discussion on study designs that would allow a more appropriate attribution of the observed effect to the educational material instead of the repetition of the classification exercise.

The preliminary results of our study show that while educational content did not improve the classification performance of participants with high IT affinity, it improved how they classify emails. The data indicates that participants take overall less time to classify emails. The educational material has highlighted common measures to identify phishing, and the analysis has shown that participants focus more on phishing indicators. They *lose* less time during email analysis to investigate benign indicators and spend their time more efficiently.

Author contributions. Contributions according to the CRediT Framework [1]: **Daniel Köhler:** Writing, Conceptualization, Supervision, Project Administration, Investigation **Michael Büßemeyer:** Methodology, Software, Formal Analysis, Data Curation, Visualization **Christoph Meinel:** Funding Acquisition.

References

1. Allen, L., O'Connell, A., Kiermer, V.: How can we ensure visibility and diversity in research contributions? How the contributor role taxonomy (CRediT) is helping the shift from authorship to contributorship. Learn. Publishing **32**(1), 71–74 (2019). https://doi.org/10.1002/leap.1210
2. Baryshevtsev, M., McGlynn, J.: Persuasive appeals predict credibility judgments of phishing messages. Cyberpsychol. Behav. Soc. Netw. **23**(5), 297–302 (2020). https://doi.org/10.1089/cyber.2019.0592
3. Cisco umbrella: cybersecurity threat trends: phishing, crypto top the list (2021). https://umbrella.cisco.com/info/2021-cyber-security-threat-trends-phishing-crypto-top-the-list
4. Furnell, S.: Phishing: can we spot the signs? Comput. Fraud Secur. **2007**(3), 10–15 (2007). https://doi.org/10.1016/S1361-3723(07)70035-0
5. Jampen, D., Gür, G., Sutter, T., Tellenbach, B.: Don't click: towards an effective anti-phishing training. A comparative literature review. Hum.-centric Comput. Inf. Sci. **10** (2020).https://doi.org/10.1186/s13673-020-00237-7
6. Kumaraguru, P., et al.: Getting users to pay attention to anti-phishing education: evaluation of retention and transfer. In: Proceedings of the Anti-phishing Working Groups 2nd Annual eCrime Researchers Summit, pp. 70–81 (2007)
7. Kumaraguru, P., Sheng, S., Acquisti, A., Cranor, L.F., Hong, J.: Teaching Johnny not to fall for phish. ACM Trans. Internet Technol. **10**(2), 1–31 (2010). https://doi.org/10.1145/1754393.1754396
8. McAlaney, J., Hills, P.J.: Understanding phishing email processing and perceived trustworthiness through eye tracking. Front. Psychol. **11** (2020). https://www.frontiersin.org/articles/10.3389/fpsyg.2020.01756
9. Parsons, K., McCormac, A., Pattinson, M., Butavicius, M., Jerram, C.: Phishing for the truth: a scenario-based experiment of users' behavioural response to emails. In: Janczewski, L.J., Wolfe, H.B., Shenoi, S. (eds.) SEC 2013. IAICT, vol. 405, pp. 366–378. Springer, Heidelberg (2013). https://doi.org/10.1007/978-3-642-39218-4_27
10. Williams, E.J., Polage, D.: How persuasive is phishing email? The role of authentic design, influence and current events in email judgements. Behav. Inf. Technol. **38**(2), 184–197 (2019). https://doi.org/10.1080/0144929X.2018.1519599

Salsa20 Cipher: Assigning Values to Probabilistic Neutral Key Bits

Nitin Kumar Sharma$^{(\boxtimes)}$ and Sabyasachi Dey

Department of Mathematics, Birla Institute of Technology and Science Pilani,
Hyderabad, Jawahar Nagar, Hyderabad 500078, India
sharmanitinkumar685@gmail.com

Abstract. In this paper, we present how to choose the actual value for so-called probabilistic neutral bits optimally. Because of the limited influence of these key bits on the computation, these are fixed to a constant value, often zero for simplicity. As we will show, despite the fact that their influence is limited, the constant can be chosen in significantly better ways, and intriguingly zero is the worst choice.

Keywords: Salsa20 · Cryptanalysis · Probabilistic Neutral Bits · Backward bias

1 Introduction

Salsa20 is, as part of the eSTREAM portfolio for software and is the base design for the cipher ChaCha used in TLS, one of the most important and analyzed stream ciphers today. It was designed by Daniel J. Bernstein in 2005 and was submitted to the ECRYPT Stream Cipher Project (eSTREAM).

The detailed structure and the use of various tools in its design have been discussed in [2]. Below we discuss the structure of 256-bit key version of Salsa20 cipher. The cipher is represented in a 4×4 matrix form consisting of 16 words, where each word is of 32 bits. The 256-bit key version of cipher takes 8 key words $(k_0, k_1, \ldots, k_7)$, 4 constants words (c_0, c_1, c_2, c_3), 2 IV words (t_0, t_1) and 2 counter words (v_0, v_1) as input and generates a 512-bit output. The constant words (c_0, c_1, c_2, c_3) for 256-bit key version have fixed value as: $c_0 = \text{0x61707865}, c_1 = \text{0x3320646e}, c_2 = \text{0x79622d32}, c_3 = \text{0x6b206574}$. The state matrix form of the Salsa20 is given by:

$$X = \begin{pmatrix} X_0 & X_1 & X_2 & X_3 \\ X_4 & X_5 & X_6 & X_7 \\ X_8 & X_9 & X_{10} & X_{11} \\ X_{12} & X_{13} & X_{14} & X_{15} \end{pmatrix} = \begin{pmatrix} c_0 & k_0 & k_1 & k_2 \\ k_3 & c_1 & v_0 & v_1 \\ t_0 & t_1 & c_2 & k_4 \\ k_5 & k_6 & k_7 & c_3 \end{pmatrix}.$$

In Salsa20 cipher algorithm, the function operated in each round is a nonlinear operation which transforms a vector (a, b, c, d) into (a', b', c', d') by performing

M. Andreoni (Ed.): ACNS 2024 Workshops, LNCS 14587, pp. 209–213, 2024.
https://doi.org/10.1007/978-3-031-61489-7_16

the $\oplus, \boxplus$ and $\lll$ operation for each round. Here, $\oplus$ denotes XOR operation between the bits, $\boxplus$ is the addition modulo 2^{32}, $\lll$ is left cyclic rotation operation.

$$b' = b \oplus ((a \boxplus d) \lll 7),$$
$$c' = c \oplus ((b' \boxplus a) \lll 9),$$
$$d' = d \oplus ((c' \boxplus b') \lll 13),$$
$$a' = a \oplus ((d' \boxplus c') \lll 18).$$

(1)

This function described in Eq. 1 is known as the quarterround function. This function is applied to each column and row of the matrix X. The application of this function along columns is known as column-round. The ordering of (a, b, c, d) along the columns is $(X_0, X_4, X_8, X_{12}), (X_5, X_9, X_{13}, X_1), (X_{10}, X_{14}, X_2, X_6)$ and $(X_{15}, X_3, X_7, X_{11})$. After columns the quarterround function is operated along the rows called row-round. The ordering along the rows is (X_0, X_1, X_2, X_3), $(X_5, X_6, X_7, X_4), (X_{10}, X_{11}, X_8, X_9)$ and $(X_{15}, X_{12}, X_{13}, X_{14})$. In the Salsa20 cipher algorithm, if the quarterround function is performed on X matrix up to n rounds, then we denote the obtained matrix by $X^{(n)}$. The final output matrix is denoted by Z and achieved by the addition of input matrix X and iterated matrix $X^{(n)}$, i.e., $Z = X + X^{(n)}$. The quarterround function is reversible and known as the reverse quarterround function. This function is used to obtain the relation between the intermediate state and ciphertext by operating in the reverse direction.

2   Finding Probabilistic Neutral Bits

Now we explain the probabilistic neutral bits (also called as non-significant key bits) and the procedure of finding those bits. Using this procedure we partition the key bits into significant key bits and non-significant key bits. Non-significant key bits are those which influences the output difference bit with low probability. The aim of partitioning the key bits is that, instead of searching over all 2^{256} feasible possibilities of the key bits (for 256 bit key), if, for example m bits are significant and the remaining $(256 - m)$ bits are non-significant, at first we aim to search the m significant bits only. As a result, the maximum number of guesses is reduced to 2^m. Once we achieve these bits, we can find the remaining bits by exhaustive search.

Let us define the non-significant bits or PNBs formally. For an initial state matrix X, after introducing a suitable non-zero input difference ($\mathcal{ID}$) we get another state X'. Running X, X' for r-rounds $(1 \leq r < n)$ we observe the output difference ($\mathcal{OD}$) at position (p, q), i.e., $\Delta X_p^{(r)}[q]$. The bias is given by ϵ_d. After completing the n-rounds we obtain the final state $X^{(n)}$ and $X'^{(n)}$ which are operated with the respective initial states X and X' to obtain keystream blocks Z and Z'. We get $X^{(r)} = F^{-1}(Z - X)$ and $X'^{(r)} = F^{-1}(Z' - X')$.

In the procedure of finding the PNB we will alter one key-bit say l among the total keys (128 or 256) in the initial states X and X'. $\bar{X}$ and $\bar{X}'$ are the new altered states. We apply the reverse round function on $Z - \bar{X}$ and $Z' - \bar{X}'$ by

$(n - r)$-rounds and obtain the state matrices $\bar{M}$ and $\bar{M}'$ i.e., $\bar{M} = F^{-1}(Z - \bar{X})$ and $\bar{M}' = F^{-1}(Z' - \bar{X}')$. For a non-significant bit, the probability of the event $\Delta\bar{M}_p[q] = \Delta X_p^{(r)}[q]$ is expected to be high. We denote γ_l to be the bias of this event, i.e.,

$$\Pr_{v,t}\left[\Delta X_p^{(r)}[q] \oplus \Delta\bar{M}_p[q] = 0 | \Delta X = D_{ID}\right] = \frac{1}{2}(1 + \gamma_l). \tag{2}$$

To construct the set of PNBs, in the work of [1], at first a threshold γ is chosen. Each of the key bits for which $\gamma_i \geq \gamma$ are considered to be probabilistically neutral.

3   Assigning the Values to Probabilistic Neutral Bits

We observe that the PNBs are located in the form of blocks, i.e., collections of consecutive bits. We decompose the subspace k_s in the form of subspaces k_{s_i}, where each k_{s_i} corresponds to a block. Now, consider one such block of PNBs of size b at X_i from $X_i[j]$ to $X_i[j+b-1]$. In our attack, after assigning the vector β at the PNBs, we compute $Z - \tilde{X}$ and $Z' - \tilde{X}'$. We know that $\tilde{M} = F^{-1}(Z - \tilde{X})$ and $X^{(r)} = F^{-1}(Z - X)$. Therefore, in order to get a good backward bias, we aim to find out how closely $Z - \tilde{X}$ replicates $Z - X$. In simple words, more the number of bits of $Z - X$ matches with $Z - \tilde{X}$, more is the backward bias.

During the subtraction $Z - \tilde{X}$, the difference between X and $\tilde{X}$ can also propagate to the bit at the position $j + b$ and onwards of $Z - \tilde{X}$ due to carry-propagation. Now, we observe that this probability of propagation varies based on the assigned values at the PNBs. So, if the assigned values at $\tilde{X}[j] \cdots \tilde{X}[j + b - 1]$ can be chosen in such a way that the probability of this propagation can be reduced, we achieve a higher backward bias. We next analyze how the values can be chosen so that this probability of propagation is minimal.

Which Values of β Minimizes the Probability of Propagation: For each of Z_i, X_i and $\tilde{X}_i$, if we consider the PNB block from j to $j+b-1$ bit, each of them is a number between 0 to $2^b - 1$. Let us denote them z, k_n and β respectively. From attackers prospective, z and k_n are unknown, and β is decided by him/her. We aim to find which value of β would be most suitable. The difference between $Z - X$ and $Z - \tilde{X}$ would propagate to $j + b$-th bit if either $k_n > z \geq \beta$ or $\beta > z \geq k_n$.

Theorem 1. *Let for some $\beta \in \{0, 1, 2, \cdots 2^b - 1\}$, $S_\beta = \{(z, x): either\ x > z \geq \beta$ or $\beta > z \geq x\}$. Then $|S_\beta|$ is minimum if $\beta = 2^{b-1} - 1$ or $\beta = 2^{b-1}$, and maximum if $\beta = 0$ or $2^b - 1$.*

Proof. Possible values of (x, z) such that $x > z \geq \beta$ is $^{2^b-\beta}C_2$, since x, z can be any integer in the range $[\beta, 2^b - 1]$. Similarly, possible values of (x, z) such that $\beta > z > x$ is $^\beta C_2$, and possible values such that $\beta > z = x$ is β. Therefore,

$$|S_\beta| = {}^{2^b-\beta}C_2 + {}^{\beta}C_2 + \beta = \frac{(2^b-\beta)!}{(2!)(2^b-\beta-2)!} + \frac{\beta!}{(2!)(\beta-2)!} + \beta$$

$$= 2^{2b-1} - 2^b \times \beta - 2^{b-1} + \beta^2 + \beta.$$

We aim to find the β for which $|S_\beta|$ is minimum. For this, we can write it as:

$$|S_\beta| = 2^{2b-1} - 2^{b-1} + \beta^2 - (2^b - 1) \times \beta$$

$$= 2^{2b-1} - 2^{b-1} - \left(\frac{2^b-1}{2}\right)^2 + \left(\beta - 2^{b-1} + \frac{1}{2}\right)^2.$$

The term $(\beta - 2^{b-1} + \frac{1}{2})^2$ is non-negative. Since β is an integer, $(\beta - 2^{b-1} + \frac{1}{2})^2$ gives minimum value either at $\beta = 2^{(b-1)} - 1$ or at $\beta = 2^{b-1}$, and at both of them $(\beta - 2^{b-1} + \frac{1}{2})^2 = \frac{1}{4}$. So, in both these cases, we get $g(2^{(b-1)} - 1) = 2^{2(b-1)}$ and $g(2^{b-1}) = 2^{2(b-1)}$. Similarly, to find the β for which $|S_\beta|$ is maximum, we focus on the term $\left(\beta - 2^{b-1} + \frac{1}{2}\right)^2$. It gives the maximum value when $\beta = 0$ or $2^b - 1$.

4 Observation for 7-Round 128-Bit Key Version of Salsa20

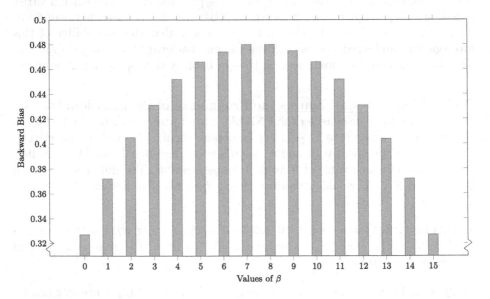

Fig. 1. Graphical Representation of the backward biases for different values of β for the PNBs $\{13, 14, 15, 16\}$

We experiment on a set of four consecutive PNBs $\{13, 14, 15, 16\}$ for 7 round 128-bit key version of Salsa20 from the PNB set. We know that there can be 2^4 possible values of this PNB set, i.e., $\{0, 1, 2, \cdots 15\}$. For each of these values, we will find the value of ϵ_a (backward bias). We observe that we got a maximum backward bias for the values $7, 8$ and a minimum backward bias at $0, 15$. In this case b=4, hence from above theorem $|S_\beta|$ is minimum at $\beta = (2^{b-1} - 1) = (2^3 - 1) = 7$ or $\beta = 2^{b-1} = 2^3 = 8$.

5   Conclusion

In this paper, we present how one can improve the backward bias by choosing optimal values of so-called probabilistic neutral bits.

We observe that we got a maximum backward bias for the values $\beta = 2^{b-1} - 1$ and $\beta = 2^{b-1}$ for block size b. We have shown that value of PNBs should be chosen in significantly better ways, and intriguingly zero is the worst choice. This technique gives a significant improvement in the backward bias and hence improve the attack complexity. Also, we are very hopeful that our ideas can work on other ARX designs.

References

1. Aumasson, J.-P., Fischer, S., Khazaei, S., Meier, W., Rechberger, C.: New features of Latin dances: analysis of Salsa, ChaCha, and Rumba. In: Nyberg, K. (ed.) FSE 2008. LNCS, vol. 5086, pp. 470–488. Springer, Heidelberg (2008). https://doi.org/10.1007/978-3-540-71039-4_30
2. Bernstein, D.J.: The Salsa20 family of stream ciphers. In: Robshaw, M., Billet, O. (eds.) New Stream Cipher Designs. LNCS, vol. 4986, pp. 84–97. Springer, Heidelberg (2008). https://doi.org/10.1007/978-3-540-68351-3_8

A Versatile and Unified HQC Hardware Accelerator

Francesco Antognazza[1]([✉]) [iD], Alessandro Barenghi[1] [iD], Gerardo Pelosi[1] [iD], and Ruggero Susella[2] [iD]

[1] Department of Electronics, Information and Bioengineering - DEIB, Politecnico di Milano, Milan, MI, Italy
{francesco.antognazza,alessandro.barenghi,gerardo.pelosi}@polimi.it
[2] STMicrolectronics S.r.l., Agrate Brianza, MB, Italy
ruggero.susella@st.com

Abstract. This work presents a hardware design for the post-quantum Hamming Quasi-Cyclic (HQC) Key Encapsulation Mechanism (KEM). We present a novel unified design allowing a runtime selection of both the cryptosystem primitive being computed (i.e., key generation, encapsulation, and decapsulation) and the parameter set suitable to provide a security margin equivalent to the one exhibited by AES-128, AES-192, and AES-256, respectively. Despite the provided flexibility, our design improves the latency (from 1.56× to 2.38×) and efficiency (from 1.24× to 1.88×) with respect to the state of the art on a HQC hardware accelerator exhibiting a security margin equivalent to the one of AES-128, while providing original designs and benchmark points also for the other security margins. To the best of our knowledge, this is the first hardware design with full compliance with the HQC specification.

Keywords: Post-quantum Cryptography · Hardware Security

1 Introduction

Recently, we have observed continuous advancements in the computational capabilities of quantum computers. IBM has been following a tight roadmap doubling the number of qubits in a single quantum processor unit (QPU) every year, surpassing in 2023 the barrier of $1,100$ qubits. Following this trend, in a few decades, the application of Shor's algorithm will be able to solve the computationally hard problems underlying most of the currently and widely deployed asymmetric cryptographic algorithms, namely the integer factorization and discrete logarithm problems used in RSA and ECDSA algorithms, respectively. In response to this, the USA National Institute of Standards and Technology (NIST) started a standardization process to evaluate cryptographic primitives able to withstand cryptanalysis aided by a quantum computer. While the lattice-based KEM named Kyber was selected as the first quantum-resistant (post-quantum) Key Encapsulation Mechanism (KEM) to be standardized, NIST will

M. Andreoni (Ed.): ACNS 2024 Workshops, LNCS 14587, pp. 214–219, 2024.
https://doi.org/10.1007/978-3-031-61489-7_17

also select a code-based algorithm in the near term, choosing one among BIKE, Classic McEliece, and HQC. HQC [2] received a wide interest from the industrial and academic communities as it exhibits good performance figures as well as strong security guarantees coming from the polynomial reduction of its underlying random quasi-cyclic (QC) syndrome decoding problem to a computationally hard problem, without relying on the indistinguishability of a hidden QC medium density parity check code from a QC random parity check code. Within the standardization context, efficient and highly optimized hardware realizations like [3–5] are necessary to thoroughly assess each proposed algorithm.

Contributions. We present a novel unified hardware design allowing a runtime selection of both the cryptosystem primitive being computed (i.e., KeyGen, Encap, and Decap) and the parameter set suitable to provide a security margin equivalent to the one exhibited by AES-128, AES-192, and AES-256, respectively. The original aspects of the proposed design are in the effective resource sharing for the realization of the distinct encoders and decoders required to manage the specific error correction codes required by the HQC functionalities to provide all the prescribed security margins.

2   Background

The HQC scheme follows the arithmetic of the binary polynomial ring $\mathbf{R} = \mathbb{F}_2[x]/\langle x^p - 1 \rangle$, where p is a prime number. With $\omega(a)$ we denote the Hamming weight of the polynomial $a \in \mathbf{R}$, and with $\mathbf{R}_w$ the set of all polynomials with weight w. We also consider a polynomial $a = a_0 + a_1 x + \ldots + a_{p-1} x^{p-1} \in \mathbf{R}$ also as a p-dimensional binary vector composed by its coefficients listed in the little-endian format (i.e., $\mathbf{a} = [a_0, a_1, \ldots, a_{p-1}] \in \mathbb{F}_2^p$). A $[n, k, d]$ binary linear code is a subspace of $\mathbb{F}_2^n$ with dimension k containing elements (codewords) with a minimum distance d. HQC uses a random quasi-cyclic $[2p, p, d]$ code, which provides the security of the scheme, and a fixed public, efficiently decodable, $[n_e n_i, k_e k_i, d_e d_i]$ code $\mathbf{G}$ derived by the concatenation of a shortened Reed-Solomon (RS) $[n_e, k_e, d_e]$ outer code with a duplicated Reed-Muller (RM) $[n_i, k_i, d_i]$ inner code. We denote with $\mathrm{CSPRNG}(\eta, \mathbf{S})$ the uniform sampling of an element from the set $\mathbf{S}$ using a Cryptographically Secure Pseudo-Random Number Generator (CSPRNG) seeded with $\eta \in \{0, 1\}^l$. HQC uses SHAKE256 as a CSPRNG, and also to build the hash functions HASH-G and HASH-K. The full HQC KEM is described in Algorithm 1. The HQC specification defines three parameter sets hqc-128, hqc-192, and hqc-256, which match the security levels of AES-128, AES-192, and AES-256, respectively. Operatively, higher security parameters imply larger polynomials, encoders/decoders, and longer messages.

3   HQC Hardware Design

Polynomials are encoded in memory blocks as sequences of $B = 128$ binary coefficients in little-endian order (dense encoding). Given the low number of

HQC.KEM-KEYGEN

Ensure: sk=$(\sigma \in \{0,1\}^{320}, \delta \in \{0,1\}^k)$,
   pk=$(\varphi \in \{0,1\}^{320}, s \in \mathbf{R})$

1: $(\sigma, \varphi) \overset{\$}{\leftarrow} \{0,1\}^{320} \times \{0,1\}^{320}$
2: $\delta \overset{\$}{\leftarrow} \{0,1\}^k$, $h \leftarrow$ CSPRNG$(\varphi, \mathbf{R})$
3: $(x,y) \leftarrow$ CSPRNG$(\sigma, \mathbf{R}_w \times \mathbf{R}_w)$
4: $s \leftarrow x + h \cdot y$
5: **return** sk $= (\sigma, \delta)$, pk $= (\varphi, s)$

HQC.KEM-ENCAPSULATE

Require: pk=$(\varphi \in \{0,1\}^{320}, s \in \mathbf{R})$
Ensure: $K \in \{0,1\}^{512}$
   ctx=$(u \in \mathbf{R}, v \in \mathbb{F}_2^{n_e n_i}, \text{salt} \in \{0,1\}^{128})$

1: $m \overset{\$}{\leftarrow} \{0,1\}^k$, salt $\overset{\$}{\leftarrow} \{0,1\}^{128}$
2: $\theta \leftarrow$ HASH-G$(m \| \varphi \| \text{salt})$
3: $(e, r_a, r_b) \leftarrow$ CSPRNG$(\theta, \mathbf{R}_{w_e} \times \mathbf{R}_{w_r} \times \mathbf{R}_{w_r})$
4: $h \leftarrow$ CSPRNG$(\varphi, \mathbf{R})$
5: $u \leftarrow r_a + h \cdot r_b$
6: $v \leftarrow$ ENCODE$_G(m)$+TRUNC$(s \cdot r_b + e)$
7: $K \leftarrow$ HASH-K$(m \| u \| v)$
8: **return** K, ctx $= (u, v, \text{salt})$

HQC.KEM-DECAPSULATE

Require: ctx=$(u \in \mathbf{R}, v \in \mathbb{F}_2^{n_e n_i}, \text{salt} \in \{0,1\}^{128})$,
   sk=$(\sigma \in \{0,1\}^{320}, \delta \in \{0,1\}^k)$,
   pk=$(\varphi \in \{0,1\}^{320}, s \in \mathbf{R})$
Ensure: $K \in \{0,1\}^{512}$

1: $(x,y) \leftarrow$ CSPRNG$(\sigma, \mathbf{R}_w \times \mathbf{R}_w)$
2: $m' \leftarrow$ DECODE$_G($TRUNC$([v \| 0^{p-n_e n_i}] - u \cdot y))$
3: $\theta' \leftarrow$ HASH-G$(m' \| \varphi \| \text{salt})$
4: $(e', r_a', r_b') \leftarrow$ CSPRNG$(\theta', \mathbf{R}_{w_e} \times \mathbf{R}_{w_r} \times \mathbf{R}_{w_r})$
5: $h \leftarrow$ CSPRNG$(\varphi, \mathbf{R})$
6: $u' \leftarrow r_a' + h \cdot r_b'$
7: $v' \leftarrow$ ENCODE$_G(m')$+TRUNC$(s \cdot r_b' + e')$
8: **if** $(u, v) \neq (u', v')$ **then**
9:    $K' \leftarrow$ HASH-K$(\delta \| \text{ctx})$
10: **else**
11:    $K' \leftarrow$ HASH-K$(m' \| \text{ctx})$
12: **end if**
13: **return** K'

Algorithm 1: the three KEM primitives of the HQC cryptographic scheme

coefficients set to one in the fixed-weight polynomials, such elements are encoded as a sequence of 16-bit unsigned indexes (sparse encoding), each of which is the exponent of the monomial term x^i, $0 \leq i \leq p - 1$ composing the polynomial.

The addition/subtraction of two densely encoded polynomials is performed computing the bit-wise eXclusive OR between the $\lceil \frac{p}{B} \rceil$ blocks of the two operands. If one of them is sparse, each 16-bit integer determines a memory block of the dense polynomial in which a single bit will be flipped. The number of blocks and weight values are selected from a small Read-Only Memory (ROM) with a multiplexer to adapt those components to multiple parameter sets at run-time.

A naive polynomial multiplication algorithm would require $\lceil \frac{p}{B} \rceil^2$ block-wise operations. Considering that one operand always has a fixed weight w, the *shift-and-add* algorithm is more profitable: the dense operand is shifted by a number of bits specified by each index of the sparse operand and accumulated, requiring $\lceil \frac{p}{B} \rceil \cdot w \approx \lceil \frac{p}{B} \rceil^{1.5}$ block-wise operations. We further reduce the latency by working with 4 indexes in parallel, and halve the accumulator size by immediately reducing modulo $x^p - 1$ the shifted polynomials. Each parameter set defines the number of indexes, which is selected from a ROM to initialize the counters appropriately and conditionally mask out some shift results when not required.

The encoding of a message m using the public code $\mathbf{G}$ is the result of the encoding with the Reed-Solomon (RS) code, followed by the encoding with the Reed-Muller (RM) code. Codes process blocks of 8 bits (symbols) as elements of the field $\mathbb{F}_{2^8}/\langle y^8 + y^4 + y^3 + y^2 + 1 \rangle$. An efficient encoder for the RS code consists in the use of a Linear Feedback Shift Register (LFSR) to compute $m(x) \cdot x^{n_e - k_e} \bmod g(x)$, where $g(x) = (x - \alpha) \cdot (x - \alpha^2) \cdot (x - \alpha^3) \cdots (x - \alpha^{d_e - 1})$ is the generator polynomial of the RS code of a specific parameter set (α is the primitive element in $\mathbb{F}_{2^8}$ having representation $\alpha = x$). LFSR registers are initialized to zero, and

Table 1. HQC top-modules w/o SHAKE256. Area × Time product is expressed in eSlices · ms. If a unified top-level is not provided, the sum of the resources of the three KEM modules, and the minimum working frequency, are considered.

HQC designs			Resources					freq.	Keygen		Encap		Decap	
sec. margin	design	unified	LUT	FF	BR	DSP	eSlice	MHz	μs	AT	μs	AT	μs	AT
AES-128	[6] balanced	✓	13865	6897	22.0	8	6283	164	96	603	203	1281	293	1847
	[6] high speed	✓	15214	7293	24.0	8	6876	178	88	608	125	866	208	1436
	[1] HLS, perf	✗	36807	26828	34.0	–	13554	150	269	3652	594	8051	1287	17446
	our	✓	20735	10834	27.5	0	8704	150	37	324	80	696	123	1075
AES-192	our	✓	20735	10834	27.5	0	8704	150	91	798	194	1688	239	2554
AES-256	our	✓	20735	10834	27.5	0	8704	150	173	1505	365	3181	552	4805

each tap of the feedback network contains a fully combinatorial $\mathbb{F}_{2^8}$ multiplier with a coefficient of the polynomial $g(x)$ as the first operand and the symbol fed back in the network as the second operand. In the first k_e cycles the symbols of the message $m(x)$ are introduced in the LFSR and also exposed to the output. Afterwards, the content of the LFSR registers is read out obtaining the codeword $c(x)$ in systematic form. To support multiple parameter sets, we instantiated the largest LFSR, selected the appropriate symbol to feedback, and determined the correct generator polynomial $g(x)$ using multiplexers. For the Reed-Muller code, we apply the standard encoding process, multiplying the RS codeword vector by the RM generator matrix. Finally, the duplication is performed by copying the resulting 128 bits blocks depending on the multiplicity of each parameter sets.

In contrast, correcting a corrupted codeword is a more complex task. The received codeword is de-duplicated, accumulating the bit-wise sum of the 128-bit replicas in a buffer using 128 adders. Since the code is a first order $RM(1,7)$ code, we use the Maximum Likelihood (ML) decoder applying the fast Hadamard transform to reduce the cycle count to only $\mathcal{O}(n_i \log(n_i))$. Finding the accumulator index containing the maximum absolute value determines the correct message symbol. Decoding the RS codeword requires initially the computation of the syndrome polynomial $S(x)$ given by the evaluation of the codeword with the first $n_e - k_e$ power of α in parallel (Horner's method). Next, the *error locator polynomial* $\Lambda(x)$ is computed through the Berlekamp-Massey algorithm, and searching for its zeros via the Chien search reveals the inverse values of the error locations. Finally, the error values are retrieved from the constructed *error evaluator polynomial* $\Omega(x)$. We based our design, for all the security levels, on the algorithms introduced in [7] to provide an efficient and highly parallelized module. Finally, the SHAKE256 module is implemented with a high-performance design performing a Keccak-$f[1600]$ transformation in 24 clock cycles, using 64 bits wide input/output ports connected to a shared buffer to maximize the throughput.

4   Experimental Evaluation

Our design is realized with a description at the Register Transfer Level (RTL) using the SystemVerilog language and validated via a behavioral simulation using the `cocotb` framework and the Universal Verification Methodology. We realized a module unifying the three KEM primitives (key generation, encapsulation, decapsulation) to maximize the reuse of the shared modules. In Table 1, we report the results of the synthesis using `Vivado` and targeting the `xc7a200tfbg484-3` Artix-7 FPGA. To fairly compare our results with other works, we use an *equivalent slices* (eSlice) synthetic indicator to summarize the use of lookup tables (LUT), flip-flops (FF), and block memories (BR) heterogeneous resources of our the target. We use the same convention of [6] extracting the resources required by the SHAKE256 module and employing the Area×Time (AT) product as efficiency metric. Our unified design substantially improves the latency (from 1.56× to 2.38×) and efficiency (from 1.24× to 1.88×) of the current state-of-the-art, while also supporting the more conservative `hqc-192` and `hqc-256` parameter sets. Digital Signal Processing units (DSPs) are not considered in the eSlice and Area-Time product figures; thus, the efficiency of solutions in [6] is actually lower.

Concluding Remarks. Our unified design is the first solution to fully support the HQC specification and be compatible with all parameter sets and KEM primitives. We improve the current state-of-the-art on HQC-128 in terms of latency and efficiency, while providing original designs and benchmark points also for the other security margins mandated by the HQC official documentation.

Acknowledgement. This work was carried out with partial financial support of the Italian MUR (PRIN 2022 project POst quantum Identification and eNcryption primiTives: dEsign and Realization (POINTER) ID-2022M2JLF2).

References

1. Aguilar Melchor, C., et al.: Towards automating cryptographic hardware implementations: a case study of HQC. In: Deneuville, J.C. (ed.) CBCrypto 2022. LCNS, vol. 13839, pp. 62–76. Springer, Cham (2022). https://doi.org/10.1007/978-3-031-29689-5_4
2. Aguilar Melchor, C., et al.: HQC documentation (2023). http://pqc-hqc.org/doc/hqc-specification_2023-04-30.pdf
3. Antognazza, F., Barenghi, A., Pelosi, G., Susella, R.: A flexible ASIC-oriented design for a full NTRU accelerator. In: Takahashi, A. (ed.) Proceedings of the 28th Asia and South Pacific Design Automation Conference, ASPDAC 2023, Tokyo, Japan, 16–19 January 2023, pp. 591–597. ACM (2023). https://doi.org/10.1145/3566097.3567916
4. Antognazza, F., Barenghi, A., Pelosi, G., Susella, R.: An efficient unified architecture for polynomial multiplications in lattice-based cryptoschemes. In: Mori, P., Lenzini, G., Furnell, S. (eds.) Proceedings of the 9th International Conference on Information Systems Security and Privacy, ICISSP 2023, Lisbon, Portugal, 22–24 February 2023, pp. 81–88. SciTePress (2023). https://doi.org/10.5220/0011654200003405
5. Antognazza, F., Barenghi, A., Pelosi, G., Susella, R.: Performance and efficiency exploration of hardware polynomial multipliers for post-quantum lattice-based cryptosystems. SN Comput. Sci. **5**(212) (2024). https://doi.org/10.1007/s42979-023-02547-w

6. Deshpande, S., et al.: Fast and efficient hardware implementation of HQC. IACR Cryptol. ePrint Arch. (2022). https://eprint.iacr.org/2022/1183
7. Wu, Y.: New scalable decoder architectures for reed-solomon codes. IEEE Trans. Commun. **63**(8) (2015). https://doi.org/10.1109/TCOMM.2015.2445759

Applying Self-recognition Biometrics to Live Deepfake Detection in Video Conferences

Hendrik Graupner[1,2(✉)] [ORCID], François-Nima Thobae[3,4], and Christoph Meinel[1]

[1] Hasso Plattner Institute, University of Potsdam, Potsdam, Germany
{hendrik.graupner,christoph.meinel}@hpi.de
[2] Bundesdruckerei GmbH, Berlin, Germany
[3] Institute of Computer Science, Free University Berlin, Berlin, Germany
thobafr@zedat.fu-berlin.de
[4] neXenio GmbH, Berlin, Germany

Abstract. This work-in-progress research addresses the pressing issue of deepfake detection in video conferencing, proposing a novel self-recognition biometric method. It addresses the increasing sophistication of cyber threats, particularly deepfakes and other face presentation attacks, by developing a user-centric verification system. This system utilizes eye tracking to detect participants' self-recognition, effectively distinguishing between genuine users and fraudulent attackers. This contribution outlines the integration of this technology into a video conferencing prototype, offering an overview of its functionality and initial performance outcomes. Our preliminary findings suggest that this method could be a groundbreaking tool for enhancing digital communication security.

1 Motivation

Face presentation attacks are a propagating issue in cybersecurity. Sophisticated impersonation, e.g., based on silicone masks, represented a primary challenge of the past. More recently, the additional threat of video and audio deepfakes drastically increased the attack potential in communication systems.

Most research in presentation attack detection (PAD) focused on attacks in face recognition systems, e.g., electronic border control. A 2019 review by Bhattacharjee et al. [2] provides an overview of the field. Known approaches are based on image analysis of either visible light imagery or extended-range imagery. Typically, they use statistical or machine-learning approaches to discriminate genuine and manipulated face images. E.g., a sophisticated method by George et al. [5] uses multiple video channels as input for a deep neural network (DNN).

The emerging field of video deepfake detection was summarized by Rana et al. [8]. Of the reviewed publications, 98 % are either based on statistical methods or machine learning (including deep learning). Machine-learning-based detection does not generalize well beyond the deepfake algorithm it was trained for.

Biometrics-aware solutions are promising, since they are based on learning typical features and behavior of people, which can not reliably be reproduced in

M. Andreoni (Ed.): ACNS 2024 Workshops, LNCS 14587, pp. 220–224, 2024.
https://doi.org/10.1007/978-3-031-61489-7_18

deepfakes. E.g., the works of Agarwal et al. [1] and Cozzolino et al. [3] train DNNs based on biometric features of their cohort. In 2022 Intel introduced a generic method based on behavior (e.g., visible blood flow in veins) in face videos [7].

Contrary to former research, our work leverages the users' ability to recognize themselves when perceiving their own faces. The approach is based on our previous work that investigated the relation between visual self-recognition and pupil behavior [10] based on the public data set [9] of a psychology study we conducted in 2022. In a recent publication, we showed the feasibility of visual self-recognition as a cognitive biometric trait [6]. This *work-in-progress research* applies our former results as a live identity validation mechanism that is robust to face presentation attacks, including deepfakes and face masks. In an online video conference scenario, we are currently implementing and analyzing the feasibility of this hypothesis.

We are happy to discuss our experiences and welcome ideas from the community to improve the method. In addition, we are actively seeking further cooperation with academia and industry to investigate potential application scenarios.

2 Video Conference Prototype

Online video conferences are increasingly part of daily life, e.g., business meetings. People commonly share sensitive information on such calls. Hence, the importance of communication security is an urgent issue.

The implementation of this prototype serves multiple goals:

1. Investigate the feasibility of identity validation via self-recognition in a real-world environment
2. Provide a research application for the collection and publication of eye-tracking data during video conferences that involve face presentation attacks
3. Contribute to video conference security by establishing the groundwork for a productive implementation

2.1 Attack Scenario

Malicious actors may initiate or join online video conferences with the intention of fraud. Today's technology provides low-threshold video and audio deepfake applications that can be deployed on affordable hardware. If an attacker impersonates a person known to other participants of the call, they may be able to get sensitive information or encourage detrimental actions. In past years, CEO frauds have been successful in stealing money from enterprises by impersonated phone calls, including the theft of up to €38 million in Paris, France, by a globally operating gang [4].

2.2 Proposed Solution

We propose identity validation based on visual self-recognition to detect face presentation attacks in online video conferences. This approach includes the utilization of eye-tracking hardware and integration into video conference software.

Users are required to enable video streaming via a webcam and to have an uncovered eye-tracking device in place. Both preconditions can be enforced by policy as conditions to be allowed to participate in high-security video conferences. The live face presentation attack detection works as follows (see Fig. 1):

1. An attacker may use *deepfake software* to alter their video stream.
2. During the video conference, users' *webcam* video streams and *eye tracker* data streams are recorded.
3. The remote *validation service* classifies the perceived faces of all participants based on the eye-tracking data and compares the result to the expectation based on the origin of the video stream.
   (a) User's own video stream: If the classification outputs the non-self label, confidence is shifted towards a potential face presentation attack.
   (b) Other participant's video stream: The classification result is used as a control condition to confirm correct functionality.
4. When a preset confidence threshold of a potential face presentation attack is reached, a suspected attack will be reported as the *validation result*.

Fig. 1. Online video conference scenario. An attacker impersonates a person known to the other participants using deepfake software. The validation service utilizes data from the video conference and eye tracker to detect the attack.

2.3   Implementation

The video conference integration builds on the open-source software OpenVidu[1]. It consists of the implementation of four components (see architecture in Fig. 2). The *training client* is required to collect data and train a binary classifier which is later deployed in the *validation service*. The *validation service* provides an API for eye-tracking and scenario-specific data and returns the classification result. *Plugins on the client and server side* of the video application are required to collect data, i.e., eye tracker data and video stream information in the user's visual focus. The utilization of the detection result, e.g., a monitoring board or alerting system, is out of the scope of this prototype.

---

[1] https://github.com/OpenVidu/openvidu (last accessed 2023/12/20).

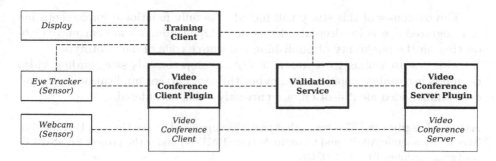

Fig. 2. The architecture of identity validation integration in a video conference system. Four sophisticated components (bold labels) had to be implemented for this scenario.

3 Preliminary Results

The implementation of the components introduced in Sect. 2 was completed by the end of November 2023. Based on this application, we collected a first small data set of 12 volunteers including deepfakes to verify the proper functionality of our pipeline. An initial test on the anonymized data set implies that the approach is promising.

Table 1 shows our first training results of four different models using different parameter sets. The best model *B-2* performs with AUROC = 0.82 on our formerly collected clinical data [9].

Table 1. Accuracy metrics of prototype models based on data from a previous study.

Model	AUROC	F_1-Score	EER
A	0.61 ± 0.03	0.59 ± 0.03	0.41 ± 0.03
B-1	0.74 ± 0.08	0.63 ± 0.06	0.34 ± 0.12
B-2	0.82 ± 0.07	0.76 ± 0.03	0.23 ± 0.07
C	0.62 ± 0.15	–	0.41 ± 0.12

As of January 2024, the collection of a representative data set of eye-tracking data in the video conference scenario is ongoing. This data will include the participation of genuine users and malicious users employing video deepfakes. We expect to conclude the data collection in the first quarter of 2024.

4 Expected Outcomes

We will compare our research to other face-PAD approaches in similar scenarios. The analysis will be based on a data set of eye-tracking data including the perception of self-videos altered by deepfake technology. We aim to provide public access to this labeled data set.

The outcomes of this study will include the fully functional implementation of integrated live video deepfake detection in OpenVidu. We are currently elaborating on the possibility of publishing the source code of our prototype.

This research aims to represent a critical step towards safeguarding video conferencing against sophisticated cyber threats. Further application scenarios, e.g., online video identification, are currently being considered.

Acknowledgments. This research is partially supported by the German Federal Ministry for Economic Affairs and Climate Action (BMWK) under the project SENSIBLE-KI (grant number 01MT21005B).

Disclosure of Interests. This research is funded by Bundesdruckerei GmbH. Software development is carried out by neXenio GmbH on behalf of Bundesdruckerei GmbH. At the time of publication, author H. Graupner is employed by Bundesdruckerei GmbH and author F. Thobae is employed by neXenio GmbH.

References

1. Agarwal, S., Farid, H., El-Gaaly, T., Lim, S.N.: Detecting deep-fake videos from appearance and behavior. In: IEEE International Workshop on Information Forensics and Security 2020, pp. 1–6. IEEE (2020)
2. Bhattacharjee, S., Mohammadi, A., Anjos, A., Marcel, S.: Recent advances in face presentation attack detection. In: Marcel, S., Nixon, M.S., Fierrez, J., Evans, N. (eds.) Handbook of Biometric Anti-Spoofing. ACVPR, pp. 207–228. Springer, Cham (2019). https://doi.org/10.1007/978-3-319-92627-8_10
3. Cozzolino, D., Rössler, A., Thies, J., Nießner, M., Verdoliva, L.: ID-reveal: Identity-aware deepfake video detection. In: IEEE/CVF International Conference on Computer Vision 2021, pp. 15108–15117. CVF (2021)
4. Europol: Franco-Israeli gang behind EUR 38 million CEO fraud busted (2023). https://www.europol.europa.eu/media-press/newsroom/news/franco-israeli-gang-behind-eur-38-million-ceo-fraud-busted. Accessed 20 Dec 2023
5. George, A., Mostaani, Z., Geissenbuhler, D., Nikisins, O., Anjos, A., Marcel, S.: Biometric face presentation attack detection with multi-channel convolutional neural network. IEEE Trans. Inf. Forensics Secur. **15**, 42–55 (2019)
6. Graupner, H., Schwetlick, L., Engbert, R., Meinel, C.: Unconventional biometrics: exploring the feasibility of a cognitive trait based on visual self-recognition. In: IEEE International Joint Conference on Biometrics 2023, pp. 326–335. IEEE (2023)
7. Intel Corporation: Intel Introduces Real-Time Deepfake Detector (2022). https://www.intel.com/content/www/us/en/newsroom/news/intel-introduces-real-time-deepfake-detector.html. Accessed 20 Dec 2023
8. Rana, M.S., Nobi, M.N., Murali, B., Sung, A.H.: Deepfake detection: a systematic literature review. IEEE Access **10**, 25494–25513 (2022)
9. Schwetlick, L., Engbert, R., Graupner, H.: Data Set: Face- and Self-Recognition Effects on Pupil Size and Microsaccade Rate. OSF (2023)
10. Schwetlick, L., Graupner, H., Dimigen, O., Engbert, R.: Self-recognition generates characteristic responses in pupil dynamics and microsaccade rate. arXiv (2023)

GAN and DM Generated Synthetic Image Detection in the Age of Misinformation

Tanusree Ghosh[(⊠)] [ID] and Ruchira Naskar [ID]

Department of Information Technology, Indian Institute of Engineering Science
and Technology, Shibpur, Howrah, India
2021itP001.tanusree@students.iiests.ac.in, ruchira@it.iiests.ac.in

Abstract. Synthetic images generated by artificial intelligence, particularly those created by Generative Adversarial Networks (GAN) and Diffusion Models (DM), have achieved hyper-realistic quality in recent years, often indistinguishable by the human eye. These fake images are critical in spreading misinformation across Online Social Networks (OSNs), commonly used as profile pictures in fake social media accounts and paired with false news to gain user trust. While many state-of-the-art solutions can identify synthetic images produced by GANs with high accuracy, their effectiveness diminishes when dealing with images circulated on OSNs.

Our study finds that selecting the right features, in combination with a deep learning-based classification model, can enhance the performance of synthetic image detectors under challenging conditions. We propose two innovative solutions: a Gradient-based method and a novel Sine Transform Feature-based Network (STN Net). Both methods perform better than existing state-of-the-art solutions for post-processed images, achieving over 99% accuracy in detecting synthetic images and over 91% detection accuracy in challenging scenarios.

Additionally, we introduce a transfer learning-based approach for identifying images generated by DMs. This solution not only excels in detecting synthetic images but also demonstrates satisfactory generalization performance.

1 Introduction and Problem Identification

In recent years, the rapid development of Generative Artificial Intelligence technologies, such as Generative Adversarial Networks (GANs) and Diffusion Models (DM), has brought forth a new era of hyper-realistic synthetic images. While these advancements have enriched industries like entertainment and gaming, they have been used to spread misinformation in Online Social Networks (OSNs), which ushered in a formidable social peril[1,2]. Fake face images are widely used

---

[1] https://www.livemint.com/news/world/aigenerated-image-of-explosion-at-pentagon-goes-viral-creates-chaos-in-stock-market-see-here-11684774645223.html.

[2] https://www.cbsnews.com/news/is-that-facebook-account-real-meta-reports-rapid-rise-in-ai-generated-profile-pictures/.

© The Author(s), under exclusive license to Springer Nature Switzerland AG 2024
M. Andreoni (Ed.): ACNS 2024 Workshops, LNCS 14587, pp. 225–229, 2024.
https://doi.org/10.1007/978-3-031-61489-7_19

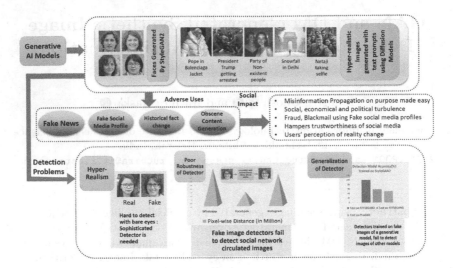

Fig. 1. Current Scenario of AI-generated image detection

as profile pictures of fake social media profiles that eventually propagate fake news or scam. On the other hand, photorealistic synthetic images are used with fake news to increase their trustworthiness, as shown in Fig. 1.

Hence, the problem at hand is the detection of synthetic images. While it is already a challenging task to detect such images due to their photo-realism and similar statistical properties to camera-generated images, in real-life scenarios, an ideal fake image detector should be able to detect OSN circulated images that go through unknown OSN-specific post-processing changes and should detect any given fake images, as it is impossible to know prior from which generative model a given image possibly could belong. Hence, with correct detection, robustness and generalisation are crucial for synthetic image detectors.

1.1   Potential Approaches

Initially, GAN-generated images were identifiable through visible artifacts [5,6,8] like mismatched eye colors, irregular pupil shapes, and inconsistent corneal highlights, allowing trained observers to spot fakes. However, advancements in GANs have erased these artifacts, reducing the observer's ability to discern synthetic images, and increasing susceptibility to misinformation.

Existing detectors fall into two categories: Deep Learning (DL) based, using complex feature sets derived automatically, and those using selected features, based on statistical properties and machine learning classifiers. DL methods typically employ models like VGG-Net and modified Xception-Net. However, using these directly in GAN-generator models can render synthetic images undetectable. On the other hand, selected features-based detectors use domain knowledge, such as statistical properties of facial landmarks with classifiers like Support Vector Machines, co-occurrence matrices, cross co-occurrence matrices, etc.

Recently, combining statistical properties with Deep Neural Network classifiers has proven effective in detecting synthetic images, an approach we adopt in our work.

Detection of fake images can broadly be viewed as efficient coordination of two sub-modules, identification of differentiating features and classifier, as shown in Fig. 2. Here it is evident that in certain feature spaces, they have visible differences. Here we have shown, a pixel-wise average of 500 gradient magnitude and direction and luminosity components for both real and fake images.

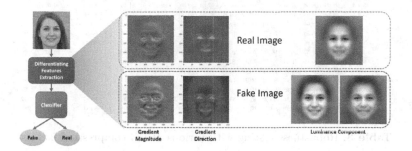

Fig. 2. Broad overview of working of fake image detector.

1.2   Proposed Solutions

As discussed in earlier section, our solution for synthetic face detection largely consists of: a feature extractor and a classifier. Based on this framework, two of our proposed solutions are as follows:

- **Gradient-Based Detection**[3]: This method utilizes the image gradient as its principal feature. Images are first converted to grayscale, from which gradient magnitude and direction matrices are derived using approximation filters such as Sobel and Scharr. Leveraging these gradients, we construct four distinct networks for an image of size $n \times n \times 3$. The GM (Gradient Magnitude Net) processes $n \times n \times 1$ dimension gradient magnitude data in a designed deep learning (DL) classifier. Similarly, the GD (Gradient Direction Net) is designed to handle gradient direction input. The GF-Net (Gradient Fusion Net) combines both gradient magnitude and direction features. Lastly, the DCG-Net (Dual Channel Gradient Net) operates as a dual-channel network integrating both GM and GD for its analysis. After extracting the features, we use a CNN based classifier.
- **STN-Net:** [4] In this case, we propose a novel feature set: Sine Transformed Noise (STN). STN extraction method begins by converting the image into grayscale, followed by the application of a Gaussian filter and then a Laplacian

---

[3] T. Ghosh and R. Naskar, "Leveraging Image Gradients for Robust GAN-Generated Image Detection in context of OSN", 38th IEEE International Conference on Visual Communications and Image Processing (VCIP) 2023. (*To appear*).

Table 1. Detection Performance Comparison on Test Set. Metric: Accuracy (%)

Metric	STN-Net (Best Model)	GF-Net (Best Model)	Qiao [11]	Nowroozi [10]	Nataraj [9]	Chen [1]	Frank [3]	Yu [12]	Li [7]
Accuracy (%)	99.53	99.80	99.95	99.33	96.11	97.70	98.58	97.70	99.50

Table 2. Robustness testing with various post-processing operations.

Operations	Parameters	Gradient based Variants								Qiao [11]	Nataraj [9]	Nowroozi [10]	STN-Net Variants		
		GM-Net		GD-Net		GF-Net		DCG-Net					Baseline (STN-Net)	STN-Net	Dual layer STN-Net
		Sobel	Scharr	Sobel	Scharr	Sobel	Scharr	Sobel	Scharr						
Median Filter	3 x 3	98.20	98.36	97.54	97.57	98.56	98.45	97.54	98.54	99.35	81.48	85.13	91.62	96.92	98.78
	5 x 5	88.88	91.96	80.53	85.62	88.12	91.89	85.57	92.53	93.80	75.98	83.65	91.12	63.77	78.92
Gaussian Noise	1.0	99.04	98.96	99.13	98.74	99.18	98.89	98.54	98.88	94.43	76.35	93.68	91.82	99.21	99.38
	2.0	99.01	98.93	99.21	98.55	99.02	98.83	98.61	98.98	74.25	76.73	96.80	91.84	99.28	99.33
CLAHE	3 x 3	98.74	98.86	99.08	98.86	98.86	98.81	98.66	98.81	94.70	51.43	50.32	85.54	97.10	98.99
Average Blurring	3 x 3	76.54	88.57	96.35	90.80	98.09	97.88	97.47	96.88	97.30	93.68	86.90	91.37	86.11	94.84
	5 x 5	50.02	50.19	70.14	85.57	75.15	82.99	81.85	78.89	82.68	88.23	76.63	90.40	50.12	53.77
Gamma Correction	0.8	98.74	98.93	99.28	98.71	99.12	98.99	98.51	98.99	95.08	82.28	86.90	90.10	99.28	99.26
	0.9	98.96	98.91	99.13	98.59	99.11	99.03	98.56	99.01	98.00	87.23	90.98	91.69	99.23	99.45
	1.2	98.88	98.93	99.08	98.66	98.96	98.99	98.66	98.91	96.90	87.20	85.53	89.56	99.40	99.36
Resizing	0.5	63.44	79.69	95.66	90.50	97.95	97.27	96.92	95.24	79.80	57.93	92.47	91.42	72.40	86.31
Average	-	88.22	91.11	94.10	94.74	95.63	**96.54**	95.53	95.96	91.48	78.04	84.11	90.58	87.53	**91.67**

Table 3. Robustness testing with various JPEG compression factors.

Quality Factor	STN-Net Variants			Qiao [11]	Nowroozi [10]	Nataraj [9]	Gradient-based Variants							
	Baseline (STN Net)	STN-Net	Dual-Layer STN-Net				GM-Net		GD-Net		GF-Net		DCG-Net	
							Sobel	Scharr	Sobel	Scharr	Sobel	Scharr	Sobel	Scharr
90	91.38	99.33	99.33	97.53	94.50	95.58	98.71	98.99	99.40	98.56	98.96	98.89	98.67	98.99
80	91.37	98.71	99.08	97.44	88.66	94.93	98.49	98.76	99.06	98.34	98.83	98.81	98.39	98.60
70	91.29	97.99	98.69	97.23	83.50	94.03	98.41	98.54	98.77	98.29	98.59	98.55	98.19	98.44
60	91.34	96.90	98.26	96.83	94.00	94.65	98.39	97.94	98.26	97.42	98.39	97.99	97.77	98.16
50	91.22	96.88	**97.89**	96.51	80.05	96.66	98.19	97.30	97.69	96.60	**98.31**	97.79	95.12	97.72

filter. The resulting feature set undergoes Sine Transformations, enhancing the extracted features. We develop two variants in this approach: The first utilizes the aforementioned feature set directly. The second variant employs a two-layer feature, each layer using different Gaussian blur values.

Results for detection accuracy for both cases are shown in Table 1. We test our solution models with various post-processed images. The results are shown in Table 2, whereas detection performance with varied JPEG compression levels is shown in Table 3.

- **Transfer learning-based solution for DM image detection:** [2] A universal detector and source model attributor based on ResNet-50 have been proposed. This approach attains over 96% accuracy for detecting DM images, along with source attribution accuracy over 93%.

1.3   Conclusion and Future Work Direction

Our existing techniques for identifying GAN-generated facial images demonstrate remarkable effectiveness when tested on synthetic images from the same dataset. These methods focus on identifying features that withstand common transformations in online social networks (OSNs).

Moving forward, our research aims to enhance both the generalization and robustness of these detection methods. With the proliferation of diverse generative models, the creation of a universal detector capable of recognizing synthetic images from any model is increasingly crucial.

Additionally, there is an unexplored potential in examining artifacts produced by Diffusion Model (DM) generated images across various domains, such as spatial and frequency, which warrants further investigation.

References

1. Chen, B., Liu, X., Zheng, Y., Zhao, G., Shi, Y.Q.: A robust GAN-generated face detection method based on dual-color spaces and an improved xception. IEEE Trans. Circuits Syst. Video Technol. **32**(6), 3527–3538 (2021)
2. Das, S., Dutta, D., Ghosh, T., Naskar, R.: Universal detection and source attribution of diffusion model generated images with high generalization and robustness. In: Maji, P., Huang, T., Pal, N.R., Chaudhury, S., De, R.K. (eds.) PReMI 2023. LNCS, vol. 14301, pp. 441–448. Springer, Cham (2023). https://doi.org/10.1007/978-3-031-45170-6_45
3. Frank, J., Eisenhofer, T., Schönherr, L., Fischer, A., Kolossa, D., Holz, T.: Leveraging frequency analysis for deep fake image recognition. In: International Conference on Machine Learning, pp. 3247–3258. PMLR (2020)
4. Ghosh, T., Naskar, R.: STN-net: a robust GAN-generated face detector. In: Muthukkumarasamy, V., Sudarsan, S.D., Shyamasundar, R.K. (eds.) ICISS 2023. LNCS, vol. 14424, pp. 141–158. Springer, Cham (2023). https://doi.org/10.1007/978-3-031-49099-6_9
5. Guo, H., Hu, S., Wang, X., Chang, M.C., Lyu, S.: Eyes tell all: irregular pupil shapes reveal GAN-generated faces. In: 2022 IEEE International Conference on Acoustics, Speech and Signal Processing (ICASSP), ICASSP 2022, pp. 2904–2908. IEEE (2022)
6. Hu, S., Li, Y., Lyu, S.: Exposing GAN-generated faces using inconsistent corneal specular highlights. In: 2021 IEEE International Conference on Acoustics, Speech and Signal Processing (ICASSP), ICASSP 2021, pp. 2500–2504. IEEE (2021)
7. Li, H., Li, B., Tan, S., Huang, J.: Identification of deep network generated images using disparities in color components. Signal Process. **174**, 107616 (2020)
8. Matern, F., Riess, C., Stamminger, M.: Exploiting visual artifacts to expose deepfakes and face manipulations. In: 2019 IEEE Winter Applications of Computer Vision Workshops (WACVW), pp. 83–92. IEEE (2019)
9. Nataraj, L., et al.: Detecting GAN generated fake images using co-occurrence matrices. arXiv preprint arXiv:1903.06836 (2019)
10. Nowroozi, E., Mekdad, Y.: Detecting high-quality GAN-generated face images using neural networks. In: Big Data Analytics and Intelligent Systems for Cyber Threat Intelligence, pp. 235–252 (2023)
11. Qiao, T., et al.: CSC-net: cross-color spatial co-occurrence matrix network for detecting synthesized fake images. IEEE Trans. Cogn. Dev. Syst. (2023)
12. Yu, Y., Ni, R., Zhao, Y.: Mining generalized features for detecting AI-manipulated fake faces. arXiv preprint arXiv:2010.14129 (2020)

Extremely Simple Fail-Stop ECDSA Signatures

Mario Yaksetig[✉]

Parfin, London, UK
`mario.yaksetig@parfin.io`

Abstract. Fail-stop signatures are digital signatures that allow a signer to prove that a specific forged signature is indeed a forgery. After such a proof is published, the system can be stopped.

We introduce a new simple ECDSA fail-stop signature scheme. Our proposal is based on the minimal assumption that an adversary with a quantum computer is not able to break the (second) preimage resistance of a cryptographically-secure hash function. Our scheme is as efficient as traditional ECDSA, does not limit the number of signatures that a signer can produce, and relies on minimal security assumptions. Using our construction, the signer has minimal computational overhead in the signature producing phase and produces a signature indistinguishable from a 'regular' ECDSA signature.

Keywords: Fail-stop signatures · Formal Methods Analysis · ECDSA

1 Introduction

Presently, the Internet relies heavily on the Elliptic Curve Digital Signature Algorithm (ECDSA) as this signature scheme represents the backbone for the issuance of digital signatures online. This issue is even more relevant in the cryptocurrency landscape, where the majority of blockchain platforms use ECDSA to secure their transactions. Effectively, this signature scheme secures a hundreds of billions of dollars since the cryptocurrency funds of each user are secure only as long as no one can steal their funds. Therefore, strengthening the ECDSA scheme, which secures these funds, is of extreme importance.

In this work, we introduce a new protocol that allows legitimate users to prove whether or not a specific signature is a forgery. This is particularly useful in a setting involving a dispute between the real user and an adversary who maliciously obtained the secret key.

1.1 Motivation

Blockchains are not designed to be easily upgraded, and such upgrades are traditionally very controversial. To cause no friction and no need for any type of hard forks, we introduce a new fail-stop variant of the ECDSA scheme that allows

M. Andreoni (Ed.): ACNS 2024 Workshops, LNCS 14587, pp. 230–234, 2024.
https://doi.org/10.1007/978-3-031-61489-7_20

users to prove whether or not a signature using a specific key is legitimate or not without requiring any change to existing ECDSA verification algorithms. This is useful as it implies that smart contracts and existing wallet and node infrastructure can remain unchanged.

Fail-stop signatures, which can detect and halt forgery attempts, represent an innovative step forward in cryptographic security. In a world where ECDSA-based cryptocurrencies face relentless security breaches leading to substantial financial losses, the integration of fail-stop signatures could provide a powerful defense. This approach significantly reduces the risk of fraudulent transactions, and enables a dispute resolution in case of a key compromise.

1.2 Our Contributions

We introduce a very lightweight addition to the traditional ECDSA to encode quantum-secure secret key information in the nonce used to produce each ECDSA signature. This encoding allows the signer to, in an event of a dispute, selectively open the nonce used in that signature and prove whether or not a signature is well-formed. Unlike the original failstop signatures [4], our proposal does not set a limit on signatures that can be constructed using the same secret key and does not affect the signature size, which remains exactly the same as a traditional ECDSA signature. Our approach can be integrated in any elliptic-curve based digital signature scheme and also complements existing fallback designs as proposed by Chaum et al. [1,2].

Arguably, the most important part of our construction is that an adversary able to break the ECDLP is not able to obtain the secret preimage used to generate the nonce for any individual signature. This feature allows the real owner of the signing keys to prove that a specific signature is a forgery.

1.3 Fail-Stop Signatures

Fail-stop signatures operate similarly to traditional digital signatures. The signer has a secret key that is used to produce signatures. These signatures can then be verified by any party who knows the corresponding public key. A signature that is successfully verified under the public key is considered acceptable. Fail-stop signatures introduce an additional property where a signer can prove that a specific signature is forged. Therefore, in the case of a dispute, a signer can provide a judge with a proof of forgery. The judge can then test if the signature is correct and provide a verdict of whether or not the provided signature is a forgery. If the proof is accepted, then there is substantial evidence that the computational assumption of the system is broken.

Definition 1 (Fail-stop Signatures). *A fail-stop signature scheme (FSS) is a 5-tuple* (Gen, Sign, Test, Prove, Verify), *where:*

- Gen(params, r_A, r_C) $\rightarrow$ (sk, pk). *This is a polynomial-time two-party protocol for generating the keys. The protocol is executed by the signer A, and a trusted* *center C, who both get params $= (k, \lambda, N)$ as input. Furthermore, each party has a secret random string, r_A and r_C. N is the maximal number of signatures that the signer is willing to construct using the same secret key. k is the security parameter for the recipient and λ is the security parameter for the signer.*

- Sign(sk, i, m$_i$) $\to$ σ. *This is a polynomial-time algorithm that on input the secret key sk, a message number $i \leq N$, and a message sequence $m = (m_1, ..., m_i)$ from $\mathcal{M}$, constructs a signature on m_i if the previously signed messages were $\{m_1, ..., m_{i-1}\}$. The output σ is called the correct signature.*

- Test(pk, m, σ) $\to$ OK/NotOK. *This is a polynomial-time algorithm that on input the public key pk, a message $m \in \mathcal{M}$, and a signature σ on m outputs either OK or NotOK. If Test(pk, m, σ) = OK, then σ is an acceptable signature on m.*

- Prove(sk, m, σ', hist) $\to$ π. *This is a polynomial-time algorithm that on input the secret key sk, a message $m \in \mathcal{M}$, a possible signature σ' on m, and the history hist of previously signed messages (plus their signatures) either outputs the string π = "not a forgery" or a bit string proof $\pi \in \{0, 1\}^*$.*

- Verify(pk, m, σ', π) $\to$ Accept/Reject. *This is a polynomial-time algorithm that on input the public key, a message $m \in \mathcal{M}$, a possible signature σ' on m and a string proof π outputs either Accept or Reject. If the result is Accept, the proof π is called a valid proof of forgery.*

A proof of forgery is always non-interactive so that it can subsequently be shown to others, and the system can be stopped in consensus. The proof must satisfy two requirements[1]:

- The ability to prove forgeries must work independently of the computational power of potential forgers.
- It must be infeasible for the signer to construct signatures that she can later prove to be forgeries[2].

Since it is equally important that fail-stop signatures cannot be forged, the signer still has to take part in choosing the keys. However, the recipients of signatures must be sure that the signer cannot disavow her own signatures. It is therefore necessary that the recipients or a center trusted by the recipients also participate in the key generation.

2 Simple Fail-Stop ECDSA

The core idea behind our construction is that a signer can secretly hide special information when generating the nonce for each ECDSA signature.

Our design proposes two simple changes to the traditional ECDSA protocol. First, the signer generates an additional secret value α. Second, the signer uses

---

[1] It can be shown that these two properties imply security against forgery.

[2] We skip this requirement as we do not desire the involvement of additional parties during key generation. Our construction, however, also supports this functionality.

this extra secret value and hashes it along with the message and its index, to generate the nonce for each signature. This ensures that the nonce is unique for every message and that it is random, assuming the hash function behaves as a random oracle. We refer the reader to Table 1 and Table 2 for a detailed protocol description.

Table 1. Extended ECDSA Construction

Keygen(1^λ)	Sign(α, i, m)	Test($\mathsf{pk}, \mathsf{m}, \sigma$)
$\alpha \overset{\$}{\leftarrow} \mathbb{Z}_q$	$z \leftarrow H(\mathsf{m})$	Parse: $(r, s) \overset{p}{\leftarrow} \sigma$
$\mathsf{sk} \leftarrow H(\alpha)$	$k \leftarrow H(\alpha, i, m)$	If $(r, s) \notin \mathbb{Z}_q$
$\mathsf{pk} \leftarrow \mathsf{sk} \cdot G$	$(e_x, e_y) \leftarrow k \cdot G$	Return NotOK
return (α, pk)	$r \leftarrow e_x \mod p$	$w \leftarrow s^{-1}$
	If $r = 0 \mod p$	$z \leftarrow H(\mathsf{m})$
	Pick another k	$u_1 \leftarrow zw \mod p$
	and start again	$u_2 \leftarrow rw \mod p$
	$s \leftarrow k^{-1} \cdot (z + r \cdot \mathsf{sk})$	$(e_x, e_y) \leftarrow u_1 \times G + u_2 \times \mathsf{pk}$
	If $s = 0 \mod p$	If $(e_x, e_y) = (0, 0)$
	Pick another k	Return NotOK
	and start again	If $r = e_x \mod p$
	Return $\sigma = (r, s)$	Return OK

3   Discussion

Verifpal Formal Verification. We analysed our construction using Verifpal [3]. We defined an active attacker, where the adversary is in charge of delivering the messages and define a quantum adversary. To do so, we use the *leak* command and expose all the secret values that are considered 'protected' by the ECDLP. The tool output that regardless of the compromise of the ECDSA secret key value, only the honest owner of the secret preimage α is able to produce well-formed signatures.

Implementation. The authors are implementing the protocol as an extension to EthSigner. Upon completion, the team intends to obtain a security audit by independent reputable external parties.

Formal Security Proofs. Presently, we are producing the adequate complete proofs of security of our construction. The next step is to, upon completing the formalization, publish an extended version exposing the construction and corresponding proofs.

Table 2. Prove and Verify algorithms of Fail-Stop ECDSA

Prove($\alpha, m, \sigma', hist$)	Verify($\mathsf{pk}, \mathsf{m}, \sigma, \pi$)
Parse: $(r, s) \xleftarrow{p} \sigma'$	Parse: $\pi' \xleftarrow{p} \pi$
Parse: $i \xleftarrow{p} hist'$	If $\pi' =$ "Not a forgery"
$k \leftarrow H(\alpha, i, m)$	Return Reject
$(e_x, e_y) \leftarrow k \cdot G$	If $\pi' = (\alpha, i)$
$r' \leftarrow e_x \mod p$	$\mathsf{sk}' \leftarrow H(\alpha)$
If $r' \neq r$	$\mathsf{pk}' \leftarrow \mathsf{sk}' \cdot G$
$\quad \pi \leftarrow (\alpha, i)$	If $\mathsf{pk}' \neq pk$
If $r' = r$	Return Reject
$\quad \pi \leftarrow$ "Not a forgery"	If $\mathsf{pk}' = pk$
Return π	Parse: $(r, s) \xleftarrow{p} \sigma$
	$k \leftarrow H(\alpha, i, m)$
	$(e_x, e_y) \leftarrow k \cdot G$
	$r' \leftarrow e_x \mod p$
	If $r' \neq r$
	Return Reject

4   Conclusion

We introduce a new very simple and cheap fail-stop signature scheme. Our construction is very useful and practical, however, slightly differs from the original fail-stop signature definition for usability and practical deployment reasons. We expect this work to set a foundation for a fruitful debate around key compromise in the cryptocurrency space.

References

1. Chaum, D., Larangeira, M., Yaksetig, M.: Tweakable sleeve: a novel sleeve construction based on tweakable hash functions. Cryptology ePrint Archive, Paper 2022/888 (2022). https://eprint.iacr.org/2022/888
2. Chaum, D., Larangeira, M., Yaksetig, M., Carter, W.: W-ots(+) up my sleeve! a hidden secure fallback for cryptocurrency wallets. Cryptology ePrint Archive, Paper 2021/872 (2021). https://eprint.iacr.org/2021/872
3. Kobeissi, N., Nicolas, G., Tiwari, M.: Verifpal: cryptographic protocol analysis for the real world. In: Proceedings of the 2020 ACM SIGSAC Conference on Cloud Computing Security Workshop, pp. 159. CCSW 2020, Association for Computing Machinery, New York, NY, USA (2020)
4. Pedersen, T.P., Pfitzmann, B.: Fail-stop signatures. SIAM J. Comput. **26**(2), 291–330 (1997). https://doi.org/10.1137/S009753979324557X

Physically Unclonable Fingerprints
for Authentication

Navajit S. Baban[1]([✉]), Jiarui Zhou[1], Sarani Bhattacharya[2], Urbi Chatterjee[3],
Sukanta Bhattacharjee[4], Sanjairaj Vijayavenkataraman[1], Yong-Ak Song[1],
Debdeep Mukhopadhyay[2], Krishnendu Chakrabarty[5], and Ramesh Karri[6]

[1] New York University Abu Dhabi, Abu Dhabi 129188, UAE
{nsb359,jz4301,vs89,rafael.song}@nyu.edu
[2] Indian Institute of Technology Kharagpur, Kharagpur 721302, India
{sarani,debdeep}@cse.iitkgp.ac.in
[3] Indian Institute of Technology Kanpur, Kanpur 208016, India
urbic@iitk.ac.in
[4] Indian Institute of Technology Guwahati, Guwahati 781039, India
sukantab@iitg.ac.in
[5] Arizona State University, Tempe 85287, USA
Krishnendu.Chakrabarty@asu.edu
[6] New York University, New York 11201, USA
rkarri@nyu.edu

Abstract. We have developed an innovative fingerprinting method
using the melt-electrospinning printing process for product authentication. This method generates unique, unclonable fingerprints that can
be made tamper-proof with a transparent polymer coating. We have
successfully tested this approach by printing 393 unique fingerprints
on glass substrates, achieving a 95.8% deep learning-based authentication accuracy. Furthermore, fluorescent ink can be employed to enhance
fingerprint visibility, enabling analysis through fluorescence microscopy
and facilitating spectral authentication. Additionally, the transparent
polymer coating obfuscates and encrypts the fingerprint, which can be
decrypted using Speeded-Up Robust Features (SURF) techniques. Our
ongoing research focuses on assessing the vulnerability of fingerprint
images to adversarial attacks, as well as conducting analyses of uniqueness, uniformity, and reliability. We are also ensuring their robustness
through machine and deep learning techniques. The proposed authentication scheme aims to provide a dependable solution tailored to the
complexities of modern manufacturing and supply chains, effectively mit-
igating potential intellectual property threats.

Keywords: Fingerprints · Physically Unclonable · Security ·
Intellectual Property · Deep Learning · Transfer Learning · Trusted
Third Party

1   Introduction

In an era marked by untrusted third-party manufacturers, outsourcing, and intricate horizontal supply chains, the need for product authentication has never

M. Andreoni (Ed.): ACNS 2024 Workshops, LNCS 14587, pp. 235–239, 2024.
https://doi.org/10.1007/978-3-031-61489-7_21

been more critical [1]. In the realm of medical devices, defense equipment, and other security-critical fields, the imperative for product authentication is paramount [2].

Robust authentication measures are essential safeguards to ensure the reliability, quality, and authenticity of these life-saving and security-sensitive items, instilling confidence and protecting against potentially life-threatening counterfeit or substandard products. Thus, we have proposed a fingerprinting scheme using a melt-electrospinning printing process to authenticate manufactured products. We employ a melt-electrospinning printer to create unique physical unclonable fingerprints on each product.

We have demonstrated the effectiveness of this novel scheme using microfluidic biochips [2]. We printed 393 unique fingerprints on glass slides, and their images were captured using an optical microscope. For the authentication of the instances on which they were printed, we employed deep learning (DL) techniques. Moreover, we leveraged transfer learning achieving a high authentication accuracy of 95.8%.

Additionally, by infusing the ink with a fluorescent dye, the fingerprints can be made visible in the UV range, thereby allowing them to exhibit spectral features. Moreover, the clear polymer layer, used as a seal for tamper protection, obfuscates and encrypts the fingerprint. This encrypted fingerprint can be decrypted using the Speeded-Up Robust Features (SURF) matching feature algorithm [3].

2   Motivation

The manufacturing of security-critical products, like medical and defense equipment, involves multiple stages and entities, raising risks of IP theft, particularly through reverse engineering [4]. Untrustworthy supply chain entities might access product details, design, materials, functionality, and operational protocols using reverse engineering to commit IP piracy, counterfeiting, and unauthorized overproduction, undermining the product's integrity and value [5]. Previous IP protection efforts in these sectors have relied on watermarking [2], microvalve based physically unclonable functions and obfuscation schemes [4], vulnerable to cloning through reverse engineering. However, fingerprint authentication for securing these products against IP infringement has seen limited use. Our research tackles this by introducing a novel fingerprinting scheme. This scheme utilizes a melt-electrospinning printer to create unique, obfuscated, encrypted, and tamper-proof unclonable fingerprints for product authentication through SURF-based algorithms.

3   Preliminary Results

3.1   Melt-Electrospinned Fingerprints

Figure 1(a) illustrates the melt-electrospinning setup, utilizing a RegenHu 3D Discovery bioprinter, to generate these fingerprints. For this process, we use

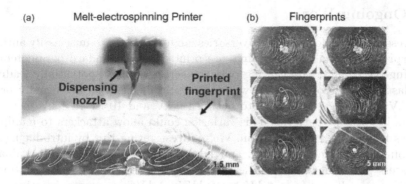

Fig. 1. Fingerprints created using the melt-electrospinning printer. (a) Melt-electrospinning printing set up. (b) Six unique fingerprints printed using the same process parameters.

Polycaprolactone (PCL) pellets with a molecular weight of 45,000. The printing parameters are carefully set, including a temperature of 85°C, a 6 mm distance between the needle and substrate, a pressure of 0.125 MPa, and a voltage of 8.0 kV. These specific settings result in the formation of random spiral fibers characteristic of the fingerprints. The print head is precisely maneuvered to a predetermined position and activated for a duration of 5 s to achieve this effect. Figure 1(b) shows the six unique fingerprints printed using the same process parameters.

3.2 Fingerprint Classification

Image preprocessing techniques, such as noise reduction, binarization, and thinning, were applied to the images of 393 unique fingerprints. After that, we tested five DL classifiers: DenseNet121, MobileNetV2, ResNet50, EfficientNetV2B0, and NASNetMobile, each with distinct image classification capabilities. We utilized transfer learning from ImageNet to enhance these classifiers, improving efficiency and generalization. Optimization involved the Adam optimizer (learning rate: 0.0001), and the dataset, split into 80% training and 20% validation, was used to evaluate performance. Training, with a batch size of 50 and early stopping at 98% accuracy, helped prevent overfitting. Transfer learning notably increased accuracy, with EfficientNetV2B0 and NASNetMobile as top performers at 95.8% and 93% accuracy, respectively. DenseNet121, MobileNetV2, and ResNet50 showed lower accuracy, possibly due to incompatibilities with our specific task or differences from ImageNet. EfficientNetV2B0's compound scaling and NASNetMobile's architecture, informed by reinforcement learning, demonstrated their effectiveness in complex pattern recognition, underscoring the value of specific models and transfer learning in DL-based authentication.

4   Ongoing Work

Our research is exploring how adversaries might use noise to misclassify authentic fingerprints. Normally, fingerprints are printed using standard parameters, but altering these can create varying patterns across batches, potentially leading to misclassification. For example, while authentic fingerprints are usually printed at 8 kV, changing the voltage to between 6 kV and 10 kV in 1 kV increments results in different patterns. This variation could allow attackers to manipulate images for incorrect classification. We're investigating this by introducing noise into our dataset and using ML and DL methods for analysis and evaluation. To assess potential vulnerabilities, we're conducting experiments printing fingerprints at voltages from 6 kV to 10 kV in 1 kV increments, creating varied patterns that attackers might use. We're analyzing these with machine learning and deep learning to understand their susceptibility to noise-based classification tampering. Our focus also includes experiments evaluating the fingerprints' uniqueness, uniformity, and reliability.

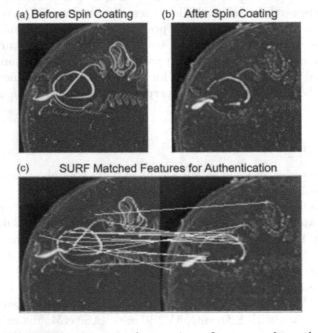

Fig. 2. Obfuscation cum encryption scheme using a fluorescent dye and spin coating a polydimethylsiloxane (PDMS) layer with 750 rpm for 1 min. (a) Fluorescent fingerprint before spin coating. (b) Fluorescent fingerprint after spin coating. (c) Authentication done by SURF algorithm.

Moreover, we've developed an encryption and obfuscation technique using a perylene-based fluorescent dye [2] in the fingerprinting ink, making it resistant to reverse engineering and physical tampering. This is achieved by applying an irreversible PDMS layer through spin coating. Figure 2(a) shows the fluorescent fingerprint before coating, while Fig. 2(b) displays it after coating, where it becomes obscured and unreadable due to the loss of features. Authentication occurs by matching post-coating images with pre-coating data stored in the trusted third-party (TTP) database. We use a SURF-based algorithm (done in Matlab) to detect and describe local image features [3]. Figure 2(c) shows successful authentication matching features in images before and after spin coating. Authentication effectiveness depends on factors like zoom level, microscope and camera quality, environmental background, and optical noise. We're creating more dye and quantum dot-doped fingerprints to evaluate the scheme's cryptographic strength, considering zoom, camera types, environmental noise, and analyzing uniformity, uniqueness, and reliability.

5   Conclusion

We have developed melt-electrospinning-based physically unclonable fingerprints for product authentication. Utilizing 393 unique fingerprints, we achieved a 95.8% authentication accuracy using deep learning methods. The use of polydimethylsiloxane (PDMS) spin coating and fluorescent ink effectively encrypts the fingerprints. Furthermore, we demonstrated the efficacy of Speeded Up Robust Features (SURF) techniques in decrypting these encrypted fingerprints, offering a robust mechanism for product authentication.

Acknowledgments. We thank the National Science Foundation (NSF) for providing us with the grants: Prof. R. Karri was supported in part by NSF awards 1833624 and 2049311, and Prof. K. Chakrabarty was supported in part by NSF under grant no. 2049335.

Disclosure of Interests. We have no competing interests.

References

1. Baban, N.S., et al.: Structural attacks and defenses for flow-based microfluidic biochips. IEEE Trans. Biomed. Circu. Syst. **16**(6), 1261–1275 (2022). https://doi.org/10.1109/TBCAS.2022.3220758
2. Baban, N.S., et al.: Material-level countermeasures for securing microfluidic biochips. Lab Chip **23**(19), 4213–4231 (2023). https://doi.org/10.1039/D3LC00335C
3. Bay, H., Tuytelaars, T., Van Gool, L.: SURF: speeded up robust features. In: Leonardis, A., Bischof, H., Pinz, A. (eds.) ECCV 2006. LNCS, vol. 3951, pp. 404–417. Springer, Heidelberg (2006). https://doi.org/10.1007/11744023-32
4. Mohammed, S., Bhattacharjee, S., Song, Y.A., Chakrabarty, K., Karri, R.: Security of Biochip Cyberphysical Systems. Springer, Berlin, Germany (2022)
5. Shayan, M., et al.: Thwarting bio-IP theft through dummy-valve-based obfuscation. IEEE Trans. Inf. Forensics Secur. **16**, 2076–2089 (2021). https://doi.org/10.1109/TIFS.2020.3047755

Author Index

M. Andreoni (Ed.): ACNS 2024 Workshops, LNCS 14587, pp. 241–243, 2024.
https://doi.org/10.1007/978-3-031-61489-7